P9-DXO-796

BEYOND THE URBAN FRINGE
Land Use Issues of Nonmetropolitan America

BEYOND THE URBAN FRINGE

Land Use Issues of Nonmetropolitan America

Rutherford H. Platt
and
George Macinko
Editors

UNIVERSITY OF MINNESOTA PRESS Minneapolis

Published by the University of Minnesota Press,
2037 University Avenue Southeast, Minneapolis, MN 55414
Printed in the United States of America.

Library of Congress Cataloging in Publication Data
Main entry under title:

Beyond the urban fringe.

Includes index.
1. Land Use, Rural—United States—Congresses.
I. Platt, Rutherford H.   II. Macinko, George.
HD256.B49 1983   333.76'13'0973   83-3518
ISBN 0-8166-1099-1

The University of Minnesota
is an equal-opportunity
educator and employer.

This volume is dedicated
to the memory of James R. Anderson,
Chief Geographer of the
U.S. Geological Survey 1972-80
and Vice-President of the Association
of American Geographers 1980.

Acknowledgments

The editors on behalf of the Association of American Geographers express their gratitude to the National Science Foundation, which funded the conference from which this volume emerged. Particular thanks are extended to Dr. Barry M. Moriarty, director of the N.S.F. Geography Program. Additional funding was contributed by the Office of Water Research and Technology and by the Geography Program of the U.S. Geological Survey, both of the U.S. Department of the Interior.

Editorial assistance in the preparation of the papers in this volume was provided by Ellen McLelland Lesser prior to the conference in June, 1980, and by Freddie Morrill thereafter. Judith Stark and Dorothy Morrison retyped many of the papers.

We also thank the authors for unfailing cooperation in the preparation and revision of their papers.

Preface

In 1785 Thomas Hutchins, the "Geographer of the United States," departed for the wilds of Ohio to initiate the survey of America's public domain. Thus began the federal rectangular land survey that was to be continued westward from the "point of beginning" on the Ohio-Pennsylvania boundary to the Bering Strait. The results of this labor may be viewed by any air traveler crossing the continent on a clear day. The federal survey grid is the basis for property ownership, political boundaries, and land-use management for most of the nation west of the Appalachians.

Few if any geographers have equalled Hutchins in their professional impact upon the use of land in this country, in part perhaps because there has been no "Geographer of the United States" since Hutchins's death in 1789. Yet geographers in a broad sense have played key roles in the exploration, mapping, resource assessment, and policy formulation for the nation's hinterland. John Wesley Powell, for instance, as founder of the U.S. Geographical and Geological Survey of the Rocky Mountains in 1870, profoundly influenced public policy regarding the arid regions of the United States.

Geographers in a stricter sense (i.e., those trained in geography after its advent as an academic discipline in the United States in 1903) have contributed in many ways to the elucidation of resource-management issues. During the 1930s, for instance, University of Chicago geographers Harlan H. Barrows and Charles C. Colby played key roles respectively on the water and land committees of Franklin D. Roosevelt's National Resources Planning Board (with their graduate student Gilbert F. White serving as staff to both committees in Washington).

The present volume grows out of a recent gathering of professional geographers and fellow researchers held during June 1980 in College Park, Maryland under the aegis of the Association of American Geographers with grants from the National Science Foundation, the Office of Water Research and Technology, and the Geography Program of the U.S. Geological Survey. The papers presented there and in this volume reflect a broad spectrum of research on problems of land use in nonmetropolitan areas. It is perhaps a new "point of beginning" for the application of geographical inquiry to the understanding and resolution of land use issues of the nation's hinterland.

Rutherford H. Platt
George Macinko

Contents

X. Nuclear and Toxic Wastes

TABLES

FIGURES

Introduction

Land Use Issues of Nonmetropolitan America: An Overview

Rutherford H. Platt

LAND USE RESEARCH AND POLICY: TOWARD SYMBIOSIS

Since the advent of zoning in the 1920s, public efforts to influence land use in the United States have been more concerned with matters of *process* than of *problem* — "how" rather than "why." For decades, innovative techniques for the management of land use have sprung from the pages of legal and planning journals into national, state, and local laws, e.g., subdivision control, planned unit development, cluster zoning, floating zones, conservation easements, timing and growth controls, transfer of development rights, and so on. By and large, the adoption of new techniques and programs for land use control have not been based upon specific findings and recommendations of land use researchers. Rather, they have emerged from an apparent consensus within a community, state, or the nation as a whole that "something must be done" about overcrowding, loss of natural areas, housing shortages, historical preservation, coastal areas, billboards, or whatever.

Zoning itself is a case in point. The appearance of zoning virtually coincided with a major demographic threshold—in 1920 the nation's urban inhabitants first outnumbered rural population. The rise of urbanism was called to the attention of the U.S. Supreme Court by planning lawyer Alfred Bettmann, who argued in support of the constitutionality of the new technique that: "Zoning is based upon a thorough and comprehensive study of the developments of modern American cities, with full consideration of economic factors of municipal growth, as well as the social factors." (Bettman 1926, p. 174) In other words, the constitutionality of zoning depended upon its basis in comprehensive planning and sound geographical analysis.

The Court was convinced, noting in its landmark 1926 decision in *Ambler Realty Co.* v. *Village of Euclid* (272 U.S. 365): "Until recent years, urban life was comparatively simple; but with the great increase and concentration of

3

population, problems have developed, and constantly are developing, which require and will continue to require, additional restrictions in respect of the use and occupation of private lands in urban communities." (272 U.S. at p. 386) States and communities across the nation were also convinced; by 1930, 981 municipalities representing 46 million people had adopted zoning (Haar 1971, 173).

Is it conceivable that all of these communities, at the dawn of the Depression, actually conducted detailed land use studies and prepared comprehensive plans upon which their zoning was based? Clearly not. Furthermore, the results of these early zoning laws were remarkably similar—what was good for New York was presumed to be good for Grand Rapids, Michigan; Greenville, South Carolina; or anywhere else. From the very outset, therefore, zoning was disconnected from "sound geographical analysis" and was simply adopted to suit the best interests of each municipality.

It was soon apparent that the best interests of a community were not necessarily the best interests of a region or the nation. Bettmann's argument to the Supreme Court conveniently ignored the reality that metropolitan America was already by 1920 becoming fragmented politically. Annexation to central cities had virtually ended (except in the southwest), and suburban jurisdictions were becoming increasingly insular. Far from being based on a comprehensive regional perspective, zoning quickly became a tool of localism, widely used to legitimize racial and economic stratification among communities. Had zoning in fact been subordinated to sound assessment of land use conditions, trends, patterns, and implications, as Bettmann had predicted, the course of metropolitan development in this nation might have been very different.

The 1960 Census yielded another demographic landmark—suburban areas for the first time outnumbered central cities. A new surge of public interest in land use management arose, this time in protest against the results of thirty years of "Euclidean Zoning." The manifesto of the 1960s land use movement was a short, punchy essay by journalist William H. Whyte Jr. (1958). Whyte noted that zoning had failed in its objective of promoting orderly use of land. Instead, planning and development control was exercised by thousands of municipalities, each vying for tax "ratables." The result was perceived by Whyte to be fiscally wasteful in the need to provide public services to scattered new development, and aesthetically a disaster as open space and "countryside" disappeared, at least within metropolitan areas. Other critics, such as planning lawyers Richard Babcock and Fred Bosselman (1963), deplored the exclusionary effects of local zoning regarding lower-cost housing, apartments, and mobile homes.

Again the focus shifted quickly from problems to solutions. A variety of legal techniques for preserving open space was developed, including cluster zoning, scenic easements, land trusts, preferential taxation for farmland. In an effort to reform "Euclidean zoning," the American Law Institute (1976) drafted a "Model Land Development Code." This process overlapped with widespread efforts to strengthen the role of state governments in land use planning and management, especially for "critical areas" of unusual scenic, ecologic, or other importance (Bosselman 1971). "Growth management" came into vogue in the 1970s through experiments with such concepts as timing controls, building permit quotas, urban extension lines, and population caps (Urban Land Institute 1976). Unlike the zoning movement of the 1920s, such measures were limited to a rather select handful of communities such as Boulder, Colorado; Ramapo, New York; and Boca Raton, Florida (Godschalk et al. 1978).

It is apparent that the driving intellectual force behind the land use reforms of the 1920s and 1960s did not originate with land use researchers per se, but instead emanated from other sources: lawyers, journalists, architects, civic leaders, conservation "activists," and others. Except for a few notable researchers who successfully reached a wider audience—e.g., Jean Gottmann, Ian McHarg, Gilbert F. White—most academics communicated chiefly with each other. At best, land use researchers before 1970 supplied a muted refrain to the chorus of public indignation regarding the misuse of land. How often have the results of serious land use research appeared in academic journals years after an issue was tried and resolved, for better or worse, in the mass media and political chambers?

This lack of symbiosis between research and policy meant that land use decisions at all levels of government were deprived of the benefit of research findings and insights. It also meant that researchers were deprived of the challenge and discipline of being taken seriously. Is it a contradiction of terms for academic research to be timely?

Not necessarily, as experience of the mid-1970s began to suggest. The National Environmental Policy Act of 1969 and its surrogates in certain states required assessment of potential environmental impacts *before* major public actions were undertaken. The preparation of "environmental impact statements" brought researchers into the policy-making process and often funded their efforts. Other federal programs eliciting the skills of land use researchers have included the Coastal Zone Management Act of 1972, Areawide Wastewater Planning under Section 208 of the Water Quality Amendments of 1972, and river basin studies under the Water Resources Planning Act of 1965. Researchers also became more closely involved in state, county, and local land use policy-making as these governmental bodies became more sensitive to the threat of environmental litigation and outraged citizenry.

Against this background of a more assertive role for land use research, a new demographic landmark was reached in 1975. After a century of decline, the population of nonmetropolitan America was found to be increasing at a faster rate (7.1 percent between 1970-75) than the United States as a whole (4.9 percent) or SMSAs as a whole (3.9 percent) (Berry and Dahmann 1980, p. 19). Furthermore, this nonmetropolitan resurgence was found not be be limited to counties adjoining SMSA but to be widespread among America's small towns and rural areas (Beale and Fuguitt 1976, p. 15).

Although not as clearcut as the demographic thresholds of 1920 or 1960, the "nonmetropolitan reversal" of the 1970s signalled the emergence of a broadened interest in the land resources of the rest of America. In common with the earlier phases of concern with urban and metropolitan land use problems, there is a widespread concern that nonmetropolitan land resources are in jeopardy and that some form of enlightened public response is called for. This time, however, researchers are investigating the nature of the issues before specific public policies are selected. An example has been the National Agricultural Lands Study undertaken jointly by the U.S. Department of Agriculture and the Council on Environmental Quality (1981) during the Carter administration.

The nature and magnitude of land use change in nonmetropolitan America is not readily characterized or understood. There is no convenient shibboleth such as "urban sprawl" to describe what is happening to land beyond the urban fringe. Population growth is in fact merely the tip of the iceberg of nonmetropolitan land use change. A great transformation of the American landscape is in progress, much of it scarcely reflected in immediate (or measurable) population growth. Second-home leisure developments, for instance, occupy millions of acres in California, Arizona, Florida, and elsewhere, yet they generally account for little population shift, inasmuch as they remain predominantly undeveloped. The legal and physical characteristics of the land, however, may be altered permanently by such enterprises. Energy boom towns of the northern Great Plains and west slope of the Rockies may generate instant "cities" that lack basic public services, amenities, and infrastructure. Like the old silver-mining towns, these may prove to be transient communities, or where long-term mining is in prospect they may become permanent central cities for their regions, albeit with little planning forethought.

In general, urban America is placing unprecedented demands upon the resources of its rural hinterland for the products of its soils and forests, for water, for energy, for recreation and scenic amenities, and for sites to accommodate its wastes, both hazardous and benign. These in turn raise further issues involving, e.g., rural transportation, natural hazard mitigation, rural housing and sanitation, siting of power plants and transmission lines, waste disposal sites, and so on.

The Association of American Geographers Conference on Nonmetropolitan Land Use Issues was an attempt to mobilize a broad array of professional land use researchers to address a series of problems in advance of the crystallization of public consensus and response. It was intended to identify, document, analyze, and recommend lines of response before policies are fully settled. The metamorphosis of nonmetropolitan America from a rural hinterland to whatever it may become is now in progress and is expected to continue over the rest of this century and beyond. This book is evidence that land use researchers were heard from when it mattered.

GENESIS OF THE AAG CONFERENCE

Inquiry into nonmetropolitan change is multidisciplinary and diffuse. As the bibliographies in this volume attest, the late 1970s produced an outpouring of pertinent literature in many fields: rural sociology, agricultural and resource economics, political science and public administration, ecology, plant and soil science, forestry, geology, physical and human geography. This state of ferment prompted the organization of the Association of American Geographers Conference on Land Use Issues of Nonmetropolitan America. The field of professional geography has traditionally served as integrator of diverse subject material and bridge between the physical and social sciences. As stated in the AAG proposal to the National Science Foundation, which led to funding of the Conference:

> Geographers are self-selected for their curiosity about, and ability to handle, a wide range of scholarly approaches. Geographical training generally fosters these traits and expands the range of accessible insights and materials. This is especially true for interactions between man and environment, for which geographers are apt to assume that any subject matter may be germane and must be taken into account more or less systematically (Association of American Geographers 1979)

Perhaps equally important is the willingness, even eagerness, of geographers to engage in multidisciplinary enterprises, particularly those that involve application of scholarly research to the understanding of public policy questions

The conference was held June 24-25, 1980, in College Park, Maryland, with funding from the National Science Foundation, the U.S. Geological Survey, and the Office of Water Research and Technology of the Department of the Interior. The program was carefully designed to promote interaction—among land use issues, among regions, among geographers and nongeographers, and among academic researchers and governmental officials. Nineteen principal papers were presented and discussed; altogether about 200 persons participated in or attended the conference representing 32 states, 3 Canadian provinces, and some 20 governmental agencies. The conference was coordinated by Rutherford H. Platt of the University of Massachusetts at Amherst with the assistance of a steering committee of ten geographers: Edward Fernald, Florida State University; John F. Lounsbury, Arizona State University; Lawrence M. Sommers, Michigan State University; James Anderson, U.S. Geological Survey; Nicholas F. Helburn, University of Colorado; George Macinko, Central Washington University; Kenneth E. Corey, University of Maryland; Richard E. Lonsdale, University of Nebraska; Philip R. Pryde, San Diego State University; and Wilbur Zelinsky, Pennsylvania State University.

The scope and objectives of the conference and of this volume may be briefly stated. Geographically speaking, the conference was directed primarily to land use issues arising outside the nation's 281 Standard Metropolitan Statistical Areas as defined in 1977. Federal lands, including the public domain, were excluded from consideration, since they are the subject of many other symposia and their management involves special policy considerations, doctrines, and laws. Likewise, water-resource management (in which geographers have a longstanding interest) was not a major emphasis of this conference.

With these three exclusions—SMSAs, federal lands, and water resources—there remained a vast portion of the land surface of the United States to be considered: approximately 1.3 billion acres, according to Healy and Short. This enormous land area is seldom studied in a systematic or comprehensive manner.

The objectives of the conference were to:

- examine and evaluate emerging trends and issues about nonmetropolitan land resources in the United States;
- disseminate and discuss recent research in geography and other disciplines relating to nonmetropolitan land use;
- identify issues requiring further investigation;
- stimulate multidisciplinary research efforts;
- facilitate communication between the research community and public agencies;
- promote cross-fertilization among public agencies; and
- lead to the publication of a proceedings volume on nonmetropolitan land use.

TOPICS AND PERSONAE

The broad parameters set forth in the conference proposal granted license to address an array of topics and to recruit participants without regard for conventional disciplinary or substantive boundaries. The result was the opportunity to attract individuals and to consider material not normally found within the framework of a single conference or between the covers of a single book. To fit within the limits of a two-day conference—plenary in format to maximize attention to each session and paper—painful choices had to be made between important topics and worthy participants. The selections made could not represent every key land use issue or research interest. As the summary of topics below indicates, however, much was accomplished. It is hoped that the reader of this volume will not only benefit from the substantive material contained herein, but will also experience vicariously the excitement of common purpose and shared insight that prevailed at College Park.

1. Geographic Perspectives on Nonmetropolitan Land Use Change

The opening paper by Penn State geographer Peirce F. Lewis resembles in its cosmic perspective and use of aerial photographs the paper by E. A. Gutkind in the classic *Man's Role in Changing the Face of the Earth* (which similarly opened the 1955 Wenner-Gren Conference). According to Gutkind:

> . . . our present situation is one of aggressiveness and conquest. Adjustment to the environment develops into exploitation. The objectives are unlimited and grow in diversity but also in disunity . . . . With the ruthlessness of a pioneer, man expands his living space and, with a complete

disregard of the danger of a primarily quantitative expansion, he deludes himself into the role of an omnipotent remark of his environment . . . . Neglect and exploitation of the natural resources, rural isolation and urban expansion, have produced an unexampled disunity of the social and economic structure. (Gutkind 1956, pp. 21, 27)

Yet Gutkind perceived a new era dawning:

Faintly the outlines of this new epoch are discernible. It will be an age of responsibility and unification . . . . Expansive ruthlessness is gradually merging into a careful adjustment to environmental conditions and new possibilities. Man begins to be aware of his real responsibility and of the limitations which the closing frontiers of the world impose upon him. The objectives are gaining in precision, foresight, and co-ordination. (Gutkind 1956, p. 27) [Hoover Dam was cited by Gutkind as a symbol of the new age.]

A quarter-century later, Lewis asserts that the urban frontier has largely vanished in the United States. In his view, the economy and culture of metropolitan America have become ubiquitous through the media of television, franchise merchandising, and the interstate highway system (begun in the year of Gutkind's essay). Do the resulting conditions satisfy Gutkind's prediction of a new age of "precision, foresight, and coordination?" Despite a generally optimistic view of the "galactic metropolis," Lewis expresses serious reservations on three points: (1) how to cope with energy shortages that challenge the viability of a land use pattern predicated upon cheap and plentiful energy; (2) how to mitigate visual blight and monotony; and (3) how to provide equality of access to the benefits of the "galactic metropolis" to all racial and economic classes. Since these issues—plus some others raised during the conference—have not been solved, it would seem that we have not moved as rapidly toward the new era as Gutkind expected, unless an interstate highway is the equivalent of Hoover Dam as a symbol of rationality and coherence.

In their comments on Lewis's paper, Professors Stone of the University of Georgia and Borchert of Minnesota concur with the list of unresolved issues, yet they question whether nonmetropolitan America has ceased to exist. Strictly in terms of land use, as distinct from life-style or products available in markets, both commenters feel that much of the United States remains relatively rural. By implication, it is perhaps not too late for Gutkind's era of rational forethought to influence the use and disposition of the remainder of the nation's land resources—provided the relevant issues are identified and resolved quickly.

2. Elements of Rural Growth and Change

The movement of people to nonmetropolitan locations and the role of interstate highways as conduits for this movement are examined respectively by

David L. Brown and Calvin L. Beale of the USDA Economics, Statistics and Co-operative Service, and by Ronald Briggs, a geographer at the University of Texas at Dallas. Brown and Beale first summarize the nature and extent of demographic shifts toward the suburbs, toward the south and west ("Sun Belt"), and particularly toward nonmetropolitan areas. The last is found to be not merely a revival of small towns but a phenomenon occurring extensively in open country not necessarily adjacent to any city or metropolitan area. Nevertheless, the authors' economic analysis of the "nonmetropolitan turnaround" lends support to Peirce Lewis's contention that "the metropolis is almost everywhere." In 1976 only 13 percent of jobs in nonmetropolitan counties were in agriculture, which trailed wholesale and retail trade, government, and manufacturing. This represents a nationalization of the trend toward rural nonfarm activities noted by Gottman (1961) for the east-coast megalopolis. Furthermore, manufacturing jobs in nonmetropolitan areas increased by 335,000 between 1970 and 1976 as compared with a loss of 741,000 manufacturing jobs from SMSAs (Chapter 4, Table 3). And much of this new manufacturing employment is found to be in "fast growth" activities, traditionally found in metropolitan areas.

In assessing the implications of these trends upon land use in nonmetropolitan areas, Brown and Beale distinguish between counties with the highest proportion of their work force in farming and counties with the highest value of agricultural output. The former, largely in the Corn Belt and Great Plains, display a relatively static population (compared with an 11-percent decline during the 1960s), while the latter group experienced population growth of 13.5 percent between 1970-78, nearly twice the national average. Many of the high-production counties, including many in California, Arizona, and Florida, thus are experiencing acute urban competition for land. Additional pre-emption of farmland may be expected in the form of highways (which occupied 21 million acres of rural land in 1977), reservoirs (60 million acres) strip mining (1.5 million acres), and power transmission lines (nearly 4 million acres nationally in 1974).

Briggs, reporting on his research for the U.S. Department of Transportation, examines the particular influence of the interstate highway system upon growth in nonmetropolitan counties. Controlling for adjacency to SMSAs and size of largest community within counties, Briggs reports that "as a group counties with freeways experienced higher rates of migration . . . than counties off the system." In terms of employment, Briggs finds a positive relationship between availability of interstate highways and total employment, retail employment, tourism, and trucking; but curiously he finds no such relationship in the case of manufacturing and wholesaling. He theorizes that these activities benefit from interstate highways without necessarily being located in counties traversed by them. In any event, the development of the interstate system has now largely run its course. With little mileage remaining to be added, particularly in nonmetropolitan areas, and with fuel costs of increasing concern, Briggs expects a "weakening of the tie between interstate highways and development."

3. The Rural Land Market

Promiscuous subdivision of rural land, whether or not resulting in subsequent development, has been a pervasive phenomenon during the 1960s and early 1970s in Sun Belt states and extending into the upper Midwest and northern New England. "Leisure-oriented" land developments have prompted several states, notably Florida, Vermont, New York, and California, to adopt state-level programs for land planning and management. Nationally, the Office of Interstate Land Sales Registration of the U.S. Department of Housing and Urban Development, since its creation in 1968 has registered 11,600 land developments involving some 6.5 million acres (as of March 31, 1981). These include only developments marketed on an interstate basis, not smaller subdivisions and individual land transactions which cumulatively may radically alter the nature of land tenure and usage in rural areas.

Two chapters examine the nature of the rural land market, one nationally, the other regionally. Robert G. Healy of The Conservation Foundation and James L. Short of the San Diego State University College of Business summarize their research on rural land tenure sponsored by Resources For the Future. Their findings from six rural study sites in West Virginia, Virginia, Vermont, Texas, California, and Illinois confirm three trends: (1) emergence of new demands for rural land, particularly from "nontraditional" investors; (2) fragmentation of rural land into smaller parcel sizes; and (3) decisively rising costs of rural land. The authors suggest the need to create new models or archetypes for rural land development that will avoid the stereotypes of suburban tract development of the traditional family farm. The need for new institutions to hold and manage rural land is also indicated.

Stephenson reviews several issues associated with the proliferation of leisure-oriented land developments in the Southwest. These enterprises place county governments on the horns of a dilemma. If a development is laid out, marketed, but not developed (as frequently happens), the land is left physically defaced and legally fragmented, with consequent losses to lot-buyers and the county tax base. On the other hand, if a development is actually built up and populated, the rural county faces several fiscal and environmental problems.

4. Small Cities and Villages: Growth and Decline

Howard Roepke, an economic geographer at the University of Illinois (Urbana), finds that industry in nonmetropolitan areas has grown significantly over the past two decades: for the period 1962-78, nonmetropolitan manufacturing jobs increased by 1.8 million as compared with 1.4 million within SMSAs. Factors in this growth have included improved highways (providing access to areas poorly served by railroads), available labor, and favorable tax policies by local jurisdictions. Counties with sizable urban communities have gained most new industry as compared with more rural counties. Roepke cautions that energy costs and possible deregulation of trucking rates could hinder future nonmetropolitan industrial development.

Population and business trends in villages of fewer than 2500 people are examined by Harley E. Johansen, a geographer at West Virginia University (now at the University of Idaho), and Glenn V. Fuguitt, Professor of Rural Sociology at the University of Wisconsin (Madison). On the basis of a five-percent sample of such communities, the authors identify an overall increase in levels of village growth since 1950. This increase is not limited to larger villages or those accessible to urban centers, although variation among villages in growth rates is increasing. The typical "Main Street" business district has declined in number of establishments despite population growth, reflecting the impact of improved transportation upon lower order central places. Evidence from a telephone update suggests, however, that retailing may be resurging in larger villages, perhaps because of population increase and energy costs.

5. Public Policy on Prime Farmlands

In terms of written words, numbers of conferences, workshops, and reports, the preservation of prime farmlands is probably the most prominent rural land use issue. Whether there is in fact a "problem" for public concern is itself an issue. It is interesting to note that President Roosevelt's National Resources Board in 1934 recommended that land in agriculture be *reduced* by 75 million acres to control soil erosion. Public purchase, rural zoning, easements—all the tools recommended for preserving prime farmlands today—were proposed for the *removal* of submarginal crop and pasture lands from production and resettlement of people living thereon. The report cited the destruction of 35 million acres of land and the substantial loss of topsoil from 218 million acres due to soil erosion and predicted decline in agricultural productivity:

> This wastage of the most basic and indispensable resource of the country—the soil—has become one of the most important problems confronting the Nation. From a country with a large proportional area of rich agricultural land we are plunging, almost heedlessly, in the direction of a nation of predominantly poor agricultural land, as a result of unrestrained erosion. (National Resources Board 1934, p. 161)

Although soil erosion continues to defy the best efforts of the Soil Conservation Service, the predicted crisis has not yet arrived. The total value of farm output increased from $22.5 billion in 1935 to $47.5 billion in 1970 (in constant 1958 dollars) (U.S. Bureau of the Census 1972, Series K 220-239). The composite index of crop yields has doubled during the past 25 years (Wittwer 1980, p. 66). Irrigation, chemical fertilizers and pesticides, and improved genetic strains have helped to offset soil losses, with possible long-term adverse effects of their own.

But what about urban encroachment upon prime farmland? At the Wenner-Gren Conference, Harris (1956, p. 889) expressed qualified skepticism:

It is obvious that neither the present nor potential total land pressures of urban agglomerations are critical. Special problems, however, may arise in connection with (1) the type of urban expansion into rural areas and (2) the pressure of urban land use in certain areas of high urbanization and sharply limited agricultural land, such as Japan, Britain, and California.

A net "loss" of 30.5 million acres of cropland between 1967 and 1975 was reported by the USDA Soil Conservation Service (Dideriksen et al. 1977). This apparent loss of 7 percent of our cropland base in 8 years sparked widespread consternation (e.g., U.S. Council on Environmental Quality 1978, p. 270). The accuracy of the SCS data, however, has been criticized by Frey (1981) of the USDA Economic Research Service. Frey feels that federal data from various sources are in conflict as to the extent of farmland conversion, and no clear implication for public policy is discernible. He is also critical of efforts by the National Agricultural Lands Study to resolve such data conflicts (Personal letter from H. Thomas Frey to Rutherford H. Platt, October 29, 1981). In discussion of the Zinn and Berry papers at the AAG conference, geographer John Fraser Hart cited Frey's position and his own oft-stated view (e.g. Hart 1977) that there is little reality to a "crisis" in farmland availability.

Further clouding the issue, the U.S. gross farm product rose by 9 percent between 1970 and 1978 from $31.1 billion to $34.2 billion in constant 1972 dollars (U.S. Bureau of the Census 1979, p. 694). But reports abound of local and regional crises in agriculture. The following are recent headlines in *The New York Times*:

- "Farmers in Florida Ponder Energy Gap" (December 16, 1979)
- "New York Reports 2.2% Fewer Farms (February 17, 1980)
- "Suffolk Plan to Save Farms is Still at Issue after 4 Years" (April 2, 1980)
- "In Plymouth County, Iowa, the Rich Topsoil's Going Fast, Alas" (July 11, 1980)
- "Soil erosion Threatens U.S. Farms' Output" (October 26, 1980)
- "Urban Shadow Darkens San Francisco Farm Life" (November 11, 1980)

Norman A. Berg, who addressed the conference as Administrator of the Soil Conservation Service (SCS), stated that the problem is not "a matter of absolute physical limits on the amount of land. Rather the problem is one of rising economic and environmental costs of large-scale conversions of pasture, range, and forest lands to crops . . . ." (Chapter 10). SCS data indicate that the nation may need to bring an additional 75-100 million acres into crop production over the next twenty years *without even considering continued conversions of existing cropland to other uses.* Such lands, Berg warns, would be "much inferior to present cropland with respect to economic productivity and susceptibility to erosion." In short, we would be returning to submarginal lands, which the National Resources Board recommended should be abandoned for agriculture.

According to David Berry (Chapter 11), soil erosion in the 48 contiguous states averages 6.9 tons per acre per year; new topsoil forms at an average rate of about 1.5 tons per acre per year, although losses up to 5 tons per acre per year are tolerable for some soils. Former Secretary of Agriculture Bob Bergland has stated that 48 million acres, or about 10 percent of the United States cropland, are experiencing losses of more than 14 tons per acre per year (*The New York Times* 1980, p. 1). Meanwhile, conversion of cropland to urban purposes between 1967 and 1975 apparently occurred at twice the rate of the previous decade, amounting to about 1 million acres per year. Berry cites measures proposed for the mitigation of soil erosion and urbanization as threats to existing prime land.

The relationship of American agriculture to the balance of trade and national energy needs is examined by Zinn. Agricultural exports grew from $5.2 billion in 1970 to approximately $37 billion in 1980 (current dollars), even with an estimated reduction in exports to the Soviet Union of $2.6 billion. In 1978, farm exports reduced the U.S. foreign trade deficit by one-third, from $46.8 billion to $32.6 billion. U.S. agriculture thus indirectly subsidizes the nation's energy imports.

Farmland and energy are interrelated in several other respects. Energy development competes with agriculture for (1) land to be strip-mined; (2) water; (3) sites for energy facilities (one nuclear plant in Illinois preempted 8,000 acres of prime cropland for a cooling lake); (4) transmission line corridors (although not prohibiting farm use of underlying land, fears of ozone pollution have aroused rural opposition in some states); and (5) land for the production of biomass for conversion to energy. (See chapter 23 by Fowler et al.)

6. Remote Sensing and Rural Land Use Data

This session was arranged by the late James R. Anderson, Chief Geographer of the U.S. Geological Survey, to whose memory this volume is dedicated. Detailed land use and land cover mapping in rural areas are relatively recent; growth of such mapping has been dependent upon the development of advanced but economical technology for the acquisition, storage, and presentation of remote sensing data. Progress in this area has been promoted through federally supported land planning programs, notably the Coastal Zone Management Program and the Section 208 Nonpoint Source Water Quality Program. Pioneering efforts at rural land mapping such as those of MacConnell at the University of Massachusetts have concentrated on the spatial distribution of existing uses, e.g., farmland, forests, and wetlands. Others have addressed land suitability through a variety of factors: soil types, slope, microclimate, parcel size, etc., as noted in MacDougall's introductory comments. According to Cowen (Chapter 14), other uses for computer-generated maps available to state and county governments include

"remonumentation of the geodetic controls, creation of high quality aerial photography, and digital production of new tax maps. Another project currently
under way [in Greenville County, S.C.] involves an analysis of the energy available from existing timber stands." Cowen reports on experience at the University
of South Carolina in applying advanced technology for digital processing and
integration of land use data to these and other nonmetropolitan land use management needs. His appraisal of results to date is optimistic.

Baumann, a geographer at SUNY Oneonta, is more skeptical about the value of
a computer-based land-mapping system as developed for Schoharie County, New
York, at the edge of the Catskills. He raises the issue of how to get the horse to
drink after you have led him to water. Under a contract with the County,
Baumann's Department of Geography assembled land use data involving 155
variables, which were digitized for the entire county. With accompanying hardware and software, this facilitated the generation of an infinite variety of county
land use maps. But the county officials and planners had no idea what to do
with this resource. Baumann reports their expectation that the "magic black
box" would deliver answers to any problem instantly. He concludes that rural
public officials must be given some training in the nature and operation of such a
system and that the system should be kept as simple as possible, with complexity added only as the need arises.

7. Coping with Natural Hazards: Floods and Drought

Geographers have long been concerned with problems of human adjustment to
natural hazards, e.g., riverine and coastal flood, hurricane, earthquake, volcano,
tornado, blizzard, and drought. Avenues of inquiry have focused upon (1) ways
and means of reducing natural hazard losses; (2) human perception of hazards;
and (3) ways to shift the economic burden of losses when they occur. A strong
tradition of interaction between academic researchers and governmental policymakers has been fostered, especially through the efforts of Gilbert F. White, a
geographer at the University of Colorado. Hazard specialists, however, like members of other interest constituencies, tend to talk to each other more than to their
colleagues interested in, say, farmland protection, economic development, or
energy facility siting, despite obvious points of common interest. The papers in
this volume by Baker and Platt and by Reibsame briefly acknowledge the role of
natural hazards as constraints upon the use of nonmetropolitan land.

Floods in the United States are usually thought to be metropolitan phenomena;
and indeed, much of the rapid increase in average annual flood losses—to nearly
$4 billion—is occurring in urbanizing metropolitan watersheds. Specific data on
flood losses outside SMSAs are not readily available, but many recent rural flood
disasters may be cited—e.g., Big Thompson Canyon, Colorado (1976); the
Red River of the North (1979); the "Hill Country" of Texas (1979); and the
Pearl River Valley of Mississippi (1979). While less dramatic and therefore less

newsworthy than floods in urban areas, floods in outlying areas inflict major losses upon agriculture and small cities. Yet public jurisdictions in nonmetropolitan America are reluctant to undertake remedial measures in the form of floodplain zoning, land acquisition, or emergency planning. Among 17,000 communities (including counties) participating in the National Flood Insurance Program in 1980, only 4,477 had adopted land use controls over floodplain development, most of them in metropolitan areas. Baker and Platt review some of the policy issues presently confronting federal, state, and local officials who attempt to mitigate flood losses in rural areas and small cities.

At the opposite end of the hydrological spectrum, drought has long been thought to be chiefly a rural hazard, at least until the urban droughts of the 1960s and early 1980s. According to William Reibsame, a post-doctoral researcher in geography at Clark University, the effects of rural drought upon crop production remain drastic despite a century of technological tinkering. But the social/economic impacts of drought upon the farm population have been greatly lessened through a variety of public assistance programs, insurance, tax policies, and other means.

8. Institutions for Managing Rural Land

Nonmetropolitan America, especially its rural areas, has always lagged behind developing urban areas in the establishment of public mechanisms for land planning and management. Most of the land in question (outside New England) is unincorporated and therefore, lacking any local municipality, comes under the jurisdiction of county governments. Except for the large metropolitan counties such as Dade, Cook, and San Diego, county governments are prevalently disinterested in land management. In 1968 the National Commission on Urban Problems (the "Douglas Commission") found that among counties outside SMSAs, only 48 percent had a planning board and 19 percent had a zoning ordinance, as compared with 80 percent and 49 percent respectively for counties inside SMSAs (Manvel 1968). Although this level of interest in land use management has undoubtedly improved, nevertheless the administration of land use controls where they do exist is notoriously lax in nonmetropolitan areas. The lack of institutional capabilities and commitment is a major obstacle to the achievement of progress in dealing with the many substantive land use issues considered in this volume and elsewhere.

According to Marion Clawson, this perception is not simply the product of recent experience. During the 1930s, President Roosevelt's national planning units envisioned comprehensive land and water planning for the entire nation. These entities encouraged the establishment of state and regional planning boards. Clawson's chapter, in which he summarizes his new book (1981) on the National Resources Planning Board, considers the activities of the board under two classifications: (1) planning and coordination, and (2) idea stimulation. To the extent that the former is "quiet and unobtrusive" and the latter "controversial," the tension between these two functions, in Clawson's view, severely hampered NRPB, leading to its demise at the hands of Congress in 1943. Nevertheless, NRPB produced a brilliant series of reports on land and water issues, a testimony to the art of "idea stimulation" in the planning process.

Recent experience in the management of rural land by a large and sophisticated county is considered in a paper by Philip R. Pryde, a geographer at San Diego State University, and David Neilson, Growth Management Director of San Diego County. Despite a 37-percent increase in county population to 1.8 million between 1970 and 1980, two-thirds of San Diego County (about 3,000 square miles) is inhabited by only 22,000 people. This hinterland of desert, mountain, and irrigated farmland, despite remoteness and water scarcity, is experiencing development pressure. Pryde and Neilson summarize the county's efforts to manage new growth through application of existing California laws and through development of a self-executing "Regional Growth Management Plan."

An instance of Clawson's "idea stimulation" as applied to rural resource management is the "Mediated Agreement" developed for the Snohomish River Basin in Washington State. Following a mediation process underwritten by the Ford Foundation, the agreement comprised a "blueprint for the future growth of the Basin" involving limited structural flood control measures, land acquisition, land use regulations, and other provisions. It was signed by the governor of Washington, two counties, thirteen municipalities, and the "Tulalip Tribes," all of which share jurisdiction over the basin in question. At the time of its signing in 1975, David A. Aggerholm reports that it was viewed as the "agreement to end all agreements." In retrospect, however, Aggerholm, like Paul Baumann on land use data, finds the reality has not lived up to the promise (or the publicity).

9. Land Use Impacts of Energy Development

Energy and nonmetropolitan land use are interrelated in diverse and complex ways. First, the cost of energy is obviously a factor in the spatial pattern of nonmetropolitan growth—to what extent does the rising cost of gasoline influence the migration of households and business to nonmetropolitan areas? Second, the extraction and processing of energy resources is significantly nonmetropolitan in location. If one examines the entire system of sites and linkages by which energy is discovered, extracted, processed, stored, and utilized, and its waste products dumped, a taxonomy of impacts upon nonmetropolitan land and society is disclosed. Third, energy development competes with agriculture and other pre-existing activities for land (e.g., for strip mining), for water (shale oil development), and for those special nonmetropolitan resources, fresh air and visibility.

Three papers in this volume address respectively these forms of interaction between energy and land use. Sommers of Michigan State University and Ziegler of Old Dominian University interpret historic and contemporary settlement patterns of North America in terms of energy constraints. Lloyd Bender of Montana

State and his colleagues report on their EPA-sponsored research on the impacts of coal mining and conversion upon pre-existing communities of the northern Great Plains with particular attention to the problem of taxation, cost-sharing among jurisdictions, and timing of public infrastructure in relation to revenue flows.

Another team of researchers led by Gary Fowler, a geographer at the University of Illinois Circle Campus, examines the potential impacts of coal and biomass developments in the Ohio River Basin upon the region's land, water, and air resources. The imminent development of a federally sponsored synthetic fuels industry is expected to exacerbate demand for Ohio Basin energy resources, particularly strippable coal and cropland for the production of biomass. Existing or probable environmental impacts include acid mine drainage, soil erosion, and solid waste disposal.

10. Toxic Wastes and Nuclear Hazards

The Herndon and Mitchell predictions offer a gloomy benediction to the volume—but perhaps one that is more realistic than the Currier and Ives image that many of the would-be "preservers of the countryside" would prefer to perpetuate. Since Love Canal came to public attention as an environmental catastrophe in 1978, discoveries of promiscuous dumping of hazardous wastes have been myriad, both within an outside metropolitan areas. The U.S. Environmental Protection Agency in 1979 estimated that there may be 32,000 to 50,000 hazardous waste dumps in the United States of which 1,200 to 2,000 could pose significant risks to health and the environment. Most disheartening is that all but 500 to 800 of these dumps are still actively used. (U.S. Council on Environmental Quality 1979, p. 174.)

Roy Herndon, a physicist at Florida State University, reviews some physical and legal aspects of hazardous waste management, both toxic and nuclear. The Resource Conservation and Recovery Act of 1976, now in process of implementation, affords some hope for the exercise of public surveillance and monitoring over hazardous wastes. Yet this does not resolve where such wastes should go. Ultimately, Herndon warns, land disposal will continue to be the primary and most feasible practice, and rural land managers are advised to plan accordingly.

The pariahs of advanced technology, nuclear power plants, and disposal sites for nuclear, hazardous, and toxic wastes are quintessential threats to the peace of mind and environment of nonmetropolitan America. Such facilities emphasize the vulnerability of America's hinterland to metropolitan demands. The need for such facilities arises from the urban appetite for electrical power and exotic technologies. Yet metropolitan areas do not want these facilities close at hand. As a *New York Times* editorial has stated: "The best way to assure safety—and allay anxiety—is to put the reactors where they would cause the least damage in the event of an accident. In the past reactors were allowed near cities on the theory that safety equipment could protect the public. That policy is now undergoing revision. New reactors should probably be put in remote sites—50 miles or more from population centers. . . ." (*The New York Times* 1979, p. 12E) The writer fails to define "population center," apparently equating it with New York City, Boston, or Washington. (One is reminded of Steinberg's delightful *New Yorker* cover depicting New York's perception of the world with the Great Plains starting just west of "Jersey.")

Mitchell's chapter (especially his first figure) indicates that no location in the east coast megalopolis is farther than 50 miles from an existing nuclear plant, and much of nonmetropolitan America lies within such distance from existing or proposed nuclear plants. Mitchell argues that reactor technology is not sufficient protection against more "Three Mile Islands," nor does remote siting alleviate the need for improved emergency planning and land use control.

References

American Law Institute 1976. *A Model Land Development Code*. Philadelphia: The Institute.

Association of American Geographers 1979. Proposal to the National Science Foundation for a Conference on Land Use Issues of Nonmetropolitan America. Washington: The Association (mimeo).

Babcock, R. F., and Bosselman, F. P. 1963. Suburban Zoning and the Apartment Boom. *University of Pennsylvania Law Review* 111: 1040-1072.

Beale, C. L., and Fuguitt, G. L. 1976. *Population Change in Nonmetropolitan Cities and Towns*. Agricultural Economic Report No. 323. Washington: Economic Research Service, USDA.

Berry, B. J. L., and Dahmann, D. C. 1980. Population Redistribution in the United States in the 1970s. In *Population Redistribution and Public Policy*, ed. Brian J. L. Berry and Lester P. Silverman, pp. 8-49. Washington: National Academy of Sciences.

Bettmann, A. 1926. Brief filed in U.S. Supreme Court re *Ambler Realty Co.* v. *Village of Euclid*. In *City and Regional Planning Papers of Alfred Bettmann*, ed. A. C. Comey, pp. 157-193. Cambridge: Harvard University Press, 1946.

Bosselman, F. P. 1971. *The Quiet Revolution in Land Use Control*. Washington: U.S. Government Printing Office.

Clawson, M. 1981. *New Deal Planning: The National Resources Planning Board*. Baltimore: The Johns Hopkins Press for Resources for the Future.

Dideriksen, R. I.; Hidlebaugh, A. R.; and Schmude, K. O. 1977. *Potential Cropland Study*. Statistical Bulletin No. 578. Washington: Soil Conservation Service, USDA.

Frey, H. T. 1981. Farmland Conversion: Some Comments on the Potential Cropland Study. Unpublished paper available from the author at USDA Economic Research Service, 500 12th St. S.W., Washington, D.C. 20250.

Godschalk. D. R.; Brower, D. J.; Herr, D. C.; and Vestal, B. A. 1978. *Responsible Growth Management: Cases and Materials*. Chicago: American Society of Planning Officials.

Gottman, J. 1961. *Megalopolis*. Cambridge: M.I.T. Press.

Gutkind, E. A. 1956. Our World from the Air: Conflict and Adaptation. In *Man's Role in Changing the Face of the Earth*, ed. William L. Thomas, Jr., pp. 1-48. Chicago: University of Chicago Press.

Haar, C. M. 1971. *Land-Use Planning: A Casebook on the Use, Misuse and Re-Use of Urban Land*. Boston: Little, Brown & Co.

Harris, C. D. 1956. The Pressure of Residential-Industrial Land Use. In *Man's Role in Changing the Face of the Earth*, ed. William L. Thomas, Jr., pp. 881-896. Chicago: University of Chicago Press.

Hart, J. F. 1977. Urban Encroachment on Rural Areas. *The Geographical Review* 66: 3-17.

Manvel, A. D. 1968. *Local Land and Building Regulation.* National Commission on Urban Problems Research Report No. 6. Washington: U.S. Government Printing Office.

National Resources Board 1934. *Final Report.* Washington: The Board.

The New York Times 1979. Nuclear Risks: How Remote? (December 23):24.

————1980. Soil Erosion Threatens U.S. Farms' Output (October 26): 1. Urban Land Institute 1976. *Management Control of Growth.* Washington: ULI.

U.S. Bureau of the Census 1972. *Historical Statistics: Colonial Times to 1970.* Washington: U.S. Government Printing Office.

————1979. *Statistical Abstract of the United States.* Washington: U.S. Government Printing Office.

U.S. Council on Environmental Quality 1978. *Environmental Quality — 1978.* Washington: U.S. Government Printing Office.

————1979. *Environmental Quality — 1979.* Washington: U.S. Government Printing Office.

U.S. Department of Agriculture/Council on Environmental Quaility 1981. *National Agricultural Lands Study: Executive Summary of Final Report.* Washington: USDA/CEQ.

Whyte, W. H., Jr. 1958. Urban Sprawl. In *The Exploding Metropolis*, ed. The Editors of Fortune, pp. 115-140. Garden City, N.Y.: Doubleday Anchor Books.

Wittwer, S. H. 1980. Future Trends in Agriculture Technology and Management. In *Long Range Environmental Outlook*, pp. 64-106. Washington: The National Academy of Sciences.

I. Geographic Perspectives
on Nonmetropolitan Land Use Change

The Galactic Metropolis

Peirce F. Lewis

THE END OF THE URBAN FRONTIER

Shortly after the 1890 Census returns were tallied, the Census Bureau announced that it would no longer try to define the location of the American settlement frontier. There was little purpose, the Bureau declared, in trying to define a boundary between settled and unsettled land, so small was the extent of that unsettled land, so patchy was its distribution, so thoroughly had Americans spread themselves across the national territory. It was an epochal event, the closing of the frontier, for it meant that America was a different kind of country from what it had been before. Henceforth Americans would have to talk and think about their country in new and unfamiliar ways. No wonder that historians and geographers have been debating the basic meaning of that event ever since. It is no small matter to try to redefine a whole nation.

Now, almost a century later, Americans are approaching another such landmark in the evolution of their national territory. We are, I believe, witnessing the rapid disappearance of an urban frontier, and in some parts of the country the frontier has already disappeared. By that I mean that the boundary that has separated city from country throughout American history is now almost gone, and that is true whether one talks about physical boundaries or about more subtle forms of intellectual or psychological boundaries. To some degree, in most parts of America's inhabited domain *the metropolis is almost everywhere.*

That idea is hard for most Americans to absorb—despite the fact that the metropolis is all around them. In the first place, this new ubiquitous metropolis is unprecedented. We have no historical models to gauge it by, and we even lack

I am grateful to George Macinko of Central Washington University, John Borchert of the University of Minnesota, and Kirk Stone of the University of Georgia, for their careful reading and criticism of early forms of this manuscript.

23

a common vocabulary to describe it. Furthermore this new metropolis is huge and diffuse, including both people and landscapes that do not look very urban — at least as we have traditionally used that word.[1] Most difficult of all, the emergence of a new kind of metropolis and the disappearance of a traditional urban frontier compel Americans to rethink some basic ideas about their native land. That is not an easy or comfortable thing to do.

The signs of unprecedented change were emerging fifty years ago, if we had only known what to look for. Just as it had done in 1890, the Census Bureau gave early warning that something new was afoot. There was no bold announcement that a frontier had closed — simply the coinage of an awkward but necessary term, "rural-nonfarm," to describe people who lived in what looked like rural areas but who failed to behave in conventional rural ways.[2] The Census Bureau repeated the warning in the 1950s and 1960s when it reported that central cities were losing population to the suburbs — and not just a few cities either. By the end of the 1970s, the Census was reporting what it called "a major reversal" in America's metropolitan population trends. For the first time since the Depression, areas "defined as metropolitan had a lower percentage population increase than nonmetropolitan territory."[3] Both the 1970 and 1980 censuses, furthermore, reported that in certain parts of the country — notably the north-central and northeast — not just central cities but whole metropolitan areas were losing population.[4] As early as 1958 the editors of *Fortune* had published a little book that spoke of an "exploding metropolis," but a continuing explosion was more than most Americans had bargained for.[5] The nation's cities seemed to be coming apart.

But one doesn't require Census statistics to know that something major has happened in the United States. Travelers on airplanes simply need to sit by the window and keep their eyes open. From the air, the signs are everywhere (Fig. 1). One is rarely out of sight of a primary highway or a freeway, with its interchangeable interchanges, and most of the interchanges come equipped with one or a cluster of low, flat, slablike buildings (a shopping center, a small factory, a warehouse, who knows which?). One sees the neat little subdivisions with their proper setbacks and curvilinear streets and big driveways and little swimming pools; some even come with their own lakes and their own marinas. Along the sides of what used to be called "farm-to-market" roads is a predictable spattering of split-levels and ranchers and immobile mobile homes, the quintessential "rural nonfarms" of Census definition (Fig. 2). Inevitably one sees a consolidated school with its baseball diamonds and running tracks and ranks of yellow buses that look like clusters of shiny insects. (One suspects that it is called Riverdale District High School, but downtown Riverdale may be nowhere nearby. Indeed, there may *be* no downtown Riverdale). And everywhere, next to the big low-slung buildings, are the ubiquitous asphalt parking lots — like the buildings, often at quite improbable distances from any town or city, but during business hours full of cars from somewhere. And the bulldozers are everywhere, making more of the same. From 30,000 feet, bulldozer tracks all look alike, differing only in

Figure 1. The ubiquitous metropolis is best seen from the air. Its basic element is the interchangeable interchange with loosely spaced low-slung buildings which contain nearly all the necessary functions of a traditional nucleated city. This could be almost anywhere, but happens to be near the Greater Pittsburgh airport in southwestern Pennsylvania, 1979.

the regional color of the dirt—red tracks on the Georgia and Carolina Piedmont, black on the peat of Louisiana or North Dakota, pale yellow on the sandy coastal plain of New Jersey or Texas, butterscotch-colored in the loess of Nebraska or Washington.

THE TWO FACES OF METROPOLIS

There is, of course, nothing new about country schools, or bulldozers either, in rural parts of the United States. What *is* new is the colossal geographic extent of the changes, and that is presumably what the organizers of this conference meant when they first spoke of the "problems of land use in nonmetropolitan America." Although I sympathize with the organizers' semantic difficulties, I would submit that the term "nonmetropolitan" is seriously misleading in describing the bulk of America's human landscape. I would submit further that the changes afoot are truly metropolitan in almost every important sense of the word. That is what I mean when I say that the urban frontier is rapidly vanishing in the United States.

Figure 2. What used to be called "farm-to-market roads" are spattered with rural-nonfarm houses, dwellings for ubiquitous metropolitan people. Near Terre Haute, Indiana, 1979.

That idea needs explaining, for we are not accustomed to the notion of a metropolis spreading over the bulk of America's national territory. But that appears now to be happening in the United States, and in much of the country it has already happened. And that event did not occur overnight. Indeed, American metropolitan functions have always been dispersed to a greater degree than in most parts of the old world, whence came America's urban heritage. What we are seeing today is the culmination of a long-standing process of metropolitan dispersion.

To understand how that dispersion occurred, we need to recall that the word "metropolitan" embraces two kinds of meaning. "Metropolitan" in one sense connotes tangible things. But in another equally important sense, the word concerns intangible cultural ideas. One meaning is morphological, the other functional. We use the word in a morphological sense when we speak of the skyscrapers and docks and public statues of metropolitan New York. It is a very tangible and visible New York, which we can recognize with our eyes and measure with tangible instruments. When we use the word functionally, however, we are talking about people and institutions that partake of a metropolitan culture—who are bound together by common ideas about how the world operates, how society should be organized, and how people should behave. In the cultural sense, the word "metropolitan" implies a high degree of complexity, sophistication, and interdependence. This kind of metropolitanism is often intangible—often hard to measure. It is closely related to the word "cosmospolitan"—of the cosmos, of the world. A metropolitan person may or may not be refined or dainty, but he is a man of the world, and connected with the world's ideas by an intricate web of communication lines. A metropolitan person, furthermore, is not necessarily an urban person—as Jefferson, Thoreau, and whole counties-ful of English statesmen have repeatedly demonstrated.

THE CULTURAL METROPOLIS AND ITS LONG-STANDING DISPERSION IN AMERICA

Metropolitan communication lines were best developed in cities, and that explains why metropolitan people were normally urban people also. (That, of course, is how we got the word "urbane.") But the relationship doesn't hold any more. The underlying thing that gave New York and London their peculiarly metropolitan character was their extreme accessibility to the ships that brought goods and wealth, and the mails and cable lines that brought information and ideas from the farthest margins of the earth. Lesser places in the United States didn't use to have that kind of accessibility, but they do now. The change began on a grand scale with Rural Free Delivery—experimental in 1889, permanent by 1902—and it culminated with the building of an all-weather high-speed national

Figure 3. Once upon a time, cities had a monopoly on metropolitan connections, but the primary highway system put an end to all that. Interstate Highway 5, in the central valley of California.

highway system. Today it is a rare American town that does not have good quick access to those primary highways and the fleets of trucks that move eternally among them (Fig. 3). Any one of those individual trucks can carry the most exotic goods literally anywhere there is a paved road, and deliver those goods to Miles City, Montana, as easily as to the upper east side of Manhattan. And, given the cost of moving trucks through New York traffic, it may do so more cheaply too. Indeed, the rural shopping center outside of Miles City may carry the same brand of gefilte fish as Horowitz's Delicatessen on 50th Street. And even without gefilte fish, the TV viewer in Miles City sees the same programs and is urged to buy the same products as the viewer in Manhattan. Thanks to cable and satellite transmission, the TV viewer in Montana may even have better reception and richer choices of programming than his New York cousin. That is not an unimportant matter in a day when most Americans get most of their ideas about the world by way of television—where children spend more waking hours watching TV than doing anything else, including sleeping or attending school.

There are, to be sure, very real differences between life in Manhattan and life in places the size of Miles City. The residents of both places relish those differences and will gladly tell you about them. Despite those obvious differences, the residents of both places have increasing access to the same tangible objects and the same intangible ideas. When it comes to the things that have historically made people metropolitan, many of the most obvious differences between big-city New York and small-town Montana pale into insignificance. The similarities are even more striking when one travels beyond the fringes of New York and Miles City, where metropolitan tissue pervades the once-rural countryside. In such new metropolitan territory, where so many Americans now live and work, cultural and physical differences are remarkably small.

Metropolitan dispersion occurs in other cultures, of course, but in contrast with the United States, that dispersion is usually weak and of recent origin. The reason for the differences arises from a fundamental difference between American cities and their Old World progenitors.

Most big European cities—and especially the old and famous ones—performed a much wider range of functions than their American offspring. From Roman and medieval times, the greatest cities flourished as centers of commerce, but even more as thrones of authority—civil, military, or religious, and commonly all three. The seats of those institutions were architecturally formidable, and deliberately so. Thus the walls of a medieval city functioned to keep enemies at bay, but they also served as symbols of power, a very tangible boundary line between the rulers and the ruled (Fig. 4). The palaces of the urban nobility were likewise grandiose, and for similar reasons. And ecclesiastical authority built the great cathedrals, surely the most awe-inspiring architectural creations of western man. Within the safety of the city walls, the nobility could afford to live well, so that art, music, literature, and architecture flourished under the patronage and protection of an urban ruling elite. It was a quintessentially metropolitan arrangement—and in the Old World it was quite naturally an urban arrangement too.

Figure 4. In traditional cities the boundaries of the metropolis were formidable and obvious, a boundary between the rulers and the ruled. These Roman walls around Ávila, Spain, were rebuilt in the last decade of the eleventh century.

Old-World cities were economic centers too of course, but economics often played a subordinate role to the military or religious or political function of the city (Fig. 5). So it was that marketplaces flourished in cathedral squares, and merchants hawked their goods in the shadow of the city's walls. It was the safest place to do business, just as it was a safe place to enjoy the fine arts. The countryside was the haunt of robbers and Philistines, an extramural wilderness.

The American experience was quite different. Almost without exception, American cities flourished if—and only if—they were successful economic enterprises. The main business of American cities was business, and it showed. If an American city possessed a central square, it was a market square, rarely a military plaza. And as soon as Americans learned to build high buildings, they were office buildings for businessmen, seldom cathedral spires for the glory of God. (Fig. 6).

It was no accident that noneconomic activities were absent or incidental to the American urban experience. Take the military, for example, which played so central a role in locating and designing so many Old World cities. In the absence of foreign invasion, Americans saw no need to build elaborate military fortresses, urban or otherwise; when forts were built to fend off Indians, they were ad hoc affairs that were promptly abandoned as soon as the Indian menace disappeared. Most Americans considered the professional military to be an expensive and

Figure 5. In cities of the Old World, economics commonly played a subordinate role to military, religious, and political functions. The marketplace in Batalha, Portugal.

VIEW FROM THE CAMPUS. SHOWING UNION TRUST. BUHL. PENOBSCOT.

DIME BANK, MAJESTIC BUILDINGS, AND CITY HALL, DETROIT, MICH.   280

Figure 6. The business of American cities has traditionally been business, and it shows. America's greatest urban cathedrals are commercial skyscrapers. Downtown Detroit in the late 1920s, from a contemporary postcard.

dangerous nuisance, to be starved or kept busy at a safe distance in the wilderness or on the high seas.

As for the church, it too was insignificant in shaping the morphology or culture of American cities. Indigenous American religion, after all, often had its deepest roots in the country, and of America's major native religions, only the Mormons turned a big city into an important religious center. When Methodists or Baptists paid attention to big cities, it was often the kind of horrified attention that any good Christian paid to barbarians in overseas colonies. The Methodist Church, for example, long sent "home missionaries" into the bowels of American cities, in much the same spirit as Livingstone was sent off to Africa to preach the message of redemption to the heathen.

Nor did America's biggest cities play important political roles—again in sharp contrast with practices in the Old World. In Europe, political authority routinely lodged itself in a strong central government, and that authority was permanently quartered in the national or provincial capital, always the biggest, richest, and most glittering city in a region or nation. Americans, by contrast, nourished a pathological suspicion of political authority, and made it a matter of high policy to weaken that authority. The doctrine of states' rights was just one natural outcome of that policy. The same policy dictated that power within the states be deliberately banished from the state's biggest city, lest the political machinery be corroded by urban iniquity, lest the power of the city exert too strong an influence upon weak and corruptible politicians. With few exceptions, state capitals were carefully located or relocated in *little* cities, places like Frankfort or Lansing or Jefferson City—emphatically not in Louisville or Detroit or St. Louis. In consequence, most of America's big cities lacked the architectural symbols of political authority, and they also lacked the periodic assembly of the state's political leaders, some of whom would inevitably be sent off to Washington to become congressmen or senators or national cabinet members or even presidents. It was a rare American president who could truly be called a city man.[6] America's political metropolis has traditionally distrusted both cities and city people.

The academic metropolis was also dispersed, and for similar reasons. College and university students were sent off to campuses in the countryside, quarantined from the perils of urban corruption. Small private college or great university, it made no difference. Ann Arbor and Berkeley and Urbana were chosen as seats of learning precisely because they were *not* Detroit or San Francisco or Chicago. Quite late in its urban career, of course, Chicago got its version of the Sorbonne, courtesy of Mr. Rockefeller, but Chicago was more properly known as hog-butcher to the world, only incidentally as a center of intellect.

Thus American cities were systematically deprived of their most potent metropolitan functions and were greatly impoverished thereby. That fact may help explain some of America's traditionally anti-urban prejudices. I suspect that Americans are not so much antagonistic to cities as they are antagonistic to America's one-sidedly economic cities. As Upton Sinclair and George F. Babbitt both demonstrated, cities that are single-mindedly engaged in laissez faire economics are not likely to be very uplifting places. New Jerusalems are hard to build when the raw materials are real-estate agencies and dark satanic mills.

There is an opposite side to the coin, to be sure. The dispersion of metropolitan cultural functions into nonurban parts of America permanently enriched the nation's rural and small-town culture to a degree that would be hard to match anywhere else in the world. In Charlottesville and East Lansing and Northfield and Oberlin and a thousand other little college towns across the country, students were reading Plato and Shakespeare and learning calculus and microbiology to become bona fide members of a metropolitan society without ever going near a city. And at each of the little state capitals, country lawyers came up to the state legislature and then went on to Washington to take their seats in the councils of the mighty.

THE DELAYED ARRIVAL OF THE PHYSICAL METROPOLIS IN AMERICA

So it was that much of nonurban Amercia has been functionally and culturally part of the metropolis for a long time. It remained only to make the countryside physically metropolitan, and that is now happening at a very rapid rate. The process began to occur when the economic metropolis began to follow the cultural metropolis into the countryside. We have just recently begun to see the tangible results of that economic dispersion on a grand scale, but the process itself is not new.

In fact, the economic boundaries between rural and urban America have always been less than clear, and farmers have done everything they could to blur the boundaries. From the times of earliest colonial settlement, Americans rejected the idea of subsistence farming; except in a few isolated places, there has seldom been anything resembling a traditional peasantry in the United States. The model American farmer was a businessman who sold his surplus at a profit; his desire for financial gain was not very different from that of the industrial capitalist or petit bourgeois shopkeeper who lived and worked in the city. The "best" farmers were those who used the tools and knowledge of the metropolis to make their land profitable. Farmers discovered that specialized farming brought higher profits than general farming. While many farmers spoke warmly of their "independent" rural life, the most successful ones were those who stuck to their commercial specialties and scorned the helter-skelter range of crops and animals that might have made them truly independent. Special crops, furthermore, required special seeds and fertilizers and machinery and buildings, so that "modern" farmers often bought as much as they sold, financing their purchases through metropolitan banks—often to their sorrow. The key to all this was connections with the metropolis, which provided not just higher profits but also the things and ideas that would free the farmer from drudgery and boredom.

Money and culture came in the same package. The farmer's son went off to the state agricultural college to learn about scientific crop management and double-entry bookkeeping, but he also learned the proper way to speak and dress and part his hair. The same railroad that hauled in fertilizers for the fields also delivered fashionable furniture for the parlor. Rural Free Delivery brought both hybrid seeds and stylish clothes from urban mail-order houses. Rural electrification powered milking machines but also the radio and TV sets that brought the metropolis into every farmhouse in America. Furthermore, by the second third of the twentieth century, running a commercial farm had become a very sophisticated financial venture, and a simple rustic did not survive in such an enterprise for very long. To a New Yorker, whose world ended at the Hudson, the idea of a sophisticated farmer seemed bizarre, but it was not bizarre to anybody who had paid attention to American farming. In cultural and economic terms as well, much of the American countryside was already very sophisticated and metropolitan, but in ways that were invisible to untutored city folk.

But we can see the metropolis now, and no doubt about it, because it is spreading very tangibly into almost every corner of the country. We can see it from the airplane window at 30,000 feet, or we can see it as a photographic cliché in planning publications—those long oblique air photos of endless tract housing (usually in Los Angeles or Long Island), designed to prove that America's farmland is being eaten up by suburbia (Fig. 7). When those photographs first began to appear in the 1950s, Americans were badly scared, partly because they

Figure 7. No planning document after World War II was complete without a photo-
graph like this—a long aerial oblique shot of suburbia creeping out from the city to
eat up the world. This was taken over Long Island in 1979, looking southward
toward Long Beach and the Atlantic.

had never seen anything like it before; partly because they didn't understand the
logic that lay behind this new apparently shapeless thing; partly because they
didn't even have a name for it. From the airplane window, it rather seemed as if
Americans were unwilling participants in a full-color horror movie, complete
with mindless, nameless, amoeboid creatures that obeyed no rules of reason but
were determined to devour the world—and us along with it.

The phenomenon came to be called "suburban sprawl," but the term was
badly misleading. The adjective "suburban" was simply wrong. Although much
of the new urban tissue lay adjacent to large cities, much of it did not, either in
location or in function. Instead of crowding around the edges of existing nucleated cities as proper suburbs used to do, this new metropolitan tissue often
flourished at great distances from established centers, its people and buildings
arranged in loose separated clusters. The residential subdivision, the shopping
centers, the industrial parks seemed to float in space; seen together, they resem-
bled a galaxy of stars and planets, held together by mutual gravitational attraction, but with large empty areas between clusters.

The pejorative "sprawl" was misleading too, for it seemed to suggest that this
new galactic urban tissue was some kind of unfortunate cosmetic eruption, rather like a bad case of pimples that Americans might grow out of some day if

only they learned to lead a clean life and apply the right kind of medication. But it is not temporary, and it is not cosmetic, and it will not go away. This *galactic metropolis*[7] is the standard tangible form that the American metropolis has taken. Furthermore, it is not suburban, and it is not an aberration. To be sure, one can find plenty of galactic metropolitan tissue on the fringes of Chicago, filling in the interstices between old established suburbs; but one can find it equally widespread across the once-rural tobacco country of eastern North Carolina,[8] on the Llano Estacado in Texas, in the Red River Valley of North Dakota, and on the edges of Rocky Mountain National Park—in sum, wherever people in the United States are building places to live and work and play. It is a fundamental geographic fact that since 1915, when the millionth Model-T rolled off the Ford assembly line,[9] there has not been a single large new city in America that has grown up with a traditional nucleated morphology. For more than half a century, Americans have been building their cities in the form of a galactic metropolis—and in no other way.[10]

THE GALACTIC METROPOLIS, AND HOW IT CAME TO BE

What happened is no mystery, but it is worth recalling just *how* it happened— how the dispersed tangible metropolis went out into the countryside to join the dispersed cultural metropolis that had been there for so long. One needs to remember that the old nucleated city, the city with a clearly-marked central business district and a clearly-marked edge, was a pre-automotive city. What kept that city from flying apart was the economic magnetism of the city's center, the place where transportation lines converged, and where business and industry competed for easy access to that transportation. Those old pre-automotive cities are easy to recognize on a road map: the maps of Cleveland and St. Louis and Detroit and Chicago all look like spiderwebs, and Boston was called "the hub" for good reason. City folk knew the importance of centrality, and they celebrated it. Skyscrapers served as signals that midcity land was expensive, and thus were tangible advertisements of commercial success. Americans decorated their skyscrapers with gargoyles and flying buttresses to show that they were proud of them. The ultimate symbol of urban accessibility, perhaps, was the railroad station, which Americans built in the same spirit that Europeans had built their castles and cathedrals—as temples to the American city's commercial gods (Fig. 8).

The new democratized automobile put an end to all that, for it allowed people to go almost anywhere they chose. To begin with, they chose to live outside the crowded city, and the period between 1915 and 1930 saw an unprecedented boom in suburbanization.

Americans didn't really understand that they were building the foundations for a wholly unprecedented kind of metropolis. After all, some of America's most magnificent downtown skyscrapers were built during the 1920s, testimonies to continued confidence in the magic of centrality. As for the suburbs, they had

Figure 8. Railroad stations were more than places to catch trains. They were monuments to centrality and temples to the city's commercial gods. Union Station, Columbus, Ohio, c. 1920, from a contemporary postcard. The station was demolished in 1978 amid lamentations from historic preservationists.

been around since the early nineteenth century. Brooklyn Heights, Philadelphia's Main Line, or Pasadena—the phenomenon seemed to be nothing new: after all, people for a long time had been riding ferry boats or horse cars or commuter trains from those suburbs to go downtown to work and shop. That judgment was dead wrong, of course, for the new automotive suburbs differed fundamentally from the old railroad and streetcar suburbs. The new suburbanites of the 1920s did not depend on any railroad's fixed schedule or fixed rails either, and those auto commuters presently discovered that they didn't need to go downtown to work or shop either.

There was some delay in making the discovery. The delay may help explain why most observers—foreign and domestic alike—failed to comprehend immediately the automobile's destructive effect on the old nucleated city. The Depression of the 1930s, followed by World War II, put a twenty-year moratorium on most privately financed building. During that period of frozen time, urban downtowns continued to do business more or less as usual. But downtown's time was borrowed. That time ended finally and abruptly as soon as World War II veterans returned home, clamoring for new houses, new cars, and a fair share of the new postwar prosperity.

The postwar housing boom was so colossal that many observers were distracted by its sheer scale. Only a few scholars were perspicacious enough to see that the new suburbanization was not just big, but that it represented a profound and permanent rearrangement of America's urban functions. The city was literally flying apart, for the simple reason that its nucleus had lost each of the three economic magnets that had held it together: commerce, industry, and residential housing.

It all seemed to happen at once. By the early 1950s, with the suburban housing boom in full blossom, Victor Gruen built Northland Shopping Center on the edge of Detroit, and the J. L. Hudson Company, the city's biggest and most prestigious department store firm, learned that it could make more money selling goods to suburbanites in the suburbs than by dragging them downtown to do the same thing. Hudson's sensational success provoked a stampede. Within twenty years, downtown Detroit was a commercial desert. Similar things were happening all over the country, but most conspicuously in the South and West, where nearly all big cities grew up in the automotive era and thus took on the classic galactic form. Houston was typical. Little more than an overgrown country town before World War II, by the 1970s it had more than two million people and was the tenth largest city in the country. A report from that period remarked that only eight percent of the city's retail trade was transacted in the central business district.[11]

Industry moved out too. Manufacturers found they could increase dividends

Figure 9. Multistoried urban factories were efficient only as long as cities were compact, and autoless workers necessarily lived closeby. Horizontal factories at freeway interchanges made factories like this obsolete. The old H. J. Heinz food-packing plant, Pittsburgh, c. 1910, from a contemporary postcard.

if they abandoned multistoried urban factories and built anew on cheaper land in the outskirts (Fig. 9). That cheap land encouraged the building of low-slung horizontal buildings, great space-consuming things that often looked from the air like shopping centers, what with their vast parking lots and loading docks for trucks. Simultaneously, of course, the new factories were closer to the work force, much of which had already abandoned the city for the green suburbs. As for the magnificent railroad stations, those monuments to centrality stood idle, waiting for the wrecking ball.

The federal urban renewal programs of the 1950s and 1960s have often been blamed for the plight of America's post-war cities. To be sure, in cities like Buffalo and St. Louis and Detroit and Syracuse, urban renewal laid waste to so much of downtown and near downtown areas that a visitor was reminded of Dresden after the fire-bombings and began to wonder who really won the war (Fig. 10). But urban renewal merely administered the coup de grace to cities whose centers were already moribund. (Fig. 11).

Of all federal projects, however, the interstate highway program really finished the job. On the one hand, those new fast highways sapped the vitality of anemic downtowns by making any area near an interchange more accessible than downtown ever was (Fig. 12). The combination of fast transportation and

Figure 10. After urban renewal, Buffalo, New York, looked like Dresden in 1945 and made one wonder who had really won the war. 1969.

Figure 11. A good many downtown areas were already moribund.
1880s San Diego, 1975.

Figure 12. The building of fast new highways sapped the vitality of downtowns. Highway construction, Cleveland, Ohio, 1958.

cheap land in the country proved an irresistible lure to commercial and industrial establishments that in an earlier time would have located downtown. Thus emerged the basic unit in the new galactic metropolis: typically a cluster of space-consuming buildings near an interchange, all equally and easily accessible by automobile and by truck, and all lavishly furnished with "free" parking. (From the airplane window, the single most visible constituent of the new landscape was the parking lot). Meanwhile, would-be house-owners discovered to their delight that they could live almost anywhere they wanted, if only they lived within a reasonable distance of a good highway, and preferably close to a freeway interchange (Fig. 13). Banks and real-estate developers were happy to oblige such folk; marginal farmers all over the country discovered with astonishment and pleasure that they could sell off the back forty for a sum that would buy a condominium in St. Petersburg and support them during their sunset years, playing shuffleboard in the sun. By the time American scholars and planners realized what was going on, the average freeway interchange had collected its share of the galactic metropolitan tissue that was erupting all over the country. By then the metropolis was on its way to becoming ubiquitous— functionally, psychologically, and physically too. For practical purposes, the urban frontier had disappeared in much of America, and it was disappearing fast in much of the rest.

Figure 13. Would-be house-owners could live almost anywhere, providing they were close to a high-speed road. Mobile home park (sic) and Interstate Highway 70, on the Great Plains east of Denver, 1978.

ACCEPTING THE FACTS OF
GALACTIC METROPOLITAN LIFE

Seen from a contemporary vantage point, none of this seems very remarkable, for most of it is very familiar. Most Americans have lived with these events all their lives; nearly all at some time work or live or do business in some part of the ubiquitous galactic metropolis. But it is worth recounting those familiar events, if only to recall how revolutionary recent American urban history has been—how radically the new urban rules have departed from those that America grew up with—and to remind ourselves how extraordinarily powerful are the forces that have gone to shape the cultural character and geographic patterns of the new metropolis.

Americans need to remind themselves of all these things when they confront the inevitable question: what is to be done with this unprecedented metropolitan structure they have built?

This is not the place to write a bill of particulars designed to reform the American metropolis. It is past time to remind ourselves, however, that whatever is done about the galactic metropolis, it is not going to go away. Planners may groan when they look out airplane windows and reach for the airsick bag, but

Americans are not going to abandon those freeways, nor their ranch-houses on those cul-de-sacs in the woods. Nor will the old nucleated city be restored to its former eminence. Historic preservationists may weep nostalgic tears about the good old days in downtown Detroit, but both the fact and the idea of downtown Detroit are gone, and the folk who left to settle the exurban countryside of Oakland and Washtenaw and Macomb Counties have no intention of returning to the inner city to live—and few show much inclination even to visit the place. Americans simply have too much capital invested in their present geographic patterns to abandon them wholesale, and that capital is emotional as well as economic. It is a plain fact that Americans overwhelmingly prefer the galactic metropolis to the nucleated city they abandoned fifty years ago. It is equally obvious, if one looks at the average American's not-so-average back yard, that most Americans really *like* the space that the galactic metropolis provides in such abundance (Fig. 14). That is what Sam Bass Warner meant when he remarked that Los Angeles was the kind of city that provided Americans with a "new freedom."[12] That prized freedom helps explain why Americans built the kind of city they did in Southern California and why, despite the lamentations of planners, they continue to build more.

What shall be done about the new ubiquitous metropolis? The answer is simple to phrase, but not so simple to execute. We must learn to live with it. I don't mean that as a counsel of despair. Learning to live with it is a literal guide for future behavior. The emphasis is on the word *learn*.

Figure 14. New freedom in the average American's not-so-average backyard. Exurban Washington, D.C., 1979.

We must learn three things about this new metropolis: how it is arranged, why it is arranged that way, and how it works. We should start with *description*. I am permanently surprised at how little good description there is of the galactic metropolis in the academic literature.[13] The paucity of such description suggests that many urbanologists have spent very little time looking at the galactic metropolis, or even its main constituent parts. The exceptions, however, are heartening—literate, perceptive scholars who have cultivated the habit of attention and know how to write lucid, forceful English.[14] We need more folk like that—people who refuse to think in bromides about "urban sprawl," who do not recoil in horror when they look out the airplane window. Vivid, accurate, dispassionate description is essential, not incidental, before we start thinking about reform.

We need to ask *why* the metropolis is arranged the way it is, and how it works That means asking hard questions about culture, not just economics. Too many geographers have talked for too long as if American cities were economic machines, and a good deal of urban geographic theory is sterile, not because it employs statistics, but because it is culturally incomplete. And we need history. We need to remember that much of America's metropolitan landscape—the pre-automotive part in particular—was created according to a cultural and economic logic that has long since ceased to operate. We can't hope to understand that antique landscape (much less manage it) unless we know the historical circumstances under which it was created. The moral is clear: to study the natural history of urban landscapes is not a frivolous pursuit.

Finally, when we get around to discussing reform, we need to start where we are, not in some mythical world where we would like to be. We need to accept the ubiquitous galactic metropolis as a permanent given, not as a temporary excrescence. Once we recognize that fact, we can begin to ask the right questions—and, just as important, we can couch those questions in realistic language that offers some hope of yielding plausible answers.

I would propose four such questions—or, rather, sets of questions—as examples of what I mean. Note that each set of questions begins with the same litany: *given* the existence of the galactic metropolis, *given* its culture, *given* its morphology, and *given* its historic origins—what can be done to solve or to ameliorate metropolitan problem X, Y, or Z?

1. Consider a set of *economic* questions first:
   given that the galactic metropolitan population is spread over a huge area, in clusters of differing density, separated by large sparsely populated spaces, and *given* that motor fuel is expensive and surely will grow more expensive:
   QUESTION: How can transportation be provided for that dispersed population that will provide good access to jobs and shops and neighbors, and will simultaneously use a minimum amount of fuel?
2. Consider a related group of *political* questions:
   given that the galactic metropolis operates as a single integrated system, yet is sliced into a myriad of political jurisdictions by geographic boundaries that are utterly irrational now because they were established long ago to meet conditions which have long since disappeared; and

given that established political boundaries are notoriously hard to change: QUESTION: What kind of political machinery can be invented that will allow the galactic metropolis to be governed in a just and economical way? QUESTION: What techniques will provide this fragmented American metropolis with reasonable municipal services—not just fire and police protection, but environmental protection as well—and do so at reasonable cost (Fig. 15)?

3. Consider some *aesthetic* questions (humans, after all, don't live by motor fuel alone):

given that residents of the galactic metropolis spend uncounted hours in motor vehicles, with their attention necessarily fixed on an automotive landscape: QUESTION: What can be done to relieve the visual squalor that encrusts that landscape? In particular, is it possible to banish the mind-numbing boredom of the national freeway landscape, the visual wastelands that are called parking lots, the wretchedness of the average strip development where the galactic metropolis transacts so much of its routine commercial business? Is it necessary for Americans, simply because they inhabit a novel metropolitan environment, to endure a half-life of ennui and ugliness (Fig. 16)?

Figure 15. What techniques can provide the galactic metropolis with environmental protection at reasonable cost? In the marshes west of Atlantic City, 1972.

Figure 16. Must Americans, simply because they inhabit the metropolis, endure a half-life of ennui and squalor? San Antonio, 1972.

4. Finally, consider what is perhaps the most grievous and intractable social question of our time, the matter of *race*—not just an "urban" question, but one that confronts the whole metropolis:

given that the poor black population of the United States is largely lodged within the archaic political boundaries of old nucleated cities, isolated by distance and by hatred from the mainstream of affluent metropolitan culture, and

given a fundamental paradox, that many of America's urban black people are really *non*metropolitan, inhabiting parts of old nucleated cities that have long since lost the economic connections with the metropolis that once made them hotbeds of opportunity:

QUESTION: What can be done to relieve the condition of poor black people who are trapped within the boundaries of those old cities, where for miles and miles, poor black people meet nobody but other poor black people, in an environment where children are routinely maleducated, teen-age males grow up without ever knowing the rewards of productive work, violence is endemic, where family life is a travesty, and racial hatred is a normal and accepted part of the local *Weltanschauung?*[15] (Fig. 17)

QUESTION: At the most primitive level, how can the geographic and institutional metropolis be altered so that it becomes easy and attractive for

Figure 17. It is a cruel paradox that much of America's urban population has very bad connections with the metropolis. Boston, 1974.

young blacks to smash out of that vicious iron circle of hatred and poverty, to join the metropolitan mainstream before their adult lives are permanently poisoned?

If there are cheap or easy answers to these questions, I have not yet heard of them. And each of these questions begets a dozen more, each as stubborn as the other.

But we can't even phrase intelligent questions until we face up to the ineluctable fact that the old urban frontier is almost gone—that nonmetropolitan America is rapidly disappearing—and that most Americans are living today in a kind of metropolis that neither they nor anyone else in the history of the world has ever inhabited before.

Notes

1. For an elaboration of this idea, see Peirce Lewis, "The Unprecedented City," in the Smithsonian Institution's *The American Land*, W. W. Norton & Co., New York, 1979, pp. 187-193.

2. Although the 1930 Census included the first general use of the term "rural-non-farm," U.S. census officials had been struggling with the problem of distinguishing rural from urban population for a long time. There had always been a nebulous shadow-zone between the two categories, but it was small enough to cause no special problem. By 1920, however, that intermediate population had grown so large that it could no longer be ignored, and it was necessary to devise another category. The three-fold classification of "urban," "rural-farm," and "rural-nonfarm" was invented to meet the need. For a historical survey of how the definitions emerged, see Henry S. Shryock, Jacob S. Siegel, and Associates, *The Methods and Materials of Demography* (Vol. 1), U.S. Bureau of the Census, Washington, D.C., 1975, pp. 158, 170 ff. See also Leon E. Truesdell, *Farm Population: 1880 to 1950*, U.S. Bureau of the Census Technical Paper No. 3, 1960.

3. "Standard Metropolitan Statistical Areas and Standard Consolidated Statistical Areas: 1980," U.S. Department of Commerce, Bureau of the Census, Supplementary Report PC80-S1-5, Washington, D.C., October, 1981, pp. 1-2. The report notes that numerous changes in boundaries of statistical areas between 1970 and 1980 tended to mask the true magnitude of change: "A large portion (of metropolitan growth) has stemmed from expansion of metropolitan territory through addition of counties as suburban development reached them, and through reclassification of smaller urban communities as they grew large enough to qualify as metropolitan. During the 1970s it was only this geographic expansion that caused the SMSAs to increase their share of the national population." And even if those artificial boundary changes are ignored between 1970 and 1980, the population of areas defined as metropolitan increased by 10.2 percent—less than the national increase of 11.4 percent, and substantially less than the "nonmetropolitan" rate of 15.1 percent.

4. During the 1960s, 23 of 243 SMSAs recorded population decrease. During the 1970s, 29 of 318 decreased, of which 28 were located in the northeast or north-central parts of the country.

5. The Editors of *Fortune, The Exploding Metropolis*, Doubleday & Company, Garden City, New York, 1958. The book caused considerable stir because it was one of the first widely distributed books to sound an alert that Americans were really building a new kind of city. Contributors to the book, who included William H. Whyte, Jr. and Jane Jacobs, thought the new urban form was detestable and urged Americans to change their ways. Most Americans, however, were evidently not convinced.

6. Al Smith was the first candidate for president who deliberately eschewed a countrified image and advertised himself as a big-city man. His thumping defeat in 1928 resulted as much perhaps from his New York hat and accent as from his religion and his views on drinking. Typically our most urbane presidents have been men like Thomas Jefferson of Monticello (carefully situated well outside the limits of urban Charlottesville), Theodore Roosevelt of Sagamore Hill, Franklin Roosevelt of Hyde Park, Woodrow Wilson of Staunton and Princeton, and John Kennedy of Hyannisport. Never mind that Kennedy was quite at home in the heart of Irish Boston, and that Theodore Roosevelt was a highly realistic police commissioner of New York City. Both men took pains to cultivate a nonurban image, whether by breaking broncos in North Dakota or walking barefoot on the beaches of Cape Cod.

7. I greatly dislike pretentious jargon, so I offer this coinage with reluctance. But "galactic metropolis" describes the phenomenon accurately, and I know of no other word or phrase that adequately describes the morphology or function of our new metropolitan tissue. When Harris and Ullman defined cities with "multiple nuclei" in 1945, their phrase came closer than most; Ullman's revised description of 1962 came still closer when he spoke of "cities [that] have been growing in size, expanding even more in area, and declining in overall density." But Harris's and Ullman's multinucleated cities still looked much like traditional cities; they had traditional names, like Chicago or Detroit; and the new tissue of their multinucleated cities was organically attached to such old cities. The galactic metropolis is quite a different kind of creature, both in location and in form. Furthermore, much of it has no name, unless one settles for the name of some local shopping center or accepts postal codes in lieu of names. (See Chauncey D. Harris and Edward L. Ullman, "The Nature of Cities," *Annals of the American Academy of Political and Social Science* CCXLII (November 1945), pp. 7-17. Also Edward L. Ullman, "The Nature of Cities Reconsidered," *Papers and Proceedings of the Regional Science Association* 9 (1962), pp. 7-23. The quotation is from p. 7).

8. See John Fraser Hart and Ennis Chestang, "Rural Revolution in East Carolina," *The Geographical Review* 68 (October 1978), pp. 435-458. Hart and Chestang's essay ostensibly concerns the mechanization of flue-cured tobacco production in eastern North Carolina, and American urban geographers have traditionally paid little attention to such matters. In fact, the essay should be required reading for any serious student of the contemporary American city, for it is a forceful and careful account of how the galactic metropolis is invading and conquering some of America's remotest rural areas.

9. John B. Rae. *The American Automobile, a Brief History*. University of Chicago Press, 1965, p. 65.

10. P. Lewis, "The Unprecedented City," Note 1.

11. The figure was cited in a report by New Orleans Planning Commission in 1970 in order to warn of the fate that would befall New Orleans if it went the way of Houston. Although New Orleans's downtown was marvellously healthy in contrast with many other American cities, all but 24 percent of the metropolitan area's retail business was conducted outside the central business district.

12. Sam Bass Warner, Jr. "The New Freedom," chapter 5 in *The Urban Wilderness: a History of the American City*, Harper & Row, New York, 1972. Warner is talking about "freedom from spacial restrictions [which] offered an unprecedented array of urban arrangements. . . ." (p. 119). Warner cites Los Angeles as the supreme example of that new freedom.

13. Suburbanization and urban sprawl, however, have been treated exhaustively. For a careful summary and large bibliography, see Peter O. Muller, *The Other City: Geographical Consequences of the Urbanization of the Suburbs* Resource Paper No. 75-2, Association of American Geographers, Washington, D.C., 1976. B. J. L. Berry and Quentin Gillard have noted the enormous expansion of metropolitan commuter fields in *The Changing Shape of Metropolitan America: Commuting Patterns, Urban Fields, and Decentralization Processes,*

1960-1970, Ballinger Publishing Co., Cambridge, Mass., 1977. Even closer to the idea of the galactic metropolis is Joseph C. Doherty's astute discussion of the "rural-urban continuum" and "the countrified city" in his essay, "Public and Private Issues in Nonmetropolitan Government," the final section of Glenn V. Fuguitt et al., *Growth and Change in Rural America*, The Urban Land Institute, Washington, D.C., 1979, pp. 53 ff.

14. Three authors come immediately to mind. Grady Clay, the landscape architect and journalist, has been describing cities with attention and care for a long time. *Close-up: How to Read the American City* (University of Chicago Press, 1973 and 1980) is probably the best and most elaborate exposition of his work. Thomas Baerwald is a geographer who has written a careful description of what happened between 1953 and 1976 to the margins of Interstate Highway 494, a freeway that is part of the bypass system around Minneapolis-St. Paul and that Baerwald describes as "The Emergence of a New 'Downtown.'" It is, in fact, an elementary constituent of the galactic metropolis. *The Geographical Review* 68 (July 1978), pp. 308-318, 378. Baerwald completed his graduate work in the geography department at the University of Minnesota, whose faculty and graduate students include some of America's most attentive and perceptive observers of the urban landscape. And, of course, Sam Bass Warner's works (note 10) constitute essential basic reading for anyone who wants to understand the origins of the galactic metropolis.

15. Racial hatred is not randomly distributed in space. For documentation, see John S. Adams, "The Geography of Riots and Civil Disorders in the 1960's," *Economic Geography* 48 (January 1972), pp. 24-42. See also Harold M. Rose, "The Geography of Despair," *Annals of the Association of American Geographers* 68 (December 1978), pp. 453-463.

The Galactic Metropolis: Misguided Misnomer

Kirk H. Stone

Two or more scholars studying the same topic commonly disagree. This is as it should be. And, as the title of Professor Lewis's chapter indicates, he and I disagree sharply. But it should be understood that we have agreed to disagree, and that this analysis of his observations is impersonal and objective, laced with respect for a fluid presentation on urban development in the United States but knotted by provocative generalizations and murky aim at the conference.

The assigned topic is Geographic Perspectives on Non-Metropolitan Land Use Change. Study and interpretation of Professor Lewis's words might be simplified to the theme that metropolitan form is everywhere and exclusive. One may think this is euphuistic, at least in part—and I do. One also may think it less than omnipresent—and I do. Further, one may think it omnipotent—and I do not. Or one may think it based on logic rather than belief, or upon various geographic scales rather than one—but I still do not. The paper may appear to many too much like the Bostonian's map of the United States, drawn to scale for Massachusetts but everything progressively smaller in scale to the south and west! Or an analyst might ask: what is the land-use issue in nonmetropolitan America, the conference theme, if there is no nonmetro? And for the future it is written that galactic metropolitanism is here to stay in its present form, patently challengeable on both historic and geographic bases.

DEFINITION

Disagreement in scientific discourse often stems from differing definitions. Such may be part of the case here.

The major unfortunate quality in current analyses is the acceptance and employment of the metropolitan-nonmetropolitan classification of population. Dichotomies commonly are weak; here they are dangerous. Nonmetro has been taken to mean whatever is left over after metro is delineated—in the United

51

States a misunderstood and major part of the population. Further weakening of nonmetro is the 1980 census subdivision of the metro part into nine classes, leaving people in places of less than 50,000 in just one class.

Professor Lewis uses nonmetro and nonurban synonymously. One may agree when he notes that "the term nonmetropolitan is seriously misleading." But he provides no alternative, while saying little about that part of our settlement landscape. There is no justification for accepting another colleague's statement that the dichotomy is all we have to work with; there is nothing to stop other ways being suggested. And it is discouraging to note that most of Lewis's examples are drawn from large metropolitan areas, not the topic of the conference.

The caveat following this is the notation that "metropolitan" has two definitionals, one cultural and one physical. Few could debate that urban culture is widespread and continues to be so via television, telephone, and other aural and visual means. But to state or infer that these United States are morphologically metropolitanizing all over, particularly because of increasing access, is unnecessarily disputatious, regardless of varying definitions.

POSSIBLE NONMETRO LAND USE ISSUES

Rather than urban development, the assigned topic of land use issues in the nonmetro landscape might have been approached directly. There are many examples: the concentration of specialized vegetable production in the southwestern corner of the country (areas surely rural in morphology); the disappearance of cotton in favor of cattle and chickens in much of the South; a zoning against farming in certain rural areas; in parts of the Plains states increasing farm sizes related to major total population losses; and in widespread localities the development of rural retirement communities. Others overseas are possible forerunners of the U.S. rural landscape: abandonment of farms in Iceland and parts of Argentina, and new rural settling for agriculture, fishing, and/or forestry in Norway, Spain, Middle America, southern Africa, Indonesia, and the Philippines.

The point that all kinds of nonmetropolitan issues may accompany metropolitanizing trends draws support from some experiences of just the past half century. In Sweden the planners sponsored new rural settling in the north, then withdrew enabling actions, and now are again supportive. In Finland the government wholeheartedly espoused new farming in the north, but in 1970 completely reversed that position. Here in the United States, supporting legislation and funds advocated new rural settling all over in the 1930s, and then the soil bank and similar measures reversed the process. Other changes might occur, either by fiat or because of an increase in prices of gasoline, or more rural zoning, or changes in lifestyles, or whatever it was that made great Middle Eastern and southern Asian cultures, including well-established large cities, collapse.

SELECTED DISPUTATIONS

Geographers will applaud the small scaling of Professor Lewis by his flying his readers at 30,000 feet. It should also be remembered, however, that these days such flight will be at 450-550 miles an hour. So one might be out of sight of a large city or freeway in only some parts of the nation. Further, after studying the interstate highway system map of the whole country and thinking of using these routes at 55 miles an automobile hour, one might ask, is the ever-present urban aspect the same?

Not incidentally, is the statement "bulldozers are everywhere" really accurate from 30,000 feet or from an automobile—and in the great C-shaped part of our nation that has been losing population for at least 30 years?

Reconsideration of Broken Bow, Nebraska as Lewis's example of metropolitanized small towns discloses facts for disagreement. What "good quick access" means is not clear, but this small town has only State Route 2-92 and the Burlington Northern railroad, beside each other and oriented northwest-southeast, and is some 40 miles north of Interstate 80; the location is 650 miles west of Chicago at the 100th meridian in the center of the state. These represent varying degrees of isolation. The city's population of about 3700 makes it rural by most definitions; the "rural shopping center" consists of a few stores and a drive-in theater half a mile east of the city limits and near the fairgrounds. It is possible that many things available in New York City could be freighted in, but the questions are: 1) do the few people in a rural shopping center near a rural place like Broken Bow provide market enough so they really do or could have the same choices and prices as New Yorkers; and 2) is this small and highly nucleated county seat truly metropolitanized morphologically, even if its citizens could believe that it is so culturally? If these questions do not make the point that metropolitanization has a mighty long way to go in Broken Bow, then one might consider similar places like Cedar Springs in Georgia, Black River Falls in New York, Gabbs in Nevada, Turner in Montana, and hundreds of others.

Three points made by Professor Lewis are puzzling: "We have no historical models to gauge it [the galactic metropolis] by"; "whole SMSAs-ful of people are migrating to the countryside"; and American college and university students were "sent off to campuses in the countryside, quarantined from the perils of urban corruption." For the first statement let us ask about India, northeast China, and the Tigris-Euphrates area if Japan really is only now "taking place"? For the second, which SMSAs, and is the "countryside" rural? And for educational centers' rural locations one may query how Harvard and the Universities of Minnesota, Washington, Los Angeles, and Miami fit the generalization.

Professor Lewis's notation that "any near an interchange (in a city) is more accessible" is a reminder of a geographer's comment about trying to stop overnight in Atlanta near I 75-85. He spoke blasphemously of finally getting off the I route, of struggling valiantly to reach the correct one-way street leading toward the motel's sign, and then noted most irreverently finally getting back on the Interstate and leaving. Access indeed! Anyway, is this related to the nonmetro land uses assigned us?

THE SOUTHERN EXAMPLE

Professor Lewis implies that there is no nonmetropolitan classification by stating that nearly everything is metropolitan. Two other viewpoints are possible: 1) that there is a nonmetro, however inadequately defined, that applies to large parts of our country's rural settlement morphology; and 2) that change—and not merely increasing metropolitanizing—characterizes it.

Recent published research on the South demonstrates both points (Stone et al. 1980). Nearly four-fifths of the region's counties are in the non-metro category. When the counties are classified on the basis of degree of rurality of a county's population in combination with the size of its largest place, a considerable rurality (as defined by the Bureau of the Census) is disclosed. For example, some 32.9 percent of the 1098 nonmetro counties are Totally Rural and another 28.5 percent are High Majority Rural with only a Town (Stone et al. 1980, Table 2, p. 13). The maps of these show the Totally Rural to be rather evenly widespread (Fig. 1) with some clustering in western Texas and Oklahoma, while the High Majority Rural counties are evenly and closely distributed, excepting

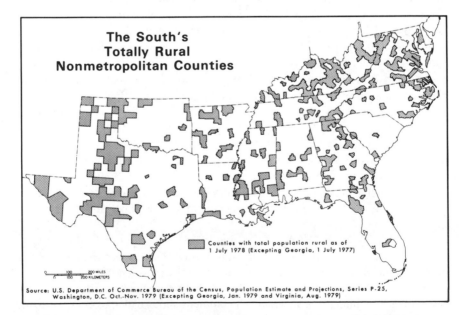

Figure 1. The South's totally rural nonmetropolitan counties. Reprinted from *The South's Nonmetropolitan Counties: Categories, Changes, and Consequences,* Kirk H. Stone, Ernest E. Melvin, and John C. Argo, ©1980, Institute of Community and Area Development, The University of Georgia, by special permission.

western Texas and Oklahoma, and mostly with Towns as the largest places (Fig. 2) (Stone et al. 1980, Figs. 3 and 4, pp. 14 and 15). On the other hand, the High-Majority Urban counties, making up only 5.1 percent of the regional types, are highly concentrated in western Texas and Oklahoma and are nearly absent eastward (Stone et al. 1980, Fig. 6, p. 18).

Further, there have been many changes in the South's nonmetro counties in recent times. Since 1940, for example, the numbers and locations of Southern counties losing and gaining in total population have been quite fluid (Melvin et al. 1978). In addition, the comparison of maps of the same and similar categories for just 1974 to 1979 show continued variety in their numbers and distributions while detailed research on selected examples shows many trends of settlement in the region (Stone et al. 1980, Figs. 1 and 3-5, pp. 6 and 14, 15, 17 and *passim.*). So forecasts about nonmetropolitan county changes in the South at least have few bases at detailed scales and have not proved to be better in more general considerations.

Thus at least most of the South, which is a large part of our nation, is far from metropolitanized in the physical quality of its settlement, this in spite of the 17.1 percent increase in its nonmetro population from 1970 to 1980. With the total population losses that have occurred in the C-shaped area from the Plains states eastward, one might therefore estimate that other large parts of the United States are not only functionally nonmetropolitan but are becoming more

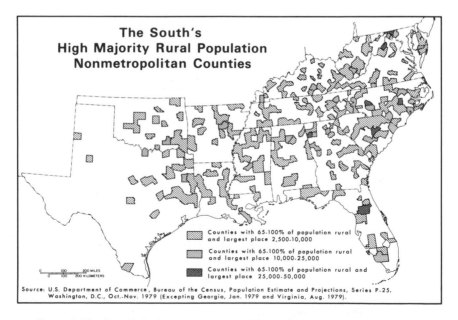

Figure 2. The South's high majority rural population nonmetropolitan counties. Reprinted from *The South's Nonmetropolitan Counties: Categories, Changes, and Consequences*, Kirk H. Stone, Ernest E. Melvin, and John C. Argo, ©1980, Institute of Community and Area Development, the University of Georgia, by special permission.

so, rather than less. And why not? Have not the great centuries-old megalopolitan areas of the Far and Near East experienced severe losses on occasion?

CONCLUSION

In retrospect, "The Galactic Metropolis" is a misguided misnomer. Professor Lewis slights the assigned topic of nonmetropolitan land use change, and his proposed new term is neither necessary, as a step towards Gottman's megalopolis, nor valid as applied to major parts of our nation's total settlement landscape.

References

Stone, K. H., Melvin, E. E., and Argo, J. C., 1980. *The South's Nonmetropolitan Counties: Categories, Changes, and Consequences*. Institute of Community and Area Development, The University of Georgia, Athens, Georgia.

Melvin, E. E., Stone, K. H., and Hardaway, T. F., 1978. *The South's Changing Population and the Georgian Example*, Institute of Community and Area Development. The University of Georgia, Athens, Georgia.

Further Geographical Perspective

John R. Borchert

In one sense there is no question about Peirce Lewis's main thesis. The nation is indeed one big metropolitan system. A very substantial body of work in geography, regional science, economics, transportation, demography, and related fields amply documents that fact. And, as Professor Lewis asserts, the physical pattern of today's metropolitan system is here to stay. Or it will dissolve only very slowly into whatever follows it. More than half of all the floor space built in all of American history has been built during the automotive age. Much of it is not yet paid for. And given the average housing replacement rate in this century, the life expectancy of buildings standing today is one to two centuries. So regardless of what is said, the necessity to adapt life-styles and transportation systems to the existing settlement pattern far exceeds the opportunity to throw away the auto-age settlements and replace them with something that might appear more rational.

Hence there is also no question about the desirability of setting goals, making plans, and trying to solve problems within the auto-age settlement framework. The three families of problems that Professor Lewis describes are certainly major ones. The neglect of aesthetics and environment is a part of the larger and fundamental lack of attention to systematic maintenance and replacement, to which Americans are finally beginning to awaken. The concentration of poor and segregated people in the oldest, most decrepit areas reflects a set of equally fundamental problems in our approach to income redistribution, through both the housing system and the education system, to which the society has barely begun to awaken. The third major family of problems, which Professor Lewis notes in passing, is surely as important as the other two. That is the political-geographical fragmentation of the metropolis—whether it is ubiquitous or not. There are thousands of overlapping jurisdictions without regional or national priorities; national publics who are quite willing to trample over the domain of local minorities and individuals without making adequate, humane compensation to those who are injured; and separation of authority from responsibility in many aspects of both the land development process and the regulatory process.

It is also true that these problems are not new. There has been a tendency to call them "urban" problems or even "the urban problem." Yet, at least since the 1960s, many people have said repeatedly that these are actually *national* problems that happen to be most visible at this time in the cities. They are by no means confined to cities, certainly not caused by cities, and certainly not corrected by railing against cities. Now Professor Lewis seems to tell us that they are, after all, city problems, but the "city" is everywhere. So we have reframed the problem. But there still are no "quick or easy solutions." Can we suggest, then, some "long and difficult" solutions and the first practical steps toward them that could be taken through geographical research and teaching? There is something else here that is not new. That is our predilection in the social sciences to reframe and reframe and reframe a problem, while the problem persists, is seldom solved, and eventually fades away in favor of another problem that assumes greater urgency or stylishness.

Finally, I would caution that one could go too far with the concept of the ubiquitous metropolis. There are of course still great differences in the actual and future amount and type of development. Freeway interchanges are not everywhere. There are perhaps two hundred junctions—intersections of two or more inter-city segments of the interstate system—in the nation; and fewer than twenty of those are outside Standard Metropolitan Areas. "The metropolis" is obviously not everywhere, even though the slides used in presenting the paper gave that impression; one could easily put together an equal number of slides that would suggest the country is empty. Thirty high-order metropolitan clusters occupy about one-fifth of the nation's land area and contain nearly three-quarters of the population. Shifts from one major land use to another are concentrated within a relatively small part of the national land area. Such shifts involved only about ten percent of the total area of the United States in the last fifty years. Of that, most of the change was simply oscillation in and out of crop, pasture, and woodland, within the farm framework. It reflected the fitfully increasing intensity and geographical concentration of American agriculture. Only two percent of the land was involved in the shift from other uses to urban subdivision, and only one percent in the expansion of mines, airfields, other rural transportation or industrial facilities, and improved open space. Reasonable expectations over the next fifty to one hundred years could involve another two percent of the land in urbanization, and another two percent in materials and energy production.

Thus most of the national land use pattern is relatively stable. But along the boundaries and in the gradient zones between those stable regions, there are relatively narrow but major land use tension zones; that is where we need to concentrate our attention. Our concern is with particular areas within this large, variegated metropolitan system, within these relatively narrow zones of conflict. The basic question there is what geographical information is needed to help to resolve the conflicts. There is an urgent and continuing need for description and interpretation of site, accessibility, ownership, and value patterns. For a given new development or redevelopment, among all the sites that are plausible, which should be developed first, which later? Some sites have a high suitability and priority for more than one use. Which high-priority use should prevail at each of those places? Those are questions of location. They demand geographic research and teaching. That will help improve the machinery for resolving land-use conflicts that are essentially locational decisions.

And if we can get on with the job, perhaps we can contribute in a substantive way to the actual solutions to some problems before they simply fade away. For they will indeed fade away. The "galactic city" built during the cheap oil-automotive age is here to stay, to be sure. But I have no doubt that fifty to seventy-five years hence, it will be simply the largest and newest among the historic layers of architectural memorabilia on the American scene.

II. Elements of Rural Growth

Socioeconomic Context of Nonmetropolitan Land Use Change

David L. Brown and Calvin L. Beale

INTRODUCTION

Growth, decline, and other changes that affect the structure of a community take place on the land. Yet analyses of rural community development seldom focus on the association between sociodemographic changes on the one hand and land use change on the other.

The land market is but one of many interrelated institutions that constitute the rural community. Hence the allocation of land among uses that occurs in such a market is affected by a constellation of community forces. This chapter seeks to establish the general sociodemographic context within which land-use change is taking place in rural America, and to describe generalized situations in which competition for rural land is mounting. Of particular concern are two major trends that have characterized the 1970s: (a) decentralization of population and economic activities, and (b) acceleration in the rate of conversion of rural land to urban and built-up uses. The evidence and analysis presented point to potential areas of competition; they do not establish direct empirical linkages between sociodemographic and land use change.

Between 1970 and 1978, nonmetropolitan areas gained a net of 2.9 million

The authors thank for their comments on an earlier version of this paper: Malcolm Baldwin, Council on Environmental Quality; Leon Bouvier, The Population Reference Bureau; Kenneth Deavers, Economic Research Service, USDA; Glenn V. Fuguitt, University of Wisconsin; Fred Hines, Economic Research Service, USDA; Larry Long, Center for Demographic Studies, Bureau of the Census; Wilbur Zelinsky, Department of Geography, Pennsylvania State University.

The views expressed herein are those of the authors, not necessarily those of the U.S. Department of Agriculture, the Council on Environmental Quality, or the ten other federal agencies participating in the National Agricultural Lands Study. Editorial assistance was provided by Stuart Diamond and Ernest McGill.

Table 1. Population Change by Metropolitan Status

| Area | Population | | | | | | Net Migration | | | | | |
| | Number (Thous.) | | | Percentage Change | | | 1970-78 | | 1960-70 | |
	1978	1970	1960	1970-78	1960-70		Number Thou.	Rate* Pct.	Number Thou.	Rate* Pct.
Total United States	218,063	203,301	179,323	7.3	13.4		3,402	1.7	3,224	1.8
Metropolitan Counties†	157,942	148,877	127,191	6.1	17.0		523	.4	6,018	4.7
Large Core Counties‡	59,554	59,862	53,547	-.5	11.8		-3,108	-5.2	470	.9
All Other Urban Counties	88,044	80,566	66,746	9.3	20.7		2,305	2.9	4,824	7.2
Rural Counties	10,344	8,449	6,898	22.4	22.5		1,326	15.7	724	10.5
Nonmetropolitan Counties	60,121	54,424	52,132	10.5	4.4		2,879	5.3	-2,794	-5.4
Adjacent Counties§	31,184	28,033	26,116	11.2	7.3		1,724	6.2	-621	-2.4
Nonadjacent Counties	28,937	26,391	26,016	9.6	1.4		1,155	4.4	-2,172	-8.4

*Net Migration Expressed as Percentage of the Population at Beginning of Specified Period.
†Metropolitan Status as of 1974.
‡Central Counties of Metropolitan Areas of More Than 1 Million.
§Nonmetropolitan Counties Adjacent to Standard Metropolitan Statistical Areas.

Table 2. Conversion of Rural Land to Urban, Built-up, and Water Use, 1958-75

Conversion	Area in Use			Average Annual Conversion	
	1975	1967	1958	1967-75	1958-67
	----------Million Acres----------			----Million Acres----	
Total	140.15	116.76	99.77	2.92	1.87
Urban and Built-up*	77.64	60.99	50.77	2.08	1.14
Water	62.51	55.77	49.20	.84	.73

Source: Soil Conservation Service 1965; U.S. Department of Agriculture 1971; and Dideriksen et al. 1977.
   *Includes transportation uses.

migrants from metropolitan areas, reversing the conditions of rural outmovement of the previous decade (Table 1). During roughly the same period (1967-75), an average annual rate of 2.1 million acres of rural land were converted to urban and builtup uses. This compares with 1.1 million acres a year during 1958-67 (Table 2). Hence land conversion trends appear to be consistent with the increased decentralization of population and economic activity.

DEMOGRAPHIC TRENDS

Since at least 1920, the United States has undergone a curious demographic pattern in which accelerations of population growth have brought a greater concentration of people, and slackenings have witnessed population deconcentration. The more rapidly national population growth occurs, the fewer are the counties showing any growth. Conversely, slowdowns in the national growth rate from one decade to another have invariably been accompanied by an increase in the number of growing counties. The nature of the relationship is obscure and could conceivably even result from chance. But in any event, the decade of the 1970s was consistent with this rule. The rate of U.S. population growth during that decade dropped by nearly a third compared with the 1960s (9.1 percent versus 13.4 percent), but through 1978, 770 more counties had increased in population than in the previous decade. Decentralization has included a continuation of suburban growth, net migration from north to south and west, and a revitalization of rural areas.

Nonmetropolitan Turnaround

Most nonmetropolitan counties in the 1970s emerged from their decline in population to a period of growth; or, if already growing, they increased their rate of growth. From 1970 to 1978, the nonmetropolitan counties grew in population by 10.5 percent, compared with a growth of just 4.4 percent in the entire 1960-70 decade. This was accomplished, despite a declining birth rate, by a shift in the flow of migration. A net outmovement of 2.8 million nonmetropolitan people in the 1960s shifted to a net inflow of 2.9 million in the first eight years of the 1970s. Nearly two-thirds of the hundreds of declining nonmetropolitan counties of the 1960s are estimated to have grown since 1970.

Within the metropolitan areas themselves, there are many counties that are predominantly rural in scale of settlement and in land use patterns. Extended commuting has integrated such counties into metropolitan labor markets. On the basis of 1970 population data, 212 metropolitan counties were solely or primarily rural in population (39 had no urban population at all). These counties contained 10.3 million people in 1978. Their growth of 22.5 percent over the 1970-78 period was somewhat more rapid than it had been during the 1960s, when annual inmigration doubled. By contrast, predominantly urban metropolitan counties grew by just 5 percent and shifted from inmovement to outmovement.

It should be emphasized that the resurgence of nonmetropolitan population growth is not simply a revival of small towns. Small towns and cities have participated in the trend, but Bureau of the Census estimates indicate that the highest rate of growth has occurred in the open country and in unincorporated hamlets. From 1970-75, the nonmetropolitan population in incorporated places grew by 4.6 percent, whereas that in the open country and hamlets rose by 7.6 percent. Growth within municipalities was moderately ahead of that of the 1960s, but growth outside town limits was nearly 5 times as great as in the 1960s. In other words, population pressures on land were distinctly in the form of decentralization out of established towns—whether metropolitan or not—and much greater entry into rural settings.

There seem to be several major reasons for the trend. Ever since the mid-1960s, residential preference surveys have consistently shown a higher percentage of the population expressing a preference for rural or small-town living than actually live there. Thus there has been a reservoir of sentiment favoring the direction of movement that has actually occurred. Some of it is based on positive notions of the advantages of living in small-scale communities; some of it is expressed in terms of negative views of big city life.

Improved rural and small-town employment conditions have helped put residential preferences into effect. In the decades between 1940 and 1970, heavy losses of farm and mine employment displaced many rural people and were only partly offset by such increases in other types of work as the local areas obtained. For example, in the 1950s the United States lost an average of 170,000 primary agricultural jobs per year. This increased to 200,000 per year in the 1960s. By contrast, the average annual figure was only 8,000 in the 1970s. Losses in mining occurred from a much smaller base, but losses of 19,000 annually in the 1950s and 9,000 annually in the 1960s shifted to a growth of 25,000 per year in the 1970s, recovering the 1950 to 1970 loss. Thus the 1970s saw much less displacement of rural people from traditional extractive industries.

Perhaps even more important, employment in every major industry group increased nationally at a more rapid rate in nonmetropolitan counties than in metropolitan areas in the 1970s. This situation was true of manufacturing in the 1960s but then spread to trade, services, construction, public administration, utilities, communications, real estate, and all other industry groups. Nonmetropolitan wage rates lag behind those of metropolitan rates, but employment opportunities have become much more numerous than they used to be. A fully adequate explanation of employment decentralization is not yet available, but it is known that manufacturing employers tend to emphasize labor factors such as supply, attitude, productivity, and wages as incentives for their decisions to locate in nonmetropolitan areas.

The propensity of retired people to move to small communities, and the greatly increased number of them who have large enough pensions to be mobile, have also been factors in recent population shifts. Mobility rates are not high for older people, but their degree of net flow to nonmetropolitan locations is much greater than that of other age groups. For example, from 1970-75, 210 persons aged 55 and over moved to nonmetropolitan areas for every 100 who moved in the opposite direction. The comparable figure for younger persons was 115 per 100. Although many more counties can be defined as retirement destinations than used to be the case, retirement movement is still sufficiently concentrated that many of the most rapidly growing nonmetropolitan counties have retirement—along with recreational services—as their basic source of economic and demographic growth.

The development of conditions fostering movement into nonmetropolitan areas and accelerating outmovement from larger and older metropolitan areas has occurred much faster than anyone foresaw, as evidenced by the demographic projections of the period 8 to 12 years ago which confidently predicted a continuation of higher metropolitan growth. The experience is not uniquely American, judging by analogous international trends shown by Vining and Kontuly (1978) and by Wardwell (1977).

Regional Trends

Regionally, growth of the U.S. population has been overwhelmingly in the west, the timbered areas of the South, northern New England, and parts of the Upper Great Lakes area. In fact, the South and the West alone account for 90 percent of the growth since 1970; for the first time these areas have more than half of the nation's total population. The basic regional drift is not new; the center of population has moved both westward and southward in each decade since 1920. But the extent of the shift has been greater than was expected, partly because the near cessation of population increase from Massachusetts to Illinois was not foreseen.

The regional shift of population from the North to the South and West has also tended to transfer population to lower-density settlement forms, quite apart from the urban to rural shift. Northern urbanized areas have had a higher density than have those in the South and West. About three-fifths of northern urbanized areas had overall densities of 3,000 or more people per square mile in 1970.

From the point of view of population distribution policy, the nation has achieved just about what it wanted ten years ago. The pace and apparent necessity of rural to urban migration were widely deplored at that time. Also deplored were the impact on already congested urban receiving areas and the distress caused in rural source areas. "Balanced growth" was the theme of the day; legislation such as the Rural Development Act of 1972 made it the explicit policy of the government to encourage the revitalization of rural areas.

One aspect of recent trends has been to put much more of the nation's growth into the public land states. The eleven western states (excluding Alaska), which have seven-eighths of all federal land and in which nearly half of all land is federal, have been getting double their proportionate share of population increases. Furthermore, for the first time in many years, most of the increase in the western states is now occurring outside California. This growth is almost certainly a contributing cause for the debate, popularly called the "sagebrush rebellion," over future control of public lands.

Trends in Household Growth

The discussion to this point has dealt with overall population change and spatial distribution. But demographic pressures on land use cannot be understood adequately without reference to trends in the size and number of households. Although we lack the same degree of area detail for households that we have for population, we know that the central feature of household change—the rapid further decline in average number of persons per household—has affected the entire nation. We have had declining household size since the nineteenth century, but in the 1970s the rate of decline accelerated to twice that of the previous decade. A low birth rate; increasing numbers of older, one- and two-person households; high rates of marital breakup; and an increased propensity for the young to leave the parental home before marriage have all contributed to the decline in household size. The effect was enhanced by the unprecedented number of young adults reaching household formation age as an outcome of the high birthrates of the 1950s. The result was an increase of 22 percent in number of households from 1970-79, compared with a growth of just eight percent in total population. In effect, a growth of about 14 percent in the number of occupied housing units was required, in the absence of any population growth at all, just to accommodate the increase in numbers of young adults and the redistribution of the population into smaller household units. Thus, in the great majority of cases, even communities with declining total population have been expanding their housing stocks.

The pace of household growth seems destined to slacken in the late 1980s as the smaller birth cohorts of the 1960s come of age and as the smallest of all cohorts from the 1930s reach early retirement age. Figure 1 and Table 3 show household growth rates and projections for metropolitan and nonmetropolitan areas between 1970 and 1995. Regardless of type of residence, the average annual rate of household growth was at a high level in the 1970s and remains so

Table 3. Household Growth by Metropolitan-Nonmetropolitan Residence, 1970-95

Residence	1970	1977	1985	1995	1970-77		1977-85		1985-95†	
					Growth	Average annual rate	Growth	Average annual rate	Growth	Average annual rate
Metro-politan*	43851	50414	59181	68746	6563	1.99%	8767	2.00%	9565	1.50%
Nonmetro-politan	19596	23728	29333	35448	4132	2.72	5605	2.64	6115	1.89

*Official 1970 definition of SMSAs as announced in 1974.
†Figures for 1985 and 1995 area based on Census Bureau Projections.
    Source: U.S. Bureau of the Census, *Current Population Reports*, Pc-23, No. 75 and Pc-25, No. 850.

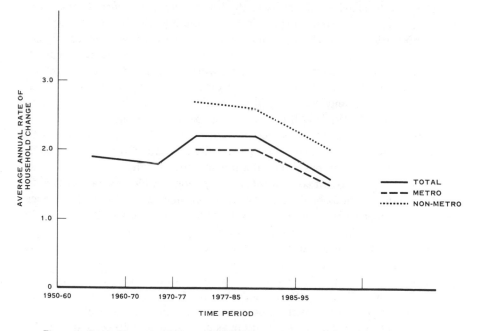

Figure 1. Rate of household growth 1950-1995, U.S. Bureau of the Census, 1974. Comparable data for the metropolitan and nonmetropolitan areas are available only for 1970-77. 1977-95 data are projected.

in the early 1980s but is projected to decline sharply between 1985 and 1995. The increased rate of household growth in the 1970s compared with previous years appears to have been a major factor in the acceleration of agricultural land conversion during that decade; the projected decline in household growth between 1985 and 1995 supports a conclusion that pressure from this factor on agricultural land will diminish during the later part of the century (Table 3 and Fig. 1). The long-term trend in the rate of household growth is much less extreme than that suggested if the 1970-85 situation were extrapolated into the future.

Households may continue to decentralize into nonmetropolitan areas, as they have during the 1970s, but the volume of the migration stream will diminish as the average annual growth in the number of households declines. In nonmetropolitan areas alone, this means about 2.6 million fewer households in 1995 than would have been present had the previous rate of household growth persisted.

Although growth in the number of households, particularly those headed by persons aged 25-34, is a major determinant of the demand for housing, demographic factors are only one part of the equation. The economic situation resulting from inflation and interest rates affects the purchasing power in the economy and therefore the effective demand for housing. Public policies—economic development policy, tax policy, financial incentive, and subsidy programs—also affect supply/demand relationships in the housing market. Hence demographic factors alone give an incomplete picture of the determination of housing demand.

Econometric models have included a wide range of demographic, economic, and institutional factors to predict housing starts over the next decade. Generally, these models show a stable or slightly growing annual addition to the housing stock through 1990. The amount of projected growth varies considerably depending on the assumptions used, however. For example, the Joint Economic Committee of Congress (1979) estimated that between 1.9 and 2.3 million new housing units will be constructed per year during the 1980s. This compares with about 2.1 million units annually during the 1970s. Variation in these estimates is due to different assumptions about inflation and interest rates.

These estimates do not cover most of the period in which the rate of growth in the number of households is projected to decline—e.g., after 1985. Hence there is no apparent inconsistency between them and the post-1985 decrease in the rate of growth in the number of households discussed earlier.

Another factor, the affordability of housing, supports an expectation that the rate of housing construction may decline during the next 20 years. Data prepared for the President's Council on Development Choices for the Eighties indicate a worsening situation (Byrne and Holland 1980). In 1988, according to these data, the income required to purchase a new home will exceed the median income for 60 percent of the population, as compared with 40 percent in 1978. Other studies predict this percentage will be lower, particularly if inflation eases and real income growth occurs.

Impacts upon Agriculture

Perhaps the most obvious land-use concern resulting from growth and decentralization of households and population is the potential effect on agriculture. The pattern of redistribution carries mixed implications. If one looks at population growth trends in counties that are most heavily dependent on farming, as measured by the percent of employment in that sector in 1970, little overall demographic pressure is evident. Counties with 30 percent or more of employed residents in agriculture had an overall population increase of just 0.2 percent from 1970 to 1978 and experienced a net outmigration of 48,000 people. This represented a marked stabilization of population levels compared with the past, given the fact that population in these counties dropped by nearly 11 percent in the 1960s.

It should be noted that counties heavily dependent on farming employment are located mainly in the Great Plains and western Corn Belt. Such areas are not among the top U.S. counties in value of agricultural output. Indeed, if one looks at the top 100 counties in value of products sold from the farm, an entirely new list emerges. Many have large populations, and, in fact, 33 are central counties of metropolitan areas. They include the counties that contain such cities as Phoenix, Fresno, Monterey, Stockton, Riverside, San Bernardino, Bakersfield, and Lancaster, Pennsylvania. The 100 top farm-production counties had a population growth rate of 13.5 percent from 1970-78. This was nearly double that of the country as a whole. If Los Angeles County, California, is removed from the list, the rate was 19.3 percent. In a few cases, farmland is located in one part of the country and the urban population in another—for example, Palm Beach County, Florida. But more typically, county population is located within farming areas in a manner that makes expansion automatically encroach on farms. The top 100 counties produced 22 percent of the value of all U.S. farm products in 1974. It is unlikely that much of the current growth of population in these counties results from farm-related activities, although some have substantial agricultural supply, handling, and processing employment.

A related and partly overlapping concern is the rate of population growth in areas with warm winter climates. Such areas produce the nation's domestic supply of citrus fruits and much of the winter vegetable and sugar-cane crop. Not all the land in these regions is of prime quality, but production is high and the climate is unique. If one defines the warm winter climate zone as those counties in which citrus fruits are produced (Florida Peninsula, Lower Rio Grande Valley, southwestern Arizona and southern California), the population growth from 1970-78 is 18 percent or 27 percent if Los Angeles is excluded. Winter or subtropical crops displaced from these rapidly developing areas are essentially irreplaceable except through importation. Much of this unique acreage has already been converted to nonagricultural uses.

Demand for Residential Land

At the national level, data on the extent of land use for residential purposes in rural areas are sketchy. Unpublished data from the 1970 Census indicate that the number of rural nonfarm people who had 10 or more acres in their home place was just as large as the number of farm residents with ten or more acres. Both groups numbered about 7.5 million persons. In addition, there were 16.5 million people living on rural nonfarm sites of less than 10 acres, exclusive of city or suburban lots. Until the 1980 Census is fully analyzed, no trend data are available on this topic. In any case, the 1970 data make it clear that there were more than 2 million households in that year occupying nonfarm tracts of rural land of 10 or more acres each. The nature of the land is not clear from the limited information. Some was undoubtedly suitable for farming and some not.

The major single difference between urban and rural housing is the percentage of units that are attached or in multiple-unit structures. In 1977, 40 percent of urban units were of this nature, compared with only 8 percent of rural units. Attached houses and apartment dwellings are increasing at a rapid rate in rural areas, but from a very small base. The mass of recent rural growth (87 percent) continues to be detached homes and mobile homes, whereas over half of urban growth since 1970 has been in attached units and apartments. Detached and mobile home developments, especially if they utilize septic systems for waste disposal, are likely to be more land-extensive than attached dwellings and apartments. Indeed, 80 percent of rural housing units constructed between 1970 and 1977 used septic tanks (U.S. Bureau of Census 1979). Hence the post-1970 decentralization of population and households has probably consumed more rural land than a similar demographic change would have required in more urbanized settings.

There is some question as to how long this land-consuming, low-density settlement pattern will continue. The single family detached home is still the overwhelming choice of the American public, but statistics on housing starts cited by the chief economist of the National Association of Homebuilders reveal a changing market distribution of types over time. Single-family detached units dropped from 77 percent of total private starts in 1975 to a projected 65 percent in 1981 (Sheehan 1981). The data also show an increase in higher-density dwellings in multi-unit structures as a proportion of total starts. Moreover, a survey reported in the *Professional Builder* (1979) indicates that smaller houses may be gaining in market share.

ECONOMIC TRENDS AND CONDITIONS
IN NONMETROPOLITAN AREAS

In addition to a decentralization of population, there has been a decentralization of employment during the 1970s. Nonmetropolitan employment grew by 12.3 percent between 1970 and 1976 compared with 8.0 percent in metropolitan areas (Table 4). Nonmetropolitan areas contained 25.5 percent of all jobs in 1976, but they accounted for 33.6 percent of all post-1970 job growth (2.7 million of 7.9 million jobs). Moreover, employment in nonmetropolitan America has undergone basic structural changes. Rural economic structure was primarily agricultural until World War II. Since 1940, the number of farms and farm people has declined precipitously. More than 23 million people lived on farms in 1950; today only 8 million live there—less than 4 percent of the nation's total population (or 6.5 million under the new Census definition of farm). Even within rural America, farm residents are a minority. Since 1920, the farm component of the rural population dropped from over 60 percent to less than 20 percent in 1970.

Table 4. Employment and Employment Change by Metropolitan Status, 1976 and 1970

Industry	Metropolitan				Nonmetropolitan				Percentage of Jobs Nonmetropolitan	
	Employment		Employment Change 1970-76		Employment		Employment Change 1970-76			
	1976	1970	No.	%	1976	1970	No.	%	1976	1970
Total	70507	65257	5250	8.0	24179	21521	2658	2658	25.5	24.8
Agriculture	1424	1350	74	5.5	3216	3336	−120	−3.6	69.3	71.2
Mining	298	273	25	9.2	459	334	125	37.4	60.7	55.0
Manufacture	14220	14962	742	−5.0	4812	4476	335	7.5	25.3	23.0
Trade	14277	12346	1931	15.6	3675	2927	748	25.6	20.5	19.2
Services	13167	10847	2320	21.4	3119	2604	514	19.8	19.2	19.4
Government	12945	12009	936	7.8	4666	4132	534	12.9	26.5	25.6
Other	14176	13470	705	5.2	4231	3712	520	14.0	22.9	21.6

Source: Unpublished Data, Bureau of Economic Analysis, U.S. Department of Commerce.

Farm Employment

Fewer farms and fewer farm workers per farm are direct results of the application of modern technology to agricultural production, especially farm machinery and agricultural chemicals. Smaller farm families and perceived relative attractiveness of cities as places to live and work are other contributing causes, but changes in the methods and structure of farming are dominant.

The range of economic activities in contemporary rural America has become more similar to that in urban areas. In 1976, nonmetropolitan counties contained 24.2 million jobs. By major industry group, the largest number was 4.8 million in manufacturing followed by 4.7 million in government, 37. million in wholesale and retail trade, and 3.1 million in services. Only 3.2 million jobs were in agriculture. Thus only 13 percent of nonmetropolitan jobs were in agriculture as compared with 20 percent in manufacturing.

As with other rural conditions, there are important regional variations. For example, there are many rural counties in which the vitality of the community is determined largely by farming. As of 1970, there were 331 counties, concentrated mainly in the Plains and Corn Belt, in which 30 percent or more of total employment was in agriculture (Beale 1978). Such counties tend, after decades of farm consolidation and outmigration, to be thinly populated. They typically average 10,000 or fewer people. In contrast, there were more than 1,000 rural counties with less than 10 percent of their employment in agriculture. These counties are more populous, averaging more than 35,000 population.

A number of nonfarm industries can be demonstrated to be fully or directly tied to agriculture, such as the manufacture and sale of agricultural machinery. Moreover, numerous trade, service, and manufacturing businesses are partly agricultural or serve an agricultural clientele. It has been estimated that about two other rural jobs are supported for every one farm production job in highly productive and commercial agricultural areas such as the Great Plains (Beale 1980). If a similar ratio holds for other regions, then about nine million nonmetropolitan jobs were farm-related or dependent on farm generated income in 1976. They would employ about two-fifths of all nonmetropolitan workers, leaving three-fifths with little or no direct dependence on agriculture.

Off-Farm Employment

Farm operators and their families are increasingly combining farm work with full- or part-time employment in nonagricultural industries. This income supplement appears to be an effective way to maintain a farming way of life for many operators of relatively small farms. As such, the availability of off-farm work may be among the most effective mechanisms for maintaining the competitiveness of farm uses of land vis-à-vis other uses. By doing so, it may retain rural land in agricultural production and/or forestall further farm consolidation.

Since World War II, the proportion of all farm operators working off the farm 200 or more days a year has increased from about six percent to about one-third (Carlin and Ghelfi 1979). Off-farm employment is more prevalent among operators of relatively small farms, although the proportion of income from off-farm sources has increased among all size classes of farms. In 1975 only 8 percent of all farm families derived their entire income from farming. The remaining 92 percent had at least one other source of economic support. Even among farms with $100,000 or more in gross sales, 20 percent of farm family income was from off-farm sources (USDA 1978).

Off-farm income is more common in the South, where only about one-half of farm operators report farming as their principal occupation. Within the South it is more common among whites than blacks. Off-farm work is also common for farm women. In 1978, 72 percent of farm women aged 16 or older who were in the labor force held off-farm jobs (Carlin and Ghelfi 1979).

Other Natural Resource-Based Industries

Mining and wood products employed about 1.4 million workers in 1976. Both industries are heavily concentrated in nonmetropolitan counties, and employment in both industries has begun to grow after decades of decline.

Manpower in mining declined from about 1.2 million jobs in the late 1920s to about half that many workers in 1970. More recently, mining employment has begun to increase again. About three-quarters of a million workers were employed in 1976. Almost all post-1970 employment growth in mining occurred in nonmetropolitan counties. In fact, six out of every ten mining jobs are now located outside of SMSAs.

The dramatic post-1970 turnaround in mining employment is attributable to increased efforts to produce fossil fuels — oil, gas, and coal. Some of these efforts are occurring in established mining regions such as southern Appalachia, but in the Northern Great Plains and in other parts of the West this activity represents a new element of economic structure.

Except for furniture and paper products, the wood products industry is also concentrated outside of SMSAs. As in the mining industry, mechanization and reduced product demand combined to diminish employment in the wood products industry in the 1950s and 1960s. Employment in this industry stabilized in the 1970s but has now begun to decline once more. This renewed decline is in response to the downturn in housing construction. It is particularly marked in the Pacific Northwest.

Manufacturing

Manufacturing is not a growth industry nationwide, but growth did occur during the 1970s in nonmetropolitan areas. In fact, nonmetropolitan counties added 335,000 manufacturing jobs between 1970 and 1976, compared with a loss of 741,000 manufacturing jobs in SMSAs (Table 4).

Recent research indicates that nonmetropolitan areas gained a diversified mix of manufacturing jobs during the 1970s. These areas experienced employment growth in 18 of 20 manufacturing industries monitored during the 1968-73 period (Petrulis 1979). To be sure, nonmetropolitan areas acquired some plants in slow-growing manufacturing sectors. They also gained more than their share of fast-growth manufacturing, however. Hence the traditional filter-down process in which nonmetropolitan areas received slow-growth economic establishments from SMSAs, does not appear to be characteristic of post-1970 nonmetropolitan manufacturing growth. Some nonmetropolitan manufacturing is resource-based —e.g., logging and wood products (except furniture), primary aluminum, and poultry processing—but much of it is not.

Many reasons are given by firms for moving to nonmetropolitan areas or for expanding operations already located there. The supply and quality of labor are almost always mentioned. Nonmetropolitan labor is considered to be more reliable, less costly, less apt to organize, and more willing to permit seasonal layoffs and part-time schedules, than metropolitan labor. Other nonmetropolitan advantages may include economic inducements like tax incentives, bond financing, and modern infrastructure such as transportation access, water and sewer service, and improved industrial sites. A prodevelopment orientation in many rural communities is also important. Whatever the specific reasons, many firms appear to feel that rural locations are more suitable than metropolitan ones.

Service and Recreation

The increasingly service-oriented nature of our society characterizes nonmetropolitan areas as well as SMSAs. Service jobs grew by almost a fifth during 1970-76 in both residential sectors (Table 4). Services now account for 13 percent of nonmetropolitan jobs and 19 percent of metropolitan jobs. The nonmetropolitan service base includes a wide range of jobs in professional and business services, finance, insurance and real estate, personal services, and recreation.

Rural communities now provide many services that were not adequately available until recently. This is especially true of professional activities such as health, education, and social services. The increased size, changing composition, and higher incomes of the nonmetropolitan population also affect the ability of communities to support a diverse and wide-ranging service economy. This is due in part to the fact that recent inmigrants from metropolitan areas have become used to a certain minimum level of services. They have the economic resources and organizational ability to create an effective demand for services in their new communities. Moreover, a large proportion of workers inmigrating to nonmetropolitan areas hold service jobs. Between 1970 and 1975, 22.9 percent of recent migrants to nonmetropolitan areas were employed in professional service occupations; another 7.5 percent were in other services (Bowles 1978). Hence the population turnaround in nonmetropolitan areas has increased the demand for services through the increased size and affluence of the population, through tastes and preferences developed in metropolitan settings, through migrants' own occupations, and through the ability to organize the community to provide new services.

Considerable resort and recreation development has occurred in environmentally attractive rural areas. In addition, a rural retirement trend has emerged, bringing many older persons into rural counties. Retirement is particularly characteristic of areas such as the Ozarks, the Southwest, central Texas, Florida, and the Upper Great Lakes. For example, metropolitan to nonmetropolitan migrants in the Upper Great Lakes region had a median age of 46 years, much older than that of most migration streams (Voss and Fuguitt 1979). Retirement and recreation create increased demand for many goods and services, a demand that is often noticed only after the migration itself has taken place.

Recreation and retirement growth has been stimulated by such factors as increased affluence, more leisure and vacation time, more adequate pensions and retirement incomes, opportunity to retire at an earlier age, improved access to rural areas, proliferation of reservoirs and public parks, and a generally greater interest in the out-of-doors.

Government Activity

Government employment (state, local, and federal) accounts for about one out of five nonmetropolitan jobs. Government jobs increased by 13 percent in nonmetropolitan counties between 1970 and 1976. This is somewhat higher than the rate of growth of metropolitan government jobs (Table 4), reflecting the growing importance of public involvement in the nonmetropolitan economy.

Consider the activities of the federal government. In fiscal year 1976, the federal government spent about $54 billion in nonmetropolitan areas. About $3 billion was for targeted economic development, $9 billion for public and private infrastructure, $5 billion for human capital programs, and $36 billion for transfer payments (the majority of which was social security). These expenditures, and the level of federal activity they indicate, are markedly higher than in previous times. They are responsible for generating many new government jobs (Deavers and Brown 1979).

State and local government employment is also high in nonmetropolitan counties. These governments provide such functions as education, health care, police and fire protection, highways, public welfare, and a wide variety of other services. At all levels, then, governmental activities are an important and growing source of employment in nonmetropolitan America.

Some Implications of Changing Economic Structure

The economic changes described in this section have a number of implications for rural land use. Most obviously, economic establishments and supporting infrastructure require land for their construction and operation. The amount of land actually converted to accommodate economic growth is not known, but in the aggregate it is probably not large.

The indirect effects of economic growth and development are probably much more substantial. An improving economic climate is one of the contributing factors in the resurgence of rural population growth. Economic opportunities attract migrants from other areas (often SMSAs) and help to retain lifelong residents who otherwise might be forced to move to another community. Hence economic development may have an indirect effect of forcing up the demand for housing and subdivision development.

As described earlier, there is reason to believe that the availability of non-agricultural jobs tends to stabilize the agricultural structure of many rural areas. Opportunities for off-farm income help farmers, especially small farmers, to maintain ownership of their land and thus to avoid its being consolidated with other larger enterprises or being converted to nonagricultural uses.

Hence, although rural economic development appears to be somewhat competitive with agricultural and other open-space uses of the land, there are reasons to expect that it is a stabilizing force leading to a more balanced farm structure. This situation doubtless differs by location, with farmland being more vulnerable to conversion in suburban fringe areas than in small towns and the open country.

OTHER NONAGRICULTURAL USERS OF RURAL LAND

Population growth and economic development are the two most obvious socio-demographic trends affecting rural land, but other factors also bear potential relationships with land use. Potential competition exists between open space (agricultural land, wetlands, and forests), transportation facilities and rights-of-way, manmade reservoirs, surface mining, and other energy-related activities.

Transportation

Highways covered 21.4 million acres of rural land in 1977. This was about 458 thousand acres more than in 1964. Divided state primary roads (including the interstate system) accounted for most of this increase. Divided highways consume about 41 acres of land per mile for right-of-way, adjacent shoulder, median strip, drainage, and access. Acreage covered per mile of other types of highway is much less, typically between 6 and 12 acres.

Most interstate highway growth took place before 1970. The average annual conversion to state primary divided roads declined from 112,000 acres between 1964 and 1969, to 83,000 acres between 1969 and 1973, and 42,000 acres between 1974 and 1977. Significant additional highway development is not expected to occur during the balance of this century. Some states have ambitious road-building programs slated for the 1980s, but increased construction costs are likely to limit the mileage that is actually built.

With marked increase in cost of motor fuel since 1979 and the downsizing and improved fuel efficiency of new car models, the consumption of fuel has dropped. For example, gasoline consumption from January through May 1980 was 6.5 percent less than that in the same period of 1979 (U.S. Department of Transportation 1980). Thus receipts from motor fuel taxes, which are used for highway construction and maintenance purposes, have also declined, and inflation has lessened the purchasing power of the taxes received. All in all, the reduced availability and value of highway construction funds and the substantial completion of the interstate system imply that highway construction will not be a serious competitor for additional open space in the foreseeable future.

Airports occupied 2.2 million acres of nonmetropolitan land in 1977. As with highways, the rate of land conversion to airport use is declining. Between 1968 and 1973, 259,000 acres were converted, whereas only 151,000 additional acres were converted between 1973 and 1977.

Reservoirs

About 60 million acres of former rural land were covered with water in 1977, an increase of about ten million acres since 1958. The average annual rate of conversion to water has been relatively constant since 1967, (.84 million acres a year between 1967 and 1975 and .73 million acres a year between 1958 and 1967) (Soil Conservation Service 1965; USDA 1971; and Dideriksen et al. 1977).

New reservoirs will probably be constructed at a slower rate during the 1980s than in the past two decades. Reasons for this decline include fiscal stringency, adverse environmental impacts, and enhanced ability of these factors to impede the construction of new reservoirs. During 1967-78, 17 Corps of Engineers' water projects were publicly challenged on grounds of farmland preservation (Esseks 1979).

Coal Strip Mining

Coal strip mining adversely affects the quality of land and water in various ways. Direct disturbance comes from excavation of the land itself and from bulldozing and/or filling additional acres for haul roads, storage, and other mining-related facilities. Stripping may also disrupt drainage on adjoining land, degrade surface water quality, and disturb underground hydrology.

In the long run, effects on water quality are probably more serious than those on the land itself. In many instances, land reclamation is now technically possible, if not economically feasible. To date, no effective method has been developed to abate serious water quality problems.

It is estimated that about 1.5 million acres of land are currently disturbed by surface mining of coal (Esseks 1979). Increased dependence on coal for the generation of electricity and other fuel-related uses will undoubtedly increase strip mining activity during the remainder of the century. It has been estimated that about 1 million additional acres will be disturbed by the year 2000. Another 800,000 acres will probably be needed for new coal and nuclear plants and associated facilities (Barse 1977).

The degree to which cropland is disturbed by coal strip mining varies by region. For example, in Illinois 52 percent of the land on which permits were granted for strip mining was in cropland, 27 percent in forest, and 21 percent in pasture (Esseks 1979). Large acreages of cropland are also underlain with strippable coal in Indiana, Kentucky, and North Dakota. In contrast, much less cropland is disturbed by strip mining in Appalachia or in Wyoming or Montana.

Electrical Transmission Lines

The installation of electrical transmission lines is expected to increase substantially between now and the year 2000. Rights-of-way for electrical transmission lines were estimated to cover between 3.3 and 4 million acres of land in 1974. A report by René Malés in the journal of the Electric Power Research Institute (1979) estimated that such lines may cover as much as 5.2 million acres by the turn of the century. This estimate, which results from a projected increase of 113,000 circuit miles of major transmission lines during the period, includes only lines of 115 or more kVs. A report by the Environmental Policy Division of the Library of Congress that includes lines of 69 kVs or more, estimates that almost 200,000 additional circuit miles of power lines will be installed by the year 2000 (Bagee 1969).

Electric transmission lines have many and varied impacts on rural land, depending upon the size of the line itself, and the uses of the land over which it passes. For example, impacts on forests are substantially different from those on farmland, since in many cases the entire right-of-way and all service roads must be cleared of trees. Not only are trees lost, but erosion and compaction of the soil often result. These consequences are particularly severe in mountainous areas.

Effects of electric transmission lines on agriculture are difficult to quantify. Direct effects include permanent loss of productive land for area roads and towers, and disturbance of land in the right-of-way (especially during the construction phase). Indirect effects include bisection of fields, aesthetic degradation, and interference with agricultural activities such as irrigation and the operation of field equipment. Potential health hazards to humans and livestock may also result from power transmission, although a recent study by the National Research Council casts doubt on this (Handler 1981).

Summary

Taken separately, none of the factors discussed in this section presages large future conversions of agricultural land. Their total impact, however, is substantial. These factors may be particularly significant in specific areas, especially if several occur simultaneously (e.g., strip mining, power generation facilities, power transmission lines, and road construction). It is further important to note that these factors have indirect effects, apart from the obvious ones. All of these factors tend to increase the level of modernization of the communities in which they are located. They also increase access between rural and urban areas as well as social and economic interdependence. Hence they may contribute to population and nonagricultural economic growth and to other more subtle changes in community structure and life-style.

CONCLUSION

This paper has identified sociodemographic forces that are potentially competitive with agricultural and other open-space uses of rural land. Major points may be summarized as follows:

- U.S. population became less concentrated during the 1970s. Suburbanization, interregional shifts between the North and the South and West, and net inmigration to nonmetropolitan areas have all created population pressures in areas of relatively low settlement density. Moreover, in nonmetropolitan areas, the highest rates of population growth are found in open country and hamlets outside incorporated places.

- Urbanization and agricultural activity appear to be in direct competition in some of our most important agricultural counties. The rate of nonfarm population growth is high in counties with the highest value of gross agricultural sales in 1974. The determinants of this population growth are not generally related to agriculture, but rather to off-farm economic opportunities and to quality-of-life considerations such as climate and the environment.

- A growth of about 14 percent in new occupied housing units was required during the 1970s just to accommodate new household formations. These new households came about through an increase in the young adult population (a legacy of the baby boom) and through the redistribution of persons from larger to smaller families. The growth rate of the number of households is expected to decline during the later part of this century, thus moderating the demand for new housing units and for residential land.

- There has been a decentralization of employment from metropolitan to nonmetropolitan areas during the 1970s. Nonmetropolitan counties contained 25.5 percent of all jobs in 1976, but they accounted for 33.6 percent of all job growth. In addition, the nature of rural employment has changed, with manufacturing and services supplanting agriculture as primary employers. New economic establishments, and the enlargement of older ones, require land on which to locate and roads and other infrastructure to operate. They provide an economic basis for further nonfarm population growth (and for houses and community services). Off-farm job opportunities, however, enable many farm families to continue farming and avoid moving to the city. This may help to maintain rural land in agricultural production and to reduce opportunities for farm consolidation. As in population decentralization, there is little reason to expect these economic trends to reverse in the foreseeable future.

Our overall conclusion is that agricultural and nonagricultural uses are at present in considerable competition for land in many rural areas. But we have found evidence that suggests that this competition may diminish during the remainder of this century. Land will continue to be converted to the nonagricultural uses discussed above, but at a diminishing rate. We reach this conclusion because two incentives to agricultural land conversion should be declining: growth rate in the number of households and major investments in land-consuming infrastructure.

Hence, although we expect the population to continue to decentralize, the migration stream should not produce so many new households. Indeed, our analysis indicates that about 2.6 million fewer households will be present in nonmetropolitan areas in 1995 than would have been the case had the 1977-85 rate of growth persisted. Economic activity is also expected to continue to decentralize, but we feel that rural economic development may actually help stabilize participation in agriculture.

National-level conditions do not necessarily reflect the wide range of regional and local situations. The local land-use policy context should thus be considered separately. Nationally, the rate of agricultural land conversion may moderate after 1985, but some communities and states may actually experience accelerated transfer of farmland to urban and built-up uses. New suburban regions are a case in point, and the situation in the 100 top agricultural counties requires close scrutiny as well.

References

Bagee, C. E. 1969. Environmental Effects of Producing Electrical Power. Statement before the Joint Committee on Atomic Energy. Washington: U.S. Government Printing Office.

Barse, J. R. 1977. Agriculture and Energy Use in the Year 2000. Discussion from a Natural Resources Perspective. *American Journal of Agricultural Economics* 59 (December): 1073-1074.

Beale, C. L. 1978. Making a Living in Rural and Smalltown America. *Rural Development Perspectives* 1 (Nobember): 1-5.

_____1980. Nonfarm Rural America. In *Farm Structure*, ed. Committee on Agriculture, Nutrition and Forestry, pp. 96-102, 36-48. Washington: U.S. Senate.

Bowles, G. K. 1978. Contributions of Recent Metro/Nonmetro Migrants to the Nonmetro Population and Labor Force. *Agricultural Economics Research* 30 (October): 15-22.

Byrne, R. M., and Holland, L. 1980. *Development Choices for the 80's: Background Information Summary*. Washington: Urban Land Institute.

Carlin, T. A., and Ghelfi, L. M. 1979. Off-Farm Employment and the Farm Structure. In *Structure Issues of American Agriculture*, ed. Economics, Statistics, and Cooperatives Service, pp. 270-274, Washington: USDA.

Deavers, K. L., and Brown, D. L. 1979. *Social and Economic Trends in Rural America*. Washington: The White House.

Dideriksen, R. J.; Hidlebaugh, A. R.; and Schmude, K. O. 1977. *Potential Cropland Study*, Stat. Bull. 578. Washington: Soil Conservation Service, USDA.

Electrical Power Research Institute, 1979. R. and D. Status Report: Electrical Systems Division. *EPRI Journal* (December): 51-56.

Esseks, J. D. 1979. Nonurban Competition for Farmland. In *Farmland, Food and the Future*, ed. M. Schnepf, pp. 49-67. Ankeny, Iowa; Soil Conservation Society of America.

Handler, P. 1981. On Bias: Does Where You Stand Really Depend on Where You Sit? *The National Research Council, 1980: Issues and Current Studies*, pp. 1-15. Washington: National Research Council.

Joint Economic Committee, Congress of the United States. 1979. *Mid-Year Review of the Economy: The Outlook for 1979*. Washington: Government Printing Office.

Malés, René. 1979. R & D Status Report, Energy Analysis and Environment Division. *EPRI Journal* (December): 57-60.

Petrulis, M. F. 1979. *Regional Manufacturing Employment Growth Patterns*. Rural Development Research Report No. 13. Washington: Economics, Statistics and Cooperative Services, USDA.

Professional Builder 1979. What 1980 Buyers Want in Housing (Dec.)

Sheehan, R. J. 1981. The Outlook for Housing. *Family Economics Review* (Spring): 26-27.

Soil Conservation Service. 1965. *Soil and Water Conservation Needs — A National Inventory, 1958*. Misc. Pub. 971. Washington: USDA.

U.S. Bureau of the Census 1979. Urban and Rural Housing Characteristics, Series H-150-77. Washington: U.S. Department of Commerce.

U.S. Department of Agriculture 1971. *Basic Statistics — National Inventory of Soil and Water Conservation Needs*. Stat. Bull. 461. Washington: USDA.

————1978. *Farm Income Statistics*. Stat. Bull. 609. Washington: Economics, Statistics, and Cooperatives Service, USDA.

U.S. Department of Transportation 1980. *Monthly Motor Gasoline Reported by States* (May). Washington: Federal Highway Administration.

Vining, D. R., Jr., and Kontuly, T. 1978. Population Dispersal from Major Metropolitan Regions: An International Comparison. *International Regional Science Review* 3(1): 49-73.

Voss, P., and Fuguitt, G. V. 1979. *Turnaround Migration in the Upper Great Lakes Region*. Population Series 70-112 (August): 1-281.

Wardwell, J. M. 1977. Equilibrium and Change in Nonmetropolitan Growth. *Rural Sociology* 42 (Summer): 156-179.

The Impact of the Interstate Highway System on Nonmetropolitan Development, 1950-75

Ronald Briggs

Improved access to transportation is frequently cited as a factor underlying the resurgence of nonmetropolitan areas of the United States in the 1970s—e.g., McCarthy and Morrison (1977), Hansen (1977), Berry (1978), and Beale (1977). The interstate highway system is probably the single most significant recent change in the nonmetropolitan transportation system. This paper explores its effect on net migration and employment change in nonmetropolitan areas over the period 1950 to 1975.

THE EXISTING LITERATURE

There is a surprising lack of research on the role of the interstate highway system as an agent of regional change. This is the case despite the cultural dominance of highways in American life, the enormity of the investment in these highways, and the changes currently occurring in the spatial pattern of development in the United States. Although an abundance of impact studies exists in the highway-planning and engineering literature, the vast majority, particularly in nonmetropolitan areas, emphasize the short-range impact of individual highway projects on land parcels, on land use at interchanges, or on a few selected case-study communities—a fact that is readily apparent from reviews of this literature (Federal Highway Administration 1972; 1974; 1976). There are but a handful of studies,

The research reported in this chapter was supported by the U.S. Department of Transportation, Office of University Research under contract DOT-RC-92040. The results and views expressed are those of the author and do not necessarily reflect those of the sponsors. The author expresses his appreciation to Florence Mills and John Kassis of the Federal Highway Administration, John Wardwell of Montana State University, Calvin Beale of the U.S. Department of Agriculture, and Glenn Fuguitt of the University of Wisconsin for making data available.

for example, that even encompass more than one state (Longley and Goley 1962; Wheat 1969), and the case-study approach continues to be utilized (Lineham and Walton 1976). Few of the empirical studies on recent nonmetropolitan trends have included a transportation variable in their analyses, despite a conceptual stress on its importance. Generally, emphasis has been on the role of four factors: 1) the spillover of metropolitan populations into nonmetropolitan areas; 2) the development of retirement and recreation communities; 3) the renaissance of industrial development, either manufacturing or energy-related, and 4) government activities such as educational and military establishments and aid to depressed areas (Beale 1977; McCarthy and Morrison 1977; Long and De Are 1980; Heaton, Clifford, and Fuguitt 1980). Each of these factors has been shown to have a significant association with recent nonmetropolitan growth, but it can be argued that improved transportation is a common contributing force.

The few studies that address the impacts of the interstate highway system on development in nonmetropolitan areas are generally limited in scope and do not permit a definitive assessment of the system's role. In particular, there has been a failure to control adequately for other factors that impinge upon the relationship between highways and growth, especially growth rates prior to the opening of interstates, overspill from metropolitan areas, urban population concentrations in nonmetropolitan areas, and regional differences.

Studies by the Federal Highway Administration (FHWA) (1972; 1974) making simple comparisons between counties with and without freeways have shown that nonmetropolitan counties with freeways experience higher population growth rates than those without. The work of Humphrey and Sell (1975) and Fuguitt and Beale (1976), however, suggests that these places may have been experiencing faster growth even before freeways were constructed. Controlling for prefreeway growth rates, a later FHWA study finds that: "While the differences (in growth rates) are not necessarily caused by freeways, it should be noted that the chance of these nonmetropolitan counties being crossed by freeways occurs almost randomly, since the Interstate System was located primarily to connect metropolitan areas." (FHWA 1976, p. 75) But Hansen (1973, p. 26) notes that counties bordering Standard Metropolitan Statistical Areas (SMSAs) have a greater chance of being traversed by a freeway, since freeways focus on metropolitan centers. In his study of counties in six regions of the United States, he concludes that it is adjacency to SMSAs that largely accounts for the higher growth rates of freeway counties. Furthermore, since nonmetropolitan counties served by freeways more frequently contain larger uban population concentrations than those not served by freeways, any relationship between freeways and nonmetropolitan growth may be confounded by the known link between growth and the size of the urban places in nonmetropolitan regions (Fuguitt and Beale 1976; Humphrey and Sell 1975; Humphrey et al. 1977). Finally, regional differences need to be considered. Wheat (1969), in a carefully controlled study of 106 city pairs (freeway-located cities matched by similar nonfreeway-located cities), found that freeway cities grew faster primarily in areas east of the

Mississippi and in the Pacific Northwest. This was attributed to mountainous terrain, high traffic volumes, and/or numerous small communities impeding traffic flow along regular highways in these areas. Similar conclusions were drawn in a study of southern nonmetropolitan cities (Wheat 1976). District regional differences are also noted by Bohm and Patterson (1972).

To date, the most comprehensive study by far of the impact of the interstate highway system on nonmetropolitan development, which is free from most of the above shortcomings, is that of Lichter and Fuguitt (1980). Examining demographic change from 1950 through 1975 and employment change from 1950 to 1970 for all nonmetropolitan counties in the United States, they suggest only a modest impact of limited-access highways on nonmetropolitan development, with particularly weak relationships for manufacturing employment and for more remote, purely rural counties. These findings differ from the commonly-held assumption that the interstate highway system plays a significant role in nonmetropolitan development.

THE ROLE OF THE INTERSTATE SYSTEM

The resurgence of nonmetropolitan areas should be viewed in conjunction with changes in metropolitan areas rather than as a process in and of itself. (See Morrill 1980; Wardwell 1977; Vining and Kontuly 1978.) Also, approximately 70 percent of the U.S. population still resides in metropolitan areas, and much of what happens in nonmetropolitan America is conditioned or controlled by the actions and needs of the metropolitan population (Dicken 1976; Pred 1976). Consequently, a theory of the role of interstate highways in nonmetropolitan development must encompass the entire metropolitan-nonmetropolitan system.

The interstate highway system, by reducing time costs, facilitates travel. This has two immediate effects. One is to increase the total amount of travel in aggregate, since costs per unit are decreased. Undoubtedly, along with rising incomes, this has been a major contributor to the marked increased in highway travel that has occurred since the inception of the interstate highway program (a 34 percent increase in passenger miles per capita, and a 56 percent increase in vehicle miles per capita, between 1960 and 1975). The other effect is to channel movement along fewer paths. Even though the 31,161 miles of rural interstate highway curretly open to traffic comprise only 12 percent of the major (arterial) road mileage in the United States, they carry 33 percent of the traffic. This travel, of course, has both an origin and a destination. Accordingly, four types of movement may be recognized: 1) travel between metropolitan centers through nonmetropolitan areas, 2) travel from a metropolitan base to a nonmetropolitan destination, 3) travel from a nonmetropolitan base to a metropolitan destination, and 4) travel within nonmetropolitan areas. These types of movement have two potential effects on the spatial distribution of development: to influence the balance of metropolitan vis à vis nonmetropolitan development, and to alter the spatial pattern of development within nonmetropolitan areas.

Travel Between Metropolitan Areas

The movement of people through a transportation network generates a "linear demand surface" for certain goods and services. To meet this demand within metropolitan areas, retail and service establishments are attracted to transportation arteries, resulting in highway strip developments that contain such functions as gasoline and vehicle repair services, restaurants and other types of eating places, motels and other forms of lodging (hotels, campsites, truck stops, etc.), and convenience stores that provide an assortment of retail goods. In nonmetropolitan areas such development arises in response to demand from travelers between metropolitan areas, and tends to cluster around highway interchanges.

The U.S. Census of Transportation reports that 72 percent of all U.S. households took at least one trip to a place one hundred or more miles from home in 1977; the number of person-trips of this type increased by 81 percent between 1967 and 1972, and by a further 18 percent between 1972 and 1977, with 82 percent of trips being by automobile in 1977. (U.S. Bureau of the Census 1979, pp. XXIII-XXVI.) Of these trips, about two-thirds originated in metropolitan areas (which is equivalent to the proportion of the population residing in metropolitan areas in 1970) and a little over 50 percent had their destination in metropolitan areas (Table 1A). This implies a substantial amount of movement between metropolitan areas, much of which must cross nonmetropolitan regions. The marked increase in this type of movement, presumably spurred to a significant degree by improved highways, and its impact on retail and service activities, are one way in which interstates may have contributed to development in nonmetropolitan vis à vis metropolitan areas.

Travel from Metropolitan to Nonmetropolitan Areas

Travel from metropolitan origins to nonmetropolitan destinations has many of the same characteristics as trips between metropolitan areas, although the former is more likely to have a vacation or outdoor recreation purpose (Table 1B). Consequently, in addition to highway-oriented services, an impact can be expected in nonmetropolitan areas on amusement and recreation services, on construction and maintenance of second homes, and on general retail and service activities to the extent that metropolitan residents reside temporarily in nonmetropolitan areas. These visitors are likely to be particularly important in more remote, recreational, and amenity areas. Their contribution to the economy is further augmented by the tendency for visitors to spend money at a higher rate than residents.

Travel from Nonmetropolitan to Metropolitan Areas

This movement has two components: 1) industries located in nonmetropolitan areas but serving metropolitan markets must move their products to these centers, and 2) residents of nonmetropolitan regions needing access to metropolitan centers, particularly for employment, may travel there on a frequent basis. Many writers suggest that good highway linkages make it possible for industry to

Table 1. Characteristics of Nonlocal Travel in the United States

A. Travel Origins and Destinations, 1977

	U.S. Population, 1975		Origin of Travel, 1977		Destination of Travel, 1977		
Location	Millions	Percentage	Thousands of person trips	Percentage	Thousands of person trips	Percentage of Total	Percentage of Domestic
Metro*	155.	72.8	376,079	69.7	290,313	53.8	55.7
Nonmetro	58.	27.2	163,210	30.3	231,114	42.9	44.3
Outside U.S.					17,862	3.3	
Total	213.	100.0	539,289	100.0	539,289	100.0	100.0

B. Purpose of Travel, 1977

All Trips: Main Purpose of Travel (Person trips in thousands)

Location of Travel Destination	Vacation Travel		Personal Visits		Business		Outdoor Recreation		Sightseeing and Entertainment	
	Number	Percentage	Number	Percentage	Number	Percentage	Number	Percentage	Number	Percentage
Metro*	94,802	50.5	107,188	55.1	71,157	69.0	15,856	23.2	40,850	64.3
Nonmetro	92,778	49.5	87,239	44.9	31,930	31.0	52,317	76.8	22,697	35.7
Total Domestic	187,580	100.0	194,427	100.0	103,087	100.0	68,173	100.0	63,547	100.0

Source: U.S. Bureau of the Census, 1977 Census of Transportation: Travel During 1977, Washington, D.C.: U.S. Government Printing Office, 1979, Tables 2A, 2B, 2J, 2K, 2L, 2M, 3A.

*SMSAs as of 1976 for Population data, as of 1977 for Travel data.

relocate or expand in nonmetropolitan areas, enjoying less congestion, lower land costs, lower labor costs, and improved labor productivity, yet retaining access to metropolitan markets and resource inputs (Lonsdale and Seyler 1979). Manufacturing is the most obvious candidate, but other industries, such as long-distance trucking and warehousing, may favor a nonmetropolitan location.

Nonmetropolitan residents who require access to metropolitan employment include both former metropolitan residents who have moved farther "out-of-town" and long-time nonmetropolitan residents who use the highway to reach metropolitan employment. Contributing to these patterns have been changes in the structure of job markets, including increasingly common three- and four-day work weeks; occupations that do not require daily attendance at job sites (such as sales, writing, and consulting jobs); and jobs that can rely on communications systems (such as computer software development) rather than physical travel. The frequency with which trips must be made to metropolitan centers is reduced by these trends, yet access to these centers remains important.

Travel Within Nonmetropolitan Areas

The interstate highway system may play a redistributive role within non-metropolitan areas. Lichter and Fuguitt (1980) suggest that interstate highways, by improving accessibility, expand the market-area of places located along them, with implications for subsequent growth in basic trade and services in these places compared to those off the system. The process may not simply be an expansion of market areas through improved accessibility, however, since this expansion would occur along the axis of the interstate highway and merely redistribute development among places along the freeway. Rather, the attractiveness of free-way-located places as trade centers for nonmetropolitan residents may be increased as a result of the development of highway and tourist services that meet needs originating from movement along the freeway. This leads to general expansion of the trade area of such places as compared to those not on a freeway.

A Model of Highway Impact

Figure 1, based upon the work of Lichter and Fuguitt (1980), shows how these various types of movement interrelate and affect nonmetropolitan development. Movement between metropolitan areas, and movement from metropolitan to nonmetropolitan areas, primarily affect employment in tourist-type activities in nonmetropolitan regions (Link 1A), which in turn affects migration (Link 2). Movement from nonmetropolitan to metropolitan areas is reflected by the effect of the interstate highway on manufacturing employment (Link 1B) and subsequently on migration (Link 2), as well as the direct effect of long-distance suburbanization on net migration (Link 3). Movement within nonmetropolitan areas and the expansion of trade areas affects employment in nonlocal services (Link 1C), which in turn affects migration. Also, there is a circular relationship (which will not be considered in the following empirical analysis) between migration and employment in local retail and service activities in which population

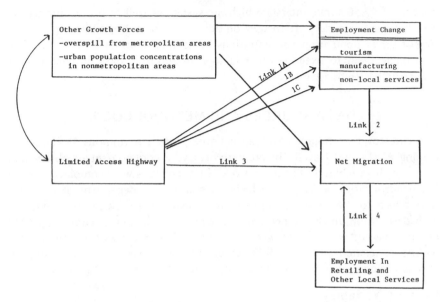

Figure 1. Model of the impact of limited access highways on employment and demographic change in nonmetropolitan areas. Based upon Lichter and Fuguitt, 1980.

growth generates increases in retail and service activities, which in turn stimulate further population growth (Link 4). Finally, other growth forces, including proximity to metropolitan areas and urban population concentrations in nonmetropolitan areas, are also included because of their known relationship with both metropolitan development and the interstate highway system.

OBJECTIVES OF EMPIRICAL ANALYSIS

The following analysis is an attempt to assess empirically the effect of the interstate highway system upon net migration and employment change in nonmetropolitan areas. Particular emphasis is placed upon controlling factors that may covary with the interstate highway system and lead to a spurious relationship between demographic and economic change and the presence of interstate highways. The literature review above suggests at least three key factors that need to be considered: 1) net migration rates prior to the date of highway opening; 2) the effect of population overspill from metropolitan areas; and 3) the role of urban population concentrations in nonmetropolitan areas. The study progressively controls each of these factors, then compares net migration rates and employment change in counties with and without interstate highways.

To some extent, the analysis revalidates the results obtained by Lichter and Fuguitt (1980), although there are some key differences in conceptual and methodological detail. The present study examines the impact of the officially designated 42,500 mile interstate highway system as well as that of limited-access highways generally. It focuses on adjacency to metropolitan regions and size of urban population concentrations in nonmetropolitan areas rather than controlling them to examine other factors. In addition, data on employment change in the 1970s are included here.

DATA SOURCES AND METHODOLOGY

The data cover all nonmetropolitan counties in the coterminous 48 states, excluding Alaska and Hawaii. In order to achieve a common set of observation units for all variables at all time periods, a few counties were combined and the independent cities of Virginia (which are politically independent of counties) were added to their respective geographical counties, to achieve comparability with observation units in other states. The result was a data set containing 3070 observations, of which 2044 were nonmetropolitan counties using the official SMSAs designated after the 1970 census, and 2660 were nonmetropolitan in 1960 on an equivalent basis. County-equivalent SMSAs were used in New England.

Highway Variables

Officially, the interstate highway system comprises approximately 42,500 miles of limited-access highway authorized by Congress in the Federal Aid Highway Act of 1956. There are also limited-access highways that are not a part of the official interstate system. In order to differentiate between these types, two sets of codings were used: an *interstate* coding, referring to the official interstate system, and a *freeway* coding, referring to all limited-access highways. Toll roads were not differentiated in either case.

The "interstate" coding was derived from a computerized administrative data file made available by the Interstate Reports Branch of the Federal Highway Administration. This file contained data on the length and date of official opening to traffic of all segments of the interstate system. A county was classified as: 1) "with an open interstate" if 50 percent or more of the planned interstate system mileage in the county was open to traffic by a given date (1960, 1970, and 1975); 2) "on system without interstate" if less than 50 percent of the planned mileage was open; or 3) "off system without interstate" if the county had no interstate mileage, open or planned, within its boundaries. The "freeway" coding was essentially the same but included limited-access highways not a part of the official interstate system. A limited-access highway link had to be completed to a metropolitan center before a county was considered to have an open freeway.

Development Variables

Individual net migration rates for each county were calculated by taking net migration (the number of inmigrants minus outmigrants) over a given time period, dividing by the population at the beginning of the period, multiplying by 100, and dividing by the number of years elapsed. Annualized rates of employment change were similarly calculated, using Census of Population data for

1950 to 1960 and 1960 to 1970, and Bureau of Economic Analysis (BEA) data for change in the 1970s. Note that the Census data are based upon place of residence and count people, whereas the BEA data are based upon place of work and count jobs. In addition to total employment, the industrial categories used are: 1) retailing; 2) tourist related industry, including eating and drinking establishments, lodging places, and amusement and recreation services; 3) manufacturing; 4) trucking; and 5) wholesaling. Choice of these categories for individual analysis was conditioned by the conceptualization of the effect of interstate highways discussed earlier. In general, these industries were those for which an effect from freeways might be expected on theoretical or previous empirical-study grounds (see Gamble, Raphael, and Sauerlender, 1966; Garrison, 1959; Kiley, 1964; Kuehn and West, 1971; Lonsdale and Seyler, 1979; Rees, 1980; Wheat, 1969, 1976).

Variables identifying nonmetropolitan counties on such characteristics as adjacency to metropolitan areas and size of largest urban place are based upon categorizations formulated by Calvin Beale (1977) and coworkers at the U.S. Department of Agriculture.

DEMOGRAPHIC CHANGE AND THE INTERSTATE SYSTEM

Does a causal link exist between the presence of an interstate highway within a county and demographic change in that county? In every decade, counties with an interstate highway experienced higher rates of migration than those without

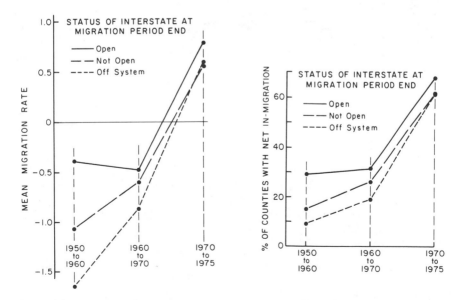

Figure 2. Annual migration rates 1950-60, 1960-70, and 1970-75 according to the status of interstate highway at the end of the migration period.

Table 2. The Relationship Between Interstate Highways and Annual Net Migration in Nonmetropolitan Counties of the U.S., 1950-75

Migration Period	All Nonmetro Counties (1970)			Interstate System Counties			
	With Interstate	Without Interstate[a]		Date of Opening			
		On System	Off System	Before 1960	1960-69	1970-74	After 1974
	1	2	3	4	5	6	7
1. Mean Annual Rate of Net Migration[b]							
1950-60	-.393	-1.092	-1.673	-.393	-1.209	-.884	-.874
1960-70	-.495	-.609	-.886	-.434	-.505	-.585	-.648
1970-75	.790	.538	.586	.370	.864	.765	.538
2. Group Annual Rate of Net Migration[b]							
1950-60	-.268	-1.023	-1.588	-.268	-1.051	-.971	-.945
1960-70	-.410	-.344	-.707	-.148	-.464	-.272	-.439
1970-75	.702	.540	.608	.259	.791	.719	.540
3. Proportion Gaining by Net Immigration							
1950-60	28.7	15.2	9.2	28.7	14.8	18.2	12.4
1960-70	31.5	26.1	18.9	41.1	30.1	28.8	21.6
1970-75	67.8	60.8	60.6	57.6	71.9	65.0	60.8
4. Proportion Experiencing Turnaround After Net Outmigration[c]							
1960-70	25.4	18.6	15.8	28.8	25.0	23.6	13.7
1970-75	60.7	53.9	54.8	46.5	63.5	57.9	53.9
5. Number of Counties							
1950-60	73	723	1648	73	466	160	97
1960-70	539	257	1648	73	466	160	97
1970-75	699	97	1648	73	466	160	97

[a] At end of migration period concerned. The "Interstate" coding (see text) is used.

[b] Mean rates are the simple averages of the individual county rates within a particular category of counties. The group rates are obtained by aggregating net migration and population within each category of counties and then calculating migration rates. They are equivalent to weighting the individual county rates by county population and then taking the average.

[c] The number of net outmigration counties during the previous migration period is used as the base.

interstates (Figure 2; Table 2, Columns 1, 2, and 3). For example, in the 1950-60 decade, even though all types of counties experienced net outmigration, the average loss of population was considerably less for counties with an open interstate highway than for those without. This relationship is consistent regardless of the migration measure used: as a group, counties with an interstate highway experienced less net outmigration (Table 2, Box 2), and a higher proportion of counties with an interstate highway experienced net inmigration than counties without an interstate (Box 3). The same is true for the 1960-70 decade. In the 1970s, net migration losses changed to gains and counties with an interstate highway experienced higher rates of population gain than counties without an interstate highway. The same is true for the other migration measures.

Although these data demonstrate a clear association between migration and the presence of an interstate highway within a county, they are far from proving a causal link from highways to migration. For instance, it could be argued that the interstate highway system was originally planned so as to pass through counties already experiencing relatively high rates of net migration, or that the construction of interstate highways was programmed in favor of such counties. These arguments have some support from the data, since counties in which the interstate highway is yet to open (Column 2) generally experienced higher net migration than counties entirely off the interstate highway system (Column 3). But these arguments are questionable on both logical and empirical grounds. Furthermore, even if interstates were constructed by design or chance in association with higher migration rates, a subsequent impact on migration is not precluded.

The interstate system was built to link large metropolitan centers by relatively direct routes, irrespective of growth rates in intervening areas (Wheat 1976, p. 56). The system might have been planned to serve intervening counties that were experiencing high net inmigration and whose highways were inadequate. Net outmigration was the norm, however, and it is unlikely that planners would seek out areas experiencing lower rates of net outmigration. Thus the association between interstates and migration is probably not by design. Furthermore, the data suggest a definite impact of interstates on subsequent migration rates even if these highways had been constructed by chance in areas already experiencing relatively higher net migration.

If counties are classified by date of interstate opening (Table 2, Columns 4, 5, 6, and 7), migration rates for any one time period generally are highest for the counties where an interstate opened in the previous decade, and second highest for the counties where the interstate opened during the migration time period being considered. For example, mean net migration in the 1960-70 decade was highest in the counties where the interstate opened before 1960, second highest in counties where the interstate opened between 1960 and 1970, and lowest where interstates were yet to open. Similarly, mean net migration for the 1970-75 period was highest for counties where the interstate had opened in the previous decade, and second highest for counties where the interstates opened between 1970 and 1975. This pattern is consistent for all the migration measures, with the partial exception of group migration rates in the 1960-70 decade. In other words, the opening of an interstate highway during one decade is associated with above-average rates of net migration during the following decade. This temporal sequencing, in which the cause precedes in time the hypothesized effect, provides strong evidence for the existence of a causal impact of interstate highways on net migration. It should be noted, however, that this impact does not necessarily continue indefinitely, since in the 1970s, counties that had been on the interstate system since before 1960 experienced the lowest net migration rates of all types of counties.

It could also be argued that the association between interstates and net migration is solely a consequence of population spillover from metropolitan areas. Since interstates connect metropolitan areas, nonmetropolitan counties adjacent to metropolitan counties have a far higher chance of being on the interstate system than non-adjacent counties. In fact, 41 percent of nonmetropolitan counties adjacent to metropolitan counties are on the interstate system, whereas only 26 percent of nonadjacent counties are on the system. Because of population spillover from metropolitan areas, adjacent nonmetropolitan counties have generally experienced higher rates of net migration than nonadjacent counties (McCarthy and Morrison 1977). Consequently, the association between interstates and net migration based on the comparisons between counties with and without freeways could be a result of the higher incidence of interstates in adjacent counties, which have experienced faster rates of growth from metropolitan spillover, rather than a consequence of the presence of freeways. Another possible factor is urban population concentrations in nonmetropolitan areas. Nonmetropolitan counties with relatively large urban population concentrations have generally experienced higher net migration rates than nonmetropolitan counties without urban population concentrations (Fuguitt and Beale 1976), and interstates disproportionately serve nonmetropolitan counties with larger urban populations.

It is possible to show an association between freeways and net migration, which is independent of the confounding influences of adjacency to metropolitan areas and urban population concentrations. In Figure 3 and Table 3 nonmetropolitan counties are grouped into adjacent and nonadjacent categories, and then further classified according to size of largest place: A) 10,000 or more ("city"); B) 2,500-9,999 ("town"); C) less than 2,500 ("rural"). As expected from metropolitan spillover, nonmetropolitan counties adjacent to metropolitan areas have higher rates of net migration than nonadjacent counties in all three size of place categories. Also, migration rates are associated with size of place, being higher for larger vis-à-vis smaller places in the 1960s, with a reversal of this relationship apparent in the 1970s.

When the effect of freeways is examined, for adjacent and nonadjacent counties alike, migration rates generally are higher for counties with an interstate compared to those without. For the size of place cateogries, Class B counties

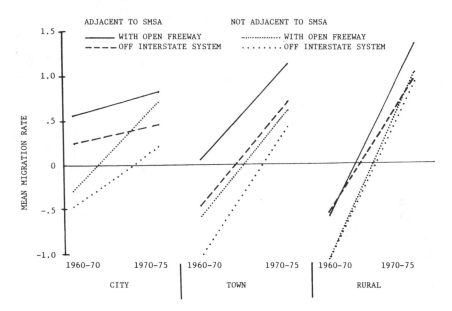

Figure 3. Annual net migration rates 1960 to 1970 and 1970 to 1975 for counties with an open limited access highway compared with counties off the interstate system, controlled for size of largest place and adjacency to metropolitan areas.

consistently experienced higher net migration if they had an open freeway. Class A counties experienced higher net migration rates if they had an open freeway than if they were entirely off the interstate system, although the rate is highest where the freeway is yet to open in nonadjacent counties in the 1960s and in adjacent counties in the 1970s. This may reflect growth due to anticipation of the completion of the freeway, in association with delays in completing the highway through these more densely populated places. Rural counties with freeways experienced higher net migration rates than those without freeways in the 1970s, but there were no differences in the 1960s between counties with a freeway and those off the interstate system. Overall, these results suggest an association between freeways and net migration even after the confounding factors of adjacency to metropolitan areas and population concentration in nonmetropolitan areas are controlled, except possibly for more remote rural regions.

EMPLOYMENT CHANGE AND THE INTERSTATE SYSTEM

Do the relationships shown in the previous section between the interstate system and demographic change also exist for changes in employment? A priori, an even stronger relationship might be expected with employment change than with migration, since jobs should be more directly responsive to the accessibility provided by the interstate system than should population. Table 4 and Figure 4 show

Table 3. The Relationship Between Interstate Highways and Annual Net Migration in Nonmetropolitan Counties of the U.S., 1960-75, Controlled For Adjacency to Metropolitan Areas and Size of Largest Place in 1970

	Mean Annual Rate of Net Migration, 1960-70				Group Annual Rate of Net Migration, 1960-70				Mean Annual Rate of Net Migration, 1970-75				Group Annual Rate of Net Migration, 1970-75			
	With an Interstate		Without Interstate		With an Interstate		Without Interstate		With an Interstate		Without Interstate		With an Interstate		Without Interstate	
Area	On System	Off System	On System	Off System	On System	Off System	On System	Off System	On System	Off System	On System	Off System	On System	Off System	On System	Off System
City																
Total	.229 (277)	.455* (84)		-.202 (285)	.267	.312*		-.157	.726 (263)	1.533* (14)		.289 (251)	.760	1.292*		2.98
Adjacent	.594 (162)	.322 (36)		.158 (103)	.568	.123		.233	.767 (154)	2.258* (9)		.375 (95)	.805	1.593*		.448
Not adj.	-.287 (115)	.554* (48)		-.406 (182)	-.314	.480*		-.475	.668 (109)	.227 (5)		.236 (156)	.674	.242		.187
Town																
Total	-.224 (241)	-.794 (157)		-.854 (714)	-.256	-.890		-.864	.784 (317)	-.063 (42)		.455 (710)	.880	-.117		.536
Adjacent	.073 (111)	.021 (59)		-.538 (233)	.040	-.233		-.511	.952 (154)	-.042 (21)		.639 (294)	1.106	-.152		.674
Not adj.	-.477	-1.284		-1.002	-.581	-1.389		-1.068	.625	-.084		.325	.590	-.085		.410
Rural																
Total	-.833 (107)	-1.096 (65)		-1.022 (714)	-.890	-1.211		-1.001	1.202 (148)	.625 (10)		.772 (689)	1.155	.720		.913
Adjacent	-.410 (43)	-.710 (15)		-.475 (139)	-.612	-.939		-.589*	1.477 (59)	.601 (5)		.983 (175)	1.303	.615		.923
Not adj.	-1.117 (64)	-1.212 (50)		-1.155 (575)	-1.122	-1.296		-1.120*	1.019 (89)	.650 (5)		.700 (514)	1.040	.811		.908

Note: Number of counties in each category given in parentheses. 1960 and 1970 SMSA definitions used for change from 1960 to 1970 and 1970 to 1975 respectively. "Freeway" coding (see text) used to identify presence of a limited access highway. See Table 2, footnote b, for difference between mean and group migration rates.

*Contradicts hypothesis of higher growth rate for counties with an open limited access highway.

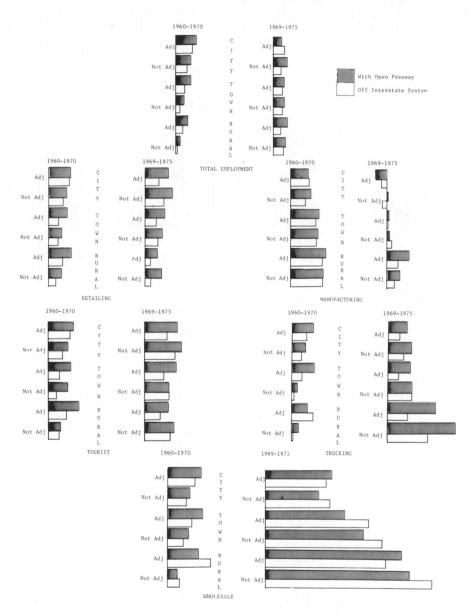

Figure 4. Employment growth rates 1960 to 1970 and 1969 to 1975 in selected industries for counties with an open limited access highway compared with counties off the interstate system, controlled for size of largest place and adjacency to metropolitan areas.

group employment change rates as annualized percentages for total employment and employment in retailing, manufacturing, tourist, trucking, and wholesaling

Table 4. The Differences in Annualized Group Net Migration Rates and Group Employment Growth Rates Between Nonmetropolitan Counties in the U.S. With Open Interstate Highways and Those Without Open Interstate Highways, Controlled For Adjacency to Metropolitan Areas and Size of Largest Place

		1960-70[a]			1969-75[b]		
		With an Interstate	Without an Interstate[c]		With an Interstate	Without an Interstate[c]	
		(rate)	On (difference)	Off (difference)	(rate)	On (difference)	Off (difference)
Migration:		0.10	0.36	0.70	0.82	0.24	0.31
City	Adj	0.57	0.44	0.33	0.80	−0.79	0.36
	Not Adj	−0.31	−0.79	0.16	0.67	0.43	0.49
Town	Adj	0.04	0.27	0.55	1.11	1.26	0.43
	Not Adj	−0.58	0.81	0.49	0.59	0.65	0.18
Rural	Adj	−0.61	0.33	−0.02	1.30	0.69	0.38
	Not Adj	−1.12	0.17	−0.00	1.04	0.23	0.13
Total Employment		1.95	0.36	0.86	1.50	−0.26	0.14
City	Adj	2.38	0.09	0.30	1.21	−1.85	−0.32
	Not Adj	1.73	−0.51	0.24	1.91	0.34	0.69
Town	Adj	1.76	0.13	0.66	1.56	0.59	0.17
	Not Adj	1.09	0.91	0.57	1.63	0.66	0.27
Rural	Adj	1.33	0.47	0.37	1.82	0.47	0.77
	Not Adj	0.57	0.39	0.48	1.63	0.45	0.14
Retail		2.49	0.42	0.87	2.90	0.73	1.07
City	Adj	2.88	0.28	0.23	2.98	−1.04	1.12
	Not Adj	2.25	−0.31	0.53	3.50	1.24	0.94
Town	Adj	2.26	−0.03	0.97	2.50	2.26	0.99
	Not Adj	1.63	0.80	0.41	2.15	0.73	0.36
Rural	Adj	2.87	1.70	1.01	1.64	3.08	0.90
	Not Adj	1.64	0.84	0.72	2.15	−0.32	1.26
Manufacturing		2.48	−0.15	−0.34	−0.50	−1.75	−0.46
City	Adj	2.10	−0.56	−0.12	−1.23	−3.86	−0.63
	Not Adj	2.44	0.30	0.47	0.17	−0.93	0.79
Town	Adj	3.54	−0.03	0.26	0.38	1.17	0.23
	Not Adj	3.49	1.04	0.17	0.21	0.03	−0.41
Rural	Adj	4.31	2.60	0.31	2.78	−4.14	2.50
	Not Adj	4.07	.088	−0.02	1.65	2.24	0.62

		1960-70[a]			1969-75[b]		
		With an Interstate	Without an Interstate[c]		With an Interstate	Without an Interstate[c]	
		(rate)	On (difference)	Off (difference)	(rate)	On (difference)	Off (difference)
Tourist		2.76	0.53	1.05	4.07	1.03	0.88
City	Adj	3.14	0.17	0.25	4.10	-1.50	1.15
	Not Adj	2.30	-0.22	0.59	4.68	2.47	0.69
Town	Adj	2.74	0.32	1.27	3.90	3.15	1.36
	Not Adj	2.32	1.45	1.29	3.17	0.10	0.00
Rural	Adj	3.78	0.13	1.56	3.00	3.83	0.96
	Not Adj	1.42	-0.03	0.09	3.69	3.07	0.46
Trucking		2.14	0.22	1.09	2.92	-0.74	0.55
City	Adj	2.65	0.43	0.77	2.47	-1.00	0.94
	Not Adj	1.69	-0.26	0.41	3.07	-1.67	0.99
Town	Adj	2.80	-1.40	1.41	2.88	0.19	1.41
	Not Adj	0.66	0.71	0.43	3.18	-0.52	0.00
Rural	Adj	2.06	-0.94	-0.55	6.17	4.14	3.62
	Not Adj	0.79	0.38	0.72	8.48	4.67	3.35
Wholesale		3.45	0.30	1.01	8.99	1.39	-2.61
City	Adj	3.98	-0.08	0.71	8.58	1.96	0.74
	Not Adj	2.86	-0.55	0.64	6.92	-1.29	-1.35
Town	Adj	4.19	-0.17	1.19	10.39	4.64	-2.78
	Not Adj	2.45	1.67	0.59	12.60	1.02	-2.18
Rural	Adj	3.78	-2.20	-1.34	17.32	9.75	1.97
	Not Adj	1.19	0.17	-0.16	18.30	14.07	-2.83

Note: The number of counties in each category is given in Table 3. The "Freeway" coding (see text) is used to identify presence of a limited access highway.

a 1960 SMSA definitions used.

b 1970 SMSA definitions used.

c The figures in these columns were obtained by taking the actual rate for counties with an open Interstate and subtracting the actual rates for counties without an Interstate. Consequently, a negative sign in these columns indicates that the hypothesis of faster growth for counties with an open Interstate highway is not upheld.

industries for the time periods under study. In order to aid assessment of the hypotheses, actual rates are given in the table only for counties with open freeways; the figures for counties without freeways are the *differences* from the rate for counties with an open freeway. Thus a negative sign for any of the values in the "without freeway" columns indicates a situation that opposes the hypothesis of higher growth in counties with freeways.

As might be expected, the results for total employment generally mirror those found for net migration. With a few exceptions in the large town category, counties with open freeways have the highest growth. Also, as might be expected since the location of retailing is closely tied to that of population, the same pattern is found for changes in retail employment. Tourism is the most consistent in exhibiting faster growth rates in counties with open interstates. Trucking is a little different, in that counties where the freeway is yet to open exhibit the highest growth rates in many instances. This may simply reflect growth in trucking in anticipation of the opening of the freeway. The major surprises occur in manufacturing and in wholesaling employment. In neither of these industries is growth clearly associated with the interstate system, especially in the 1970s. This is surprising, given the many statements in the literature suggesting that both are dependent upon accessibility.

EMPLOYMENT CHANGE, NET MIGRATION, AND THE INTERSTATE SYSTEM

Migration and employment change, hitherto analyzed separately, are interrelated. As the model of highway impact suggests (Fig. 1), limited-access highways may affect migration both directly as well as indirectly through changes in employment opportunities, which in turn affect migration. What is the relative importance of this direct versus indirect effect, and what types of industries are most affected by the presence of interstates?

In order to answer these questions, path analysis was applied to the model in Figure 1. In contrast to the earlier findings, the results suggest a weak relationship (if any at all) between freeways and demographic and employment change (Table 5). The partial correlation coefficients between the freeway and change variables (controlled for adjacency to metropolitan areas and size of largest place in nonmetropolitan areas) are very low, although in the expected direction with the exception of wholesaling in the 1970s. Likewise, the values of the standardized regression coefficients are extremely small. Apart from this, the most notable feature is the minor role of manufacturing and wholesaling and, comparatively, the overwhelming effect of employment in tourism. Indeed, for the 1960-70 decade some 57 percent of the total effect of the interstate system on net migration is due to change in tourism employment. The difference between the 1960s and 1970s in the indirect vis-à-vis direct effect of freeways on migration, which initially is striking, is probably due to the fact that employment change was measured using a residential base for the 1960s but a place-of-work base for the 1970s.

Table 5. The Effects of Interstate Highways on Employment Growth and Net Migration, 1960-70 and 1970-75: Path Analysis Results

Endogenous Variable 1960-70	Partial r with Freeway*	Direct Effect of Freeway on Endogenous Variable†:		Indirect Effect of Freeway on Migration via Endogenous Variable‡:		Indirect Effect as a Percent of Total Effect§
		b	beta	b	beta	
Net Migration	.07	.080	.020	–	–	–
Manufacturing	.04	1.174	.051	.020	.005	6.6
Tourism	.07	1.100	.090	.173	.042	57.1
Trucking	.04	1.373	.044	.015	.004	4.9
Wholesaling	.02	0.614	.028	.014	.003	4.8
All Employ. Var.				.222	.054	73.4
1970-75						
Net Migration	.08	.223	.053	–	–	–
Manufacturing	.005	.606	.005	.0006	.0001	0.2
Tourism	.03	.787	.030	.0752	.0178	25.3
Trucking	.03	2.683	.029	.0004	.0001	0.2
Wholesaling	−.02	−2.400	−.016	−.0022	−.0005	–
All Employ. Var.				.0740	.0175	25.7

Note: All regression equations include three dummy variables as exogenous controls indexing adjacency to metropolitan areas, counties with cities over 10,000 population, and counties with cities between 2,500 and 10,000 population.

　*These are the partial correlation coefficients between the freeway variable and each of the change variables, controlling for the three exogenous variables.

　†The direct effects for the employment variables are the regression coefficients of the freeway variable in models separately regressing each employment variable against the three exogenous control variables and the freeway variable. The direct effect for net migration is the regression coefficient of the freeway variable in a model regressing net migration against the three exogenous control variables, the freeway variable and the four employment variables.

　‡The indirect effect on net migration is the direct effect of freeways on an employment variable multiplied by the regression coefficients for the respective employment variable in a model regressing net migration against the three exogenous control variables, the freeway variable, and the four employment variables—the same regression equation as is used to obtain the direct effect of freeways on migration.

　§The total effect of freeways is the regression coefficient in a model regressing net migration against the three exogenous control variables and the freeway variable. The results were:1960-70: b −.302; beta −.074. 1970-75: b −.297; beta −.071.

The weak empirical link between interstate highways and manufacturing is certainly at variance with prevailing assumptions. (Similar findings were reported by Lichter and Fuguitt, however.) Fact and theory thus appear to differ. On the other hand, the predominance of the effect on tourism employment is consistent with the expectations of anyone who has witnessed the proliferation of gas stations, eating places, and lodging establishments along interstates (although the effect differs from Lichter and Fuguitt's findings). But perhaps the most critical question is why the results of the path analysis suggest a weak relationship at best between freeways and employment and demographic change, whereas the other analyses indicate a definite impact of freeways on development.

DISCUSSION AND CONCLUSION

Parts of the above analysis suggest a definite impact of freeways on development, whereas other parts suggest a weak relationship at best. Resolution of this contradiction is important in understanding the role of interstate highways in nonmetropolitan development.

For longer-term demographic and economic development, does it matter if a county is on or off the interstate system? The comparison of average net migration and employment rates between counties on and off the interstate suggested a definite impact of limited-access highways on growth. On the other hand, the measures of association between growth rates and the interstate system calculated in the path analysis were all extremely low. This apparent contradiction suggests that although counties on the system, as a group, have higher average growth rates, the experience of individual counties, which is indexed by the measures of association, has been extremely varied. That is to say, there is a great deal of overlap in growth rates between counties with and without interstates. The implication of this for policy planning is that the presence of a limited-access highway is no guarantee of community development. Neither is its absence a precursor of community demise, as may have been the case in an earlier era with the railroad.

Why is there no clear association between manufacturing, as well as other employment categories, and the interstate system? One explanation is that the interstate system has provided only an increment to an already relatively good highway network which itself has been greatly improved over the last few decades. The interstate system, in association with noninterstate highways, may have created a high level of accessibility throughout nonmetropolitan America to the benefit of many communities, not necessarily only those immediately adjacent to limited access highways. Manufacturing may still benefit from interstates, yet may not need to locate near these highways. Tourism, on the other hand, drawing much of its business directly from freeway traffic, requires physical proximity to the interstate. Perhaps the same process that can be observed on a small scale within metropolitan areas is occurring on a larger scale in nonmetropolitan areas. Within metropolitan areas, such functions as gas stations, restaurants, and motels (the "tourism" of industry, as the term is used in this study) cluster at freeway interchanges, since they are directly dependent on traffic on these arteries. Manufacturing is more distant. The results of the study suggest the operation of similar process on a larger scale in nonmetropolitan America.

How important has the interstate system been in stimulating nonmetropolitan development in the 1970s? Although this study was directed toward this question, the answer has proven elusive. In several analyses other than those reported here (see Briggs 1980), the performance of the interstate highway variable was always disappointing. The reason may lie in the type of empirical analysis conducted in these studies, which, in common with others that explore the role of interstates, assumes a locationally specific effect of interstates on development. The test of the impact of an interstate is the occurrence of growth in spatial proximity to the highway. However, an important role of the interstate highway system may have been to raise accessibility levels throughout nonmetropolitan America, as suggested in the discussion of manufacturing change. Furthermore, this may have established only a necessary, but not sufficient, precondition for development. Actual development in a particular locale may need to be triggered by other forces (see Gauthier 1970, and Kuehn and West 1971). The combination of raised accessibility levels throughout nonmetropolitan America, not just in proximity to the interstate, and the need for triggering forces not necessarily directly tied to the location of interstates, leads to development only at certain points along the interstate, as well as away from it. Consequently, the empirical link between interstates and development is weak, and the channeling of growth along interstate corridors is at best a minor, not a major, feature of the spatial pattern of nonmetropolitan development.

What relationships can be expected between the interstate system and development in the 1980s? The interstate highway system is now almost complete. In the face of tightened federal budgets, rapid escalations in highway construction costs, greater demands for maintenance and repair funds, and a general shift in federal policy away from highways and toward mass transit, we cannot expect major new highway programs (Smith 1980; Wachs and Ortner 1979). The emphasis within existing programs is likely to shift increasingly toward improving noninterstate highways. Also the rate of growth in vehicular traffic has slowed markedly as fuel prices have risen. All of these forces suggest a further weakening of the tie between the location of interstate highways and development. The "one-time" effect on employment of the construction of highways and associated tourist facilities will not be present in the future. Expansion will be primarily a function of the growth in traffic on interstates, but this growth will probably occur at more moderate rates in the future than in the past as rising gasoline costs constrain automobile travel, and other modes for freight transportation, particularly railroads, become more competitive as fuel costs rise for trucking. Also, if noninterstate highways are improved, regions off the interstate will become relatively more accessible.

Finally, in what directions should future research proceed? One obvious need is to refine the various measures used in this analysis. The county is a very gross spatial unit; the use of cities, townships, or census county divisions may explicate more clearly the relationship between interstate highways and development. Employment categories that reflect the role of highways more precisely would be helpful. As categorizations become more refined in a nonmetropolitan context, however, the problems of sampling variability, small bases for calculating change, and suppression for confidentiality increase commensurably. But these problems are overshadowed by a major conceptual problem. The impact of movement through space on in situ change is being assessed without measuring movement directly. In metropolitan areas, land-use and transportation modeling are carried out as one, with direct measures of traffic flows being incorporated. The major research challenge for the future, perhaps, is to move in the same direction in nonmetropolitan areas.

References

Beale, C. L. 1976. A Further Look at Nonmetropolitan Population Growth Since 1970. *American Journal of Agricultural Economics* 58: 952-958.

_____1977. The Recent Shift of United States Population to Non-Metropolitan Areas, 1970-1975. *International Regional Science Review* 2: 113-122.

Berry, B. J. L. 1978. The Counterurbanization Process: How General? In *Human Settlement Systems*, ed. Niles Hansen, pp. 25-49. Cambridge, Mass.: Ballinger.

Bohm, R. A., and Patterson, D. A. 1972. Interstate Highways and the Growth and Distribution of Population. *Proceedings of the American Statistical Association, 1971.* Washington, D.C.: American Statistical Association.

Briggs, R. 1980. *The Impact of the Interstate Highway System on Nonmetropolitan Growth.* Washington, D.C.: U.S. Department of Transportation, Office of University Research.

Dicken, P. 1976. The Multi-plant Business Enterprise and Geographical Space: Some Issues in the Study of External Control and Regional Development. *Regional Studies* 10:401-412.

Federal Highway Administration 1972. *Social and Economic Effects of Highways.* Washington, D.C.: U.S. Department of Transportation.

_____1974. *Social and Economic Effects of Highways.* Washington, D.C.: U.S. Department of Transportation.

_____1976. *Social and Economic Effects of Highways.* Washington, D.C.: U.S. Department of Transportation.

Fuguitt, G. V., and Beale, C. L. 1976. Population Change in Nonmetropolitan Cities and Towns. *Agricultural Economic Report No. 323*, U.S. Department of Agriculture.

Gamble, H. B.; Raphael, D. L.; and Sauerlender, D. H. 1966. Direct and Indirect Economic Impacts of Highway Interchange Development. *Highway Research Record* no. 149: 42-55.

Garrison, W. L.; Berry, B. J. L.; Marble, D. F.; Nystuen, J. D.; and Morrill, R. L. 1959. *Studies of Highway Development and Geographic Change.* Seattle: University of Washington Press.

Gauthier, H. L. 1970. Geography, Transportation and Regional Development. *Economic Geography* 46: 612-619.

Hansen, N. 1977. Some Research and Policy Implications of Recent Migration Patterns in Industrial Countries. *International Regional Science Review* 2: 161-166.

_____1973. *The Future of Nonmetropolitan America.* Lexington, Mass.: D. C. Heath

Heaton, T. B.; Clifford, W.; and Fuguitt, G. V. 1980. Temporal Shifts in the Determinants of Migration in Nonmetropolitan Areas. Paper presented at the annual meetings, Population Association of America, Denver, Col., April 10.

Humprhey, C. R., and R. R. Sell 1975. The Impact of Controlled Access Highways on Population Growth in Pennsylvania Nonmetropolitan Communities 1940-1970. *Rural Sociology* 40: 332-343.

Humphrey, C. R.; Sell, R. R.; Krout, J. A.; and Gillespy, R. T. 1977. Net Migration Turnaround in Pennsylvania Nonmetropolitan Minor Civil Divisons, 1960-1970. *Rural Sociology* 42: 332-351.

Kiley, E. V. 1964. Highways as a Factor in Industrial Location. *Highway Research Record* no. 75: 48-52.

Kuehn, J. A., and West, J. G. 1971. Highways and Regional Development. *Growth and Change* 2: 23-28.

Lichter, D. F., and Fuguitt, G. V. 1980. Demographic Response to Transportation Innovation: The Case of the Interstate Highway. *Social Forces* 59:493-512.

Lineham, R., and Walton, C. M. 1976. Interurban Transportation Networks and Rural Economic Development. *Transportation Research Record* No. 617: 39-41.

Long, L. H., and De Are, D. 1980. Migration to Nonmetropolitan Areas: Appraising the Trend and Reasons for Moving. Washington, D.C.: U.S. Bureau of the Census, Center for Demographic Studies.

Longley, J. S., and Goley, B. T. 1962. A Statistical Evaluation of the Influence of Highways on Rural Land Values in the United States. *Bulletin 327*, Highway Research Board: 21-55.

Lonsdale, R. E., and Seyler, H. L. 1979. *Nonmetropolitan Industrialization.* Washington, D.C.: Winston.

McCarthy, K. F., and Morrisson, P. A. 1977. The Changing Demographic and Economic Structure of Nonmetropolitan Areas in the United States. *International Regional Science Review* 2: 123-142.

Morrill, R. L. 1980. The Spread of Change in Metropolitan and Nonmetropolitan Growth. *Urban Geography* 1: 118-129.

Pred, A. R. 1976. The Interurban Transmission of Growth in Advanced Economies: Empirical Findings Versus Regional Planning Assumptions. *Regional Studies* 10:151-171.

Rees, J. 1980. Economic Development Trends in Nonmetropolitan and Suburban Communities. Paper prepared for the President's National Urban Policy Report.

Skorpa, L.; Dodge, R.; Walton, C. M.; and Huddleston, J. 1974. *Transportation Impact Studies: A Review With Emphasis on Rural Areas,* Austin, Texas: Council for Advanced Transportation Studies, Research Report 2.

Smith, W. S. 1980. Future of Highway Financing. *Traffic Quarterly* 34: 21-32.

Tucker, C. J. 1976. Changing Patterns of Migration Between Metropolitan and Nonmetropolitan Areas in the United States: Recent Evidence. *Demography* 13: 435-443.

U.S. Bureau of the Census 1979. *1977 Census of Transportation, Travel During 1977.* Washington, D. C.: U.S. Government Printing Office.

Vining, D. R., and Kontuly, T. 1978. Population Dispersion From Major Metropolitan Regions: An International Comparison. *International Regional Science Review* 3: 49-74.

Vining, D. R., and Strauss, A. 1977. A Demonstration that the Current Deconcentration of Population in the United States is a Clean Break with the Past. *Environment and Planning* A, 9: 751-758.

Wachs, M., and Ortner, J. 1979. Capital Grants and Recurrent Subsidies: A Dilemma in American Transportation. *Transportation* 8: 3-20.

Wardwell, J. M. 1977. Equilibrium and Change in Nonmetropolitan Growth. *Rural Sociology* 42: 156-179.

Wheat, L. F. 1969. The Effect of Modern Highways on Urban Manufacturing Growth. *Highway Research Record* No. 277: 9-24.

_____1976. *Urban Growth in the Nonmetropolitan South*, Lexington, Mass.: D. C. Heath.

III. The Rural Land Market

Changing Markets for Rural Lands: Patterns and Issues

Robert G. Healy and James L. Short

INTRODUCTION

There are about ten acres of rural land for each American. If we ignore the vast holdings of federal, state, and local governments—about two-fifths of all U.S. land—there remain about six acres per capita. This amounts to a bit less than 1.3 billion acres in all. This privately owned rural land produces nearly all of the nation's food and three-quarters of its wood fiber. It provides water, recreation, grazing, minerals, and wildlife habitat. It represents a large, and probably rising, share of the nation's wealth.

Anyone who has spent much time driving rural highways and back roads cannot fail to be impressed by the tremendous variety of the rural landscapes he encounters. In some places vast acreages are devoted to producing a single commodity, whether in the fields of soybeans or corn in Illinois and Iowa or the endless ranks of Douglas firs in the Pacific Northwest. Elsewhere, several rural land uses are jumbled together—here a farm, there a roadside business, over tnere a scrap of forest, perhaps with a dilapidated sign offering "recreation lots, 5+ acres." A significant amount of rural land seems devoted to no apparent use at all.

This landscape, with all its implications for the supply of natural resources and for the quality of the environment, is for the most part not the product of social or governmental planning or coordination. Rather, it has been formed by millions of decisions made over the years by the private owners of the land. And each day thousands of these owners continue to buy or sell land or make decisions about its use. These land use choices are decidedly individual ones, made on the basis of private economic opportunities and on personal preferences, values, and aspirations. In sum, rural land use decisions are principally private market decisions, for government regulations on rural land are few.

More often than not, the land itself mirrors these private use decisions and the underlying patterns of ownership. For example, the physical boundary between a hayfield and a woodland often corresponds exactly to the border between parcels found in land records at a county courthouse.

Increasingly, however, current land uses conceal the reality of owner identities and of owner intentions. In one rural county on the outskirts of Washington, D.C., thousands of acres of corn are planted each year. Yet the land is not owned by farmers, but by real-estate speculators, biding their time until sewers become available and zoning is changed. In many forest areas, an apparent abundance of greenery hides the fact that the best timber has been long removed and the land is owned by weekend recreationists. In several coastal areas in California, pastoral landscapes belie the reality that they occupy land long ago subdivided into building lots. Rural land of all types has become a vehicle for investors more interested in capital gains and inflation hedges than in commodity production.

Also emerging in the nation's rural areas are new patterns of migration and human habitation, which have far reaching implications for the future use and conservation of the country's rural land. For the first time in U.S. history, people whose backgrounds are urban—born, raised, educated, and employed in urban surroundings—are gravitating toward nonurban places: high-amenity areas, farms, small country towns, and exurban areas. The phenomenon appears to have multiple causes, and to be occurring in nearly all parts of the country (Beale 1975; McCarthy and Morrison 1979; Fuguitt and Voss 1979). Historically, just the opposite was the case, as generations of people with rural backgrounds were important sources of urban growth and change.

Thus America's rural land market is changing, even though evidence of the changes is often not readily apparent in the way land is currently being used. New types of owners are appearing in the marketplace. New issues are being raised about use efficiency and resource conservation. New motives are beginning to influence decisions about land use.

This paper provides some of the results of our own study, for the Conservation Foundation, of the market for rural land—how it works; what patterns are emerging; what various market trends imply for the use of land. Our final report (Healy and Short, 1981) was the first comprehensive attempt to explain the workings of and changes occurring in the current rural land market.

The Conservation Foundation's study of the rural land market was undertaken because of our belief that events in the land market precede, and often preordain, changes in the way land is used. Public concern about preserving the beauty and productivity of the rural landscape usually focuses only on the moment at which the use of land is actually changed. Our study, in contrast, looks at the much longer period during which expectations about future uses are formed and institutional arrangements created that commit land to a given use. These expectations and institutional arrangements affecting land are frequently revealed in the land market long before any change occurs on the land itself. For example, the expectation that a piece of land will be put to urban use is often reflected in the land's price years before a single building is built on it. And potentially productive timberland may be split into recreational parcels too small to produce wood products economically, yet the land itself will appear unchanged.

Despite the importance of understanding the land market, there are great gaps in existing knowledge of how it works and where market trends seem to be leading us. No one really knows "who owns rural America." Little research has been done on how rural land prices are determined. And although we now have some data on the sizes of individual landownerships, we still know virtually nothing about how they have been changing over time. Even less is known about how the diverse new demands being expressed in the rural marketplace will affect the productivity and efficiency of rural land resources.

Since the beginning of our study in 1977, there has been a significant increase in research activity concerned with rural land. Particularly important have been the development of new government data resources, such as the national land-ownership survey by the U.S. Department of Agriculture (USDA), and new data on foreign ownership (Lewis 1980; USDA 1980). Rather than duplicate these data sources, we have concentrated on collecting data at the local level. The new national data sources can serve as bench marks and for purposes of comparison with the information we have collected.

Records of land ownership and land transfers have long been available for public inspection at county courthouses around the country. We selected six representative rural places for intensive interviewing and data-collecting. The six areas chosen are widely separated geographically and include a variety of types and uses of land. They include examples of both fertile and marginal farmland, hardwood and softwood timberland, and land in demand for recreation and rural settlement. The six areas also illustrate a continuum of remoteness, ranging from places just beyond the metropolitan fringe to places quite distant from any metropolis. Although all regions of the country could not be included in a sample of this size, the areas selected cover a wide range of regional diversity. The places selected were:

> Hardy and Pendleton counties, West Virginia—a remote area of steep, timbered mountains and fertile bottomlands whose former isolation has been disturbed by urbanites seeking recreational properties;

> West Windsor, Vermont and Plainfield, New Hampshire—the first a recreational haven for persons from New York and Connecticut; the second an area of low density rural living for persons working in medium-sized New Hampshire cities;

> Loudoun County, Virginia (outlying portion)—part of Virginia's "horse country," this exurban portion of the Washington, D.C., metropolis preserves a rural lifestyle for commuters and retirees;

> Tyler County, Texas—located in the east Texas "pineywoods" in the midst of some of the nation's most productive softwood timberland;

> San Luis Obispo County, California—an area of dry, rolling grazing land,

this county along the central California coast has become a magnet for persons moving out of crowded southern California cities;

Douglas County, Illinois—an almost exclusively agricultural county in the center of the Midwestern Corn Belt, one of the most fertile farming regions in the world.

RURAL LAND MARKETS

The Geography of Rural Lands

Definitions of "rural" range from a dictionary's "sparsely settled or agricultural areas" to the approach taken by the U.S. Census Bureau that whatever is not urban is rural. That is, the Bureau defines "urban" and by implication the residual is "rural." By this definition, in 1970 there were 54 million rural inhabitants occupying 1,282 million acres of privately owned land. (In the same year, 149 million urban dwellers occupied only 35 million acres. (Provisional 1980 Census counts, released as this book went to press, reported 59.5 million rural residents and 167.0 million urban residents.

Another view is in terms of metropolitan versus nonmetropolitan. As of 1976 there were 277 government-defined SMSAs, covering some 317 million acres. The remaining 2,400 nonmetropolitan counties covered 1,580 million acres and were home to some 59 million people.

These two government ways of looking at rural land—as nonurban and nonmetropolitan—even though they result in disparities, by and large are sensible definitions; and the acceptance of each will depend on the reasons for seeking a definition. In any case, these viewpoints are the basis of all land use and population data collected by the government.

Conceptually, we prefer to think of rural land as part of a continuum of urban development. Figure 1 shows the typical range of urban development, from the central city of an SMSA, where population density may exceed 20 persons per acre, to designated wilderness areas, where government policy allows no human habitation. Using government data, we have attempted to estimate how much of the surface of the United States (excluding Alaska and Hawaii) lies in each of the categories along this continuum. Central cities and suburbs make up most of what the Census Bureau defines as urbanized areas. Allowing a few million acres for land in nonmetropolitan towns, perhaps 26 million acres of urbanized land lie within our metropolitan areas.

Beyond the suburbs is the "urban fringe." This is land that is not yet built up, nor provided with public services, but that is irrevocably committed to future urban use. Land values in this zone are set entirely by the expectation of future development; typical prices are at least several thousand dollars per acre. Some of this land may appear rural—it may even be farmed or used for grazing—yet this is only an interim use while owners await the land's "ripening" for urban development. Assuming that metropolitan areas are surrounded by a 20-year

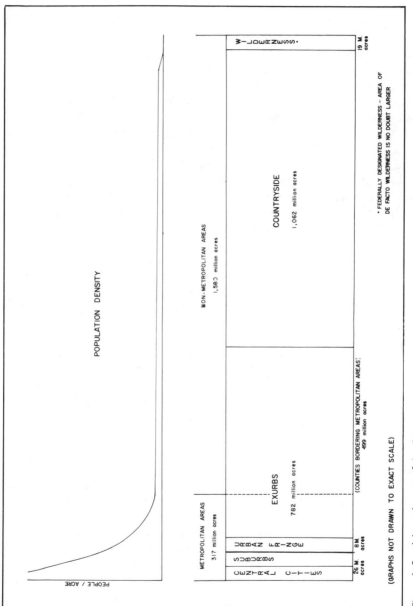

Figure 1. Spatial continuum of development.

supply of such land, we guess that perhaps 8 million acres of land should be placed within this category.

Beyond the fringe are the "exurbs." Here land is unlikely to be completely urbanized in the foreseeable future. Yet the exurbs are heavily influenced by the metropolitan zone. Exurbs are defined mainly by the possibility of commuting, and they present a diverse appearance. They contain quite a bit of agriculture, often with a visible emphasis on vegetables, dairying, and specialty crops. Exurbs typically contain a large number of suburban type houses, and occasionally a scattering of dense subdivisions—a phenomenon sometimes called "buckshot urbanization." Yet urban services generally are not available, nor is the population density likely ever to be so great as to warrant their extension. Despite the sometimes high degree of urban influence, the exurbs are still "beyond the fringe."

In trying to estimate the amount of land that could be considered exurban, we have combined the amount of land within SMSAs that is neither now urbanized nor likely to be urbanized in the next 20 years (approximately 283 million acres) and added to it the 499 million acres of land contained in counties bordering SMSAs. The total (782 million acres) represents 41 percent of the land area of the country (excluding Alaska and Hawaii), a measure of how widespread is the influence of large urban concentrations in the current United States land use picture. An alternative definition, based on worker commuting data obtained after this paper was presented, places the estimated area of exurbs at about 520 million acres, with the area of "countryside" correspondingly larger. (Healy and Short 1981.)

Beyond the exurbs is what we might call "the countryside." This is the land in the 1,500 metropolitan counties not adjacent to SMSAs. These counties do contain towns, even small cities. But unlike the large central cities of SMSAs, these urban places usually do not cast an influence on land use over a large surrounding region. Overall, this "countryside" area contains about 1,062 million acres.

Within the exurbs and countryside, approximately 550 million acres are owned by various levels of government, with the largest holdings those of two federal agencies, the Bureau of Land Management and the Forest Service. The policies of government as the holder of such a large fraction of the nation's rural landscape are particularly important, especially in the western states, where federal holdings are very large. A rather considerable literature on government land management has arisen, and government managers have increasingly relied on long-range planning and economic analysis in their decision making.

In the pages that follow, our own interest will focus on the privately held land in the exurbs and the countryside. It is this 1.3 billion acres that we shall refer to when we speak of "rural land." And it is this land that trades on the "rural land market."

Differentiating the Rural Land Market

The term "market" describes where and how buyers and sellers of a commodity get together to make exchanges. The land market, however, has no central institution, such as the stock exchanges in New York or Chicago's commodity exchange. Rather, a land market occurs in any of the varied spots where buyers and sellers get together to exchange money for land. Some rural parcels are traded at auction, some through real estate brokers, others through direct contact between buyer and seller. Land may be "put on the market" by formal advertisement or listing, or may be sold only after a buyer has taken the initiative and sought out a potential seller.

A useful analytical approach to the rural land market is to compare its workings with the economist's concept of a market as "the area within which the price of a commodity tends toward uniformity, allowance being made for transportation costs" (Stigler 1966). If there were only a single, perfectly competitive market for rural land, the price of two parcels of land of equal fertility, one in Tennessee and the other in Minnesota, would differ only by the difference in the amount it cost to haul the crop produced by each of them to the point of consumption. In fact, we do find that the more isolated a piece of land is, the lower (all other factors constant) its market price tends to be.

In a perfectly competitive market, moreover, the difference between the price of cropland and the price of timberland would be no greater than the marginal cost of converting land from one use to the other. For example, again considering two tracts of equal fertility, suppose it costs $500 an acre to clear a piece of woodland and create a field suitable for soybeans. In that case, the price of an acre of soybean land could never rise to more than $500 above the price of an acre of timberland. Clearly, if the market price difference were, say, $800 per acre, enterprising owners of timberland would start clearing their land, forcing the price of soybean land back down until the differential was eliminated.

In reality, the rural land market appears to be neither a perfectly competitive national market (as is the stock market or the cash grain market) nor a series of balkanized markets, in each of which the price of land is completely independent of the price in any other. Rather, the rural land market is *a series of interconnected local markets, joined together by fitful and imperfect flows of capital and information.*

In the main, competition between local buyers and sellers sets the price of rural land. Yet if the price in a given locality becomes unusually low, outsiders will eventually take an interest, bringing new money to the market and driving up the price. The availability of unusually cheap recreational land in the Ozarks and in northern New England during the 1960s, for example, caused urban bidders to enter the market, paying more than local people could afford or were willing to pay. Similarly, high prices for cash grain land in the Midwest have caused a few farmers to consider selling out and moving their operations to cheaper, but nearly as productive, land in the Mississippi Delta states (Bickers 1978). And there has been an increase in the demand for rural land in general from foreign investors, who find U.S. land prices low compared with those in their own countries (U.S. Senate 1979).

In addition to locally segmented markets, there are also separate, but inter-connected, markets for various *types* of land. We hypothesize that there are three basic rural land markets: an agricultural land market, a timber/recreational land market, and a development land market. These three markets are distinct, yet interconnected, and compare to those suggested in earlier studies by Crowley (1974) and Barrows and Dunford (1976). Each market is characterized by a particular group of potential buyers and by a distinct pattern of information flows between buyers and sellers. Thus, when a piece of cropland is auctioned off on the steps of a rural county courthouse, the bidders are likely to be quite different from those who would attend the auction of a piece of timberland or the sale of a rural parcel with potential for development as a housing subdivision or a shopping center.

The three types of land markets are differentiated by the amount of difficulty and expense in converting land from one use to another, by the different kinds of expertise needed to profitably manage various types of land, and by the sizes and prices of parcels that typically come on the market. Thus different types of land will appeal to different groups of buyers. For example, the aesthetic and recreational values of cropland are frequently not as great as those for other types of land; and potential buyers of recreational properties are more likely to show up at sales of timberland than they are when good cropland is being sold. The latter sales will be dominated by farmers or others with the skills necessary to farm the land.

Of course, land with development potential can come from either agricultural land or timberland. Yet only a small fraction of either agricultural or timber land has development potential, mainly because of a general lack of accessibility. Buyers in the development market are either planning to develop the land themselves or speculating (sometimes foolishly) on the possibility of later development by others. Land with development potential tends to sell in the smallest-sized parcels, but for the highest prices per acre. Most types of development simply do not require parcels as large as do most resource-based uses. And developers are typically able to pay much more for land than are farmers or forest operators. Once a piece of rural land has been sold at development market prices, it is quite unlikely that it will ever resell for farm or forest value, regardless of whether or not development takes place.

CHANGING PATTERNS IN RURAL LAND MARKETS

Rural places are undergoing some significant but as yet little understood changes. To date, most research on rural areas has focused either on aggregate demographic data (e.g., population shifts and migration to nonmetropolitan areas), or on certain types of land use policies meant to affect current uses of rural land (e.g., use-value taxation and agricultural districting). Little attention, however, has been concentrated on changes in the land market itself.

We believe that forces have been developing in rural land markets that may profoundly affect the appearance of the American countryside, the distribution of rural wealth, and the availability of rural land to provide food, fiber, and recreation. These forces are given their first expression through the market for rural land.

In our study of the rural land market we have identified three important phenomena: (1) increased and diverse demands for rural properties; (2) changes in the size distribution of landholdings—particularly the phenomenon of "parcellation"; and (3) notable increases in the price of rural lands. We have documented these changes as occurring strongly over more than a decade; we find them to be trends that cut across all types of rural land and are setting the stage for economic, physical, and social change in rural areas around the country.

Diverse New Demands for Rural Land

New names are appearing in the land ownership books in musty county courthouses. Some are urbanites buying land for use or investment; others are corporations or real-estate syndicates; still others are local people now living in cities, who have bought for retirement or have acquired the land through inheritance. Some of these new owners have moved onto the land, but many have not. Most of these new purchasers of rural land are making a long-term investment, based upon their hopes and expectations about the future. A clearer understanding of their behavior in the land market affords an unparalleled chance to explore what these hopes and expectations are, and what this implies for the future uses of rural land.

There has been a notable increase in the demand for rural land of all types, beginning in the late 1960s and continuing, only slightly diminished, to the present. Despite considerable diversity in their locations and physical geographies, five of our study sites showed marked similarities in the way land transfers varied over time. (Data on land transfers for the Illinois site were unavailable.). In each place, there was a notable acceleration in the rate of transfer in the late 1960s, usually becoming most apparent in 1969. In each, a peak level of transfers was reached in 1972-73, followed by a sharp decline in the recession/energy crisis years 1974-75. Except for one study site, land transfers subsequently recovered strongly from the recession low, with transfers in most places at or close to an all-time high. This pattern contrasts with that observed for transfers of operating farms, which—nationwide—declined steadily from 1950 to 1971, quickened somewhat in 1972-74, then went to new lows thereafter. In 1950, 280,000 transfers of farm real estate took place; in 1979, only 86,000 occurred. The drop reflects both a major drop in the number of farms, and some decline in the rate of transfer per 1000 farms (USDA 1979).

This rise in nonfarm market activity has been associated with increases in several types of demand for rural land, including speculative demand, demand for land as an inflation hedge, demand for rural primary and recreational homesites, retirement demand, and demand by foreign investors (Healy and Short 1978). The fall in farm transfers over time should be attributed not to lack of demand, but to sharply restricted supply, as farmland was accumulated by expanding farmers interested in increasing the scale of their operations, then remained in these "strong hands" as demand continued to rise.

Particularly significant in the nonfarm market has been the increase in demand for land by "nontraditional" owners. Traditional farmers or small town owners of rural land are now being joined by urban professionals whose income and flexible work schedules allow a mixture of rural amenities with urban business; by urban workers looking forward to retirement in quieter environments with lower living costs; and by young professional couples combining weekend "hobby farming" with close attention to their land's potential as a long-term investment.

Part of the increased demand for rural land is associated with the oft-noted revival in rural population growth. Its impact on the land market is most easily measured by looking at the changing number of rural housing units. Between 1960 and 1970, urban housing units grew by 23 percent, while rural units grew by only 6 percent (U.S. Bureau of Census 1979). But then came a very dramatic reversal. Between 1970 and 1977, while urban housing units grew by 14 percent, those in rural areas increased by 35 percent. Demographic studies have indicated that the rural population revival has touched all regions of the country, and rural places of all sizes (McCarthy and Morrison 1979; Fuguitt and Voss 1979). The migrants themselves, who tend to have higher levels of both education and job status than do the long-time rural residents, have helped change the composition of rural land holders and have injected new funds into rural land markets.

Rural job growth has also required a substantial amount of land. A variety of economic activities, first led by manufacturing, but increasingly including other activities, have been decentralizing to nonmetropolitan areas. Between 1970 and 1977, nonfarm employment grew twice as rapidly (22 percent) in nonmetropolitan areas, compared with metropolitan areas. Nonmetropolitan areas led in each major sector of employment (USDA 1978).

But even despite new rural growth, in many parts of the country control over land is increasingly passing into the hands of nonresidents. Some of these are interested in eventually moving to the land; others seek weekend recreation; still others are interested mainly in investment. In the areas we studied, outsiders were generally buying land even more rapidly than they were moving in. For example, in Tyler County, Texas, 31 percent of the landowners in 1954 lived outside the county; by 1976, 58 percent were noncounty residents. In western Loudoun County, Virginia, the number of parcels owned by people residing outside the county more than doubled over this same period. And in West Windsor, Vermont, only 6 percent of all land parcels were owned by persons living more than 30 miles away in 1954; but by 1976, some 39 percent of all parcels were owned by such persons, nearly all of them from out-of-state. In our "prime farmland" area, Douglas Co., Illinois, however, absentee ownership was rather high (40 percent) in 1954 and increased only slightly (to 43 percent) in 1976. Half of these absentees in both periods lived in adjoining rural counties.

Demand for rural land by corporations is another source of concern for many observers of the rural scene. But it is not clear that increased demands for rural land by corporations are a significant part of the surge in market transactions during the early 1970s. Corporations—a class of owner that may include family corporations, small groups of absentee investors, and huge multinational firms—do appear to own substantial amounts of rural land. But the exact extent of the holdings of each of these groups, and more importantly how these holdings have been changing over time, are difficult to determine. Some companies choose to keep their holdings confidential (Meyer 1979). And there is no government agency collecting comprehensive data on corporate land ownership or its rate of change, although a few states do require regular reports from corporations on their agricultural landholdings. Most data on corporate land ownership are derived from aggregate statistics of the Department of Agriculture and U.S. Forest Service. The USDA's 1978 national landownership study found total corporate ownership of 218 million acres (Lewis 1980). Of these, 59 million acres are owned by family corporations with fewer than 10 shareholders. These acres are generally family farms incorporated for tax or inheritance purposes. Some 68 million acres are commercial forest land owned by wood-producing companies, for the most part in Maine, the South, and the Pacific Northwest (U.S. Forest Service 1978). Ownership of rural land by oil companies, mining companies, and railroads is also considerable. Nonfamily corporate demands for rural land do appear to be significant (current holdings amount to about 11 percent of all land), but lack of data allows little more than speculation on how these demands have been changing in the past or how they can be expected to change in the future.

Finally, new demands for rural land also come from increasing numbers of people who are retiring or anticipating retirement. The number of people over 65 is expected to increase from 16 million in 1960 to an estimated 31 million by the year 2000. The proportion of these people who now have pensions, enabling them to buy property and retire in places they consider pleasant, is greater than ever. For example, nonmetropolitan counties with high concentrations of Social Security and Medicare recipients experienced significantly higher than average annual rates of net migration for both 1960-70 and 1970-74 (McCarthy and Morrison 1979). Many people are simply returning to areas where they lived as youngsters or had previous experience of during vacations (Fuguitt and Voss 1979). Nationally, it has been shown that sizable numbers of retirees have gone not just to traditional sunbelt destinations but to such places as the Ozarks, the North Carolina highlands, upper Michigan, and the coastal Pacific Northwest (Doherty 1979). Even sunbelt retirement havens such as southern California, Arizona, and Florida are spinning off their own rural-bound retirees, as some of these previously attractive and quiet areas become increasingly costly and congested (Gottschalk 1979).

New types of demands for rural land have grown substantially during the past decade. Demand for land by foreigners, corporations, and speculators, demands due to inflation hedging, urban conversion, and population dispersal generally, and other diverse new demands for rural land are treated in detail in our book (Healy and Short 1981).

An Increase in Parcellation

The changing nature of demands for rural land has modified the size of landholdings in rural areas. In some parts of the country, economies of scale in farming have led to land consolidation; elsewhere demand has been strongest for smaller acreage, causing some landowners and land dealers to respond by splitting lots.

The size of the parcel in which land is held is mainly a function of custom (e.g., the uniform 40 to 640 acre plots based on the rectangular survey) and the economics of past land uses. As economic forces change, the size of holdings slowly changes to reflect them. Thus, in response to technological change in agriculture, the average size of operating farms has been rising nationwide since the end of the Depression, doubling since 1950 to 440 acres per farm in 1974. In fact, in 1978 farm enlargement accounted for 63 percent of all farmland purchases, up from 29 percent in 1954 (USDA 1979).

On the other hand, there is also increasing demand for land in smaller and smaller parcels, and this raises questions about efficient usage of rural land. Even as some farmland is being consolidated, other rural land—mainly timberland and marginal cropland—is being divided. Our case-study data reveal the enormous popularity of splitting large tracts of land into a small number of small to medium-sized (6-40 acres) parcels. This practice has been encouraged by changes in both supply and demand. On the supply side, multiple-acre lot splits can be created by a local real estate agent or an individual landowner, without need for elaborate planning or legal or sales organization and with minimal front-end costs. If fewer than 50 lots are created or sales efforts are not directed across state lines, no HUD property registration is required. And in many cases, multiple-acre lot splits are not regulated by state or local subdivision laws. On the demand side, consumers appear to have become disenchanted with the recreational subdivisions so popular during the late 1960s, in part because they have found that an unimproved 10-acre parcel can cost no more than an acre in a rural development project. One Boston land dealer, who specializes in northern New England properties, stated: "Even when you do a development you have to be sure that it's not a 'development.' We have 1,000 acres in Waterville Valley (N.H.) and 100 lots. But we only sell 5 or 6 at a time because people don't want a development." Until recently, there have been little data on the size distributions of landholdings, and on how they have changed over time. The USDA's national landownership survey (Table 1) indicates that the overwhelming majority of private land acreage in the U.S. is held in ownership units large enough to permit efficient commodity production. For example, 94 percent of cropland is held in units of 50 acres or more. And for rangeland, where much larger management units are appropriate, more than 90 percent of the acreage is in units of 260 acres or more.

Table 1. Land Use in 1977 by Size of Holdings, United States
(Excluding Alaska)[a]

	Land Use						
Size of Holdings[b]	Cropland	Pasture	Range	Forest	Other[c]	Urban and Water[d]	Total
Acres				*Percent*			
Less than 10	1.28	2.59	.87	3.12	4.69	32.82	3.32
10-49	4.45	9.47	1.59	8.53	9.73	11.84	5.82
50-69	2.25	4.57	.45	3.70	3.39	3.23	2.49
70-79	5.41	9.41	1.14	6.16	8.05	4.03	5.00
100-139	6.19	9.07	.92	6.69	7.25	2.96	5.20
140-179	10.77	9.14	2.21	5.65	5.28	3.84	6.67
180-259	10.87	12.21	2.39	7.79	5.97	4.55	7.65
260-499	20.64	16.71	7.64	10.85	10.80	8.71	13.64
500-999	16.88	11.71	11.00	8.08	8.96	6.38	11.91
1,000-1,999	10.20	6.06	12.75	4.87	6.47	4.80	8.69
2,000 and over	11.07	9.06	59.04	34.56	29.40	16.86	29.63
Total	100.00	100.00	100.00	100.00	100.00	100.00	100.00

[a]Data provided by Linda K. Lee, Oklahoma State University.

[b]Landowners' total holdings within a specified county.

[c]Includes farmsteads, other land in farms, strip mines, quarries, gravel pits, borrow pits, barren land, and all other land not defined elsewhere including greenbelts and large un-wooded parks.

[d]Includes urban and built-up land, transportation uses, water, and miscellaneous land uses for which limited Soil Conservation Service data are available.

Continued parcellation, however, may impair productivity; some areas bear watching. For example, 21 percent of private forest land is held in ownership units of less than 100 acres, generally too small for efficient timber management. Similarly, although less than 6 percent of all cropland is held in parcels below 50 acres, this involves over 20 million acres of land. Considerable attention has recently been focused on the urbanization of farmland; virtually none on acreage whose production potential may have been severely limited by parcellation.

Ownership and parcel-size data for our case sites for the period 1954-76 indicate that parcellation has been quite high during the last two decades (Table 2). The increase in total number of rural parcels over the period ranged from 16 percent in Douglas County, Illinois, to 266 percent in Tyler County, Texas.

In sum, stability of returns in a future filled with economic uncertainties is not likely to lessen the demand for rural land as a way of protecting one's capital from high and rising rates of inflation. Demand for land in America's rural areas continues to be strong, and there are few signs that the relatively sluggish supply we note later will work very differently to keep price increases down. While we cannot predict the future course of land prices, rural land clearly has some fundamental reasons to attract nonfarm as well as farmer investors.

Table 2. Total Number of Land Parcels at Six Study Sites

Study Site	1954	1976	Annual Percent Change
Hardy Co., W. Virginia*	2,186	3,688	2.4
Loudoun Co., Virginia (rural portions)	4,034	6,425	2.1
San Luis Obispo Co., California (rural portions)*†	46,399	54,037	1.5
Tyler County, Texas*	3,080	11,264	6.1
W. Windsor, Vt./Plainfield, N.H.	741	1,492	3.2
Douglas Co., Illinois*	841	972	0.7

Source: Conservation Foundation Rural Land Market Project.
    *Adjoining or nearby parcels in single ownership counted as single parcel.
    †Data are for 1967 and 1977.

Despite the very dramatic increase in the *number* of small parcels, *the number of acres* affected has proven to be rather low. In Tyler, for example, although the number of parcels of less than 10 acres rose more than 5.5 times, the percentage of acres held in tracts of less than 10 acres rose only from 2.0 to 5.6 percent. In the New England site, the proportion of land area held in parcels of less than 10 acres was 1.4 percent in 1954 and 4.5 percent in 1976. The 10-25 acre parcels, on the other hand, showed more moderate growth in *number*, but increased their *acreage* more impressively. In Tyler County, they rose from 4.1 to 10 percent of total acreage; in Loudoun, from 5.3 to 10.7 percent; and in West Windsor/Plainfield, from 3.5 to 9 percent.

Nevertheless, even though parcellation has occurred, more than half the area of each county is in holdings of more than 100 acres in size. Thus, in spite of rapid change, the land-resource base apparently has not been fragmented beyond repair, so far.

Increases in the Price of Rural Land

Perhaps the most dramatic of the new rural land-market phenomena has been the notable rise in land prices. Increasing demand, smaller average parcel sizes, and a relatively sluggish supply response have combined to force rural land prices to record levels. A plethora of examples from our case study files makes it clear that even after accounting for general inflation, rural land prices have risen very rapidly over the past two decades, thus giving land a reputation as an inflation hedge that has itself fueled further increases.

The price of farmland is the best documented component of rural land values. Between 1950 and 1979, farmland prices rose more then eightfold (tripling between 1970-79), while the general price level rose 320 percent. Virtually every part of the country has participated in this long price boom, although there have been both regional and temporal differences—the more urbanized states and states in the deep south generally did better than average before 1970, while the Corn Belt showed the greatest increases after 1973.

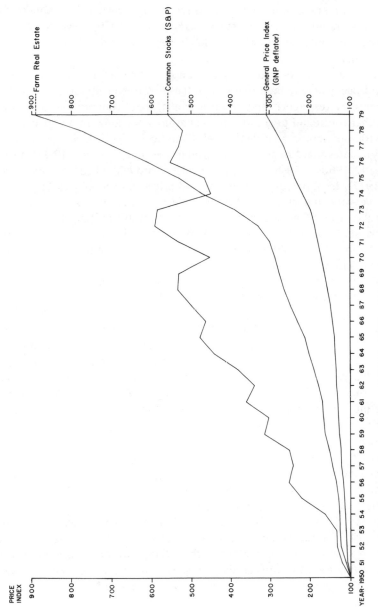

Figure 2. Comparative record of price change, 1950-79. (1950 = 100.)

Farmland prices have performed better than either the general price index or Standard and Poor's index of 500 common stocks (Fig. 2). During the 1950s and 1960s, farmland prices rose about twice as rapidly as the general price index, but not nearly so rapidly as did the stock market. Since 1970, however, farmland prices have continued to outpace inflation by far, even as the stock market average has stagnated.

There is no source of national data on nonfarm rural land prices, but anecdotal evidence generally indicated substantial increases in this sector as well. A New Hampshire researcher reports, for example, that "common talk among foresters is that forestland prices in New Hampshire have gone from $10 an acre to nearly $100 per acre in a single decade" (Wallace 1973). A U.S. Forest Service land buyer notes that low-grade timberland in Arkansas sold for $12-$18 an acre in the early 1960s, $50 by 1970, and by 1977 brought $150 or more an acre (Welsh 1977). In Minnesota, where cropland prices have been soaring, prices of land in the wooded northeastern section tripled between 1971 and 1974, leveled off, and then rose 56 percent in 1977-78 (Christianson and Raup 1979). A comprehensive study of forestland sales in Vermont found that per acre prices rose from $163 in 1968 to $398 in 1973, then were stable for the next four years (Armstrong and Briggs 1978).

Trends in values of rural land used for outdoor recreation are particularly difficult to estimate, because such land can range from waterfront on Cape Cod or Chesapeake Bay (sold by the front foot) to rugged wilderness in the far West. The chief of land acquisition for the National Park Service told a congressional committee in 1975 that land purchased by that agency was appreciating at an average of about 12 percent annually (U.S. House of Representatives 1975). In 1979 a NPS research appraiser estimated that smaller recreational tracts were rising in price by perhaps 15 percent a year (Langer 1979). Several real estate experts we interviewed pointed to the extremely high demand for water frontage, whether on the ocean or on inland lakes, and the consequent very rapid rise in the prices of such properties.

Perhaps the best approximation of the change in value of timberland and recreation land for a large area of the country might be the prices of land acquired by the U.S. Forest Service, under the Weeks Act (used since 1912 to buy land for timber and watershed purposes, primarily in national forests east of the Rockies) and the Land and Water Conservation Fund (used since 1966 to buy land primarily for recreational purposes, nationwide). Prices for land acquired under both sources rose rapidly during the 1970s, with percentage rates of increase dwarfing even those of farmland (Fig. 3). Rural land prices even outpaced existing urban home prices, as indicated by data from the National Association of Realtors (1980).

Measuring benefits to purchasers of rural land by merely noting a consistent rise in land prices, however, overlooks the important investment consideration of risk—generally measured in some way by the variability in returns received. And what little we do know about the performance of rural real estate compared to

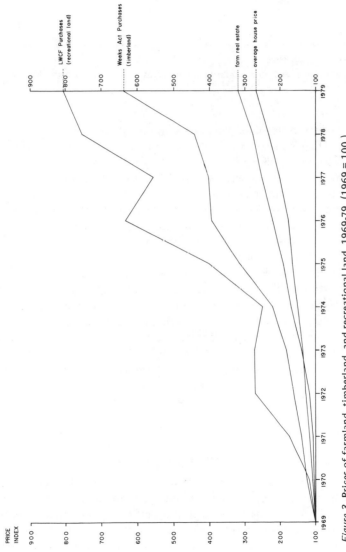

Figure 3. Prices of farmland, timberland, and recreational land, 1969-79. (1969 = 100.)

Table 3. Total Annual Return on Investment (Percentage)

Period	Farmland[a]	Common Stocks	Price Inflation
1940-50	14.0	8.0	6.3
1950-60	10.2	19.5	2.5
1960-70	8.9	7.7	2.9
1970-78	16.6	4.1	6.6
1940-78	12.9	10.8	4.5

Source: Gertel and Lewis 1980

[a]Average return for cash rented farmland in areas of Illinois, Kansas, Montana and Mississippi.

other investment vehicles underlines the stability of land's returns. Gertel and Lewis (1980) compared investors' returns from cash rented farmland (in four states) and from the stock market (measured by the S&P 500 index) with rates of price inflation for various periods since 1940. In the case of both stocks and farmland, returns include both current income, in the form of dividends or cash rents, and price appreciation over time. Table 3 indicates that during the post-1940 period, both farmland and common stocks have been good hedges against price inflation, but with widely varying performance, depending on the time period considered. Although the rates of return for the entire 1940-78 period were not markedly different between these two kinds of assets, one can note that farmland has exhibited two characteristics that seem to give it a real advantage as an inflation hedge. First, the return to farmland was highest during the two periods of greatest general inflation, the 1940s and the 1970s. Second, the inflation-adjusted returns to farmland (annual return minus annual inflation) were much more stable than those of common stocks. For example, in no decade did the inflation adjusted farmland return exceed 10 percent—but it never fell below 5 percent. Common stocks, on the other hand, produced adjusted returns that varied between 17.0 percent annually for their best decade, and −2.5 percent for their worst.

WHAT ARE THE ISSUES?

The changing patterns of ownership and use of rural land documented above raise a number of complex unresolved issues. We continue to rely on the *private* land market to allocate lands among their most efficient uses, and address *public* policies to that market for socially desirable distributions of those uses. To misinterpret motives and changing patterns in the private marketplace is to employ inappropriate public policies with very uncertain results. And the patterns of population migration and landownership now appearing in rural areas are indeed diverse. One author commented: "[G]rowth in [rural] areas does not represent a return to the land. The new residents of these areas enjoy 'rural' amenities, but they are [often] part of the nonfarm urban economy. Thus, the emerging pattern of development could be interpreted more as a dispersal of urban America than a rural renaissance." (Doherty 1979, p. 56) This does not mean, however, that measures designed to solve urban land use problems can be applied easily to the rural land market. We cannot "continue to make rules and lay down theories for a big city centered nation that is rapidly ceasing to exist" (Doherty 1979, p. 95).

Diversity Among Owners

Conflicts in the use of rural land arise from the diversity of ownership—traditional versus nontraditional, and resident versus absentee. Traditional owners tend to view land in terms of its productive capacity—farmers, ranchers, and forest managers must make a living from the soil. To such owners the economic role of the land tends to take precedence over noneconomic factors. By contrast, nontraditional landowners may focus entirely on amenity values and care little about land's economic productivity. For example, urban-oriented owners may believe that they are "conserving" the forest by not cutting trees. Yet many foresters believe that prudent long-term management includes immediate harvesting and regeneration in more usable species. This has particular significance for management of the 296 million acres of commercial forestland (59 percent of the national total) held by nonindustrial private owners.

Use by owner versus use by a tenant further affects the management of rural land. In 1978 some 282 million acres of farmland, about a third of all farmland, were rented rather than owned by their operators. Many observers contend that leased land is frequently abused by its operator, particularly when the owner lives far away and the lease is only for a year at a time. This "careless tenant" hypothesis is supported by a western Iowa study, which found that rental land was losing an average of 20.9 tons per acre of topsoil annually to erosion, while owner-operated land was losing only 15.6 tons (Timmons and Hauser, forthcoming). Further study is needed before we can judge the truthfulness of a proverb commonly cited by land-reform advocates: "The best fertilizer for the land are the footsteps of the owners."

Corporate and Foreign Ownership

We actually know very little about "who owns rural America." According to the 1978 USDA ownership survey (Lewis 1980), the biggest owners of land in the United States are farmers, who own more than half a billion acres, 38 percent of all privately held acreage. Next in importance are retirees, who hold 190 million acres, or 14 percent of all private land. Nonfamily corporations own some 151 million acres, or 11 percent of the total—about half of these acres are commercial forests owned by timber companies. Also in this category are the rather extensive holdings of mining and petroleum companies, railroads, and agricultural corporations.

The remaining owners are a diverse group—nonfarm rural families, urbanites who have inherited or purchased land in the country, and various types of partnerships and syndicates. More than 10 million acres are owned by real-estate dealers themselves. The proportion of owners who actually live on their land is unknown, but the USDA survey found that 80 percent of all noncorporate land is owned by residents of the county containing the land, and 94 percent by residents of the same state (Lewis 1980).

Foreign ownership of U.S. land has received a great deal of attention in the press. On the basis of reports filed under the 1978 Agricultural Foreign Investment Disclosure Act, USDA (1980) estimates that foreign residents own only one-half of one percent of all private agricultural land nationally. A significant proportion of these holdings are by timber companies, many of them U.S.-based but with some foreign ownership interest. Most individual foreign owners are Europeans or Canadians; very few are residents of OPEC (although some OPEC owners may disguise their identities through use of Carribbean tax havens). It appears that the bulk of foreign holdings comprise improved urban real estate (office buildings and shopping centers) rather than unimproved rural acreage.

Implications of Changing Parcel Sizes

Changes in parcel size raise questions about the efficiency of long-term resource management. There is considerable disagreement over the extent of economies of scale in both agriculture and forestry, but there is surely some parcel size below which many resource management practices become inefficient.

Considering agricultural land first: apparent economic advantages of large-scale farms have been a driving force in allowing a rapidly declining farm population to produce ever-increasing quantities of food. And we have noted earlier the continuing tendency for farm enlargement to be a major factor in farm real-estate markets. Large-scale agricultural operations also have been criticized, however, for producing a visually monotonous landscape, for reducing the rural population available to support small-town businesses, for destroying wildlife habitat, and for being slow to adjust to changing market conditions (Belden and Forte 1976; Babb 1979; Goldschmidt 1947, 1978). Clearly, the scale-of-operation issue remains unresolved.

For forest lands the parcellation issue perhaps is more focused. A timber buyer for one large lumber company notes that even just *harvesting* small tracts is prohibitive: "We have people coming to us all the time trying to sell timber in 2, 3 and 5 acre blocks. We just refer them someplace else. We hardly ever buy anything less than 25 acres, and we prefer 50 or more. Our contractor loses a day's work just moving his equipment to the next site."

One forest economist has found that tract size has substantial impacts on the financial returns to intensive forest management practices, and that scale economies are found as parcel size rises up to at least 160 acres. On the other hand, tract size influences returns from minimal management only for parcels smaller than about 40 acres. He concludes that "where tracts are small, owners may accurately perceive that *for them* intensive timber growing would not be worth the effort, unless it facilitates other objectives." (Row 1978.)

Moreover, even if a given type of management is profitable on a small tract in *percentage* terms, the *total amount* of money involved may not be large enough to make the landowner take action. For example, few urban absentee owners will bother to arrange to lease a 10-acre pasture to a neighboring farmer when the total rental is no more than $50 a year.

Certainly more research is needed on the parcellation phenomenon. This information would be particularly useful in those rapidly growing rural areas where very large minimum-lot-size zoning has been introduced in the attempt to curtail real estate market activity affecting land uses there. "Building lots" (e.g., commonly from 5 to 40 acres minimum) created by these controls may indeed help preserve an area's bucolic character, but they also drastically increase the number of acres of land locked up in parcels too small to be efficient production units.

Probably one of the most important issues associated with parcellation is the irreversibility (in the economic sense) of parcel splitting. So far much of the rural land being purchased by newly arriving exurbanites for residential or recreational purposes has been marginal land not currently in demand for either agricultural or forestry purposes. It is possible that future increases in food or timber prices could encourage owners of such land to return it to production, but they would then be faced with problems of small parcel sizes and scattered ownership.

Prices and parcel size are interrelated. In the past, when land prices were low, persons buying land for investment or recreation could afford the relatively large parcels that had formerly been used in agriculture. Rising land prices, however, mean that a given amount of money buys a smaller parcel—incentive in itself to break traditional-sized parcels into smaller ones. Once split and sold to urban owners, rural parcels can prove very difficult to recombine, even if resource prices are considerably higher than present levels. Experience with urban renewal and central city properties during the 1950-70 period suggests how fragmented ownership slows the land market's response to changing conditions.

Finally, there are other less tangible factors to consider. The small rural farm parcel (e.g., the part-time "hobby farm") has been both praised and criticized. Fields that are allowed to revert to brush are inefficient from the standpoint of commodity production, but over time they can provide habitats for wildlife. Moreover, small part-time agricultural operations may not be very productive in an economic sense, but they increase the landscape's diversity and allow people to enjoy rural living without having to become subsistence farmers.

Rising Rural Land Prices

Rising rural land prices affect farmers, investors, new and old landowners, local bankers, planners, and conservationists. For existing farmers, higher prices impede purchase of additional land despite the greater efficiency of larger units. For would-be farmers the cost of going into business may be simply prohibitive. Timber companies find it difficult to expand their holdings of new productive timber because land prices have reached levels not justified by the production of timber. On the other hand, the expectation of steady increases in land value has probably kept many farmers in business, despite low rates of current income. Capital gains from land have made it possible for farmers to borrow for expansion and to look forward to a secure retirement. And local rural bankers may oppose any new land-use policy that has the potential to reduce the market values that secure their loans.

Rising prices are not just the result of increased demands. Per-acre prices are also strongly influenced by parcel size, with smaller parcels selling (at any given time) for higher per acre prices than large parcels. As larger parcels purchased at one point in time are broken down into smaller ones, this parcel-size effect combines with increasing demand for parcels of *all* sizes to force prices up.

Factors are also at work on the supply side of the market that help keep land prices high and rising. One of the notable aspects of rural land supply is the way landowners' personal circumstances can often take precedence over economic market forces in the decision to sell land. In some areas, the supply of land is controlled by a few long-time owners who may be reluctant to sell. Estate sales and land auctions from the courthouse steps are major sources of land supply, and these have more to do with demographics and life cycles than with market phenomena and prices. Discussing the sluggish response of the local rural land supply, one rural Virginia real estate broker commented: "Divorce and death are the big things here—divorce is how we got our farm." A recent survey of farmland owners in three Vermont counties found that health and age were the two most important reasons for selling land. Ranking only third was the price-oriented response: "received a good offer for the land" (Bancroft et al. 1977).

Noneconomic factors may have more impact on the timing of sales than on the eventual outcome, however. A Texas real-estate dealer noted that today the local land supply is "mostly from estates where the heirs want their part . . . they're selling to developers . . . land values are getting to the point where you see you can make a few bucks." And a West Virginia real-estate broker noted that farmers' reluctance to sell melted away when newcomers were willing to pay what he called "extortion prices" for land—far above what it was worth for farming or forestry purposes.

Finally, even in those few rural counties where some form of zoning or land-use planning is in operation, the combined effects of controls over the land's use and rising prices seem to have affected the demand for land very little. Application in rural areas of common planning tools, such as minimum-lot size zoning and differential taxation of agricultural land, has had mixed results at best; in many cases they have done little to stifle the land appetites of the diverse new purchasers of rural real estate. For example, at one of our case sites, more than a fifth of the county is zoned for minimum parcels of 640 acres in an attempt to slow down the land market activity. Nevertheless, a planner there noted that each time the minimum parcel size was increased they "just got a more exclusive new buyer."

SOME NOTES ON PUBLIC POLICY

Nearly all of the land-market issues we have raised here are long-term ones. Perhaps the most pressing is the difficulty that high land prices pose for landless young farmers, a problem recently exacerbated by high-interest rates and low crop prices. But in the main, the issues we have described are not likely to trouble us for some years to come. Yet this lack of urgency must not blind us from realizing that the potential problems are extremely significant, and that the long time needed for them to build up is likely to be matched by an equally long time in dealing with them effectively.

If large quantities of productive rural land are devoted to urban, residential, or recreational uses; if parcel sizes are too small for efficient management; or if land and timber are neglected or abused by their owners, it may take literally decades to cope with the results. An analogy to the long decline of central cities may be appropriate. Forces that began to be noticed by economists, sociologists, and planners as early as the 1930s eventually produced an "urban crisis" in the 1960s. Today, 20 years later, we have made only modest progress in dealing with the problems. Would we not have been better prepared if we had begun to understand and monitor what was happening to our central cities as the process of decline was just beginning?

A tentative approach to rural land policy might start by recognizing that it will be neither possible, nor desirable, to try to dampen the widespread popular desire to buy land in rural areas or the desire to relocate there. Many of the impacts of new people and new money are beneficial ones, particularly if we can harness some of these private energies in the service of social goals.

An early priority for rural land policy is to create new models of rural physical development and land use. At present, a great deal of rural growth takes the form of either attempts to recreate an idealized agricultural economy and landscape long made obsolete by economic and technological change; or attempts to replicate suburban styles of development in low density areas. Both of these patterns result in wasted land, high public service costs, and rural living patterns that have little relation to a rural economy that is now overwhelmingly nonagricultural, yet scarcely suburban.

We must also create new institutions for holding and managing rural land. For example, timber cooperatives might make it possible for many small landowners to bring otherwise wasted forestland under productive management. Community land trusts, now being experimented with in several parts of the country, might be used to make rural land available on a long-term lease basis to farmers and other users who cannot afford outright purchase. The questions of absentee ownership of rural land and the role of nonfarm capital in financing agriculture — which have both good and bad points — should be faced, and new, more appropriate institutional arrangements created. Local governments might experiment with ways to use property tax incentives and penalties to encourage better land management and resource protection, particularly with respect to erosion control, public access, and forest management.

Finally, policymakers and rural residents must come to realize that new forms of rural settlement will require both a greater degree of public control of land use than has been traditional in rural places and a heightened private "land ethic." Under conditions of changing ownership, denser settlement, and new types of land uses, we cannot rely solely on either urban-style zoning or on the frontier mentality of private decisions for private profit. Education, exhortation, incentives, and controls must be combined in creative ways to address new rural issues more effectively.

As we noted at the very beginning of this chapter, something new has happened to America's rural landscape. It is now being challenged and changed as new and diverse forces have entered its land markets. There has been a "turnaround" in past migration and development patterns; rural places long accustomed to stagnation and decline are experiencing a new inflow of people and money. The important economic and social developments now occurring pose difficult long-run problems concerning the efficient and equitable use of one of our most valuable resources—rural land. Today we stand on the threshold of understanding and planning for the future growth and change facing rural America. But we should proceed carefully and with better knowledge of the potential effects of our plans and policies than we had when we sought to solve many critical but ill-understood urban issues a number of years ago. Again, it is our belief that an important starting point in this task is a thorough understanding of land markets in rural areas.

References

Armstrong, F. H., and Briggs, R. D. 1978. *Valuation of Vermont forests, 1968-1977*. Burlington, Vt.: University of Vermont, Department of Forestry.

Babb, E. M. 1979. Consequences of structural change in U.S. agriculture, in U.S. Department of Agriculture. *Structural issues in American agriculture*. USDA, ESCS.

Bancroft, R. L.; Sinclair, R. O.; and Tremblay, R. H. 1977. *Attitudes toward preserving agricultural land in Vermont*. Burlington, Vermont: University of Vermont, Agricultural Experiment Station, Miscellaneous Publication 93.

Barrows, R., and Dunford, R., 1976. *Agricultural, urban and recreational determinants of farmland values in Wisconsin*. Madison: University of Wisconsin, College of Agricultural and Life Sciences, Research Bulletin R2764.

Beale, C. L. 1975. *The revival of population growth in nonmetropolitan America*. Washington: USDA.

Belden, J., and Forte, G. 1976. *Toward a national food policy*. Washington: Exploratory project for economic alternatives.

Bickers, J. 1978. Why the southern land boom may be just beginning. *Progressive Farmer* (July): 15-17.

Christianson, R., and Raup, P. M. 1979. *The Minnesota rural real estate market in 1978*. St. Paul: University of Minnesota Department of Agricultural and Applied Economics.

Crowley, W. D., Jr. 1974. *Farmland use values versus market prices in three Oregon land markets*. Washington: USGPO, ERS Report ERS-550.

Doherty, J. C. 1979. Public and private issues in nonmetropolitan government. *In Growth and change in rural America*. Washington: The Urban Land Institute: 51-101.

Fuguitt, G., and Voss, P. 1979. Recent nonmetropolitan population trends. *In Growth and change in rural America*. Washington: Urban Land Institute: 1-47.

Gertel, K., and Lewis, J. A. 1980. Returns from investment in farmland and common stock 1940-1979. *Agricultural Finance Review* 40 (April): 1-11.

Goldschmidt, W. 1947, 1978. *As you sow: three studies in the social consequences of agribusiness*. Englewood Cliffs, N.J.: Allenheld, Osmun and Co.

Gottschalk, E. C., Jr. 1979. As some sun belt sites get crowded, retirees head for the country. *The Wall Street Journal* (November 13): 1, 44.

Healy, R. G., and Short, J. L. 1978. New forces in the market for rural land. *Appraisal Journal* 56, 2 (April): 85-199.

_____1979. Rural land: market trends and planning implications, *Journal of the American Planning Association* 45, 3: 305-317.

_____ 1981. The market for rural land: trends, issues, policies. Washington: The Conservation Foundation.

Langer, P. 1979. Washington, D.C., National Park Service. Personal interview, September.

Lewis, J. A. 1980. *Landownership in the United States, 1978*. Washington: Economics, Statistics, and Cooperatives Service, U.S. Department of Agriculture, Agriculture Information Bulletin no. 435.

McCarthy, K. F., and Morrison, P. A. 1979. *The changing demographic and economic structure of nonmetropolitan areas in the 1970s*. Santa Monica: The Rand Corporation, January.

Meyer, P. 1979. Land rush: a survey of America's land. *Harper's* 258,1544: 45-60.

National Association of Realtors. 1980. Telephone interview.

Row, C. 1978. Economics of tract size in timber growing. *Journal of Forestry* (September): 576-582.

Stigler, G. 1966. *The theory of price*. New York: MacMillan Company, 3rd Edition, p. 85.

Timmons, J. F. and Hauser, W. Forthcoming. *Soil erosion control in western Iowa: obstacles and remedies*. Department of Agricultural Economics. Iowa State University.

U.S. Bureau of Census. 1979. *Statistical abstract of the U.S.* Washington: USGPO: 782.

U.S. Department of Agriculture 1978. *Rural Development Perspectives*. Washington: ESCS-EDD (November): 8.

_____ 1979. *Farm real estate market developments*. Washington: Economics, Statistics, and Cooperatives Service, USDA.

_____ 1980. *Foreign ownership of U.S. agricultural land*. ESCS-NRED. Agricultural economic report no. 447.

U.S. Forest Service. 1978. *Forest Statistics of the U.S.*, 1977. Washington: USGPO.

U.S. House of Representatives, Committee on Interior and Insular Affairs. 1975. *Hearing, to amend the land and water conservation fund act*. Washington: USGPO.

U.S. Senate. 1979. *Foreign investment in United States Agricultural land*. Committee on Agriculture, Nutrition and Forestry (January).

Voss, P. R., and Fuguitt, G. V. 1979. *Turnaround Migration in the Upper Great Lakes Region*. Madison: University of Wisconsin, Department of Rural Sociology.

Wallace, O. P., Sr. 1973. *Some factors influencing forest land pricing in New Hampshire*. Durham, N.H.: New Hampshire Agricultural Experiment Station.

Welsh, J. F. 1977. U.S. Forest Service, Atlanta, Ga. Personal interview, August.

Remote Land Subdivisions in the Southwest

Larry K. Stephenson

INTRODUCTION

An important subset of the rural land market in the United States is the remote land subdivision boom, especially in the Southwest. This chapter reviews the dimensions of this nonmetropolitan land use phenomenon and notes certain policy issues that confront planners and decision makers as such subdivisions mature. Although only the Southwestern context is considered, many of the issues noted here apply to land developments elsewhere in the United States.

Land Subdivisions in the Southwest

The Southwest, for purposes of the following discussion, includes the "four corner" states of Arizona, New Mexico, Utah, and Colorado, as well as Nevada, California, and Hawaii. Together these states account for almost 20 percent of the land area of the United States and contain approximately 30 million people, about 14 percent of the national total.

The term "land subdivision" refers to the process of dividing a large tract of land into numerous smaller parcels for sale to individuals. Unlike conventional residential subdivisions, land subdivisions normally involve the sale of vacant lots without structures. The subdivider, however, frequently provides roads, public services, and recreational amenities. Land subdivisions are often designed and marketed for leisure or retirement usage.

Several factors contribute to the popularity of large scale land subdivisions in the Southwest. First, the region offers amenities and healthful environments. The term "Sun Belt" applies preeminently to the Southwest as defined above. A second factor is the seasons: a large influx of people occurs during the winter rather than the summer months. The participants in this modern-day transhumance descend upon the Southwest in search of both sun and snow. Demand for second homes ensues from this seasonal flow of population.

A third factor that distinguishes the Southwest from other regions is the relatively small amount of privately owned land available for development. The recent "Sagebrush Rebellion" can be viewed in part as the result of increasing pressure on these private lands (Lounsbury and Taylor 1980). In Arizona, for example, only 15 percent of all land is privately held; in Nevada, only 13 percent is presently available for development. Most land in these states is owned by federal agencies (including national forests, parks, and monuments and holdings of the Bureau of Land Management) or by states or is in Indian reservations, leaving little for private speculation.

Fourth, parcels available for development in the Southwest, particularly in the arid portions, tend to be very large in size. Early development often centered around cattle grazing that operated on a fairly large scale because of the limited carrying capacity per land unit. This was recognized, for example, in federal land-disposal policies, which allowed significantly larger acreages to be homesteaded in the Southwest than in the Midwest. These substantial acreages that could be obtained by developers often allowed certain scale economies in the financing, marketing, and disposing of the subdivided parcels.

Finally, there is simply the "frontier spirit," the notion that an individual's right to use his/her land should be only minimally constrained by government. This conviction is shared by buyers and sellers, as well as by most public authorities.

Collectively, these factors have accounted for the large number of land subdivisions scattered across the Southwest.

Magnitude and Extent

The overall magnitude and extent of land subdivisions in the Southwest can be estimated only roughly. The following paragraphs summarize data from several states at various times. The reader should not assume that the definition of land subdivision is consistent from one study to another.

An inventory of the 2,565 remote subdivisions in Arizona in 1975 revealed that 943,460 acres had been plotted into 742,829 lots (Arizona Office of Economic Planning and Development 1975). More than three-fourths of these lots are in the more than 200 subdivisions larger than a full section (640 acres) in size.

New Mexico has several very extensive land subdivisions. Data from the U.S. Office of Interstate Land Sales Registration for 1974 indicated that 81 subdivisions with 342,341 lots encompassed slightly more than 1 million acres (Council on Environmental Quality—hereafter CEQ—1976, p. 135). One New Mexico subdivision covers more than 400 sections (250,000 acres) divided into 172,000 parcels (Allan, Kuder, and Oakes 1976, p. 205).

Between 1962 and 1972, 238,000 acres in Utah were subdivided into 62,716 lots averaging 3.8 acres in size and costing approximately $3,100 each (Workman et al. 1973, p. 3). It is safe to assume that additional lots have been created since 1972, especially since the Utah legislature failed to pass proposed legislation dealing with county subdivisions and planning.

Colorado presently has perhaps 200,000 remote subdivision parcels (e.g., "ranchettes") extending over about 2 million acres, while approximately 3 million acres of California land has been transformed into what Parsons (1972) has labeled "subdivisions without homes." "In 1970 alone, subdivision applications totaling over 200,000 acres were considered by the (California) State Real Estate Commissioner" (Hansen, Johnston, and Dickinson 1976, pp. 191-192).

Nevada has experienced relatively minimal land development activity. Approximately 150,000 acres have been subdivided into about 50,000 lots. As noted earlier, only about 13 percent of Nevada is under nongovernmental ownership or management.

A detailed analysis of the Puna district of the Island of Hawaii revealed 53 remote subdivisions with over 50,000 parcels (Stephenson and Nishida 1978). Combined, there are approximately 75 to 100 thousand acres of remote subdivision in Hawaii. As in Nevada, this apparently small degree of subdivision activity reflects a scarcity of fee simple parcels of developable scale. In Hawaii, however, it is trust land rather than government land that creates the constraint.

The federal government requires registration of subdivisions that are to be marketed on an interstate basis. The Interstate Land Sales Full Disclosure Act is the statute requiring registration; the federal Department of Housing and Urban Development is the agency responsible for administering the program. Although not all large land subdivisions are registered, examination of the data on file reveals a decline of subdivision activity over the past few years (see, for example, Allan, Kuder, and Oakes 1976). Reasons for this decrease include an oversupply of lots relative to demand, varying economic conditions, and stricter subdivision regulations at the state and/or local level. It is also possible that fewer land subdivisions are being marketed on an interstate basis so as to avoid the registration requirement.

The Southwest has roughly 2.5 to 3 million parcels in land subdivisions in toto, which have been plotted on about 8 to 9 million acres of land. There may be some quibbling about the exact magnitude of this inventory, but there is no doubt that the remote land subdivision phenomenon has created a special land use and planning challenge to the states of the Southwest and to substantial numbers of rural counties in those states.

THE PRIMARY MARKET

The market for remote land subdivisions involves two distinct levels of locational decision making. First, the developer seeks large parcels of low-cost, undeveloped, undivided lands, from which a remote subdivision may be created. The second level involves the purchase of one or more parcels of remote subdivision land. This paper is concerned primarily with the level of the individual purchaser.

Purchasers

The number of remote lots available normally exceeds the number of potential purchasers. Some buyers acquire more than one lot, and many parcels remain in the possession of the developer. A study by the U.S. Council on Environmental

Quality (CEQ) (1976, p. 6) indicates certain general characteristics of lot buyers: "One U.S. family in 12 owns a piece of recreational property—either a vacant recreational lot or a second home." These tend to be "white, middle class families whose incomes and education are only slightly higher than national averages," and three-fourths of them live in metropolitan areas (CEQ, 1976, p. 6). Thus the average purchaser may be depicted as an average family in the metropolitan mainstream of the United States.

One interesting geographic characteristic of lot owners is the relatively large distances separating their primary place of residence from their parcel. In a study of developments in northern California, Hansen, Johnston, and Dickinson (1976, p. 196) found that owners resided, on the average, 555 miles from their lots.

Reasons for Buying

People purchase land in remote land subdivision developments for many reasons, but investment looms large. According to one national survey, 38 percent of the purchasers of vacant subdivision lots bought them for investment purposes (CEQ 1976, p. 25). Johnston and Hansen (1974, p. 235), in a study of Northern California, reported 45 percent of respondents bought for speculative gain. A study of four remote subdivisions in Hawaii revealed that 68 percent of purchasers originally bought their parcels as an investment, and that over time there was an increase in the proportion whose intended use was for investment (Nishida and Stephenson 1977).

The data cited above do not necessarily address the actual decision-making criteria or the high sales-pressure context in which many of these commitments are made. Anthony Wolff (1973), in an exposé entitled *Unreal Estate*, has documented some of the sales tactics used to persuade people—quite some distance removed from the developments—to purchase their speculative lots.

One result of the marketing of remote southwestern subdivision lots throughout the United States (and also foreign countries) is that many people buy their land sight unseen. Two recent studies indicate that only about one-third of the lot owners had visited their parcels prior to purchase, and another third had yet to visit their land (Hansen, Johnston, and Dickinson 1976; Nishida and Stephenson 1977).

In addition to investment for speculative purposes, two other major reasons for purchasing land in remote subdivisions are its use for recreational purposes (e.g., "second home") and for retirement homes.

The widespread sale of remote subdivision lots is in part related to their seemingly low initial cost coupled with the ease of obtaining "financing" for the purchase. In 1971, a year some consider to represent the peak of the land-sales boom (CEQ 1976, p. 20), half of the lots were priced between $4,000 and $8,000; in 1972, average selling prices were about $6,500 (CEQ 1976, p. 21). The average down payment required varied from almost nothing to 10 percent of the purchase price. Relatively low monthly payments follow a minimal initial outlay.

A controversial aspect of this "low down, low monthly payment" method of purchasing lots is the "interest" charged by the developer on the balance remaining after the down payment. In many instances the developer is not lending money for the purchase of a parcel but is instead merely accepting periodic payments toward full purchase for land which the developer owns. Critics charge that no "interest rates" should be applied to the payment schedule, since no actual monetary loan has been acquired. Despite criticism, the majority of low-cost lots are saddled with an interest schedule reflecting current money-market conditions.

There are several implications of the "low down, low monthly payment" mechanism. Depending upon respective state laws, lot purchasers may not be able to obtain legal title until full payment has been made on the lot. Often this means that lot buyers cannot build on their parcel until it is fully paid for. Furthermore, if a purchaser fails to keep his schedule of payments, the developer may repossess the lot, which has already generated some revenue, and resell it to a new purchaser.

SECOND HOMES

To buy a lot is one thing; to build a dwelling on it is yet another. The "second home" tradition is fairly old in the United States, especially among upper socio-economic classes. More recently, many households of average means have purchased lots for second homes, but many have encountered difficulty in building their dream home on them.

Buildout

For a variety of reasons, the actual numbers of dwellings constructed per development have been few in comparison with the total number of lots subdivided and sold. According to the CEQ: "Considering the entire national market, the buildout rate—the ratio of lots with homes on them to the total number of subdivided lots in a project—is very low. . . . each year housing starts occur on approximately two percent of the recreational lots sold." In the remote land subdivisions of the Southwest, the buildout rates are usually considerably lower. One California county reported only 319 houses constructed on a possible 19,317 remote subdivision lots sold during a ten-year period. In another California context that involves "24 recreational subdivisions that include a total of 107,000 lots, 3,240 homes have been built since the lots were first offered for sale. . . . it would take 150 years to fill half of the lots if past trends continue into the future" (CEQ, 1976, p. 25). In an analysis of a 50,000-acre development in southwestern Arizona, the authors noted that "if the site continued to attract population at the rate it has in its first fifteen years, it would not be fully occupied for 900 to 1,000 years" (Allan, Kuder, and Oakes 1976, p. 248). A study of residential buildout in the Puna district of Hawaii noted that "it should be about 600 years before the remaining 48,557 empty remote subdivision lots in Puna are built on" (Stephenson 1978, p. 8).

One factor in the less-than-expected buildout rate is the changing expectations of the lots owners. Research has shown that many owners who initially bought lots for second-home or retirement-home purposes change their plans subsequently and hold the lot simply as an investment (Nishida and Stephenson 1977). With a substantial proportion of lots purchased *prior* to inspection, such a shift in attitudes is not surprising.

In many developments, the sales of parcels may be less than anticipated by the developer, thus leaving many parcels unsold and vacant. Reasons for this include: a) adverse publicity, which dampens advertising claims and lessens sales; b) legal restraints on further sale of land; c) financial failure of developer; and d) changing statutory or regulatory requirements, which affect allocation or utilization of resources (such as water) assumed to be available to the land.

Infrastructure

Many developers promise a variety of services and amenities such as roads, lakes, golf courses, clubhouses, sewage systems, etc. Often the realization of these plans may lag far behind original schedules or may never materialize at all. Lack of infrastructure and unfulfilled promises serve to retard buildout in remote land subdivisions.

Ironically, the realization of the promised material support systems can likewise lead to a lower-than-expected residential buildout rate. This occurs when the costs for utilities are not included in the purchase price of the lot but are financed instead by special assessments. Assessment for improvements may even exceed the cost of the land itself (Allan, Kuder, and Oakes 1976, p. 34). High assessments thus discourage building and may influence some owners to try to resell their lots.

Nevertheless, some lot buyers fulfill their dream to reside—either seasonally or permanently—on a piece of the Southwest. Types of dwellings found in remote subdivisions vary considerably, ranging from expensive architect-designed, custom-built luxury homes to simple, self-constructed houses, to assembled prefabricated cabins, to the ubiquitous mobile homes. In some instances, the homes have been constructed or sited in a manner consistent with the larger environment; in other cases, the houses appear quite inappropriate to the setting. House types in remote land subdivisions deserve further study from aesthetic and economic perspectives.

Resale Value

By acquiring a large plot of low-cost land for further subdividing, the developer creates an artificial demand for the product. The "demand" typically results from a well-planned sales-promotion campaign, which often involves heavy "front end" expenditures such as fees for celebrities to promote the development, free all-expense-paid trips to visit the property, cocktail parties or dinners for prospective buyers, and commissions to sales personnel. Such expenses have to be reflected in the purchase price of a parcel, yet they do nothing to increase the utility of the parcel (Bleck 1972, pp. 13-14). The promotional dollars must often compete with the improvement dollars for highest priority by the developer. And promotion is usually perceived as having a higher priority and hence receives a greater share of development costs.

The high proportion of developmental dollars used in promotion indicates that lots are inflated in value above their utility (for residential or other uses). "In effect, these remote subdivision developers are selling 'futures' to the public. Lots are not valued as a present commodity, but rather as a means to participate in the future growth of an area . . . but the selling price so established is justifiable only if the developer's optimistic projections actually materialize" (Bleck 1972, p. 13).

As seen from the discussion of buildout rates, however, these optimistic projections are either misconceived or are very long-term. Speculative lot purchasers are by definition buying "land futures." According to Bleck (1972, p. 13): "By persuading buyers to purchase lots as an investment on the promise they will increase in value simply with the passage of time, the seller also persuades buyers to accept promises of amenities rather than actual installation."

There is thus a viscious circle: high promotional costs cause less money to be spent upon land improvements, which are promised as a basis for buildout and a healthy financial return on lot investments. The lack of improvements in turn retards buildout and persuades lot owners to sell. The result is a depressed secondary land market for those lot owners who desire to sell. This is especially true when an individual owner attempts to sell his lot in competition with the developer who still holds unsold lots (Allan, Kuder, and Oakes 1976, p. 32).

Thus the investment curve for land values in remote land subdivisions is not upward and linear as projected by developers, but rather follows a "U" or "J" shape with the initial value declining over time, reaching some nadir, and then eventually increasing (Stephenson and Matsunami 1977). Support for this comes from Bleck (1972), who found in Arizona that resale prices are considerably lower: resale prices ranged between 61 percent and 88 percent of their original offering prices. Another study of ten southwestern remote subdivisions found that "At three of the subdivisions . . . the only resale market was at prices lower than the original lot purchase prices. At the other seven subdivisions there is no resale market at all" (Allan, Kuder, and Oakes 1976, p. 32). In fact, this study documented the unwillingness of some local real estate agents to even list lots for resale. Evidence from Hawaii, however, indicates that some lot owners may have success in the secondary market (Stephenson and Matsunami 1977).

The inescapable conclusion is that subdivision lots are sold in such large amounts at such highly inflated prices in the primary market by the developers that the individual lot owner faces a severely limited secondary market for resale of his greatly discounted little piece of the Southwest.

COMMUNITY IMPACTS

Large remote subdivisions in sparsely populated areas in the Southwest impose a variety of impacts, both pro and con, upon host counties. Rural counties with limited economic bases often welcome large land developments in their jurisdictions. Subdivision of large tracts of low-value grazing land into thousands of individual lots would apparently increase county property tax revenue. An increase in retail sales and services to new residents is viewed as an economic bonanza.

But nonmetropolitan counties often lack planning and development control skills and experience. In many cases, "elected officials are not fully aware of the hidden costs inherent in placing a subdivision in a location distant from existing community services or where no previous development has taken place" (Thompson, Randle, and McKell 1975, p. 84).

Impact Analysis

There are numerous ways to assess costs associated with remote subdivision developments. These include cost-benefit analysis (Thompson, Randle, and McKell 1975), fiscal impact analysis (Schaenman and Muller 1974; Schaenman 1976), and environmental and social impact assessments (McEvoy and Diety 1977) or similar systemic analyses. A simple cost-benefit model has been proposed for use in Utah to analyze the aggregate impact of a land-development scheme with an assumed buildout rate (Thompson, Randle, and McKell 1975). The model considers as benefits: a) property tax revenues; b) building permit fees; and c) incremental revenues resulting from increased populations. The costs are assumed to be the loss of property tax revenue from the current use of the site, and the incremental costs of providing services due to an increased population base. A crucial assumption associated with this model is the buildout rate: the lower the rate, generally the more financially attractive the development i.e., the benefits outweigh the costs). Since, as noted previously, the buildout rates in these remote subdivisions tend to be fairly low, the implication of this model is that developments may in fact be positive economic forces in a county.

The analysis of the impact of a *proposed* development assumes that the developer (or a successor entity such as an improvement district or homeowners' association) will be fully liable to provide improvements and services, and that failure to do so will not leave the county liable. This is, of course, a naive assumption. People who buy lots will as taxpayers demand that public services be provided at county expense. The costs of such services to local governments can easily exceed the tax revenue from development (Dickenson 1974). Ironically, the county may benefit most if the development remains a "nonfunctional remote subdivision," i.e., one that lacks both residents and the need for services (Johnson 1973).

Environmental Impacts

The environmental consequences of remote land subdivisions are both short- and long-term. An immediate impact is the aesthetic alteration of the landscape due to roads, signs, lot boundary stakes, etc. Often lots are laid out in a rigid grid pattern without regard to terrain. Road cuts on slopes cause erosion and sedimentation in nearby watercourses (CEQ 1976, p. 51). Removal of natural vegetation eliminates natural habitat and ecologic diversity. The drilling of domestic wells and subsequent pumping can lower the water table. Excessive pumping can adversely affect vegetation when the water table drops below the reach of root systems (Brown and Rich 1975, p. 4).

The availability of an adequate water supply for a subdivision is a limiting factor in the Southwest, where the "surface waters were long ago legally appropriated for agricultural, commercial, and community use, with nothing left over to support additional residential development" (CEQ 1976, p. 48). Groundwater thus becomes the desired commodity. But the lack of centralized water distribution systems means that individual lot owners must sink domestic wells. In a sort of "catch-22" situation in New Mexico, wells are prohibited on lots of less than three-fourths of an acre if septic tanks are used for wastewater disposal (Allan, Kuder, and Oakes 1976, pp. 148-149). Lots smaller than this minimum are hence effectively undevelopable without linkage to central systems of water and/or wastewater. Such parcels are commonly referred to as "dry lots" or "dry lot subdivisions."

A related environmental problem in the arid Southwest is the blowing dust or sand that results from roads and decreased vegetative cover. An immediate impact is upon neighboring lots. Some lots in a New Mexico subdivision "were reported covered with as much as one and one-half feet of sand. New Mexico officials estimate that such subdivision roads are the source of 700 million tons of blowing dust per year" (CEQ 1976, p. 53).

The disposal of wastewater from remote subdivisions would be a much more serious environmental problem if there were adequate domestic water supplies and delivery systems available. Facilities for centralized collection and treatment of wastewater are rare. For some developments, septic tanks may be quite appropriate disposal systems; elsewhere they may either be ineffective due to soil conditions or prohibited because of the small size of the lot. Consideration must also be given to the potential aggregate impact on groundwater quality of potentially thousands of septic tanks discharging hundreds of thousands of gallons of sewage per day. This is especially important in the Southwest, where the ground and surface waters are often interchangeable.

Other environmental considerations apply to specific regions. Some developments in Hawaii, for example, are situated along the rift zone of active volcanoes, or along earthquake fault zones (Stephenson and Nishida 1978). Forty-three percent of a set "of subdivisions reviewed by the Colorado Geological Survey had plans inconsistent with geological conditions" (CEQ 1976, p. 51). Yet other developments in the Southwest suffer from periodic flood damage—for example, those sited on alluvial fans at bases of washes or arroyos.

LAND USE ISSUES

As a result of increased public concern for the fiscal, environmental, and social effects of remote subdivisions, there have been movements toward stronger local, state, and national regulatory policies (Platt 1973; Reilly 1973). Many counties, for example, have adopted new or strengthened subdivision ordinances designed to discourage remote land-subdivision developments by requiring developers to provide all utilities and paved roads initially. We may hope that such ordinances, combined with some states' land use planning efforts and the federal government's Interstate Land Sales Full Disclosure Act, will slow down the dissection of rural landscape in the Southwest. Even if there were no further subdivisions in the Southwest (an unlikely situation), however, there remain serious land use and policy issues raised by the existence of the present developments.

Consolidation

The large-scale remote land subdivision with fragmented and absentee ownership patterns presents a special challenge to planners. In order to "retrofit" such developments for rational land use policies and planning, it would perhaps be necessary to consolidate the numerous small parcels into large tracts. There are serious legal questions, centered about the taking issue, related to consolidation.

Should, or can, government *require* consolidation of small lots in order to have large tracts of land again that may be innovatively planned for (e.g., as cluster developments or PUDs)? And if so, on what basis? For example, could attempts be made to remove lots from the speculative market by requiring productive use of land parcels within a specified period of time, thus limiting further trading in land as a commodity?

What are the obligations of local or state government to developers with substantial lot holdings in the primary market? Are there vested rights free from any further government constraints regarding the use and sale of these lots? Or can these lots (assuming they are somewhat contiguous or clustered) be down-zoned into larger parcels? If they are down-zoned, does this then constitute a legal "taking"?

Provision of Services

The existence of remote land subdivisions with scattered residents raises the issue of the provision of services by local governments. What are the reasonable expectations of land-subdivision dwellers with respect to the range of public services usually offered? What is the obligation of local government to the individual resident and/or owners of remote subdivision lots for providing public services to those parcels? What are the costs of providing such services in relation to additional revenue generated by the subdivision? What are "reasonable" costs? How should revenue to pay for such costs be generated?

Beyond Plat Maps

In situations where it is felt that limiting typical remote land subdivisions may constrain the rights of individuals to have access to certain property or limit the opportunity to pursue speculative land purchases, alternatives may be available. The question of whether speculative gambles on large remote parcels of land by numerous small investors can be allowed without fee-simple ownership of individually plotted lots and the usual accompanying environmental disruption has been answered affirmatively by Hansen and Dickinson (1975). They explore the concept of "undivided interest" as a solution or answer to the above question.

CONCLUSIONS

The remote land subdivision has made its marks on the rural land market, the landscape of the Southwest, and the planning awareness of elected and appointed officials. There is a definite need to develop appropriate land-use policies, techniques, and tools to allow communities affected by these developments to accommodate them effectively in their plan-implementation activities. Many of these subdivisions are like time bombs—with fuses of unknown lengths—waiting to explode. We may hope that imaginative planning efforts can defuse many such situations.

References

Allan, L.; Kuder, B.; and Oakes, S. L. 1976. *Promised Lands. Volume 1: Subdivisions in Desert and Mountains*, New York: Inform, Inc.

Arizona Office of Economic Planning and Development 1975. *Arizona's Remote Subdivisions: An Inventory*. Phoenix: State of Arizona (January).

Bleck, E. K. 1972. Merchandising Remote Subdivision Lots in Southern Arizona. *Arizona Review* 21: 10-15.

Brown, B. A., and Rich J. September 1975. *Arizona's Remote Subdivisions: Environmental Concerns*. Phoenix: Arizona Office of Economic Planning and Development.

Council on Environmental Quality (CEQ); U.S. Department of Housing and Urban Development; and Appalachian Regional Commission 1976. *Subdividing Rural America: Impacts of Recreational Lot and Second Home Development*. Washington, D.C.: U.S. Government Printing Office.

Dickensen, D. R. 1974. *Utah Recreation Subdivisions: A Cost Benefit Analysis Based on Twenty-eight Subdivisions in Three Counties*. Salt Lake City: Department of Community Affairs, State of Utah.

Dickinson, T. E.; Johnston, W. E.; and Hansen, D. E. 1978. Remote Subdivisions in Northern California. Paper presented to the Association of American Geographers, New Orleans, Louisiana.

Hansen, D. E., and Dickinson, T. E. 1975. Undivided Interests: Implications of a New Approach to Recreational Land Development. *Land Economics* 51: 124-132.

Hansen, D. E.; Johnston, W. E.; and Dickinson, T. E. 1976. California Remote Subdivisions: Policy Implications for Consumers and Rural Communities. *Journal of Consumer Affairs* 10: 191-207.

Johnson, M. E. 1973. *Utah's Subdivision Problem*. Logan, Utah: Utah State University Press.

Johnston, W. E., and Hansen, D. E. 1974. Behavior Characteristics of Purchasers of Remote Recreational Subdivision Parcels in Northern California. *Erdkunde* 28: 231-237.

Lounsbury, J. F., and Taylor, P. W. 1980. Land Use Policy: The Conflict of Federal vs. State Control of Public Lands. *Proceedings of the Applied Geography Conference* 3:114-126.

146   LARRY K. STEPHENSON

McEvoy, J., III, and Dety, T., eds. 1977. *Handbook for Environmental Planning: The Social Consequences of Environmental Change*. New York: John Wiley.

Nishida, J. I., and Stephenson, L. K. 1977. Patterns of Expected Use of Hawaii's Remote Subdivision. *Erdkunde* 31:61-69.

Parsons, J. L. 1972. Slicing Up the Open Space: Subdivisions Without Homes in Northern California. *Erdkunde* 26: 1-8.

Platt, R. H. 1973. Backwoods Urban Growth: The Recreation Land Development Boom. *Proceedings of the Association of American Geographers* 5: 225-229.

Reilly, W. K. 1973. *The Use of Land: A Citizen's Policy Guide to Urban Growth*. New York: T. Y. Crowell.

Schaenman, P. S. 1976. *Using an Impact Measurement System to Evaluate Land Development*. Washington, D.C.: The Urban Institute.

Schaenman, P. S., and Muller, T. 1974. *Measuring Impacts of Land Development: An Initial Approach*. Washington, D.C.: The Urban Institute.

Stephenson, L. K. 1978. Residential Development Patterns in Hawaii's Remote Subdivisions. Paper presented to the Association of American Geographers, New Orleans, Louisiana.

Stephenson, L. K., and Matsunami, O. W. 1977. Speculative Subdivision Land Values in Puna, Hawaii. *Journal of Tropical Geography* 45: 52-57.

Stephenson, L. K., and Nishida, J. I. 1978. Little Pieces of Paradise: Remote Subdivision Ownership in Puna, Hawaii. *Geographical Survey* 8: 22-32.

Thompson, J. L.; Randle, P. A.; and McKell, C. M. 1975. Subdivisions Out in the Country Can Be Expensive. *Utah Science* 36: 83-86.

Wolff, A. 1973. *Unreal Estate*. San Francisco: Sierra Club.

Workman, J. P.; MacPherson, D. W.; Nielson, D. B.; and Kennedy, J. J. 1973. *A Taxpayer's Problem — Recreational Subdivisions in Utah*. Logan, Utah: Utah State University Press.

IV. Small Towns: Growth and Decline

Industry in Nonmetropolitan Areas

Howard G. Roepke

The shift of manufacturing industry to nonmetropolitan areas is not a new phenomenon. After a long period of increasing concentration in urban centers, the proportion of total industrial employment found in nonmetro areas began to rise as early as 1954 and has increased steadily since (Lonsdale 1980, Fig. 1). Thus increased employment in manufacturing preceded and doubtless helped cause the much-discussed absolute and relative growth in population in these areas, which has become clearly apparent only since about 1970.

The numbers of people involved in this shift of industry are considerable. From 1962 to 1978, some 1.8 million manufacturing jobs were added in nonmetro areas, compared to 1.4 million in metropolitan areas (as designated through December 1977). This increased the share of U.S. manufacturing employment found in nonmetro areas from 23.5 to 28.8 percent of the total (Haren and Holling 1979, p. 15). Since nonmetro areas contained 31 percent of the population of the United States in 1970, such areas are almost as industrialized as the nation as a whole (Lonsdale 1980, p. 6). An accompanying phenomenon that has received less attention is the fact that service and other nonmanufacturing jobs are also growing more rapidly in nonmetro areas. Absolute growth is still larger in metro areas, but the increase from 1962 to 1978 in nonmetro areas was 81.5 percent compared to 77.0 percent in metro areas. The disparity in private sector service jobs is even greater: 87.6 percent increase in nonmetro areas and only 75.9 percent in metro areas. Nearly 25 percent of all service employment was found in nonmetro areas in 1978 (Haren and Holling 1979, p. 16). This phenomenon should be studied more fully.

The present chapter will focus on industrial change. It will be useful to identify several aspects of the shift of manufacturing to nonmetro areas. Although the data do not always allow complete differentiation, it is clear that the flows differed in both timing and motivation. At least four different patterns of movement can be discerned. The earliest, well documented between 1947 and 1955, was a shift to fringe counties around metro areas—the outer reaches of suburbanization (Creamer 1969). A second pattern has been part of the broad regional shift in economic activity that has been going on in the United States. More than half the new nonmetro manufacturing jobs added from 1962 to 1978 were located in the South (Haren and Holling 1979, p. 43). Perhaps the most important pattern at present is the move to urban-centered, nonmetro counties that are not adjacent to metro areas. ("Urban-centered" in this paper is taken to mean counties containing a city with at least 10,000 population.) The fourth pattern is a shift to what might be called purely rural areas. It is clear that these categories are not mutually exclusive, but it will be useful to keep them in mind as we examine the reasons for the shifts, the types of industries involved, and the impacts on the nonmetro areas where they are occurring.

REASONS FOR SHIFTS

The reasons for the shifts are as varied as the types of moves. A major cause has clearly been changes in the transportation system in the United States. These changes include the growth in truck transportation, which both benefited from and helped cause the development of a national highway network. The interstate highway system has had the effect of increasing the accessibility of nonmetro areas to the national metropolitan economy. (See Chapter 4 above, by Ronald Briggs.) For many decades a prime industrial site could be defined most easily as one on or near a railroad line. With the development of highways and the growth of truck transportation, literally thousands of new prime industrial sites were created in all parts of the country. This was most important in those areas like the South that had been poorly served by railroads. Chinitz (1960) has pointed out the effect of this transportation change on both decentralization of industry in general and on shifts to the South and the West.

Much of the literature has explained the dispersal of industry by the concept of the product cycle. This suggests that mature industries, past the innovation and rapid growth stages, have routinized operations and no longer need immediate access to the centers of innovation and management expertise found in metro areas (Hirsch 1967; Vernon 1966; Thompson 1969). They can thus establish virtually self-contained plants to serve regional markets. There is good evidence that this thesis explains part of the move to nonmetro areas, but care must be taken to distinguish among industrial types. Some, even in the mature stage, have patterns of procurement and distribution that make them ill-suited to nonmetro areas.

A further attraction of nonmetro areas, related also to the lower skill requirements in mature industries, has been the labor supply available there. Little competition for labor in nonmetro areas has led to low wage rates and underemployment, with the result that larger supplies of labor have been available at modest cost than would have seemed likely from unemployment statistics. The move of labor from farm to nonagricultural jobs has been well documented, but many of these moves take place only when an alternative opportunity nearby becomes available. It is only when economic growth has begun that these workers appear on any employment registry.

Some idea of the role of industry in the economic structure of nonmetro areas can be obtained by examining the 576 nonmetro counties that contained a city of at least 10,000 in 1960. These counties, here called urban-centered, are likely to have sufficient services to act as a focus for economic activity. The county is a reasonable unit for analysis given present commuting patterns, and it has been shown that residents of nonmetro cities of 10,000 to 49,999 are less likely to engage in intercounty job commuting than residents of any other type of settlement (Beale 1974).

The employment structure of a county with mean employment for the group is portrayed in Table 1. Such a county had 18,455 workers in 1960 out of a population of 55,194. By 1970 this county had employed 22,465 of 62,032 persons. Five sectors—agriculture, durable manufacturing, nondurable manufacturing, retail, and professional—account for about two-thirds of all employment in both years. During the decade, employment in durable manufacturing in this mean county increased by 34.3 percent compared to a national growth rate of 19.1 percent and nondurable manufacturing increased by 16.9 percent compared to the national rate of 5.4 percent. The major declines occurred in agriculture and personal services. This will serve as a summary, although significant differences from the national mean were found when the Census divisions were examined individually. It would seem that these nonmetro, urban-centered counties led the

Table 1. United States Nonmetropolitan, Urban-centered Counties
Employment by Sector in County With Mean Employment

	1960		1970	
	Number	Percentage	Number	Percentage
Agriculture	2192	11.9	1483	6.6
Mining	387	2.1	382	1.7
Construction	1215	6.6	1438	6.4
Durable Mfg.	2192	11.9	2943	13.1
Non-Durable Mfg.	2228	12.1	2606	11.6
Transportation	1234	6.7	1393	6.2
Wholesale	516	2.8	696	3.1
Retail	2965	16.1	3729	16.6
Finance	534	2.9	741	3.3
Business Service	387	2.1	494	2.2
Personal Service	1308	7.1	1191	5.3
Entertainment	129	0.7	157	0.7
Professional	2376	12.9	4156	18.5
Public Admin.	792	4.3	1056	4.7
Total	18,455		22,465	

increase in population and employment later noted more generally for nonmetro areas. From 1960 to 1970, all but 150 of the 576 counties grew in population and nearly two-thirds of the population losers gained in employment.

To better understand the economic structure of these nonmetro, urban-centered counties and the impact of growth on their employment structure, an economic base analysis was performed. The minimum requirements technique was used to distinguish basic from nonbasic employment. This technique has been widely used to analyze the economic base of metro areas (Ullman et al. 1971), but recently it has been found to work well for nonmetro areas if a universe for comparison is selected carefully (Gibson 1975).

The multiplier for all 576 counties as a group was relatively low and changed little over the decade. The low multiplier, seen in Table 2, reflects the effect of the size of the universe on this technique—as more units are included, the chance of low values and therefore low minima is increased. More revealing are the multipliers calculated for the major census divisions. Except for the South Atlantic division, all are well above the national figure, all are increasing, and all are widening their spread above the national. The general increase in the multipliers suggests the increase in local service employment in nonmetro areas mentioned earlier. If one makes the fashionable comparison between the Manufacturing Belt and the Sun Belt, some clear differences emerge. The 1970 multiplier of 2.17 for the Manufacturing Belt compared with 1.85 for the Sun Belt clearly shows the greater dispersion of economic activity and the greater importance of local service activity in the "older" areas. There are sufficient differences within the Sun-Belt area, however, to make generalizations risky.

TYPES OF INDUSTRY

Perhaps the oustanding fact about the types of industry found in nonmetro areas is their diversity. Any notion that they are confined to the low-wage, low-skill types is simply not borne out by the facts. Swager studied the industries found

Table 2. Employment Multipliers by Census Division
Nonmetropolitan, Urban-centered Counties

	1960	1970
Northeast*	2.19	2.21
South Atlantic	1.78	1.83
East South Central	2.05	2.26
West South Central	1.99	2.11
East North Central	2.11	2.21
West North Central	2.18	2.26
Mountain	1.88	2.00
Pacific	2.20	2.45
U.S.	1.81	1.87

*Includes New England and Middle Atlantic

in the nonmetro counties of Illinois, Ohio, and Georgia (Swager 1977). (He used the Rural Development Act of 1972 definition of nonmetro counties as all those whose largest city contained fewer than 25,000 people.) In these 3 states alone he found that 104 of the 148 three-digit industries in the standard industrial classification were found in five or more counties in at least one of the three states. (This definition was designed to exclude one-of-a-kind aberrations.) Each of the states individually was found to contain about half of all the three-digit types. Certain industries, generally resources-related, were found in all three states. Many of the major growth industries in each state, however, were not of this type. Illinois was the most diversified of the three, with major growth in nonmetro areas of industries in the transportation, electrical and nonelectrical machinery, foods, textile, apparel, chemicals, and metal products groups. Nonmetro Georgia was least diversified with strongest emphasis on textiles, apparel, and resource-based paper, wood, and mineral products. Even here the machinery and equipment industries, notably including mobile homes, grew rapidly. In Ohio, machinery, metal products, transportation equipment, and chemical industry groups grew rapidly.

Two conclusions may be drawn from these findings. First, a wider variety of industries is moving to nonmetro areas than is commonly believed. Many of these are high-wage, specialized types rather than resource-oriented industries. Second, the differences between the states studied suggests that nonmetro areas are taking part in developing regional specializations rather than attracting a distinct type of ubiquitous or footloose industries.

The same study attempted to relate the presence of industry in nonmetro areas to a wide variety of socio-economic characteristics of those areas. Some 29 characteristics, which might be regarded as location factors, were subjected to a factor analysis to group them. The dimension that came out as the single most important in all three states was labelled by the author "Urban Orientation." This does not refer to proximity to a metro area but rather to the urban or agglomerated characteristics of this county's population. This supports the contention made earlier in this chapter that the urban-centered nonmetro counties are most likely to experience industrial growth. The ordering of the other factors differed sufficiently among the states that the conclusion of the regional character of nonmetro industry was reinforced.

The evidence, then, suggests that purely rural areas may have trouble attracting industry and that an area with at least a small city as a focal point is likely to be most successful. There are at least three reasons why this is likely to be true (Roepke 1973). First, the people making the location decision are likely either to own the business or to expect to manage the plant. They may be fleeing the problems of the big cities, but they will generally still insist on certain of the amenities and services available only in a population concentration. Septic tanks may make indoor plumbing possible in a purely rural setting, but it is unlikely that a dispersed rural population or a town of 1,500 will support an adequate supermarket, clothing store, or library. Second, industry usually requires that at least minimal services be available. Obviously they can be supplied by the industry itself, but industrialists usually prefer that adequate sewer, water, police, and other services be available. Third, if this move of industries to nonmetro areas is to be encouraged, it will probably require various forms of aid or subsidy that will be much more effective if focused on those places with the best chance of meeting industrial requirements.

IMPACT OF INDUSTRY

Almost the only area of complete agreement concerning the impact of industrialization on nonmetro areas is that there must be an impact. The research done thus far has several shortcomings that account for the lack of agreement on the dimensions and even the direction of the impact. A principal difficulty is lack of comparability in the studies. They cover different periods, different regional settings, and communities of varying size and economic structure (Seyler 1979a, p. 49). This variation will lead inevitably to conflicting conclusions. A second difficulty has stemmed from the insistence of some researchers that if the impact is to be labelled as positive it must bring about a change in a specific, objective, usually aggregate measure chosen by the researcher. If that measure doesn't change, any opinion by the residents that the community is a more desirable place in which to live is taken as irrelevant. Further study on the perception of change could be most enlightening. Another problem is the excessive expectations sometimes made regarding the effects of industrialization. If it does not increase employment, *and* decrease unemployment, *and* reduce the number of families at the poverty level, *and* increase public services, etc., then it has not had a positive impact. The potential for change from modest industrial growth is limited. There is also a tendency to measure immediate or at least short-run change when that may not be the primary local objective. In this author's experience, many nonmetro areas undertake programs to encourage industrialization with the modest idea that it will provide the basis for future growth and development, rather than with unrealistic expectations of instant solutions to problems.

It is easier to identify areas of life and activity in which impact might be expected than it is to measure the quantity, or to identify the direction, of change. For example, one would expect a positive impact on employment. A number of studies have noted, however, that both employment and unemployment are likely to increase with industrial growth in nonmetro areas (Seyler 1979b). In the one case the change may be an increase in jobs while in the other it may be an increase in people registered with an agency. Attempts to discover who filled the newly created jobs have also been inconclusive. Inmigrants have been found to constitute from 4.3 percent to 37 percent of the work force, while returning former residents constitute from 3.8 percent to at least 13.1 percent of the work force (Shaffer 1979, notes 10 and 40). There is evidence that more people are commuting farther in nonmetro areas (Schriver 1967), but numbers and distances remain elusive. Other employment questions include the effect on underemployment, the extent to which jobs held by the underemployed are refilled, the effect on labor-force participation rates, etc.

Social change is another probable impact of industrialization, but it has been investigated even less. Seyler points out that only two of Smith's seven macro-characteristics that differentiate well-being (employment and educational change) have received significant attention (Seyler 1979a, p. 48). An examination of the annotations in a very useful bibliography entitled *Social Impacts of Nonmetro Industrial Growth* shows that many, if not most, deal with economic effects on such matters as employment and income rather than with impacts on the social structure (Selvik and Summers 1977). One fairly large group of studies discerned little change in social participation and social interaction with nonmetro industrialization (Summers et al 1976, chap. 7). Others have suggested a tendency for newcomers brought to the community by industrialization to "take over" social institutions, but the evidence thus far seems to be more anecdotal than objective.

The fiscal impact of nonmetro industrialization simply cannot be generalized. It varies too widely with the size and type of the industry involved as well as with the quality of the service base already in existence. At best it may result in a significant increase in the tax base without adding much to the cost of services. At worst it may require costly addition to schools, water and sewer systems, and other services that can create a long-term debt burden and greatly increase taxes to present residents. The most unfortunate situation occurs when a municipality or other governmental unit, in its eagerness to attract industry, provides services outside its boundaries at standard rates. In this way it incurs all the costs of expanded service without the benefits of additional tax revenue. On the other hand, one of the reasons some nonmetro areas seek industry is that it may make possible, or at least be the occasion for, improved services that have long been needed by present residents.

We may better understand the impacts of industrialization on nonmetro areas when enough comparable research has been done to give us greater confidence in its findings. But the variation in both the industries and the areas involved is so great that generalizations will remain risky. Perhaps we may agree with Beale (1975, p. 9): "the growth of manufacturing has been a centerpiece of the revival of nonmetro population retention," and with Seyler (1979a, p. 48), who concludes that the prevailing view of those who have done research on impacts is one of "measured reserve."

EFFECTS OF NONSPECIFIC POLICY DECISIONS

I shall not discuss the need to move toward a more carefully planned national growth policy. Both the urgency of the need and some idea of the elements that would affect nonmetro areas will be obvious from many of the other papers. Instead I shall discuss briefly two kinds of policy decisions, presently being made, which can have a tremendous effect on nonmetro industrialization. It sometimes seems that most policy impacts on nonmetro areas occur inadvertently. Nonmetro effects are often not considered when policy decisions are taken by our legislative bodies, which, given population patterns, are inevitably urban-oriented.

As we grope toward a national energy policy, most of the attention has been focused on aggregates of supply and demand. Secondarily there has been some discussion of the impact on large cities—usually taken as a class rather than individually. Possibly because of a lack of geographers in high-policy positions, there has been little discussion of regional differences in the impact of scarce and expensive energy and even less discussion of the impact on nonmetro areas. When a supply crisis occurs, people always seem greatly surprised when it becomes apparent that a reduction in supply of a quantity that would scarcely affect the length of lines at gasoline stations in a large city could paralyze a nonmetro county.

From the standpoint of nonmetro industrialization, the steady increase in energy costs—especially as applied to transportation—is likely to be a significant handicap. Both the cost of assembling materials and of shipping products will inevitably increase, and the increase will be greatest for isolated plants in nonmetro areas. Much of the increase in energy costs that has occurred so far has come in a period of general inflation when prices could easily be raised to compensate. When this is no longer possible, any added requirement for transportation resulting from a nonmetro location is likely to have a major effect on the cost structure of an industry. Further, increased costs for personal transportation involved in commuting are bound to be reflected in demands for higher wages. Nonmetro industrialization often depends on an areally extensive labor shed, as shown by a number of studies that have found a commute of 20 miles one-way to be common (Shaffer 1979, p. 112). On the other hand, a study of the Chicago SMSA has shown that most workers commute 10 miles or less (Continental Bank 1978, p. 14). The instinctively suggested mass-transit solutions are not likely to be helpful in nonmetro areas.

An even more serious, and even less discussed, impact on nonmetro industrialization may arise from present moves toward the deregulation of the trucking industry. The proposals vary in detail, but greater freedom to choose routes and set rates are common features. If the experience of airline deregulation is any guide, the result is likely to be a concentration of service on lucrative, high-volume routes. Many small communities that now receive service as a condition of a franchise may be left totally without service. If we have faith in the market system, we may expect this void to be filled by new entrepreneurs, an expansion of private and contract hauling, etc. At best, however, temporary disruptions and increased costs seem inevitable. These, then, are two examples of the kinds of policy decisions that—although not designed for that purpose—are likely to do much to determine the course of nonmetro industrialization over the next decade.

CONCLUSION

The growth of industry in nonmetro areas has been going on in considerable volume for at least 25 years. In the future, however, national policy decisions on such factors as energy supply and truck deregulation may result in a slowing of the movement. The generally slow growth of the manufacturing sector and the side effects of policies created for other reasons are probably the greatest obstacles to continued nonmetro industrial development. Since a significant number of the industries moving are specialized, high-wage types, and since the service sector is growing, general economic growth may well continue anyway. The single greatest need for further research is a better assessment of the impacts of nonmetro industrialization, and that research must consider local satisfactions as well as changes in aggregate measures.

References

Beale, C. L. 1974. Rural Development: Population and Settlement Prospects. *Journal of Soil and Water Conservation* 29:26.

————1975. *The Revival of Population Growth in Nonmetropolitan America*. Washington: U.S. Department of Agriculture, Economic Research Service.

Berry, B. J. L., and Silverman, L. P., eds. 1980. *Population Redistribution and Public Policy*. Washington: National Academy of Sciences.

Chinitz, B. 1960. The Effect of Transportation Forms on Regional Growth. *Traffic Quarterly* 14: 129-142.

Continental Illinois National Bank 1978. *Industrial Labor Sheds*. Chicago: Continental Bank, Area Development Division.

Creamer, D. 1969. *Manufacturing Employment by Types of Location*. New York: National Industrial Conference Board, 1969.

Fuguitt, G. V.; Voss, P. R.; and Doherty, J. O. 1979. *Growth and Change in Rural America*. Washington: Urban Land Institute.

Gibson, L. J. Local Impact Analysis: An Arizona Case Study. *Arizona Review* 24: 1-10.

Haren, C. C., and Holling, R. W. 1979. Industrial Development in Nonmetropolitan America: A Locational Perspective. In *Nonmetropolitan Industrialization*, ed. R. E. Lonsdale and H. L. Seyler, pp. 13-45. New York: John Wiley.

Hirsch, S. 1967. *Location of Industry and International Competitiveness*. Oxford: Clarendon Press.

Lonsdale, R. E. 1980. Industry's Role in Nonmetropolitan Economic Development and Population Change. In *Population Redistribution in the Midwest*, ed. C. Roseman, A. J. Sofranko, and J. D. Williams, pp. 129-148. Ames, Iowa: North Central Center for Rural Development.

Lonsdale, R. E., and H. L. Seyler, eds. 1979. *Nonmetropolitan Industrialization*. New York: John Wiley.

Roepke, H. G. 1973. Industrial Possibilities for Non-Metropolitan Areas. *AIDC Journal* (October): 27-45.

Roseman, C.; Sofranko, A. J.; and Williams, J. D., eds. 1980. *Population Redistribution in the Midwest*. Ames, Iowa: North Central Center for Rural Development.

Schriver, W. R. 1967. The Attitude of Workers Toward Commuting. *AIDS Journal* 2: 25-32.

Selvik, A., and Summers, G. F. 1977. *Social Impacts of Nonmetro Industrial Growth*. 1979. (SRDC Series Publication No. 18) Mississippi State, Miss.: Southern Rural Development Center.

Seyler, H. L. 1979a. Contemporary Research Emphases in the United States. In *Nonmetropolitan Industrial Growth and Community Change*, ed. F. Summers and A. Selvik, pp. 43-58. Lexington, Mass.: D. C. Heath.

Seyler, H. L. 1979b. Dimensions of Social and Economic Change: The Impact of Nonmetropolitan Industrialization. In *Nonmetropolitan Industrialization*, ed. R. E. Lonsdale and H. L. Seyler, pp. 95-102. New York: John Wiley.

Shaffer, R. E. 1979. The General Economic Impact of Industrial Growth on the Private Sector of Nonmetropolitan Communities. In *Nonmetropolitan Industrialization*, ed. R. E. Lonsdale and H. L. Seyler, pp. 103-118. New York: John Wiley.

Smith, E. R., n.d. *Industrialization of Rural Areas.* (SRDC Bibliography Series No. 1) Mississippi State, Miss.: Southern Rural Development Center.

Summers, F.; Evans, S. D.; Clemente, F.; Beck, E. M.; and Minkoff, J. 1976. *Industrial Invasion of Nonmetropolitan America.* New York: Praeger.

Summers, F. and Selvik, A. 1979. *Nonmetropolitan Industrial Growth and Community Change.* Lexington, Mass.: D. C. Heath.

Swager, J. 1977. Location Requirements of Selected Industries in Nonmetropolitan Areas. *AIDC Journal* (October) 12: 7-28.

Thompson, R. 1969. The Economic Base of Urban Problems. In *Contemporary Economic Issues*, ed. N. W. Chamberlain, pp. 1-47. Homewood, Ill.: Richard D. Irwin.

Tweeten, L., and Brinkman, G. L. 1976. *Micropolitan Development.* Ames, Iowa: The Iowa State University Press.

Ullman, E. L.; Dacey, M. F.; and Brodsky, H. 1971. *The Economic Base of American Cities.* (Revised edition.) Seattle: University of Washington Press.

Vernon, A. 1966. "International Investment and International Trade in the Product Cycle." *Quarterly Journal of Economics* 80: 190-207.

Recent Population
and Business Trends
in American Villages

Harley E. Johansen and Glenn V. Fuguitt

When we hear the term "small town" or "village," most of us can bring to mind at least one, if not several, communities that we feel typify this level of urbanization. We think of rural settings with uncluttered landscapes and a simplified form of social and economic exchange between individuals compared to the complexities of our larger cities. We envision main streets, general stores, comfortable old houses, gossip between neighbors, and a general lack of excitement. Our images are based on actual experiences and literary descriptions and have often been clouded with a nostalgic desire to hold onto something constant and pure in a rapidly changing urbanized world.

Despite our images, American villages and small towns have continued to change, adapting to the social and economic forces of the automobile and telecommunications era. This chapter attempts to describe some of the changes that have occurred in American villages since 1950, and to explore some possible causes of the patterns of change in population and business that have been observed. Emphasis is on economic activities in villages, particularly the retail and service sector, which dominates the overall business offering of most villages. Data are based on a national sample of five percent of the incorporated places with less than 2,500 population as of 1960 and located outside of metropolitan counties. These were stratified according to census division, population size, location relative to SMSA central cities, and growth of population between 1950

This work was supported by the Regional Research Institute at West Virginia University and by the Economic Development Division, Economic Research Service, U.S. Department of Agriculture, through a cooperative agreement with the College of Agricultural and Life Sciences, University of Wisconsin Madison, and by a Center for Population Research grant, No. HD05876, to the Center for Demography and Ecology, University of Wisconsin-Madison, from the Center for Population Research of the National Institute of Child Health and Human Development. The assistance of Daniel Lichter is gratefully acknowledged.

and 1960 (Johansen 1974). Data for population analysis were obtained from published and unpublished census sources; economic data for this paper are from Dun and Bradstreet Reference Book listings for the years 1950, 1960, and 1970, with updated information for a subsample of villages obtained via telephone interviews with local bank personnel.

VILLAGE POPULATION TRENDS

There has been considerable variability among U.S. villages in population growth and decline. Although writers have traditionally spoken of the "dying small town," towns that are incorporated seldom disappear from successive census reports. In fact, fewer than 3 percent disappeared over the 1950-60 and 1960-70 time periods, although almost half declined in size. Of the 11,000 nonmetropolitan incorporated places in the United States with fewer than 2,500 people in 1960, about 5,000, or 45 percent, lost population between 1960 and 1970. On the other hand, about 25 percent of these places grew faster than the nation as a whole.

Little is currently known about village trends during the post-1970 upturn in nonmetropolitan population growth. We have added to our data files, however, the preliminary 1980 census figures for each sample place, making a 1970-80 growth comparison possible. For the analysis, we calculated annualized growth rates per 100, using the formula $r = [\ln (P_n/P_0)/n]\ 100$ for each place over each of the three decades, where $\ln$ is the natural logarithm and n is the number of years (10) in each growth interval (Shryock and Siegel 1971, p. 379). Earlier comparisons showed that 1950-70 growth patterns for our village sample were very similar to those for the universe of nonmetropolitan villages in the United States (Johansen 1974).

The average annualized growth rate for places in the sample increased considerably across the three time intervals (Table 1). This occurred despite an overall decline in national growth. During the 1970-80 period, 39 percent of the

Table 1. Means and Standard Deviations of Annualized Rate of Population Change per 100, Sample of Villages in the United States

Initial Size	1950-60		1960-70		1970-80	
	Mean	S.D.	Mean	S.D.	Mean	S.D.
1000-2500	.19	2.2	.74	1.8	.84	1.6
500-999	.63	2.3	.22	1.8	.79	2.2
LT500	−.44	2.4	.17	2.9	.86	2.6
Total Sample Villages	−.01	2.3	.32	2.4	.84	2.3
U.S. Total Annualized Population Change	1.70		1.25		1.08	

villages were growing more rapidly than the United States as a whole, and only 32 percent were declining according to the preliminary population figures.

A variety of studies in many settings has shown that villages initially smaller in size are more likely to decline or have lower levels of growth than larger places. As revealed in Table 1, this was the case in our sample during the 1960s; comparison of the universe figures indicates that the association also would have been positive in the 1950s had our sample not excluded places that grew to more than 2,500 between 1950 and 1960. By the 1970s, however, there was essentially no association between initial size and average growth. In fact, if places newly incorporated in 1970 had been added to the sample, the association would have been inverse, since new places tend to be small and grow rapidly.

Previous studies have also shown a tendency for the population change in small towns to be directly related to urban proximity as the urban commuting range is extended to include smaller places (Hart and Salisbury 1965; Fuguitt and Beale 1976; Roseman 1977). To examine this relationship , an index of urban accessibility was developed for each village according to the formula:

$$A_i = \sum_{j=1}^{n} \frac{P_j}{d_{ij}^2}$$

where A_i is the accessibility index for village (i), P is the population of a city within 50 miles of at least 10,000, and d is the airline distance between (i) and (j).

To show the distribution of growth levels by size of place, and the effect of urban accessibility, Figure 1 was prepared. Here villages are classed by whether they had rather substantial decline (one percent annually or more), were approximately stable, or grew one percent per year or more over the time period. Across all the bar charts, we see that smaller places continue to be more likely to decline substantially than larger ones, but this differential by size of place is getting smaller. Comparing the second and third columns of each chart, nonaccessible villages were more likely to decline than accessible villages, although this differential also diminished over time. Similarly, with one exception, accessible villages were more likely to post a greater-than-one percent growth than nonaccessible ones of the same initial size over any time interval. The patterns of rapid growth by size of village are not always consistent, however. Particularly interesting is the finding for nonaccessible places, with smaller villages more likely than larger ones *both* to decline and to grow rapidly. This is partly a regional effect, since smaller nonaccessible centers that are declining tend to be found in the Great Plains, an area that has not shared in the nonmetropolitan turnaround to the extent of most other sections of the country.

ECONOMIC ACTIVITIES IN VILLAGES

Comparative research on the economic structure of American villages at a national scale has been almost nonexistent in the literature. In 1927 Brunner

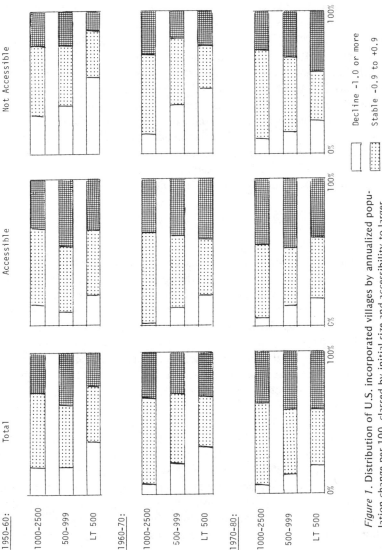

Figure 1. Distribution of U.S. incorporated villages by annualized population change per 100, classed by initial size and accessibility to larger centers, 1950-60, 1960-70, and 1970-80. Villages were divided on the median value of (A) for the total sample.

published a study of economic characteristics for a national sample of villages from agricultural areas of the United States (Brunner et al. 1927). Concerned primarily with agricultural villages, Brunner described the village economy as a system designed to serve nearby farmers in two ways: first as a center for marketing, storage, and other services designed to dispose of surplus agricultural production; and second as a center for retail goods and services necessary to the livelihood of farm and village people.

Although Brunner's description of the village economy was focused on agricultural activities, we know that villages may be dependent primarily on other industries such as forestry, fishing, mining, or manufacturing. More recently, villages have developed or have been transformed where employment is available in nearby cities through commuting, or where recreational or energy-related

Table 2. Inventory of Economic Activity in Sampled Villages

Economic Activity	1950	1960	1970
Retail—No. Establishments	11714	9721	8958
Mean per village	22.5	18.7	17.2
Total percent change		−17.0	−7.8
Service No. Establishments	2511	2368	1430
Mean per village	4.8	4.5	2.7
Total percent change		−5.7	−39.6
Manufacturing—No. Establishments	1043	1072	1169
Mean per village	2.0	2.0	2.2
Total percent change		2.7	9.0
Building Contractors—			
No. Establishments	570	875	1064
Mean per village	1.1	1.7	2.0
Total percent change		53.5	21.6
Agr. Production and Service—			
No. Establishments	511	519	470
Mean per village	1.0	1.0	.9
Total percent change		1.6	−9.4
Wholesale—No. Establishments	491	745	663
Mean per village	.9	1.4	1.3
Total percent change		51.7	−11.0
Mining—No. Establishments	101	130	95
Mean per village	.2	.2	.1
Total percent change		28.7	−26.9
Forestry—No. Establishments	5	1	3
Mean per village	0	0	0
Total percent change			
No. of villages with economic data*	520	520	520

Source: Dun and Bradstreet, *Reference Book*, 1950, 1960, 1970.

*Of the 574 villages in the total sample this is the number which were listed by Dun and Bradstreet all three years. Where villages were extremely small or adjacent suburbs of larger places, the listing had been combined with the larger place and, therefore, was not available.

developments have occurred in close proximity. To understand the recent economic makeup of American villages, we can turn to the data for our sample.

The inventory of business activities as reported by Dun and Bradstreet for 1950, 1960, and 1970 is presented in Table 2. As measured by the number of establishments, retail and service activities outnumbered all others with over 80 percent of all business establishments. These activities, however, declined during each decade in contrast to other categories such as manufacturing and construction firms.

The only consistent increases in business establishments were in the manufacturing and construction categories. Probably most important is the increase that occurred in manufacturing, because it represents basic employment within the village and has been much sought by rural communities in recent years. The net increase during both decades suggests that some villages have been successful in attracting manufacturing firms to offset declines stemming from changes in primary industries.

The increase in manufacturing shown in Table 2 disguises declines in some traditional activities such as food processing, especially canning, butter and cheese, lumber mills, and newspaper publishing, while increases occurred in animal feeds, textiles, and concrete products. Table 3 contains an elaboration of manufacturing industries found in villages and shows an increase in textile and apparel industries along with a diversified category labeled "other manufacturing." The traditional raw material-oriented industries that dominated manufacturing in the earlier village as reported by Brunner et al. (1927) were still important in recent years, but villages have gained industries less concerned with either raw materials or rural markets. These are attracted to rural areas by low land and labor costs that offset possible locational disadvantages. As suggested by Till (1974), these tend to be fabricating or apparel industries that seek low-cost labor, particularly among farm wives and other female workers in rural areas where labor unions have been slow to develop. Cheap labor is not the only reason why industries choose to locate in villages, however. Community environment, low taxes and land costs, and transport connections (which have improved for many villages) are also likely to be involved in the decision (Little 1972). Villages can

Table 3. Number of Manufacturing Firms by Type in Sampled Villages

Type of Manufacturing	Total U.S.		
	1950	1960	1970
Food, kindred and tobacco	265	263	214
Textile and apparel	79	95	130
Lumber and wood products, furniture, paper, and applied products	214	212	196
Printing and publishing	193	184	163
Other manufacturing	292	318	466
Total	1043	1072	1169

offer a pleasant environment for manufacturing and a competent labor force, both from within the local community and among residents of nearby villages or rural areas who are willing to commute.

The number of building contractors nearly doubled in villages between 1950 and 1970 (Table 2). Most of these firms were general building contractors, but gains were experienced in most major building trades, probably in response to both farm and suburban-rural construction needs. Modern-scale increases in farming have often required an increase in physical plant to accommodate innovations in livestock feeding and housing, and in machine, grain, and feed storage. Farm housing has also been changing as farmers replace old farmhouses with modern dwellings that resemble those in suburban areas. Housing and other construction have increased rapidly in near-urban locations that allow construction firms to prosper where access to the urban fringe is good.

Agricultural production and service activities were relatively stable throughout the 20-year period, with a slight decline in the latter decade. The small net change, however, includes declining numbers of cotton gins and poultry hatcheries in the South, while other agricultural business firms were increasing in such activities as dairies, poultry, and animal specialties. Wholesale business increased in villages between 1950 and 1960 and then declined between 1960 and 1970, although the loss did not offset the gain in the earlier decade and the net result was an increase between 1950 and 1970 in wholesale establishments.

Mining activities represent a minority category of business in villages as measured by the number of firms (Table 2). Listed were mining of a variety of mineral ores including iron, copper, lead, and zinc, along with bituminous coal, which was the most common mining activity as well as the most subject to decline. It dropped from 61 establishments in 1950 to 44 in 1960 and 23 in 1970. Most of these were found in the Appalachian region. Declines in coal were offset by increases in natural gas and petroleum mining activities, and also in stone quarries and construction, sand, and gravel. Together, the mining activities represented a small portion of village business firms at each time. This was also true of forestry activities, which were surprisingly almost nonexistent in these places.

RETAIL AND SERVICE ACTIVITIES

Clearly, the most visible aspect of the village community in the United States is, or has been, the "main street" business district, where retail and service activities are concentrated. "Main street" is a microscale version of the central business district of larger cities. The similarity is not only in configuration; casual observation reveals that the main streets in many villages have undergone a transition similar to the one that has occurred in central business districts of larger cities. Empty storefronts and former banks and other prominent buildings used for less important activities are signs of decay common to small towns.

Looking at the data on retail and service activities in the sampled villages, we can see that most villages experienced a net loss of these activities (Table 4).

Table 4. Retail and Service Establishments and Functions

Mean number of establishments	1950	27
	1960	23
	1970	18
Percentage losing establishments	1950-60	79
	1960-70	76
Mean number of functions	1950	13
	1960	12
	1970	10
Percentage losing functions	1950-60	60
	1960-70	76

Between 1950 and 1960, 79 percent of the sampled villages lost retail and service establishments and 60 percent lost activities or functions completely. This high rate of decline suggests the severity of the problems facing village residents and merchants. The rate was nearly as high for establishments during the next decade with 76 percent losing, and the rate of function loss also increased coincidentally to 76 percent. It should be stated here that the measures used represent the number of business units in villages rather than the volume or scale of retail business. It is possible that sales volume could remain the same or even increase while the number of establishments declined. Yet with the complete loss of a function, the decline is absolute; the high rate of this decline suggests that scale increases are not responsible for the decline in establishments observed here.

The retail sector in villages has no doubt been affected by a declining farm population throughout the country and by outmigration of young people to urban centers (Beale 1972). The increased scale of farming has displaced many farm families who shopped in village stores in the past. In addition to population decline in the village trade area, the mobility of the rural population has increased with the availability of automobiles and improvements in highway design, which allow rural residents to bypass nearby village stores in favor of larger uban centers. The recent movement of stores to peripheral shopping centers has further reduced travel time from rural areas to "urban" shopping opportunities.

It is necessary to look at specific business activities individually to understand what lies behind the changes observed in Table 4. All business activities that appeared in the sampled villages under retail and service categories are listed in Table 5. These activities are ranked by the number of villages with at least one establishment of the activity as of 1950.

Looking first at the percentage of villages with each activity, we can see that the ranking indicates the importance of common functions such as groceries, service station, and hardware compared to the less common activities such as jeweler, meat market, florist, and department store. The consistency of functional offering among villages, however, was quite low. Only 8 out of 47 functions were found in more than half of the sampled villages in 1950; this number declined to 7 for 1960 and only 3 in 1970 (Table 5).

Table 5. Individual Business Activities in Sampled Villages

Business Activity	Percentage of Places with 1950	1960	1970		Percentage of Places with 1950	1960	1970
Groceries	99	97	93	Auto parts	20	20	24
Service station	90	87	81	Liquor	20	11	11
Auto repair	68	57	27	Electrical repair	18	26	28
Eating place	68	51	47	Confections	16	5	5
Hardware	60	53	46	Radio & t.v.	13	17	16
Drug	56	51	41	Dairy	12	7	3
Lumber	55	49	45	Bakery	12	9	8
Bank	51	54	55	Meat	11	11	7
Feed	47	43	37	Florist	9	13	16
Farm implement	43	37	33	Plumbing	9	7	6
Tavern	40	42	20	Farm supplies	9	20	23
Auto dealer (new)	38	32	26	Sporting goods	7	9	10
Petroleum fuel	37	40	38	Auto body repair	6	7	5
Mortuary	35	34	23	Paint and wallpaper	6	4	3
Appliances	35	28	19	Fruit and vegetables	5	3	1
Clothing	34	31	30	Laundromat	5	4	3
Furniture	33	28	28	Department store	5	4	4
Welding and repair	33	18	7	Antique	5	8	7
Variety	32	26	26	Used autos	5	7	9
Fuel (other)	27	21	18	Watch repair	4	3	2
Laundry & dry cleaning	26	26	17	Electric supplies	4	3	1
Bowling	23	15	8	Photographer	3	5	2
Hotel	22	25	25	Furniture repair	3	4	2
Jeweler	20	15	12				

Nearly two-thirds of the business activities were found in fewer villages in 1960 than in 1950, and this proportion increased to three-fourths during the 1960-70 decade. The rate and pattern of change varied by activity and by decade. Some activities such as service station, bank, clothing, and radio and TV were relatively stable over the 20-year period, while most experienced substantial decline in one, if not both, decades. The greatest relative gains and losses were found among the less common activities—e.g., bowling, liquor, confections, and dairy suffered severe decline, while electrical repair, florist, farm supplies, and sporting goods increased rather substantially during the 20-year period. These growing activities may reflect recent growth in recreation and agriculture, which has stimulated a market for certain products handled by sporting goods, farm supply, and other stores in villages. Certainly the vastly increased output from farms has stimulated production-related business in many farming areas, while the decline in farm families has reduced the consumer goods market. Florists, on the other hand, have expanded their market through national networks that give village merchants a contact with relatives and friends of local residents who have moved away.

Despite the differential rate of growth or decline among activities, the village remains a center of common goods and services. Declining functions outnumbered the gainers at all levels of rank, but the overall makeup of village business activities remained intact over the 20-year period.

Correlates of Retail and Service Business in Villages

The extensive decline in retail and service activities shown in Table 4 suggests a universal pattern of loss among villages everywhere. Yet we know that some villages have grown in business activity and that all declining villages did not lose at the same rate. In another study based on this sample, we analyzed the effects of village location relative to larger cities, and of village population trends, on change in village retail activity (Johansen and Fuguitt 1979). On the basis of the argument that urban proximity causes greater competition for village merchants, we looked for a negative association between urban proximity and change in business in the village. Using path analysis, we discovered that urban accessibility had a direct negative effect on business change, but that it also had an indirect positive effect on business change through its association with village population change. The two factors tended to offset each other to negate the value of urban accessibility as a predictor of retail change in villages.

In an attempt to further our understanding of retail and service business change, we looked at the manufacturing and other economic activities as possible correlates of retail change. With a declining population in farming and other primary occupations, villages have sought other forms of industry to employ local residents. The most dominant growth has been in manufacturing industry, but activities such as agricultural services, construction, and recreational developments have been important also. By having a local employment base, a village can sustain a larger population and therefore greater support for local retail merchants than would be the case without it. Employment opportunities in industries such as manufacturing can also attract residents of nearby villages as employees who then may support the retail stores in the villages of their employment, thereby expanding the local market to include some residents of nearby communities. We might, therefore, expect villages with more nonretail or service industries to have more retail shops and also to show greater gains in these activities.

To test the importance of other economic activities on the retail sector in villages, we looked first at a static model of the number of retail and service establishments in villages. Using regression analysis, we included two variables: number of establishments in categories of Table 2 except retail and service, and size of village population. Given the high correlation between population size and the number of establishments (Berry 1967; Marshall 1969; Johansen and Fuguitt 1973 and 1979), it is necessary to control for population size by including it in the regression. In terms of number of firms, manufacturing is the most important component of the "other economic activity" category, and we have seen that this activity has been growing in villages over the time interval considered here. There was a consistently high association between the number of other economic activities and number of retail establishments when we controlled

Table 6. Regression Model of the Number of Retail Establishments in Villages

Independent Variable	Standardized Regression Coefficients*		
	1950	1960	1970
Population size	.534	.460	.583
Number of establishments of other economic activities	.399	.481	.377
Multiple R	.880	.890	.895

*All coefficients are statistically significant at .01 using an F test.

Table 7. Regression Results for Model of Change in Retail Establishments*

Independent Variables	Standardized Regression Coefficients[†]	
	1950-60	1960-70
Change in village population	.355	.258
Change in manufacturing activity (number of firms)	.239	.229
Accessibility to urban centers (index)	−.121	−.107
Multiple R	.439	.349

*All measures of change are residualized variables from the regression of initial with end-of-decade values. This measure of change is "Base free" and avoids problems due to small initial size values as discussed by Bohrnstedt (1969).
[†]All coefficients are statistically significant at .01 level of confidence using an F test.

for population size during each year of observation (Table 6). Given this association at each time, it should follow that change in other economic activities would lead to similar change in number of retail establishments. Table 7 contains the results of a regression model, with change in number of retail establishments as the dependent variable and change in population, change in manufacturing, and urban accessibility as the independent variables. The results indicate clearly that manufacturing change has been associated directly with retail change. This underscores the value of basic industry in sustaining retail activity in villages, regardless of changes in population size and the effects of urban accessibility.

The Village Since 1975

In an effort to update our information about business activities in villages, we selected a systematic sample of just over five percent of the total sample for a telephone survey. In each of these places a high-level bank employee was interviewed. The respondents were asked to name the businesses that had newly opened or closed in their communities during the past five years, and to answer additional questions regarding population trends and employment and shopping opportunities in the vicinity of the village. Although obviously limited as an analytical data base, the survey was informative and produced some insight into current trends in small towns.

The use of bank employees as respondents resulted in a sample of villages

Table 8. Characteristics of Villages by Reported Change in Retail
Business Activities, 1975-80*

	No. of Villages (N = 36)	X̄ Population 1970	X̄ No. Retail and Service Est. 1970	X̄ Accessibility Index
Net gain of retail stores	22	1171	29	226
No change in no. of retail stores	8	604	17	305
Net loss of retail stores	6	947	25	352

*Based on telephone interview with bank personnel in village.

that were somewhat larger than average, since the smallest places typically did not have a bank. The villages selected averaged 1,055 population and 14 retail functions in 1970, compared to 745 and 10 for the total sample. This bias in size may be responsible in part for the relatively large number of villages that reported gains in retail stores during the 1975-80 period (Table 8). Nevertheless, many of these villages lost establishments over 1960-70, so the 1975-80 reported increase in stores is often contrary to previous trends. Within the selected villages, those that gained retail stores were larger in size and less accessible to urban centers as measured by the means shown in Table 8.

Characteristics reported that seemed to be associated with growth in business establishments were new recreational developments nearby, new manufacturing activities, aggressive banking policies to attract business outlets, and population growth in the vicinity of the village due to these and other reasons such as in-migrant retirees or migrants from urban areas.

Respondents generally seemed optimistic about the future of their communities. Some stated that rising fuel prices had helped their local merchants by discouraging people from driving to larger shopping centers. On the other hand, several people expressed concern that large regional shopping centers had been opened recently that had hurt local trade.

CONCLUSIONS

Our review of village population change has shown an extension of older trends as well as emerging patterns of the new growth in nonmetropolitan areas. There appears to have been a considerable increase in levels of village growth over the 30-year period, and this is not limited to those places larger in size, or those accessible to urban centers. As is true for county patterns, increased population growth levels in the 1970s are seen in retrospect to be an extension of changes between 1950-60 and 1960-70, consistent with the view that the turnaround is not a sudden post-1970 phenomenon.

Whether or not the nonmetropolitan turnaround may be considered a "new" trend, it is an extension of population deconcentration. The apparent growth resurgence for villages of all size groups shown here, even away from cities, is consistent. Yet this growth is at a lower annualized level than a recent estimate of post-1970 total nonmetropolitan growth outside cities, suggesting that the open country may have increased even faster than villages during the 1970s (Fuguitt, Lichter, and Beale 1980).

Villages have suffered as trade centers. Whether their purpose is to serve farm families, retired people, or others, the shopping opportunities of villages have been seriously reduced. This trend has negative implications for rural residents, particularly elderly people who may find travel to larger cities difficult. Village location relative to larger cities has been a factor in both population change and business change, although the effect on each trend has been contrary to the other; i.e., urban accessibility seems to lead to growth in population but to decline in retail activity.

The latter association may be masked, however, by the fact that growing villages either gain more or lose fewer retail establishments than others. Many villages have gained manufacturing activities, and these seem to have offset the forces that caused decline in retail business. Since villages cannot change their locations, continued efforts to attract manufacturing and other basic industries seem justified by these findings.

As suggested in our survey, many villages have gained business establishments since 1975. Whether the data on which this rather surprising finding is based are consistent with the 1950-70 analysis of establishments requires further study. If so, it would be a reversal of past trends for establishments, though consistent with increased population growth. The rising cost of fuel may, as suggested in our survey, help village merchants keep their customers, but it could also inhibit population growth due to higher costs of commuting.

Finally, economic efficiency may require the demise of the trade-center function of many villages whose spatial pattern is geared to a previous settlement pattern and economy. The decline of local shopping would, however, present remaining residents with a much greater need to travel in an age of higher costs; and this possibility exists at a time when population appears to be growing in many villages. With further analysis of the results of the 1980 census and additional information on recent economic trends, we will be able to understand better, in a variety of settings, the current and emerging position of the American village in our increasingly deconcentrated settlement structure.

References

Beale, C. L. 1972. *Rural and Nonmetropolitan Population Trends of Significance for the National Population Policy*. Prepared for the Commission on Population Growth in America's Future.

Berry, B. J. L. 1967. *Geography of Market Centers and Retail Distribution*. Englewood Cliffs, NJ: Prentice Hall, Inc.

Bohrnstedt, G. W. 1969. Observations on the Measurement of Change. In *Sociological Methodology*, ed. E. F. Borgotta, pp. 113-133. San Francisco: Jossey-Bass.

Brunner, E. DeS.; Hughes, G. S.; and Patten, M. 1927. *American Agricultural Villages*. New York: George Duran Co.

Dun and Bradstreet, Inc. 1950, 1960, 1970. *Reference Book of Dun and Bradstreet*. New York: Dun and Bradstreet.

Fuguitt, G. V., and Beale, C. L., 1976. Population Change in Nonmetropolitan Cities and Towns. Washington, DC: U.S. Department of Agriculture, Agricultural Economic Report 323.

Fuguitt, G. V.; Lichter, D. T.; and Beale, C. L. 1980. Population Deconcentration in Nonmetropolitan America. Madison: University of Wisconsin, Department of Rural Sociology, Applied Population Laboratory, Population Series 70-15.

Hart, J. F., and Salisbury, N. E. 1965. Population Change in Middle Western Villages: A Statistical Approach. *Annals of the Association of American Geographers* 55 (March): 140-60.

Johansen, H. E. 1974. Recent Changes in Population and Business Activity in Rural Villages of the United States. Unpublished Ph.D. Dissertation. Madison: University of Wisconsin.

Johansen, H. E., and Fuguitt, G. V. 1973. Changing Retail Activity in Wisconsin Villages. *Rural Sociology* 38 (Summer): 208-18.

Johansen, H. E., and Fuguitt, G. V. 1979. Population Growth and Retail Decline: Conflicting Effects of Urban Accessibility in American Villages. *Rural Sociology* 44 (Spring): 24-38.

Little, J. D. 1972. Employers' Needs for Labor Market Information in Order to Locate and Operate in Rural Areas. In *Labor Market Information in Rural Areas*, ed. Collette Moser, pp. 47-50. East Lansing, MI: Michigan State University.

Marshall, J. U. 1969. *The Location of Service Towns*. Toronto: University of Toronto Press.

Roseman, C., 1977. Changing Migration Patterns within the United States. A. A. G. Resource Paper No. 77-2, Washington: Association of American Geographers.

Shryock, H. S., and Siegel, J. S. 1971. The Methods and Materials of Demography. Washington, DC: U.S. Government Printing Office.

Till, T. E., 1974. Industrialization and Poverty in Southern Nonmetropolitan Labor Markets. *Growth and Change* 5 (January): 18-24.

V. Prime Farmland and Public Policy

Can the Nation Retain Good Farmland for Agriculture?

Norman A. Berg

Land use in all its complexities has consumed my interest and energy for many years. My main concern is farmland, particularly those acres of relatively flat, deep, fertile soils we call prime farmland. Each year about three million acres of important agricultural land, about a third of which is prime farmland, are taken out of agricultural use—for good.

In my view, the primary land-use issue in the United States is the retention of our finest farmland for farming. And the primary question is how to do it. Before I attempt to answer that question, I would like to review some of the reasons for the disappearance of our agricultural land . . . and some of the other major soil and water resource problems facing the nation. We all know what urbanization is doing. A farmer in Fayette County, Kentucky, was interviewed recently by a local reporter. The farmer said that the land on which he started growing tobacco 20 years ago is now part of the Stonewall Estates subdivision. He added: "We've been in the path of progress for a long time. Now it's kind of inching out toward me."

I would say that "inching" hardly describes it. In the past 10 years, Fayette County lost about one-third of its prime farmland to urbanization, and the state of Kentucky lost more than 123 thousand acres. A serious problem in a state in which agriculture is the primary industry.

What is true in Kentucky is true throughout the nation. Former Secretary of Agriculture Bob Bergland has said: "I don't know where it is going to stop. But stop it must. Continued destruction of cropland is wanton squandering of an irreplaceable resource." Recent figures show that U.S. population growth may require more than 44 thousand new housing units a week for the next 10 years, removing additional land for roads, power plants, and job-related industry. He called these two opposing trends a "collision course with disaster."

We can't blame all of this loss of important farmland on urbanization. From 1967 to 1975, about 70 thousand acres each year were converted to water uses—farm ponds, dams, flood control structures. These needs will continue. But it is soil erosion that is the primary cause of soil loss and the main despoiler of the land. Each year, water and wind erosion removes about 6.4 billion tons of soil from nonfederal rural lands—an amount equivalent to one inch of topsoil from all such lands in the entire state of Missouri. Most of this loss—nearly 5 billion tons—is from water, or sheet and rill, erosion.

The estimated average sheet and rill erosion rate on all cropland in the conterminous United States is 4.7 tons per acre per year. SCS surveys indicate that 94 million acres of cropland—an area as large as Iowa, Ohio, and North Carolina—are eroding from water at rates that lower agricultural productivity (more than 5 tons per acre per year). Of the nation's total water erosion, 11 percent is estimated to be from streambanks, 6 percent from gullies, 3 percent from roads and roadsides, and 2 percent from construction sites. Soil compaction, which restricts root penetration and cuts down on crop yields, is another problem in many areas. Conservation tillage can help, but many farmers are slow to accept this farming method.

We also have some water problems that need attention. For instance, in some areas, water tables are falling—never to be refilled—because of an increase in irrigation, and because people are flocking to places like the Sun Belt to retire and to play. These newcomers' demands for water are high, and they compete with those of farmers.

Salinity is another water problem. In Colorado, for example, 60,000 acre-feet of excess irrigation water seep through the soil and pick up salt from the underlying mica shale deposited on ancient sea beds. This water, now saline, runs underground and eventually rejoins the Colorado River to be used and reused.

And then, of course, there are problems with upstream flood damages. About 175 million acres of nonfederal rural land are classified as flood-prone. (A flood-prone area is one adjoining a river, stream, or lake where there is a 1-percent chance of flooding in any given year). Of this total, about 106 million acres are pasture, rangeland, or forest land; 48 million acres are cropland; and 21 million acres are classified as rural land. The cost of upstream flood damages is expected to increase about 35 percent during the next 20 years, partly as a result of construction that alters patterns of water absorption and runoff.

Studies carried out as part of the Soil and Water Resources Conservation Act of 1977, which I shall discuss below, indicate that among eight major resource areas that need attention in the immediate future, two merit special emphasis: (1) protecting soil quantity and quality, and (2) preventing upstream flood damages to farms and rural areas.

I have touched briefly on some of the major natural resource problems that must be dealt with now and in the years ahead. The question that remains is this: what are we doing to solve these problems? Geographers have been a tremendous help in providing a picture of the land and waterways as they were in the eighteenth and nineteenth centuries—before the Great Plains were stripped of tons of soil; before surface mining changed land contours and killed vegetation;

before free-running rivers and streams were clogged with silt and their channels straightened; and before low-lying farmland became swamps.

Every step of our progress has brought change. Every change has had its price. The great days of reclamation are over. We can't restore this land to eighteenth-century conditions. But I believe we can and must continue to work to keep a balance between growth and new technologies on the one hand, and abundant and productive farmland and clean water on the other.

In 1975 the Soil Conservation Service issued a Land Inventory and Monitoring Memorandum defining prime and unique farmland. It inaugurated a program of county and state mapping of this land. As of mid-1980, 507 county and 8 state maps had been published. Maps of 1,300 high-priority counties—in regions undergoing rapid land-use changes or containing rich coal reserves—should be published by 1986. The importance of these maps is obvious—we have to know where our best farmland is before we can protect it. These maps already are providing a basis on which local and state governments can design programs to preserve their most valuable farmland.

In addition to retaining our best farmland for farming, it is important that we have a viable agriculture—good markets, good prices, a clear picture of the interrelationships of all the elements. To bring these essentials into a new and sharp perspective, the Department of Agriculture initiated a project called the "Structure of Agriculture" in 1979. The goals were to explore all aspects of the structure of agriculture, its present trends, and its future course—and to carry on a national dialogue with the agricultural community and the consumer public.

Another nationwide effort is being carried out in the Department of Agriculture under the Soil and Water Resources Conservation Act of 1977, or RCA. This law directed the Secretary of Agriculture to appraise on a continuing basis the soil, water, and related resources of the nation's nonfederal land; to develop a program to further the conservation, protection, and enhancement of these resources; to report to Congress and the public; and to repeat the process in 1985. RCA has been a tremendous undertaking, one of vital importance. What we do now will help determine the condition of the nation's natural resources for the next 50 years, and beyond.

The nine USDA agencies and the two White House offices that have been involved with RCA have had the benefit of a poll conducted by Louis Harris and Associates. A cross-section of the entire adult population (seven thousand people) was queried on a number of major conservation and agricultural issues). We were very gratified to learn that farmers are not alone in their recognition that soil and water conservation are among the country's most pressing concerns. Most of the people questioned consider the loss of good farmland and the misuse of soil and water resources to be serious problems; they believe that efforts to conserve soil and water must be continued regardless of cost.

The U.S. Department of Agriculture (USDA) has published three RCA draft documents, plus a summary. These documents were made available to the public; we received about 68 thousand written responses. These comments were evaluated and incorporated into a proposed RCA program, which once again went to the public. A final RCA program will go to the president and congress in 1982.

The USDA was also involved with the National Agricultural Lands Study (NALS), a joint venture with the President's Council on Environmental Quality and 10 other federal agencies. Basically, NALS examined the availability of the nation's agricultural land. How much of it is being converted to other uses? Why is it being converted? How does the retention or loss of this land affect the United States and the rest of the world now and in the future? The study was completed in January 1981.

In addition to these activities, the USDA is directing the bulk of its federal research funds for basic, rather than applied, research—crop and animal, energy, integrated pest management, food additives, human nutrition, aerospace technology for better information on how weather fluctuations affect crops, and nonpoint source water pollution. All of these efforts will help us do a better job of protecting and preserving our soil and water resources, including keeping our best farmland in farming. But we must not stop with these activities; we must spread the conservation word beyond the doors of the Department of Agriculture, a handful of other federal agencies, and a few university faculties.

I ask a question in the title of this essay—can the nation retain good farmland for agriculture? My answer is a tentative yes, it can:—if we can hold urbanization in a pattern that is not destructive to cropland;—if we can contain soil erosion within the tolerance limits;—if local, state, and federal governments can devise effective and coordinated programs for farmland retention;—if we can find the proper balance between private rights and public interest;—if we recognize that the time for more informed land use decisions is now; and—if we can make this nation's people sensitive to the land and aware of the necessity for all these actions. If we can do these things, then we can be confident that our fertile land will provide enough food and fiber for our own needs and those of our global neighbors.

Threats to American Cropland: Urbanization and Soil Erosion

David Berry

INTRODUCTION

From the viewpoint of agricultural aesthetics, there is probably no more impressive landscape than that of central Illinois and Iowa. A flight over the Midwest and Central Plains reveals cropland from one horizon to the other. Upstate New York has miles of dairy, vegetable, and fruit farms; southeastern Pennsylvania presents a classic landscape of agricultural abundance.

Despite these and other examples of a copious agricultural land base, there are serious long-term concerns regarding the future adequacy of high-quality U.S. cropland. These concerns are based on evidence of a loss of productive farmland and of continued soil erosion, in the face of a highly volatile world demand for American farm products. The recent surge of interest in converting grain to fuel products presents still another source of demand upon the agricultural base of the country (see following chapter by Zinn). At a time of short-term surplus and bulging grain elevators, it is difficult to address the need to anticipate possible future shortages. Yet as our experience with energy suggests, it is in times of excess that future needs should be considered.

Withdrawals from the agricultural resource base have many causes: urbanization (including housing, shopping centers, highways, airports, etc.); strip mining of coal and other minerals; inundation by water resource projects; soil erosion; and retirement of marginal farmland due to low productivity, isolated location, fragmented ownership, and so on (Hart 1968). This chapter examines two of these factors: soil erosion and urban encroachment.

The author wishes to thank Thomas Plaut for his many useful ideas and comments, and Eliza McClennen for preparing the maps in this paper.

Table 1. Components of America's Land Resource Base

Component	Area (millions of acres)	Source
Stock of Land, by Use		
Land area	2,264	1
Land area, excluding Alaska and Hawaii	1,897	1
Nonfederal land area, 1977	1,512	2
Cropland	413	2
Pasture and Rangeland	547	2
Forestland	376	2
Other Rural Land	107	2
Urban Land	69	2
Stock of Land, by Quality		
Prime Farmland, 1977	346	3
Cropped	230	3
Nonfederal Land by Capability Class, 1977		
Class I	38	3
Class II	287	3
Class III	288	3
Cropland by Capability Class, 1977		
Class I	32	3
Class II	188	3
Class III	132	3

Sources: (1) U.S. Dept. of the Interior 1974, Table 1.
(2) National Agricultural Lands Study 1981A, Figure 1.
(3) U.S. Dept. of Agriculture 1977-79, Tables G1, H, R1.

THE U.S. AGRICULTURAL LAND BASE

To understand the future of American cropland, it is necessary to determine the stocks of land in various categories and the changes in those stocks over time. In this section we review stocks; in later sections we look at causes of change in those stocks.

Table 1 summarizes recent estimates of stocks of the land resource base. About 18 percent of all the nation's land is in cropland; only 3 percent is in urban uses. In terms of quality, there are 230 million acres of prime cropland and 220 million acres of cropland in soil capability classes I and II. Figure 1 shows the regional distribution of prime cropland. Prime cropland is the land best suited to production of food and feed crops, in terms of soil quality, growing season, and moisture supply and the economics and technology of modern farm production (Schmude 1977). Soil in capability classes I and II is nearly all prime; some soil in capability class III is prime. Capability refers to susceptibility to erosion, excess water, climatic limitations, and other limitations. Classes I and II are the least erodable, least waterlogged soils with the fewest limitations.

In addition to land currently in crop production, there exists a stock of potential cropland (Dideriksen et al. 1977). In 1975 there were about 46 million acres of noncropland having soils in capability classes I and II with high or

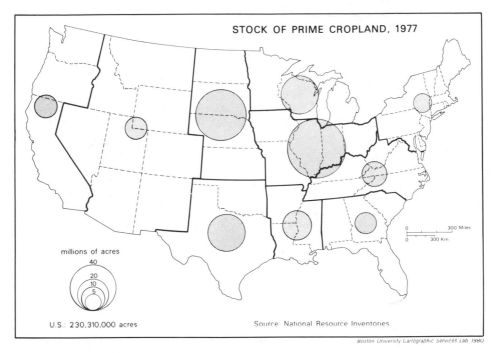

STOCK OF PRIME CROPLAND, 1977

millions of acres
40
20
10
5

U.S.: 230,310,000 acres

Source: National Resource Inventories

0   300 Miles
0   300 Km

Boston University Cartographic Services Lab 1980

Figure 1. Stock of prime cropland.

medium potential for being brought into crop production based on 1974 cost-price relationships (Lee 1978). The regional breakdown of this potential cropland is shown in Figure 2. A total of 111 million acres of high and medium potential cropland of all quality levels existed in 1975. Thus we have a high-quality base of about 230 million acres of prime cropland plus another 46 million acres of potentially good cropland that is currently in pasture and range, woodland, or wetland, or that lies idle.

Such high-quality land is of obvious value to society. It is a productive resource that cannot be enlarged without great expense in clearing, draining, fertilizing, terracing, and other land preparation activities or in removing buildings from the land. It is therefore wasteful to base the use of this land on nearly irreversible short-run economic motives rather than on its long-run capability for producing food, feed, and fiber. To minimize our risk over the next 50 years, conversions of prime cropland and high-quality potential cropland to nonagricultural uses should be discouraged.

SOIL EROSION

There is little doubt that soil erosion has had and continues to have a detrimental effect on agricultural productivity and input costs. The Dust Bowl of the 1930s illustrated what can happen under extreme conditions (Worster 1979).

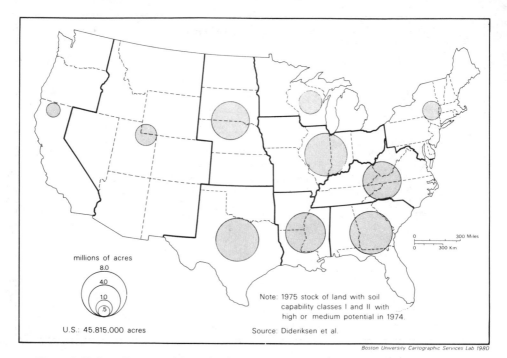

millions of acres
8.0
40
10
5

U.S.: 45,815,000 acres

Note: 1975 stock of land with soil
capability classes I and II with
high or medium potential in 1974.

Source: Dideriksen et al.

Boston University Cartographic Services Lab 1980

Figure 2. High quality potential cropland.

Pimentel et al. (1976) have reviewed studies of soil erosion and have noted four
general kinds of adverse effects: 1) selective removal of plant nutrients and organic matter; 2) loss of fine soil particles, resulting in soil compaction; 3) loss of
topsoil and therefore of a rooting medium for plants; and 4) increased water runoff. Offsetting losses in productivity as soil blows or washes away can become an
expensive proposition—as, for example, in the need to apply more fertilizer to
replace nutrients lost through erosion.

Geographically, the greatest concentration of soil losses from cropland occurs
in Texas and Oklahoma due principally to wind erosion (Table 2; Fig. 3). The
Corn Belt and Northern Plains are also major losing areas, contributing over 40
percent of the nation's soil erosion on cropland, most of it sheet and rill erosion.
Although local conditions vary enormously, a sense of the relative magnitude of
the losses reported in Table 2 can be gained from Carter's (1977) observations
that in the absence of soil erosion losses, about 1.5 tons of new topsoil are
formed per acre every year, given normal farming conditions, and that some soils
can tolerate losses up to five tons per acre per year without lowering productivity. The national average of losses on cropland exceeds this range. Moreover, approximately 48 million acres of U.S. cropland are losing more than 14 tons of
soil per acre per year (National Agricultural Lands Study, 1981B).

The physical improvements and changes in cropping practices necessary to

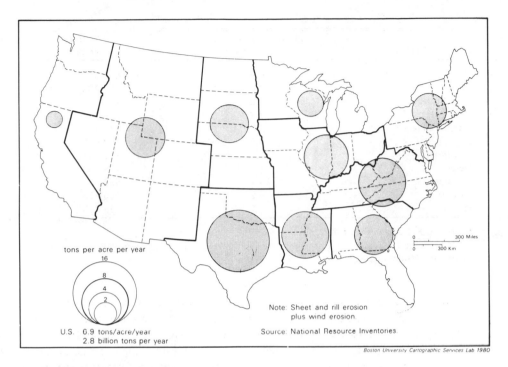

Figure 3. Soil erosion on cropland, 1977.

reduce soil erosion have been known for decades: contour farming, terracing, construction of waterways, windbreak plantings, maintenance of soil cover, adoption of certain tillage practices, and so on. Most call for a break with traditional farming practices, and some call for heavy investment by the farmer.

Soil conservation policy to promote conservation practices has generally emphasized voluntary participation and local control over such matters as erosion control techniques, determination of performance standards, inspection, and penalties for noncompliance. Sometimes state review of local district plans may be required (Seitz and Spitze 1978; Harder, Daniel, and Madison 1978). Federal and state agencies offer certain economic incentives such as subsidies, loans, and tax breaks to encourage conservation practices.

Currently the greatest interest in conservation policy centers around "green-ticket" versus "red-ticket" approaches (Benbrook 1979). A green-ticket strategy enables farmers who comply with conservation regulations or guidelines to participate in additional government programs or to receive additional benefits from existing programs. Qualified farmers receive a green ticket, which entitles them to these additional benefits. Among the kinds of benefits could be greater tax breaks, higher target prices, or better loan rates. Nonparticipants still receive some or all of the benefits of these programs but do not qualify for the incremental benefits. A

Table 2. Annual Soil Erosion on Cropland, 1977

Region	Soil Erosion,* Tons per Acre per Year	Soil Erosion*, Thousands of Tons per Year
United States (48 States)	6.9	2,842,343
Northeast	4.9	82,900
Lake States	2.6	116,746
Corn Belt	7.8	698,282
Northern Plains	5.7	537,761
Appalachia	9.3	192,671
Southeast	6.4	111,795
Delta	8.4	178,069
Southern Plains	15.1	637,957
Mountain	6.2	260,803
Pacific	1.1	25,359

Source: U.S. Department of Agriculture, 1977-79.
*Sheet and rill erosion in all regions plus wind erosion in the Northern Plains, Southern Plains, and Mountain regions.

red-ticket strategy would permit only those farmers who comply with conservation regulations or guidelines to participate in any (or at least some) governmental programs. Farmers who do not comply would receive a red ticket and would then not be eligible for program benefits. Subsidies for investing in erosion control practices and technical assistance may be offered to induce farmers to engage in conservation practices under either the green ticket or red-ticket strategy. Naturally, the green-ticket strategy has greater political appeal to farmers than the red-ticket strategy.

Two kinds of problems with either of these programs are especially vexing. One has to do with equity. Some farmers may have invested heavily already in conservation practices, while their tardier neighbors can now participate in a program that may offer them large subsidies that were not available in the past. Moreover, some farmers have land that needs only slight conservation treatment, while others with more erodable soils must invest greatly to meet conservation guidelines. Even with a subsidy, some farmers are going to face much larger costs than others in qualifying for green-ticket status or in avoiding red-ticket status.

The second problem is that of tailoring guidelines to individual farms or parcels of land. No blanket technique can be prescribed: a program must be sensitive to variations in soil types, farm types, and existing incentives and subsidies in order to allow the farmer to maximize his income subject to erosion limits (Boggess et al. 1979). Careful field work and local planning are therefore necessary to set up the criteria for attaining green-ticket status or avoiding red-ticket status.

The green-ticket and red-ticket approaches are still being developed. Whether either will be implemented successfully to help curtail soil erosion remains to be seen.

URBANIZATION OF CROPLAND

The rate of conversion of farmland (cropland, pasture, etc.) to urban uses apparently doubled between the mid-1960s and mid-1970s, from about a half million to one million acres per year. Conversions in the 1960s have been inferred from the relationships between population density and built-up acreage per person using county level data from the 1967 Conservation Needs Inventory and from regional studies of conversion using aerial photographs (e.g., Vining, Plaut, and Bieri 1977; Berry and Plaut 1978; Zeimetz et al. 1976). The Potential Cropland Study for 1975 indicates a higher annual rate of conversion of farmland to urban uses between 1967 and 1975, about twice the rate in the previous decade (Dideriksen et al. 1977).

The conversion of farmland to urban uses such as residential, commercial, industrial, transportation, and institutional uses exhibits several important spatial patterns. In areas of low population density, where there is little infrastructural capital in place and where people typically live on relatively large lots, the acreage requirements per new dwelling unit are larger than in more built-up suburbs or cities (Vining, Plaut, and Bieri 1977). In addition, the pattern of new development is often highly scattered rather than being a contiguous extension of previous development (Berry 1981). Exceptions to this may include amenity-related developments in which the developers or builders concentrate as much new construction as possible close to a lake, ridge, or other scenic attraction.

Besides the actual conversion of rural land to urban uses, there is also a process of idling of farmland in areas of intense development pressure (Berry 1978; Berry and Plaut 1978). Urban effects spill over into nearby areas. Consequently, the continuity of farming may be impeded by factors such as land speculation, regulation of routine agricultural activities that inflict noise, odors, and chemicals upon nonfarm neighbors, and proposals for new highways, reservoirs, and other public facilities. Such factors deter new farmers from taking the place of those who retire, die, or migrate elsewhere. The land, which otherwise would be productive, is idled in anticipation of conversion to urban uses or in response to other urban spillovers. This is a fairly localized phenomenon, but it can account for tens of thousands of acres of farmland that could be used productively. A gradual switch-over to less capital-intensive forms of agriculture may also occur in areas subject to urban pressure, as farmers do not wish to make investments they cannot fully depreciate. One example of this is the switch-over from dairying to cash-grain farming on the outer fringes of urban areas (Berry 1978; 1979).

The conversion and idling of farmland may seem relatively unimportant if there is potential cropland that can be brought into production to replace that which is urbanized. This reserve of potential cropland, however, is quite limited in the Northeastern and Pacific states and somewhat limited in the Lake states (Fig. 4). (The data from the Potential Cropland Study upon which Figure 4 is based have come under a great deal of criticism regarding their accuracy; thus this map can be considered as only a rough approximation.) Although there

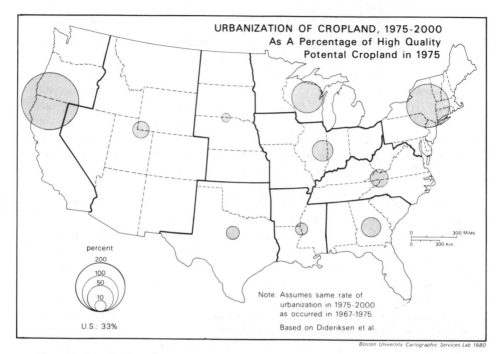

Boston University Cartographic Services Lab 1980

Figure 4. Urbanization of cropland, 1975-2000.

may be little concern over the loss of land in the Northern Plains to urban uses, we cannot be so sanguine about the advance of development into the valleys of California and into the Connecticut Valley, the Champlain lowlands, the Erie-Ontario Plain in upstate New York, the middle Mohawk Valley, the southeastern quadrant of Pennsylvania, or southern New Jersey. Compared to the Midwest, one might see the Northeast as of lesser agricultural value; but these areas are highly productive, especially for fruits, vegetables, and dairy products. By the end of this century we shall no longer have the ability to replace urbanized cropland acre for acre with good potential cropland at low or moderate cost in the Northeast and Pacific states.

CROPLAND SHORTAGES?

Is there reason to be concerned about the availability of cropland? This depends upon what crops are grown, crop yields, and domestic and foreign demand for crops. Assuming the same mix of crops currently produced, Plaut (1979) examines cropland needs for the year 2000. Assuming optimal conditions of slow rates of increase in demand and high rates of increase in productivity and yields typical of the 1960s, he estimates over 100 million acres of currently used cropland will be retired. Assuming somewhat worse conditions—moderate increase in demand, and little or no increase in productivity and yields—he estimates that between 79 million and 154 million additional acres of cropland will be needed as compared with 1977. The reserve of potential cropland that could be brought into production at low or moderate cost to supplement agricultural needs in the next two decades in this case may be just sufficient. But if we consider losses to urbanization, there will probably be a cropland deficit in 20 years.

The issue of yields is central to any prediction of cropland requirements. The twentieth century has seen remarkable increases in the production per acre of most crops and in the output of livestock and livestock products. These have resulted from agricultural research on plant hybridization and stock improvement, the retirement of marginal farmlands, the commercialization of farming, enlargement of farms, generally favorable climatic conditions, soil improvement programs, and the application of fertilizers, herbicides, and insecticides in large doses (Heady 1976). In the optimistic spirit of past technology, we might envision 200 bushel per acre corn, average dairy cows yielding 17,000 pounds of milk per year, and so on. However, there are indications of less favorable climatic conditions in the future (Schneider 1976), decreasing marginal returns to fertilizers and pesticides, and higher energy costs that will limit the use of fertilizers and pesticides and perhaps alter tillage and planting routines and crop-drying procedures. Experiments with and observations of organic and intermediate technology farming methods suggest (still inconclusively) that yields may be slightly lower on organic livestock-crop farms than on conventional livestock-crop farms in the Midwest (Klepper et al. 1977); and that reductions in yields as the use of machinery is limited varies from one part of the country to another (Johnson, Stoltzfus, and Craumer 1977). At any rate, it is reasonable to postulate much slower increases in yields over the future than in the past as the costs of inputs into agricultural production increase.

Shortages of cropland are not likely to result in food shortages in this country but rather in a shifting away from beef, perhaps to greater reliance on fruits and vegetables and to pork and poultry. Over two-thirds of our cropland is used for animal feed, principally corn, soybeans, and hay (Table 3). Since cattle are rather inefficient energy converters compared to hogs and poultry (Heichel and Frink 1975), we might very well witness a decline in the consumption of grain-fed beef and a substitution of pork, chicken, eggs, and other poultry products to supply meat protein.

Besides feeding ourselves we also supply substantial exports of food and feed to the rest of the world. Just under a third of our cropland is used to produce crops for export, up from about a quarter in the mid-1960s (Table 4). The importance of these exports is increasing in terms of volume and possibly in political leverage (Robbins 1980). Many observers have indicated that the future of United States trade lies in our agricultural potential as well as in high technology products and services. Thus the retention of productive agricultural land takes on additional importance.

Table 3. 1977 Acreage of Major Crops Used Principally for Feed

Crop	Acreage Planted
Corn	82,680,000
Soybeans	59,080,000
Hay*	60,493,000
Oats	17,793,000
Barley	10,586,000
Sorghum	16,994,000
Flaxseed	1,510,000
Sugarbeets	1,278,000
Total	250,414,000
Total for all crops	351,226,000

Feed crop acreage as a percentage of all crop acreage = 71.3%

Source: U.S. Department of Agriculture, Agricultural Statistics, 1978. Tables 39, 48, 56, 65, 178, 107, 156, 403, 629.
   *Acreage harvested

LAND USE POLICIES AND URBANIZATION

Policies to retain agricultural land in areas of urban pressure are largely a function of state and local initiative, because of the traditional desire for local control over land use and because of the states' police powers. Basically these kinds of policies fall into two categories (Berry and Plaut 1978): 1) direct, in which the use of land is controlled through zoning, public purchase of farmland, public purchase of development rights, and various innovative techniques such as transferable development rights; and 2) indirect, in which farmland owners are offered incentives to keep their land in agricultural production. Among these incentives are tax breaks, such as differential assessment and alleviation of some of the spillover effects of urbanization, as with New York's agricultural districts. Indirect

Table 4. Acreage Used for Producing Crops for Export

Year	Export Acreage Harvested (Millions)	Percentage of Total Harvested
1963	77	25.8
1967	69	22.5
1970	72	24.6
1973	96	29.9
1974	99	30.2
1975	100	29.8
1976	97	28.8
1977	111	32.3

Source: U.S. Department of Agriculture, Agricultural Statistics, 1978, 1979 Tables 630, 629 respectively.

incentives are far more widespread than direct controls, with differential assessment of farmland existing in almost all states (Coughlin, Berry, and Plaut 1978).

As for the effectiveness of land use policies, the major considerations are focus, cost, complexity, and participation patterns (Berry and Plaut 1978). Incentives are focused on rather marginal aspects of obstacles to farming, considering the profits that can be made in land speculation, while direct controls are focused on the central issue of the conversion of farmland. Both types of policies may be needed in areas of strong urban pressures where potential profits of conversion are high and where farming may be hindered by local regulation of routine farming activities to suit urban neighbors, by the use of eminent domain for public facilities, by increased taxes on land to pay for urban services, and the like.

Although direct controls may be more effective in retaining farmland, they are also expensive. The costs of zoning fall on private landowners, who may object to restrictions on the use of their land and who are often successful in watering down or blocking exclusive agricultural zoning ordinances. At a typical public hearing in a rural area, zoning is frequently regarded with hostility by local landowners. Approaches to exclusive farm use zoning at the state level are exemplified by Oregon and Hawaii and on a local level by many communities in California, Illinois, Iowa, and the Northeast. As an incentive, Wisconsin offers farmers substantial income tax breaks in areas of approved agricultural planning or zoning (Barrows and Yanggen 1978).

The costs of public purchase of development rights in areas of intense urban pressures can also be high, but here the costs fall on the public, not on landowners whose land is restricted in use. Public purchase of development rights programs have been tried in New Jersey (without success yet, principally because of the high costs involved); in Suffolk County, Long Island (with some success — 3200 acres of rights at a cost of $12 million by 1978 [Newton 1979]); and in Massachusetts (where development rights on the first 8 participating farms were purchased by the spring of 1980 at a cost of $1.6 million). Scenic easements have been used successfully along highways in Wisconsin, but these are usually much less costly than agricultural easements near urban areas, since most of the purchases in Wisconsin are in relatively rural areas (Coughlin and Plaut 1978).

Complexity is probably the most important factor in limiting the use of such programs as transferable development rights, where the markets for such development rights are quite difficult to predict and control. Local planners must create a market in transferable development rights that will permit builders to concentrate their development activities in designated "growth" areas through the purchase of development rights from landowners in "no-growth" areas. These rights permit higher-density development in the growth areas, and their purchase from landowners in no-growth areas compensates these landowners for not being allowed to develop their own land at moderate or high density. The no-growth areas would therefore presumably remain in open space, possibly in agriculture. But the fine tuning required to coax out a price for transferable development rights sufficient to compensate landowners in the no-growth areas requires capabilities beyond those of most local planning agencies.

Participation patterns in voluntary indirect incentive programs indicate that in areas of strong urban pressure, farmland owners are reluctant to commit themselves to relatively costly participation efforts, such as postponing the opportunity for conversion of farmland to urban uses for at least ten years or undertaking the paperwork and persuasion necessary to establish agricultural districts. Yet where urban pressures are weaker, participation in indirect controls is often high. This can be seen in California's restrictive agreements program or New York's agricultural districting program (Hansen and Schwartz 1976; Gustafson and Wallace 1975; and Berry and Plaut 1978).

CONCLUSIONS

Both soil erosion and urbanization are avoidable threats to American cropland. The volume of soil erosion is most significant in the Plains states and in the Corn Belt, but erosion is also intense in most other regions of the country, the only exceptions being the Lake states and the Pacific states. Urbanization of high-quality cropland presents an immediate threat in the Northeastern, Pacific, and Lake states, areas that produce a large portion of the nation's fruit, vegetables, and dairy products.

It is not possible to argue that the next twenty to fifty years will bring about an absolute shortage of cropland. Instead, the continuation of soil erosion and urbanization will probably cause a shift away from beef and, if these factors are severe enough, away from other meats as well to greater production of commodities directly consumed by people. Lower supplies and greater demand also imply higher prices.

We know how to control soil erosion and limit urban development of high-quality cropland. But these solutions are expensive, and the benefits will be realized only well into the future. This kind of temporal tradeoff has rarely been made in the United States.

References

Barrows, R., and Yanggen, D. 1978. The Wisconsin Farmland Preservation Program. *Journal of Soil and Water Conservation* 33: 209-212.

Benbrook, C. 1979. Integrating Soil Conservation and Commodity Programs: A Policy Proposal. *Journal of Soil and Water Conservation* 34: 160-167.

Berry, D. 1978. Effects of Urbanization on Agricultural Activities. *Growth and Change* 9(3) 2-8.

_____ 1979. The Sensitivity of Dairying to Urbanization: A Study of Northeastern Illinois. *Professional Geographer* 31: 170-176.

_____ 1981. Population Redistribution and Conflicts in Land Use: A Midwestern Perspective. Pp. 149-168 in *Population Redistribution in the Midwest*, ed. C. Roseman, A. Sofranko, and J. Williams, Ames, Iowa: North Central Regional Center for Rural Development, Iowa State University.

Berry, D., and Plaut, T., 1978. Retaining Agricultural Activities Under Urban Pressures: A Review of Land Use Conflicts and Policies. *Policy Sciences* 9: 153-178.

Boggess, W.; McGrann, J.; Boehlje, M.; and Heady, E. O. 1979. Farm-Level Impacts of Alternative Soil Loss Control Policies. *Journal of Soil and Water Conservation* 34: 177-183.

Carter, L. 1977. Soil Erosion: The Problem Persists Despite the Billions Spent on It. *Science* 196: 409-411.

Coughlin, R.; Berry, D.; and Plaut, T. 1978. Differential Assessment of Real Property as an Incentive to Open Space Preservation and Farmland Retention. *National Tax Journal* 31: 165-179.

Coughlin, R., and Plaut, T. 1978. The Use of Less-than-Fee Acquisition for Preservation of Open Space. *Journal of the American Institute of Planners* 44:452-462.

Dideriksen, R.; Hidlebaugh, A.; and Schmude, K. 1977. *Potential Cropland Study*. Statistical Bulletin No. 578. Washington: Soil Conservation Service, USDA.

Gustafson, G., and Wallace, L. 1975. Differential Assessment as Land Use Policy: The California Case. *Journal of the American Institute of Planners* 41: 379-389.

Hansen, D., and Schwartz, S. 1976. Prime Land Preservation: The California Land Conservation Act. *Journal of Soil and Water Conservation* 31, no. 5: 198-203.

Harder, S. M.; Daniel, T. C.; and Madison, F. W. 1978. Guidelines for Mandatory Erosion Control Programs. *Journal of Soil and Water Conservation* 33: 80-84.

Hart, J. F. 1968. Loss and Abandonment of Cleared Farmland in the Eastern United States. *Annals of the Association of American Geographers* 58: 417-440.

Heady, E. O. 1976. The Agriculture of the U.S. *Scientific American* 235: 106-127.

Heichel, G. H. and Frink, C. R. 1975. Anticipating the Energy Needs of American Agriculture. *Journal of Soil and Water Conservation* 30: 48-53.

Johnson, W.; Stoltzfus, V.; and Craumer, P. 1977. Energy Conservation in Amish Agriculture. *Science* 198: 373-378.

Klepper, R.; Lockeretz, W.; Commoner, B.; Gertler, M.; Fast, S.; O'Leary, D.; and Blobaum, R. 1977. Economic Performance and Energy Intensiveness on Organic and Conventional Farms in the Corn Belt: A Preliminary Comparison. *American Journal of Agricultural Economics* 59: 1-12.

Lee, L. 1978. *A Perspective on Cropland Availability*. Agric. Econ. Rpt. No. 406, Washington: Economics, Statistics, and Cooperatives Service, USDA.

National Agricultural Lands Study 1981A. *Final Report*. Washington: USDA and CEQ.

_____ 1981B. Soil Degradation: Effects on Agricultural Productivity. Washington: USDA and CEQ.

Newton, D. 1979. Saving Prime Farmland: The Suffolk County Experience. Presented at the Conference on Protecting and Preserving Land Uses, Fredericksburg, VA (December 5-6).

Pimentel, D.; Terhune, E.; Dyson-Hudson, R.; Rochereau, S.; Samis, R.; Smith, E.; Denman, D.; Reifschneider, D.; and Shepard, M. 1976. Land Degradation: Effects on Food and Energy Resources. *Science* 194: 149-155.

Plaut, T. 1979. *Urban Expansion and the Loss of Farmland in the United States*. Paper BP 79-5. Austin, Texas: Bureau of Business Research, University of Texas.

Robbins, W. 1980. The Policies and Politics of Wheat. *The New York Times International Economic Survey* (Feb. 3): 13.

Schmude, K. 1977. A Perspective on Prime Farmland. *Journal of Soil and Water Conservation* 32: 240-242.

Schneider, S. 1976. *The Genesis Strategy*. New York: Plenum.

Seitz, W., and Spitze, R. G. F. 1978. Soil Erosion Control Policies: Institutional Alternatives and Costs. *Journal of Soil and Water Conservation* 33: 118-125.

U.S. Department of Agriculture 1977-79. *National Resource Inventories*. Washington: Soil Conservation Service, USDA.

_____ 1978, 1979. *Agricultural Statistics*. Washington: USDA.

U.S. Department of the Interior 1974. *Public Land Statistics*. Washington: USDOI.

Vining, D.; Plaut, T.; and Bieri, K. 1977. Urban Encroachment on Prime Agricultural Land in the United States. *International Regional Science Review* 2: 143-156.

Worster, D. 1979. *Dust Bowl: The Southern Plains in the 1930's*. New York: Oxford University Press.

Zeimetz, K.; Dillon, E.; Hardy, E.; and Otte, R. 1976. *Dynamics of Land Use in Fast Growth Areas*. Agric. Econ. Rpt. No. 325. Washington: Economic Research Service, USDA.

Exports and Energy: New Factors in U.S. Agricultural Land Policy

Jeffrey A. Zinn

INTRODUCTION

Agriculture in the United States is challenged from two directions—rising world demand for American farm products and rising energy costs. The two are inter-related: increased sale of farm commodities abroad helps to offset part of the cost of importing foreign oil. Yet efforts to raise U.S. farm output to serve world demand (as well as rising domestic requirements) depend upon increased use of energy in food production; e.g., to pump water for irrigation of arid lands, for erosion control, for the preparation and application of fertilizers, pesticides, and so forth. This situation underscores the importance of maintaining the nation's base of prime farmlands for energy-efficient food production.

Patterns and trends in world demand for U.S. agricultural exports are reviewed in the first section below. Following sections consider the declining quantity and quality of U.S. agricultural lands available to meet this demand. Finally, some additional energy issues affecting agricultural policy are reviewed. Some thoughts about the interrelated nature of energy issues, world demand, and prime farmland conclude the paper.

THE WORLD MARKET

Exports of U.S. agricultural products have risen rapidly in the decade of the 1970s and are expected to continue to grow in the future. In 1970, about 1 of every 5 acres harvested supplied the export market. By 1980, this figure had

The views expressed in this paper are those of the author and do not reflect any official views of the Congressional Research Service. The author is indebted to Wendell Fletcher of the American Land Forum, whose research on relationships between energy and agriculture conducted for the National Agricultural Lands Study was very helpful in the preparation of this paper.

193

risen to 1 acre in 3 (Fletcher 1980, p. 2). In different terms, over 107 million harvested acres of cropland were devoted to exports in 1977, more than double the acreage serving that market in 1970 (U.S. Department of Agriculture—hereafter USDA—1971, p. 4). The allocation of those 107 million acres includes 40 million acres in food grains, 26 million acres in animal feed grains, and 37 million acres in other commodities (Dideriksen 1979, p. 4).

The value of exports has risen even more dramatically, from $5.2 billion in 1970 (in itself a 21-percent increase over the preceding year) to $41 billion in 1980. Adjusted for inflation, this reflects an absolute increase of about 400 percent, even with an estimated reduction of exports to the Soviet Union of about $2.6 billion in 1979 and a similar value in 1980 (USDA 1980b, I-2).

This rapid increase has not kept pace with the value of petroleum imports, which increased from $2.7 billion in 1970 to more than $80 billion in 1980, a rise of over 1200 percent in constant dollars. Agricultural exports, however, have reduced the foreign trade deficit resulting from oil imports by an estimated one-third—lowering the deficit in 1978 from $46.8 billion to $32.6 billion (Dideriksen 1979, p. 4). It is expected that rising world demand for food will continue to increase the volume (and value) of agricultural exports, and help reduce the national trade deficit. Farm policy is thus a key element of foreign policy.

The growing importance of world markets was recognized in the appraisal of future demand on land and water resources developed by the Soil Conservation Service (SCS), as required by the 1977 Soil and Water Resources Conservation Act (RCA). One of three factors used in developing different scenarios of cropland requirements in the years 2000 and 2030 is alternative levels of world market demand for U.S. products (USDA 1980a, part 2, pp. 2-7). The RCA analysis of future demands on soil resources is also based on three alternative levels of production. Table 1 lists the assumptions for the three scenarios.

The three principal exports from the United States are feed grains (primarily corn), wheat, and soybeans and soybean by-products. Each has preferred site requirements to maximize production. In 1975 75 percent of all corn, 70 percent of all soybeans, and 54 percent of all wheat were grown on prime farmland (USDA 1980a, part I, p. 3). Exports account for more than 26 percent of U.S. feedgrains, 60 percent of wheat, and 56 percent of soybeans and products (USDA 1979b, p. 77). Average annual increase in rates of yields of these crops has been generally decreasing during the 1970s (Crossen 1977, pp. 52-57). These declining rates of increase, when coupled with the high total acreage devoted to export crops and the anticipated future increase in demand, have substantial implications for future agricultural policy. One USDA projection estimates that 407 million acres of harvested cropland, an 81-million-acre increase over 1974, would be required in 1985 if projected "worse case" demand levels were to be met (Lee 1978, 3).

A recent study estimated changes in demand over the next 25 years for the three principal exports. The results, shown in Table 2, indicate that most growth in demand will come from the export market. At today's yield levels,

Table 1. Scenarios of the Future Used in the RCA Analysis

Alternatives	Population[1]	Exports	Technology[3]
Domestic consumption only	Series II	Zero	Moderate
Domestic consumption plus base exports	Series II	Constant (1975-77)	Moderate
Domestic consumption plus projected exports	Series II	Moderate[3]	Moderate

Source: USDA, 1980a, part II, pp. 2-7.

[1] The population growth rate will increase to 0.9 percent in the 1980s and decline to 0.6 percent by 2000 and to 0.3 percent by 2030.

[2] Agricultural productivity will increase by 1.1 percent per year to 2000 and by 0.8 percent annually from 2000 to 2030. (By contrast, a group of nationally known economists, discussing future production at a recent Resources for the Future symposium, reached a general consensus that the average rate would be 1.5 to 2.0 percent. This higher prediction, if true, would mean less land would be required to meet anticipated demands. But average yield figures at any rate, over an extended time hide much wider annual differences resulting from a combination of weather variation and introduction of new products and processes, which are developed on an irregular basis. Annual variations are difficult to forecast.)

[3] Exports will increase by 2.3 percent annually to 2000 and by 0.6 percent annually from 2000 to 2030.

these increases would require about 140 million additional acres. On the other hand, if yields increase at the same rate as they did between 1945 and 1973, about 3 percent per year for feedgrains and wheat, and 1.7 percent per year for soybeans), then the land requirement would decline 40 million acres by 2005 (Crossen 1980, pp. 7-8). But the higher growth rates of yield levels have not been maintained since 1973. Most experts forecast lower levels in the future. The contrasting results do demonstrate the importance of changing yield patterns when estimating this country's ability to supply the world market.

A recent study has projected planted acreage needed to meet projected

Table 2. Percentage Changes in Demand for Feedgrains, Wheat, and Soybeans in the United States, 1978-79 to 2005

Feedgrains	
Domestic demand	67%—86%
Export demand	107
Total	79—92
Wheat	
Domestic demand	—.9%
Export demand	97
Total	56
Soybeans	
Domestic demand	28%—44%
Export demand	12—45
Total	21—44

Source: Abel 1980, p. 7.

demand under three alternative yield assumptions: .75 percent gain per year, similar to the average increase between 1970 and 1979; 1.5 percent gain per year, similar to the average increase between 1960 and 1969; and 1.25 percent gain per year. This analysis concludes that between 77 and 113 million acres of additional land would need to be planted in principal crops (about 90 percent of the total historic planted acreage for all crops) by 1999 (National Agricultural Lands Study 1981a, p. 59).

DECLINING QUANTITY OF AGRICULTURAL LAND

The preceding chapter by Berry discusses current estimates of cropland and prime farmland in the United States. According to data he presents, in 1977 the nation had an estimated 413 million acres of land in crops, of which 230 million acres were "prime" (having soils in capability classes I, II, and—in certain cases—III). Another 115 million acres of prime land are devoted to other agricultural uses—pasture, range, and forestry. Prime lands are most productive, have the least erosion problems, and require relatively less energy input to obtain high yields.

There has been considerable discussion in recent years of the rate at which agricultural land, and particularly prime land, is being converted to nonagricultural purposes, often with irreversible consequences. Two branches of USDA, in fact, have developed very different estimates of the annual rate of loss. On the one hand, the Soil Conservation Service (SCS) has developed the much-quoted figure of 3 million acres of cropland converted to nonagricultural purposes annually between 1967 and 1975 (USDA 1977). On the other hand, Frey (1979) of the Economics, Statistics and Cooperative Service has estimated that the annual loss is less than one million acres per year. The discrepancy apparently results, at least in part, from the use of different definitions and an alternative set of land use inventories. The SCS figure is based on an estimated decline of 30.5 million acres between 1967 and 1975, leaving a cropland base of approximately 400 million acres (USDA 1977). Of this decline, about 8 million acres was estimated to be prime land, or an average of one million acres per year. Frey, on the other hand, concludes that an annual average of 900,000 acres was converted to urban and transportation uses between 1969 and 1974. Most of the converted lands were not in cropland.

In any event, conversion of cropland and prime land to other uses at possibly high rates stimulated a new study of U.S. agricultural land policies—the National Agricultural Lands Study (NALS)—undertaken in 1979 under the joint collaboration of USDA and the Council on Environmental Quality, and with the participation of ten other federal agencies. A number of technical reports prepared by NALS examine aspects of the agricultural land conversion issue in detail.

The goals of NALS were to review:

(1) the agricultural land resource base including quantity, quality, and ownership patterns;
(2) current pressures on agricultural land such as urban and industrial development, transportation, and energy requirements;
(3) the economic, environmental, and social effects of agricultural land conversion and retention;
(4) the impacts of federal programs and policies on agricultural land; and
(5) the actions that state and local governments have taken to ensure agricultural land availability.

The final report of NALS concludes:

The United States at present has approximately 413 million acres of cropland and about 127 million acres of potential cropland for a total of about 540 million acres. In addition there are some 268 million acres of rural land with low potential for cultivated crops.

From its research, NALS concludes that agricultural land is converted to other uses in an incremental piece-by-piece fashion. Many of the effects are local, but continued conversion of agricultural land at the current rate could have noteworthy national implications. The cumulative loss of cropland, in conjunction with other stresses on the U.S. agricultural system such as the growing demand for exports and rising energy costs could seriously increase the economic and environmental costs of producing food and fiber in the United States during the next 20 years (NALS 1981, p. 2).

In particular, a draft study for NALS projects that 22.4 million acres of prime farmland will be lost by the year 2000 if the 1967-75 conversion trends continue. This projected loss is only 7 percent of the prime land base (345 million acres), but more than half the estimated high-potential cropland/resource of 40 million acres that can be drawn on. Losses will vary from region to region, being greatest in Atlantic and Pacific coastal States, and least in the central part of the country. A few states, including Florida, New Hampshire, and Rhode Island, could lose nearly all prime lands if past rates continue. Other states, including Illinois, Iowa, and Nebraska, would lose less than five percent. But if one assumes an annual production level of 150 bushels of corn per acre in the Corn Belt, where a loss of 4 percent is projected, then 480 million bushels of corn would be lost annually by the year 2000, at the present levels of production. In the Pacific region, where the estimated loss of prime farmland is 16 percent, 150 million bushels of wheat would be lost annually by the year 2000, assuming average production of 75 bushels per acre (Hidlebaugh 1980).

Of great concern is the fact that the conversion rate has been increasing. The average annual conversion rate was 55 percent higher in the 1967-75 period than in the 1958-1967 period. Brewer and Boxley (1980, pp. 17-19) have proposed four possible explanations for the increased rate:

1. Recent internal migration trends, coupled with changes in the demographic characteristics of the U.S. population, favor large-lot sizes for housing.

2. Substantial and increasing acreages were removed from agriculture by highways and energy rights-of-way.

3. Substantial and increasing acreages of unimproved land were removed from agricultural use, divided into lots, and sold on the interstate land market.

4. Substantial and increasing acreages of agricultural land were disturbed by extractive land-use activities.

DECLINING QUALITY OF AGRICULTURAL LAND

Concern about reduced production capability due to a reduced land base is reinforced by the changing quality of the remaining cropland. SCS has estimated the annual national soil loss caused by sheet, rill, and wind erosion at almost three billion tons, averaging 6.9 tons per acre, despite more than $20 billion the Department of Agriculture has spent since 1935 for soil and water conservation programs (USDA 1979a, p. vii). Results of these expenditures include:

1. more than 115 million acres were contoured and/or stripcropped;
2. more than 2,357,000 farm ponds and impoundments were constructed;
3. on farmland, 1.8 million miles of terraces were installed; and
4. revegetation of 2.5 million acres of surface mine spoils and critical areas were completed.

The importance of the declining quality of the land base, especially the prime farmland portion, is that production potential is reduced. Installation of conservation practices has helped slow land deterioration, but erosion is taking a heavy toll on cropland productivity. (See discussion of erosion in Berry's chapter above).

When nonprime lands are brought into production to replace lost prime farmlands, more acreage is required as well as greater preparation costs per acre to produce a given level of output. Even with installation of conservation practices, these areas are inherently less productive without a substantial infusion of additives, especially fertilizers. A recent study of Guthrie County, Iowa, illustrates this problem (Schmude 1977, p. 241). The study showed that predicted yields of corn were highest "on the classes of land having the highest percentage of prime farmland." These results are shown in Table 3.

Other studies comparing yields of prime and nonprime soils in Appanoose County and Blackhawk County in Iowa indicate similar results (Table 4).

AGRICULTURE AND ENERGY

Energy and agriculture are closely interrelated. First, energy activities take large areas out of production, especially for strip mining and transmission lines. Second, agricultural production on some land may be diverted from food and fiber crops to fuel crops, depending on federal policies and changing fuel prices. Third, energy activities compete with agriculture for a number of scarce resources,

Table 3. Predicted Average Corn Yields from a Soil Survey of Guthrie County, Iowa

Cropland Capability Class/Subclass	Percentage of Land That is Prime	Average Yield Expected (Bushels/Acre)
I	100	113
IIe	87	109
IIw	86	100
IIIe	26	95
IIIw	43	87

Source: Schmude 1977, p. 241.

Table 4. Corn and Soybean Yields in Two Iowa Counties (1977)
(Bushel per Acre)

	Prime Lands	Nonprime Lands
Appanose County*		
Corn	98.5	70.7
Soybeans	37.5	19.2
Blackhawk County†		
Corn	106.0	66.0
Soybeans	40.0	25.0

Source: Dideriksen 1979, p. 3
†*Source*: USDA 1980a.

particularly water. Finally, energy facilities may adversely affect productivity, as with acid rain caused by sulphur emissions from fossil fuel power plants (U.S. Congress 1980, pp. 576-606).

The entire food system, from production through human consumption, uses about 16.5 percent of the energy consumed in this country. Farm production alone consumes three percent of the total. From a second perspective, approximately 8 percent of total farm production costs in 1975 was spent on energy. Approximately $5 billion was expended for fuels and electricity, and another $1 billion for chemical products, primarily fertilizers and pesticides (Van Arsdall and Devlin 1978, p. iii). Changes since 1975 in fuel costs per acre for two major export crops are listed in Table 5.

Energy activities that affect farmland have been summarized by Fletcher (1980 p. 19):

Direct consequences could arise from diversion of land and water resources away from agriculture in order to meet future energy development requirements. In addition, there may be indirect consequences associated with energy development that could affect the availability of agricultural land—stemming from such factors as the sudden introduction of an industrial economy in previously rural areas, increased air pollution, erosion hazards, and disruption of rural communities and their economies.

Table 5. Average Fuel Cost per Acre and Variable Cost per Acre, 1975-79

Year and Crop	Fuel Cost per Acre	Total Variable Cost per Acre	Fuel as a Share of Variable Cost (%)
Corn			
1975	$5.72	$91.21	6.3
1976	6.00	86.39	7.0
1977	7.89	96.41	8.2
1978	8.41	98.27	8.6
1979	11.10	104.80	10.6
Wheat			
1975	4.72	39.50	10.4
1976	4.55	36.20	12.6
1977	4.80	37.24	12.8
1978	5.19	37.64	13.8
1979	6.85	41.35	16.5

Source: Barton 1979, p. 442.

Strip mining is likely to be the largest source of prime farmland conversion. The U.S. Department of the Interior (DOI) has estimated that 10.1 million acres are underlain by strippable coal reserves. About one-fourth of these reserves are located under prime farmland east of the Mississippi (DOI 1979, p. 236). In Illinois, where conflict between strip mining and agricultural land will be severe, 52 percent of the land area where permits have been granted for strip mining is cropland. Indiana, Kentucky, and North Dakota also have much coal underlying prime farmland (Esseks 1979, p. 57). Because of the rapid increase in strip mining during the 1970s, 1.66 million acres already needed reclamation by mid-1977. About 15 percent of this area was cropland (U.S. Congress, 1978, p. 74). Another 430,000 acres are expected to be directly and indirectly altered by strip mining between 1980 and 1985, but new federal policies could accelerate the rate of strip mining (DOI 1979, 47). Over the next 50 years, estimates of land affected by energy development in the northern Great Plains alone range from 240,000 acres to more than 1,470,000 acres. (Northern Great Plains Resources Program 1975, p. 2) (See chapter by Bender et al. below.)

A second major source of conversion will be construction of power plants and transmission lines. A 1977 survey by the Bureau of Mines identified 450 electric generating plants that were proposed or being planned. As more plants are constructed, additional transmission lines will be extended across agricultural regions to serve urban markets. Transmission line rights-of-way occupied 3.3 to 4 million acres of land by 1974. The Federal Power Commission has estimated that an additional 3 million acres will be required by 1990, while the Electric Power Research Institute estimates that the total acreage used for lines will be 5.2 million acres by the year 2000 (Noble 1980; Fletcher 1980, p. 28). The percentage of cropland required for transmission lines in the nine Regional Electric Reliability Council Areas varies from 54 percent in the Upper Midwest to 9 percent in the western states (Noble 1980). Since easements are commonly used to establish rights-of-way, agriculture may use much of the land beneath power lines except during construction. But even after construction, herbicide applications along rights-of-way and poor location of towers can interfere with efficient use of adjacent land. In addition, the effects of high-voltage lines on human health are uncertain (Young 1973).

Other energy activities will also convert agricultural lands, although in smaller amounts. Synfuels development, which could be located in several of the 15 states identified as having adequate coal reserves, will take an unknown amount of land out of production. A small amount of bottom land could be removed by reservoirs located behind new small dams. Finally, communities to house plant construction and operation personnel will spring up in rural areas near new energy-producing facilities and require an additional, but unknown, amount of land.

In 1980 President Carter announced a national goal to produce 500 million gallons of ethanol per year by the end of 1981. If implemented, this would use the yield from approximately 1.9 million acres of corn-producing land for nonfood purposes (assuming 100 bushels per acre and 2.6 gallons of ethanol per bushel) (Fletcher 1980). With the change of administration in 1981, it is not yet clear what future goals for ethanol production will be.

The Department of Energy (DOE) (1979) has taken a broader look at the potential of ethanol production. It projects that 660 million gallons a year is a likely production level by the mid-1980s. DOE analysts also have concluded that as much as 4.7 billion gallons a year are possible, but only if all existing grain land is brought into production. They assume that 14 million acres of sweet sorghum would be needed to provide this feedstock.

The Department of Agriculture has attempted to estimate the amount of land required to produce 8 quads of energy (8 quadrillion BTUs), slightly over 10 percent of the total energy used in the United States in 1977. Eight quads of energy could be produced from 268 million acres of corn acreage of the type found in Indiana. But 724 million acres would be required to produce enough corn under conditions typical of North Dakota, according to Zeimetz (1979), who warns: "to minimize loss of soil, deterioration of soil structure, and water pollution from nonpoint sources will mean that biomass production will have to utilize high quality land and careful management practices." (p. 12)

CONCLUSION

Trends in world demand, farmland decline, and energy considerations have been reviewed. The familiar litany of concern for the preservation of prime farmland gains much force when viewed in the context of emerging export demand and growing energy production from crops. U.S. farm production is a key element of foreign policy and our balance of payments.

As world demand and biomass production continue to grow, and the present supply of prime farmland declines, new lands will be brought into production. But these new lands will usually be of lesser quality, thus requiring more land and energy per unit of output. In Appanoose County, Iowa, for example, corn would require 25 percent more acreage, and soybeans would require nearly twice the acreage, if the same size harvest were sought from nonprime lands. (See Table 4 above.) Conversion of nonprime lands to agriculture requires installation of a variety of conservation practices for drainage, erosion control, irrigation, and so on. Each requires energy for construction and maintenance. Research is needed to develop a more precise accounting of energy and monetary costs associated with bringing poorer quality lands into production.

After conversion, production on nonprime farmlands is also more expensive. For example, 78 trillion BTUs of nitrogen fertilizer per year could be saved by the year 2030 if the present rate of prime farmland conversion were cut in half (USDA 1980a, Part II, pp. 3-257). If more land of poorer quality is brought into production, costs of energy inputs to maintain production and practices will be higher. Growing a larger percentage of crops on poorer-quality lands may also have a number of potential adverse environmental effects, such as increasing rates of erosion and wetland destruction.

Protecting prime agricultural lands can contribute to energy conservation. These savings could be considerable, especially when compared with energy requirements for converting and maintaining production on lands of poorer quality. In a time when all agricultural lands will receive increased pressure to supply the world market, and when energy costs are escalating, to protect the most productive lands makes good economic sense. Additional research is needed to explore relative energy demands for production of major export crops and energy crops on various qualities of land. Such studies should contribute to the growing public dialogue concerning the need to protect prime farmland.

References

Abel, M. 1980. Growth in Demand for U.S. Crop and Animal Production by 2005. Unpublished paper prepared for Resources for the Future, Washington, D.C.

Barton, W. 1979. Energy Inputs. 1980 Agricultural Outlook. Paper prepared for the Senate Committee on Agriculture, Nutrition, and Forestry. Washington: U.S. Government Printing Office (hereafter cited U.S.G.P.O.)

Brewer, M., and Boxley, R. 1980. The Potential Supply of Cropland. Unpublished paper prepared for Resources for the Future, Washington, D.C.

Crossen, P. 1977. Demand for Food and Fiber: Implications for Land Use in the United States. *Land Use: Tough Choices in Today's World* Special Publication No. 22. Ankeny, Iowa: Soil Conservation Society of America, pp. 49-61.

————. 1980. Future Economic and Environmental Costs of Agricultural Land. Unpublished paper prepared for Resources for the Future, Washington, D.C.

Dideriksen, R. 1979. Affidavit submitted to the U.S. District Court for the Southern District of Iowa in *Star Coal Co. v. Cecil Andrus.*

Esseks, J.D. 1979. Nonurban Competition for Farmland. In *Farmland, Food and the Future,* ed. Max Schnepf, pp. 49-66. Ankeny, Iowa: Soil Conservation Society of America.

Fletcher, W. 1980. *Farmland and Energy: Conflicts in the Making.* Paper prepared for the National Agricultural Lands Study. Washington: American Land Forum.

Frey, H. T. 1979. *Major Uses of Land in the United States: 1974.* Agricultural Economic Report No. 440. Washington: USDA, Economics, Statistics and Cooperatives Service.

Hidlebaugh, A. 1980. *Projected Losses of Prime Farmland.* Unpublished paper prepared for the National Agricultural Lands Study. Washington, D.C.

Lee, L. K. 1978. *A Perspective on Cropland Availability.* Agricultural Economic Report No. 406. Washington: USDA, Economics, Statistics, and Cooperatives Service.

National Agricultural Lands Study 1981a. *Final Report.* Washington: U.S.D.A. and C.E.Q.

————. 1981b. *Summary of Final Report.* Washington: U.S.D.A. and C.E.Q.

Noble, J. 1980. Electrical Energy Transmission and the Conversion of Agricultural Lands. Unpublished paper prepared for the National Agricultural Lands Study. Washington, D.C.

Northern Great Plains Resources Program. 1975. *Effects of Coal Development in the Northern Great Plains: A Review of Major Issues and Consequences at Different Rates of Development.* Denver: NGPRP.

Schmude, K. O. 1977. A Perspective on Prime Farmland. *Journal of Soil and Water Conservation* 32: 240-242.

U.S. Congress 1978. Senate Committee on Governmental Affairs. *The Coal Industry: Problems and Prospects.* Washington: U.S.G.P.O.

————. 1980. House Committee on Interstate and Foreign Commerce, Subcommittee on Oversight and Investigations. *Hearings on Acid Rain.* Washington: U.S.G.P.O.

U.S. Department of Agriculture 1971. *Foreign Agriculture Trade of the United States.* (Economic Research Service). Washington: U.S.G.P.O.

————. 1977. *Potential Cropland Study.* Soil Conservation Service Stat. Bull. No. 578. Washington: U.S.G.P.O.

————. 1979a. Executive Summary: Activities of the Land and Water Task Force. Unpublished report prepared for the Senate Committee on Agriculture, Nutrition and Forestry. Washington: U.S.D.A.

————. 1979b. *1979 Handbook of Agricultural Charts.* Agricultural Handbook No. 561. Washington: U.S.D.A.

————. 1980a. *Appraisal 1980: Parts I and II* (Review Draft). Washington: U.S.D.A.

————. 1980b. *Outlook for U.S. Agricultural Exports* (Economics, Statistics, and Cooperatives Service). Washington: U.S.G.P.O.

U.S. Department of Energy. 1979. *Report of the Alcohol Fuels Policy Review.* Washington: U.S.G.P.O.

U.S. Department of the Interior. 1979. *Final Environmental Impact Statement on Section 501(b) Regulations* (Office of Surface Mining Reclamation and Enforcement). Washington: U.S.G.P.O.

Van Arsdell, R.T., and Devlin, P.J. 1978. *Energy Policies: Price Impacts on the U.S. Food System.* Agric. Econ. Report No. 407. Washington: U.S.G.P.O.

Young, L. B. 1973. *Power Over People.* New York: Oxford University Press.

Zeimetz, K. A. 1979. *Growing Energy: Land for Biomass Farms.* Agric. Econ. Report No. 425. Washington: U.S.D.A.

On the Need
for Farmland Policy

Barry Smit

The conversion of land from farming to nonagricultural uses has generated concern in many parts of North America. As lands once used for agriculture are converted for housing, industry, forestry, and other activities, there is reaction to the changes and anxiety over future food supplies. It is in this context that both Berry and Zinn stress the need for land use policy, or more specifically, the need for policy to preserve land for agricultural use. Of course, other items are addressed, but the fundamental question that is raised, and the one I wish to focus upon, is whether land should be retained (by policy) for agricultural activities.

In discussions of farmland policy, many people start from the assumption that we *should* preserve land (or "prime" land) for agriculture. Berry and Zinn wisely point out that the *need* for such policies must be clearly demonstrated or such policies will not be enacted. I would go further to argue that such policies should not even be contemplated unless their need is clearly illustrated. The costs of intervention in the land market, both costs to individuals and regulatory costs, are such that we have an *obligation* to ensure that policy is absolutely necessary before we devise and implement such policy. Thus, to propose some policy that might prevent or discourage nonagricultural uses on certain areas or types of land, we need first to demonstrate that it is especially important that these lands be kept available for agriculture. In other words, we need to evaluate these lands for agriculture relative to other uses, and we need to show that this land is crucial for agriculture.

Berry and Zinn address this issue in chapters 11 and 12 in this volume. I find their arguments both exciting and disappointing, an assessment that requires some clarification.

First, both authors are concerned with the use of the land resource in the long term. They acknowledge that there may be no shortage of land for agriculture now or in 5 years, but they are concerned with the situation fifty years from now. Land use for the next ten years is largely determined already, and we should be attempting to estimate the implications of these and other trends for food supply and other goals over the long run.

Second, Berry and Zinn are somewhat uneasy about relying upon the market mechanism to allocate land uses to satisfy food needs in the long term. The lack of confidence in the market mechanism has been acknowledged by others (Raup 1976; Gibson 1977). The short-term nature of the market may not ensure that fundamental societal requirements from the land are met.

Third, Berry and Zinn are concerned with the use of land from a societal point of view, rather than from the perspective of a particular local area or individual. Often these interests are not the same. For instance, it might be in the best interest of a region (from the point of view of tax base) to encourage urban-industrial development; yet if this region is the only one in the country that can produce certain needed food crops, then an urban-industrial orientation might not be in the interest of the country as a whole. It is important that some researchers address the comprehensive picture so that such implications for local areas can be identified.

Fourth, both authors acknowledge that land use planning cannot be based simply upon a knowledge of the capability of soil for agriculture. We often hear the argument: this land is prime for a particular use, therefore we should preserve it for that use. But this does not necessarily follow. To illustrate, if a vast area of land is ideally suited to pea production, should we introduce policies to retain all of this land for peas? Surely the answer depends on, among other things, how many peas we need and how much land can produce peas elsewhere.

Berry and Zinn point out that we cannot argue for the protection of land for agriculture unless we can demonstrate a need for agricultural products, to satisfy domestic or world food needs or to earn foreign exchange. Such needs represent goals from the use of the land. Land-use planning becomes necessary when it appears that such fundamental goals might not be met without some kind of control over the use of land. Whether certain areas of land are especially important for agriculture depends upon other goals and constraints as well. For example, energy availability may influence our evaluation of land: if there is less energy available to produce food, there is likely to be less flexibility in the ways in which the land can be used to meet food requirements and other goals.

Although it may not have been their intent, these papers provide a useful basis for an evaluation of land for agriculture. The importance of areas or types of land for agriculture depends upon the constraints and goals that are identified or assumed. Thus:

   —if we know that there are certain areas of different types of land available, and
   —if we know that these have certain yields and associated input requirements, and
   —if we have only so much energy available, and
   —if we want to produce certain amounts of food commodities,

then we should be able to identify:

—the degree of flexibility that exists in the use of the land—that is, under the stated conditions, can the food goals be met easily or is there little choice in how the land can be used if the goals are to be met? and

—the areas in which agriculture is especially important—that is, which particular land areas are crucial for agriculture if the goals are to be met?

This approach to identifying areas that might need to be retained for agriculture is based upon the construction of scenarios. The evaluation of land for agriculture depends upon the conditions and goals that are specified or assumed. Thus we can ask under what conditions (population growth, consumption patterns, production technologies, etc.), and with what goals (food requirements, etc.), is there little flexibility in the use of land for agriculture, and where are the critical areas? This type of approach, suggested by Berry and Zinn, provides a comprehensive alternative to the simple assessment of land capability as the basis for land planning.

The major disappointment with these chapters is that in evaluating the importance of land areas for agriculture, the authors make no explicit recognition of the *nonagricultural* demands for land. Surely it is not good enough for us to say "from the point of view of agriculture, this land is prime for agriculture, and therefore we should have policy to retain it in agriculture." Consider the reaction if someone stated, "this land is prime for forestry and therefore should be retained for forestry," or "this land is prime for housing and therefore should be retained for housing," or "this land is prime for mineral extraction and therefore should be used for extraction." Such statements are simplistic and ill-founded, largely because they do not consider all of the various requirements from the land. It is equally myopic, however, to base land use policy *simply* upon the capability of the land for agriculture and the requirements from agriculture.

I stress this point for two reasons. The first relates to our credibility as scientists. In evaluating land for agriculture, we should recognize the legitimate needs for land for nonagricultural uses. These represent additional constraints and goals pertaining to the land, which will affect the flexibility in the use of land. Some uses have much more flexibility than others. Nonagricultural uses can be incorporated into the scheme outlined earlier. Thus, given the various goals relating to land (food, timber, minerals, housing, water, recreation, etc.), we can determine the extent to which these goals are compatible (given the land base and other conditions), and we can identify areas that are crucial for particular uses. Such an approach would represent a comprehensive evaluation of one land use relative to others (Smit et al. 1979).

The second reason is a pragmatic one. If we wish to convince politicians and the public at large that land use controls are necessary, then we should be able to put forward a comprehensive assessment of the options that are open; and this assessment should be for all uses, not forestry in isolation, nor housing in isolation, nor mining in isolation, nor agriculture in isolation. We should be able to demonstrate that, given our requirements for food, timber, minerals, housing space, and so on, certain areas of land are strategically important for particular uses.

Not only is this type of comprehensive evaluation necessary, it *can* be done. Land use models already exist that include information on land areas, yields, and so on. We could modify and extend these models to examine the degree of flexibility that exists in the use of land for both agricultural *and* nonagricultural activities. Without such assessments we really have little basis for advocating land use policy.

References

Gibson, J.A. 1977. On the Allocation of Prime Agricultural Land. *Journal of Soil and Water Conservation* 32 (6): 271-275.

Raup, P.M. 1976 What is Prime Land?. *Journal of Soil and Water Conservation* 31 (5): 180-181.

Smit, B.; Phillips, T.P.; deGrosbois, E.B.; and Cipl, M.E. 1979. *Development of Land Use Allocation-Evaluation Models for Ontario.* University of Guelph, Centre for Resources Development Publication No. 93.

VI. Remote Sensing Data for Rural America

Integration of Digital Land Use Data in South Carolina

David J. Cowen

INTRODUCTION

The purpose of this paper is to demonstrate some of the current technical capabilities available to geographers for the automated analyses and display of land use information. Further, an attempt has been made to provide a comparative basis for the evaluation of the utility of the U.S. Geological Survey (USGS) Land Use and Land Cover Maps (Loelkes 1977) for different types of analyses. The presentation extracts examples from four projects that have been completed in South Carolina during the last two years. The figures used in the paper demonstrate the proficiency of the University of South Carolina's Computer Services Division in the field of geographical data processing. That group, comprised of three geographers working in conjunction with researchers in the Department of Geography, has assembled an impressive set of hardware and software capabilities designed to serve the needs of various state agencies. These services are coordinated through the Office of Geographical Statistics of the South Carolina Division of Research and Statistical Services. The establishment and philosophy of this partnership have been discussed elsewhere (Cowen et al. 1979; 1980).

Land Use/Land Cover Mapping for the Coastal Zone

In April 1978 a decision was made to utilize the USGS land use and land cover data to inventory and display land use information for the State Coastal Zone Management Plan. In order to accomplish this task, the university transferred and installed the USGS Geographical Information Retrieval and Analysis System (GIRAS) (Mitchell et al. 1977). This complex software system was

The assistance of the University of South Carolina Computer Services Division and the Department of Geography's Cartography Lab is gratefully acknowledged for the production of the illustrations used in this paper.

211

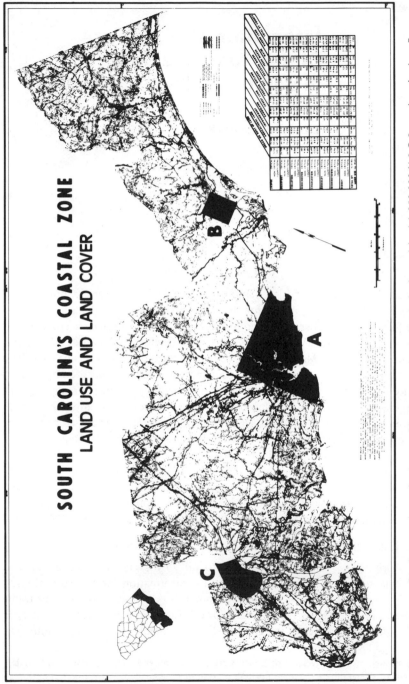

Figure 1. Base map for the coastal zone land use and land cover map. Area A is the James Island 1:250,000 U.S.G.S. quadrangle. Area B is the Georgetown South 7½ minute quadrangle. Area C is the Coosawhatchie Swamp drainage basin.

utilized to input, edit, scale, analyze, and finally map the land use and land cover for an eight-county coastal area (Fig. 1). In actuality, the area encompasses segments of five 1:250,000 maps that had been prepared previously by the USGS Geography Program as part of its nationwide land use and land cover mapping program. Two of the maps were supplied to the state in digital form; the other three had to be digitized and edited by the staff of the university.

GIRAS consists of a valuable set of tools for the geographer involved in land-use analyses. It includes an extremely efficient input algorithm (ATP) for forming topologically complete land use polygons with a minimum of map-labelling and bookkeeping. Further, it can form extremely complex polygons automatically by chaining arcs and then check for internal islands or completely surrounded land-use categories. The system also contains a versatile mapping program (SHADE) that retrieves the digital land-use files and enables users to design their own shading patterns to display the information selectively. For example, GIRAS efficiently handled the complex land-use patterns presented by the imbedded islands of wetlands and agriculture in the northeastern section of the James Island Quadrangle (Fig. 2). Another advantage of the algorithm is its ability to output single categories (Fig. 3). By means of this process, a set of polygon boundaries for the eight coastal counties was scribed on the university's flatbed plotter. Open-window negatives of Level I land use and land cover (Anderson et al. 1976) were then produced to generate the composite color map for the Coastal Zone (Fig. 4). The polygon-to-grid (PTG) and area-sum programs were used to generate land-use statistics at the county level, both inside and outside the critical area of the coastal zone. Through a cooperative agreement with the Department of Geography and the Social and Behavioral Sciences Laboratory at the University of South Carolina, the USGS is presently improving the documentation of GIRAS and developing a set of training materials that will help clarify the concepts of the system.

GEORGETOWN DEMONSTRATION PROJECT

Although GIRAS provided the university with excellent input and display programs, there remained a need for a more complete system, capable of interrelating various types of geographical information into a total geographical information system. Following an extensive survey of existing software, the university decided to acquire the PIOS and GRID systems from the Environmental Systems Research Institute of Redlands, California. The capabilities of these systems were evaluated in a demonstration project conducted for Georgetown, South Carolina (Fig. 5), an important steel and paper producing center on the coast (Area B on Fig. 1).

The demonstration project consisted of a simulation of the type of land use analysis that would be required for the evaluation of a potential site for a barge terminal. The inputs for the analysis required the digitizing of 14 different variables for a 4-quadrangle area. The complete coverage variables included land

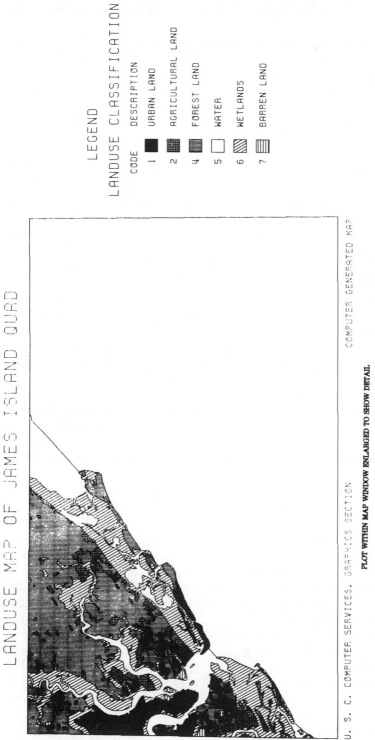

LANDUSE MAP OF JAMES ISLAND QUAD

LEGEND
LANDUSE CLASSIFICATION

CODE	DESCRIPTION
1	URBAN LAND
2	AGRICULTURAL LAND
4	FOREST LAND
5	WATER
6	WETLANDS
7	BARREN LAND

U. S. C. COMPUTER SERVICES, GRAPHICS SECTION   COMPUTER GENERATED MAP

PLOT WITHIN MAP WINDOW ENLARGED TO SHOW DETAIL

Figure 2. GIRAS computer-generated plot of Level I land use and land cover. Note the complex polygon structure created by the forest pattern.

Urban Land Use Of James Island Quad

Figure 3. Electrostatic plot of single feature Level I land use and land cover for the James Island quadrangle.

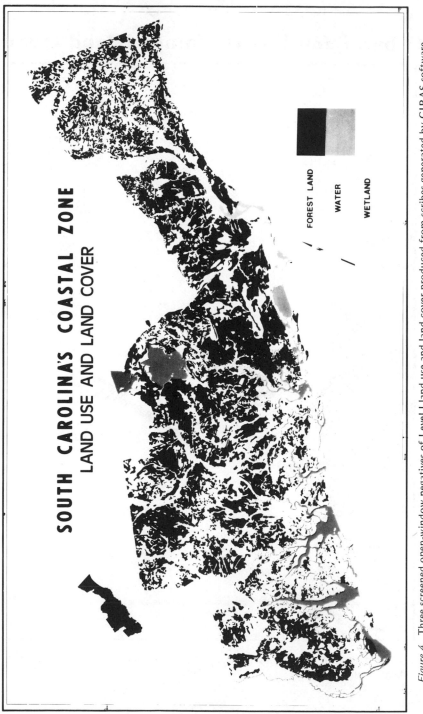

SOUTH CAROLINA'S COASTAL ZONE
LAND USE AND LAND COVER

FOREST LAND

WATER

WETLAND

Figure 4. Three screened open-window negatives of Level I land use and land cover produced from scribes generated by GIRAS software.

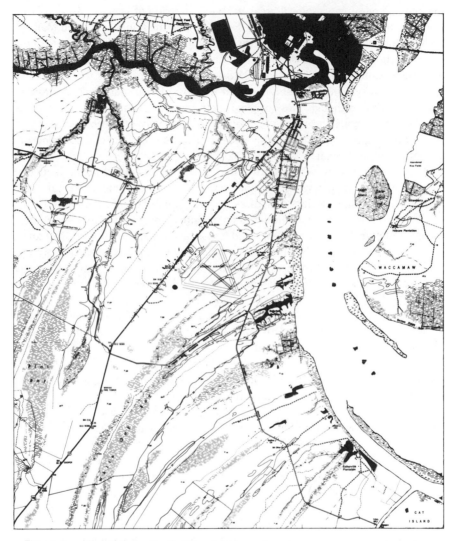

Figure 5.   Georgetown South 7½ minute quadrangle.

use/wetlands, soils, zoning, flood-prone areas, and water quality. Point data included bench marks, historical sites, and rookeries; the linear features consisted of transportation arteries and utility lines. With the GRID system, 13 additional interpreted variables, such as slope and distance from utilities, were generated from the original data. The resultant 27-layer data file formed the basis for subsequent analytical operations.

The construction of the grid-based data files represents a major advance in technical and philosophical thinking about the automatic handling of geographical information. Typically, the earlier natural-resource system relied on the manual coding of geographical areas by the conversion of irregular areas to arbitrary and usually very crude grid cells. For example, the Minnesota Land Management Information System (Robinette and Nordstand 1978, p. 262), utilized a 40-acre cell, while the Maryland Automated Geographical Information (Dangermond and Antenucci 1974) used a 91.8-acre cell. Regardless of the fineness of the grid, such systems invariably resulted in a loss of information (Tomlinson et al. 1976). Thus, although these original methods were readily adaptable to line-printer output maps and simple manipulation by matrix operations in standard statistical packages, they were also widely criticized for lack of detail and unattractive output format.

The desire for more accurate information not only resulted in the increased use of electronic digitizing devices and incremental plotters, but also created the need for more complex data-structures and programming tasks (Schmidt 1977). For example, the area calculation and composite mapping tasks that had merely involved simple frequency counts and cross-tabulations with grid structures, required sophisticated polygon overlay routines when the data elements became the actual boundaries of the areas. Furthermore, although an incremental plotter could easily draw the boundaries of such areas, it proved to be inefficient for shading or filling the areas with a dense pattern. The development of inexpensive raster-based elestrostatic plotters and color graphics terminals provided an opportunity to utilize the best of both systems (Peuquet 1979, pp. 130-132). Current concepts often incorporate manual or automated digitizing of lines (arcs) from stable base maps, interactive editing to construct clean topologically accurate data files, and software conversion of the polygons to fine cells or rasters that can be manipulated and displayed easily.

One aspect of the demonstration involved the digitizing of the land use/wetlands map (Fig. 6) as a series of chains and nodes that were plotted on mylar as a set of polygons. Once the same information was converted into one-acre cells, the task of displaying the map more clearly as a series of shaded or patterned areas on an electrostatic plotter was simplified (Fig. 7). An additional benefit of the electrostatic plotter is derived from its ability to display square cells at almost any size without the inherent distortion that often accompanies line-printer maps. The resultant data base can produce accurate line plots for a cartographic product or a grid system that can be easily displayed and integrated with other data for analytical operations. For example, in the Georgetown demonstration project, each one-acre cell contained a total of 27 individual codes. The final suitability map (Fig. 8) was generated by a grid-modelling routine that utilized a set of weights assigned by planners at the Coastal Council. This project applied current technological capabilities and data base concepts to generate a type of analysis that could never have been undertaken by simply employing conventional methods. The most significant benefit of the approach is its ability to generate easily a number of similar maps based on varying suitability weightings developed by individuals or groups with opposing viewpoints.

Flatbed Plot

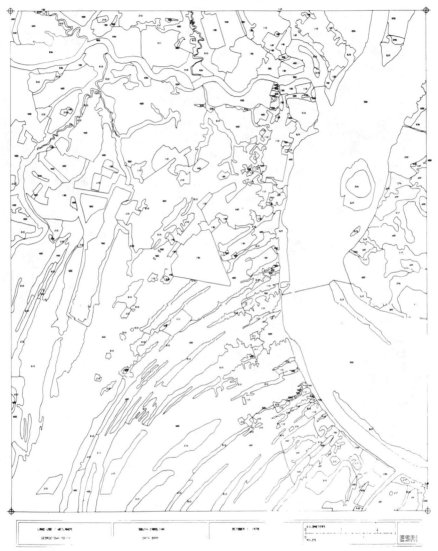

Figure 6. Georgetown South land use/wetlands data compiled from low altitude infrared photography. Map plotted on flatbed plotter with PIOS.

Electrostatic Plot

☐ RESIDENTIAL
☐ COMMERCIAL
☐ TRANSPORTATION/INSTITUTIONAL
☐ FIELD AGRICULTURE/FEEDING OPERATIONS
▦ ORCHARDS AND VINEYARDS

▦ FOREST
■ FORESTED WETLANDS
■ BRUSH AND UNFORESTED
▦ MARSH
■ ABANDONED RICE/MARSH
      AND BEACHES

Figure 7. Georgetown South land use/wetlands data represented as one acre cells. Map plotted on an electrostatic plotter with GRID program.

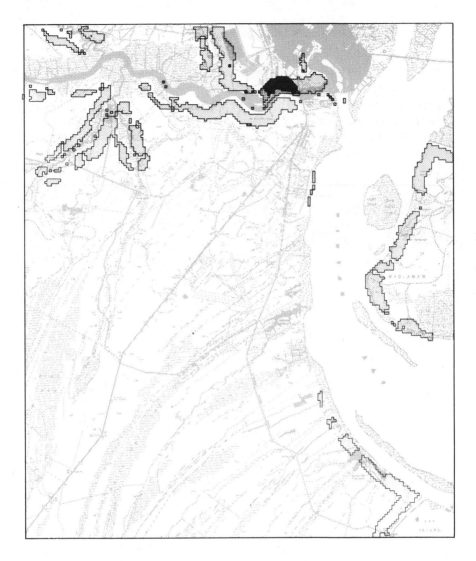

☐ VERY LOW SUITABILITY
▦ LOW SUITABILITY
■ MODERATE SUITABILITY
▦ HIGH SUITABILITY
■ VERY HIGH SUITABILITY

Figure 8. Georgetown South barge site suitability model generated from 27 layer file with ESRI software.

A COMPARISON OF USGS AND LANDSAT DATA

The analysis demonstrated in the Georgetown project utilized data that were collected and converted to digital form specifically for the analysis; but it has become increasingly possible to obtain land-use information that is already in digital form. Both the USGS Land Use/Land Cover Mapping Program and the LANDSAT program now provide such digital data. An examination of the information displayed in Figures 9 and 10 provides a visual comparison of these two data-sources for the Georgetown South 7½-minute quadrangle. These figures

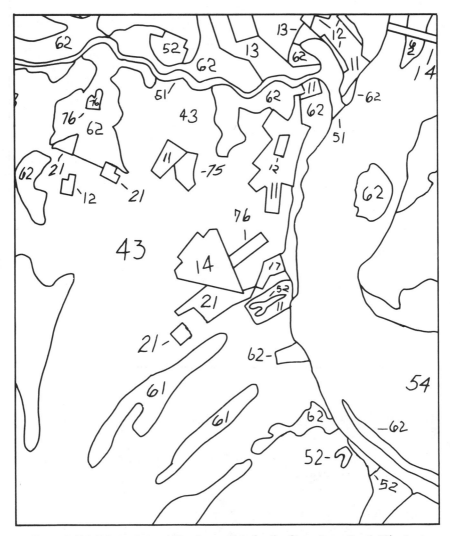

Figure 9. U.S.G.S. land use and land cover data for the Georgetown South 7½ minute quadrangle.

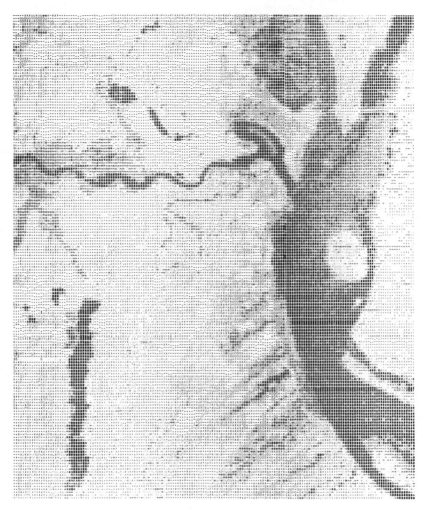

Figure 10. January 1979 LANDSAT data for the Georgetown area. Image generated on lineprinter depicting individual pixels.

can also be compared to the land use/wetlands map (Fig. 6) compiled from low-altitude photography. The USGS data, which are interpreted from high-altitude (60,000 to 65,000 feet) photography, utilize a minimum mapping unit of 40 acres except for urban and agriculture land uses or water bodies, which are identified as small as 10 acres. This photography produces a consistent Level II classification (Anderson et al. 1976) with boundary lines that are highly accurate.

The LANDSAT data have proven to be quite useful for classifying and mapping large areas of homogeneous land cover. They do not enable one to generate Level II classifications consistently and are not suitable for mapping at a large scale. The major advantage of the LANDSAT data for land use analysis are their digital raster format and the continuous coverage on a nine-day cycle. Other benefits include their objectivity, cost effectiveness, availability for large areas, and potential for temporal and spatial change detection analysis (Knapp and Rider 1979, p. 9). Some of the disadvantages of LANDSAT for land use analysis include problems of geographical registration, geometric correction, image quality, and accuracy of the classification procedures. Some of these technical problems will be alleviated as the LANDSAT system is transferred into an operational status with the Department of Commerce by 1983. Now that some of the uncertainty associated with the initially experimental program has been eliminated, data formats and processing procedures can be expected to stabilize. The USGS has experimented with the use of LANDSAT data to assist in its interpretation process, especially in areas of dense forests, tundra, icecaps and large agricultural land uses.

The academic geographer is only beginning to benefit from the availability of both automated data handling capabilities and digital data. The availability of these tools is supported by a myriad of state and federal legislation that demands that natural resource information be measured, analyzed, and displayed. A major impetus for land-use analyses has been the Environmental Protection Agency's 208 program, which addresses issues dealing with nonpoint source water pollution. A major determinant of such pollution is the land use within a drainage basin. The information needed to analyze the potential runoff can be extracted by overlaying a digital land use file with the boundaries of the drainage basins. In order to test this approach in South Carolina, a map of drainage basins was compiled and digitized for a section of the Savannah 1:250,000 land use and land cover map. An interface program was used to link the GIRAS data files to the Polygon Information Overlay System (PIOS) to elicit the land-use information for each drainage basin. One of these basins (Fig. 11) is identified as area C on Figure 1. As the land use and land cover files are completed for the state, the Department of Health and Environmental Control will be able to integrate the information into its 208 program. Unfortunately, such information was unavailable at the beginning of the project.

GREENVILLE PILOT PROJECT

The most recent project undertaken by the university's Graphics Section involves the production of a set of nine color maps and related statistical summaries of farmland in Greenville County (Fig. 12). Ideally, the Department of Agriculture would like to promote national, state, and local governmental cooperation in order to obtain a meaningful display of the nation's farmlands. Information would provide an important inventory of one of the country's most precious natural resources as well as much-needed data for assessing the value of rural land. In accordance with these needs, the Graphics Section, in cooperation with the State Division of Research and Statistical Services and the Land Resource

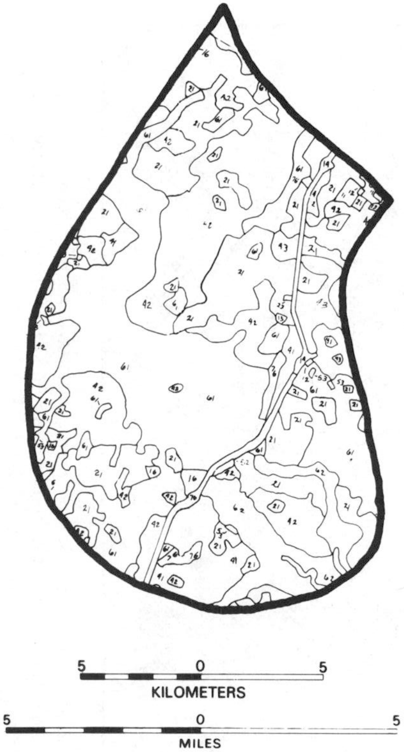

Level II Land Use and Land Cover [1]	Area (Acres)
11. Residential	475.4
12. Commercial	16.1
13. Industrial	32.4
14. Transportation, Communication and Utilities	494.6
16. Mixed Urban or Built-up Land	446.8
21. Cropland and Pasture	13,695.4
23. Confined Feeding Operations	15.4
24. Other Agricultural Land	14.5
32. Shrub and Brush Rangeland	142.4
41. Deciduous Forest Land	1,022.0
42. Evergreen Forest Land	16,728.5
43. Mixed Forest Land	616.3
52. Streams and Canals	57.1
53. Reservoirs	63.0
61. Forested Wetland	18,658.7
62. Non-forested Wetland	1,461.5
76. Transitional Areas	793.5
Total	54,733.6

1. For definitions of Level II categories see U.S. Geological Survey Professional Paper 964, A Land Use and Land Cover Classification System for Use With Remote Sensor Data, 1976, by Anderson, J.R., E.E. Hardy, J.T. Roach and R.E. Witmer.

Figure 11. U.S.G.S. land use and land cover map and statistics for Coosawhatchie Swamp drainage basin. Statistics generated by PIOS after conversion from GIRAS data structure.

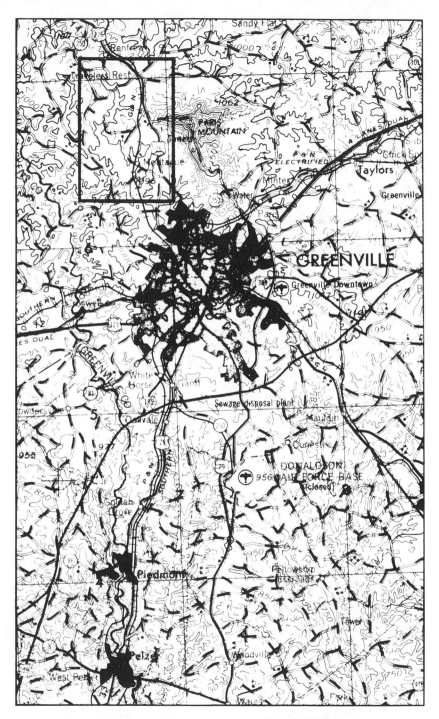

Figure 12. 1:250,000 U.S.G.S. topographic quadrangle for the Greenville, S.C. vicinity. Box indicates detailed study area for important farmlands. Mapping included in examples.

Conservation Commission, undertook the ambitious project of mapping farm-lands in the upstate county. On the basis of published soil surveys and other material relating to slope and drainage, base maps were compiled and digitized using the PIOS system. The categories consisted of prime agricultural land, land of statewide importance, urban land, water, and other lands. A section of a shaded plot depicting an area on the northern fringe of Greenville is illustrated in Figure 13. The production of the final color printed map involved the scribing of the polygon boundaries (Fig. 14) on the plotter and production of open-window negatives from peelcoats for each category. The screened negative, in conjunction with a map of the culture of the area (Fig. 15), was used by a com-mercial printer to produce 500 copies of the final maps at a scale of 1:50,000. A section of the USGS Land Use and Land Cover Map for the same area (Fig. 16) is included for comparison.

The production of the important farmlands maps represents merely one aspect of a major geographical data base presently being assembled for Greenville County. The total effort includes remonumentation of the geodetic controls, creation of high quality aerial photography, and digital production of new tax maps. Another project currently underway in the county involves an analysis of the energy available from existing timber stands. This study will combine LANDSAT data for the forest classification, with accessibility measures deter-mined from a digital road network file and slope measures derived from a digital terrain model (DTM) (American Society for Photogrammetry 1978). The DTM being used in the study was obtained from data available from the Defense Mapping Agency on computer compatible tape through the National Carto-graphic Information Center (NCIC). These data correspond to the elevation information contained on the 1:250,000 U.S.G.S. topographic quadrangles. Such DTMs represent an excellent source of digital data, which can be combined with land-use information for a variety of analytical purposes. By linking a sec-tion of the DTM to the topographic programs of the Environmental Systems Research Institute's GRID System, it was possible to generate a three-dimensional perspective view of Paris Mountain for the study area in Greenville County (Fig. 17). Additional analytical capabilities include contour mapping, diffusion, sun intensity, slope, aspect, drainage, and viewshed calculations (Fig. 18).

CONCLUSION

The purpose of this paper has been to demonstrate some of the possibilities for digital land use analysis that are now available to the research community. The examples used in the paper were generated by operational software in a pro-duction-type setting. Within the last five years, a number of public agencies and private companies have purchased entirely integrated hardware and software systems to handle a full range of geographical information systems functions. These systems often use menus and English-language commands to perform the required operations. The standardization of software, as well as the declining

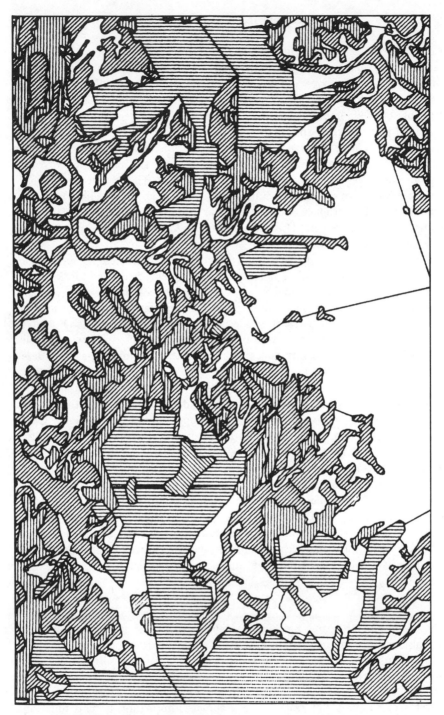

Figure 13. Shade plot of farmland categories for the study area north of Greenville. Map plotted with PIOS software on flatbed plotter.

Figure 14. Polygon outlines of farmland categories produced from a scribe produced on a flatbed plotter.

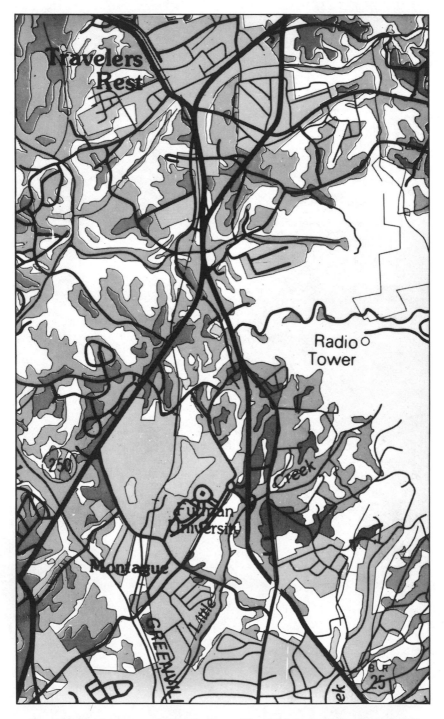

Figure 15. Screened open-window negatives of farmland categories produced from peelcoat.

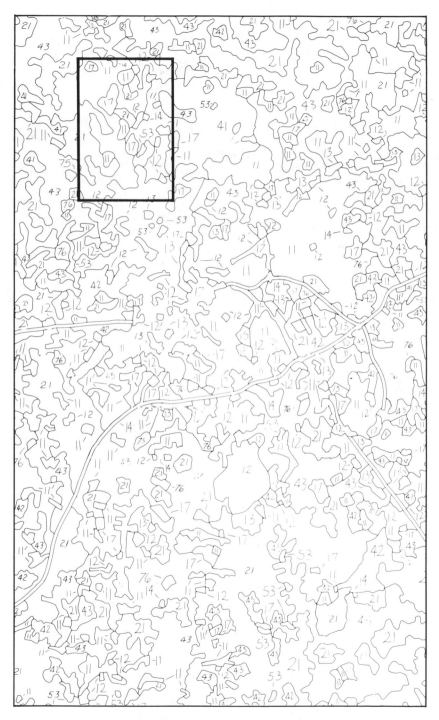

Figure 16. Land use and land cover map of the same area shown in Figure 12.

Figure 17. Three-dimensional perspective view of Paris Mountain, north of Greenville. Plot generated on electrostatic plotter from digital terrain model with VIEWS program.

cost of micro-electronics, have made such alternatives practical and cost-efficient for production-oriented organizations. In addition, the extensive research and development programs of the federal government have enabled sophisticated software systems such as GIRAS (USGS) and MOSS (Fish and Wildlife Service) to become available in the public domain. It may be suggested that the previous decades of research and development in computer graphics and related areas of geographical data handling are beginning to pay real dividends in 1980. With both the information and the analytical tools required for land-use analysis becoming increasingly available, geographers are facing a challenge to their imaginative abilities to address and analyze some of the country's most pressing problems.

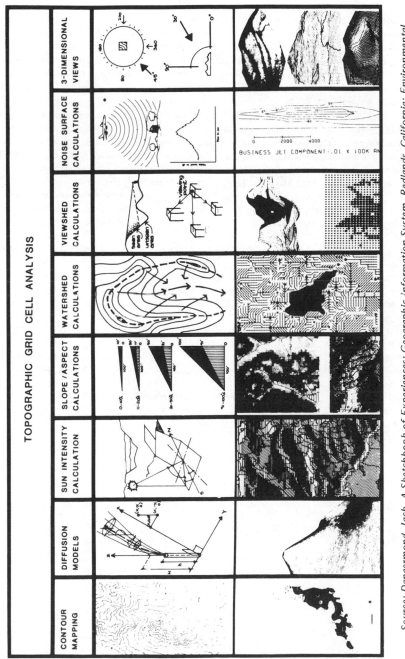

Source: Dangermond, Jack, A Sketchbook of Experiences: Geographic information System, Redlands, California: Environmental Systems Research Institute, p. 20.

Figure 18. Possible analytical and graphical products that can be generated from digital terrain models.

References

American Society of Photogrammetry. 1978. *Proceedings of the Digital Terrain Models (DTM) Symposium.*

Anderson, J.R.; Hardy, E.E.; Roach, J.T.; and Witmer, R.E. 1976. *A Land Use and Land Cover Classification System for Use With Remote Sensor Data.* U.S. Geological Survey Professional Paper 964. Washington, D.C. Government Printing Office.

Cowen, D.; Walters, G.; Feinberg, K.; Holland, M; and Vang, A. 1979. The evolution of the South Carolina mapping program. *Computer Mapping in Education, Research and Medicine.* Cambridge, Mass.: Harvard University Laboratory for Computer Graphics and Spatial Analysis, pp. 29-36.

Cowen, D.; Vang, A.; and Waddell, J. 1980. The South Carolina geographical information system: The role of the state and the university in system implementation. *Urban, Regional and State Government Applications of Computer Mapping.* Cambridge, Mass.: Harvard University Laboratory for Computer Graphics and Spatial Analyses, pp. 48-58.

Dangermond, J., and Antenucci, J. 1974. *Maryland Automated Geographic Information System.* Baltimore, Md.: Maryland Department of State Planning.

Knapp, E., and Rider, D. 1979. Automated geographic information systems and landsat data: A survey. *Computer Mapping in Natural Resources and the Environment.* Cambridge, Mass.: Harvard University Laboratory for Computer Graphics and Spatial Analysis, pp. 57-68.

Loelkes, George L. Jr. 1977. *Specifications for Land Use and Land Cover and Associated Maps.* Reston, Va.: U.S. Geological Survey.

Mitchell, W.; Guptill, S.; Anderson, K.; Fegeas, R.; and Hallam, C. 1977. *GIRAS: A Geographic Information Retrieval and Analysis System for Handling Land Use and Land Cover Data.* U.S. Geological Survey Professional Paper 1059, Washington, D.C.: U.S. Government Printing Office.

Peuquet, D. 1979. Raster processing: an alternative approach to automated cartographic data handling. *The American Cartographer* 6 (2): 129-139.

Robinette, A., and Nordstrand, E. 1978. A resource information system developed by user applications. *Proceedings — Urban and Regional Information Systems Association:* 255-267.

Schmidt, Allan. 1977. *An Advanced Study Symposium on Topological Data Structure for Geographical Information Systems.* Cambridge, Mass.: Harvard University Laboratory for Computer Graphics and Spatial Analysis.

Tomlinson, R.; Calkins, H.; and Marble, D. 1976. *Computer Handling of Geographical Data.* Paris: UNESCO Press.

Rural Land Resource Data Systems: Experience from the Catskills

Paul R. Baumann

In 1975 the Schoharie County Planning and Development Agency (New York) and the Department of Geography, State University of New York at Oneonta entered into a cooperative arrangement referred to as the Schoharie County Cooperative Program. Under this program, several projects based on computer-geographic techniques have been undertaken by the Department of Geography for the planning and development agency. One major project has been the development of a county-wide computerized environmental information system. This information system has been given the acronym SCOGIS, *Scho*harie *CO*unty *G*eographic *I*nformation *S*ystem. The primary purpose of SCOGIS is to provide the decision-makers and planning officials of Schoharie County with a means to analyze and to display environmental data related to various county planning and development problems. This chapter is a report on the development of this information system and the difficulties being encountered in persuading planning officials and decision makers to utilize the system.

Schoharie County is a large rural county located on the northern edge of the Catskill region in upper New York State. It faces the problems of high unemployment, decline in agricultural production, increase in absentee ownership of land, and demands on its water resources from the New York metropolitan area. Many planning decisions related to these and other problems must be made at the county level, but often these decisions are based only on empirical information tinted by emotions. Factual information is either not readily available or not in a format that can be interpreted easily. SCOGIS is designed to provide the county with a means to ascertain environmental data rapidly and in a format easily understood so that county officials can make informed decisions.

SCHOHARIE COUNTY GEOGRAPHIC
INFORMATION SYSTEM

Geo-Data Bank

SCOGIS consists of two integral components: a geo-data bank and a computer software package. The geo-data bank contains environmental data collected and organized to conform to the Universal Transverse Mercator (UTM) geographic reference system. Data available in this geo-data bank relate to four main categories: terrain, land use, selected cultural features, and soil. These categories, and the specific variables associated with them, were selected on the basis of the character and the needs of the county. None of these data were collected firsthand; they were either extrapolated or interpolated from secondary sources. Terrain data were acquired from the 7½-minute United States Geological Survey (USGS) maps. Elevation values were extrapolated from these maps and used to interpolate slope, relative relief, and aspect. Land-use and selected cultural data were taken from land use maps prepared for the New York State Temporary Commission to Study the Catskills. These maps are at the scale of 1:24000 and correspond in coverage with the USGS maps. Aerial photographs taken in 1973 form the data base for these maps. Land-use data taken from these maps reflect strongly the natural and man-made vegetation patterns within the county. The selected cultural data from these maps represent certain commercial, public, and semipublic institutions such as trailer parks, schools, and cemeteries. Additional cultural data were acquired from the New York State Department of Transportation's (DOT) updated 7½-minute USGS maps. The most recently updated DOT maps covering the county are for the years 1968-69. Cultural data obtained from these maps included such items as roads, political boundaries, and transmission lines—mainly man-made features relatively fixed on the landscape. Soil data were collected from maps developed for the county by the Department of Geography under another project. Developed from information obtained from a 1969 soil survey of the county done by the U.S. Soil Conservation Service, these maps are at the scale of 1:24000 and have the same coverage as the USGS maps.

The data bank is organized on a standard uniform grid network based on the UTM coordinate system. Each cell in the grid network is 1/16 km^2 in size or approximately 15½ acres. This cell size allows enough spatial detail in this rural area to meet many of the needs of the planning and development agency, and permits the overall system to be manageable with respect to data-processing operations. To cover the county at this level, approximately 26000 grid cells are needed. For each grid cell, 155 pieces of data relating to the previously discussed categories have been collected and stored on a magnetic tape file. Each grid cell is handled as one record on the tape file, and each record is organized as an array to hold the data pertaining to each cell. To identify a particular grid cell, the UTM coordinates associated with the upper left-hand corner of the cell are used. Consequently, it is quite easy to retrieve a certain piece of information on any grid cell. Only the correct UTM coordinates for the grid cell and the array element number of the data are needed.

Software Package

The SCOGIS software package consists of two computer programs. The first program performs both retrieval and transformation operations and works in conjunction with the geo-data bank. It is designed to retrieve data from the geo-data bank and to store the specified data on a temporary file to be used by the second program. This program also is designed to transform one or more variables from the geo-data bank into a different form or a new variable by the use of certain basic mathematical and conditional operations. In other words, the user of this program can write his or her own program to convert or modify data from the data bank. The transformed data are stored on a temporary file the same way as the retrieved data. The second program is a mapping program. It contains the standard cartographic functions required to produce maps for the purpose of either displaying or analyzing data. Maps are printed on a computer line printer, an output device common to most computer installations. Both programs are written in standard FORTRAN IV and are operational at the college's computer center. In addition to these two programs, SCOGIS is designed to interface with future software related to various quantitative methods, simulation models, and other cartographic techniques. Also, land use data in the geo-data bank are presently being updated by the use of LANDSAT data.

UTILIZATION PROBLEMS

As stated initially, the purpose of SCOGIS is to provide the county's decision makers and planning officials with the means to analyze and to display environmental data related to various planning and development problems. Since SCOGIS became an operational system, however, the decision makers and planning officials have shown little enthusiasm for utilizing it, even though they consider it an important resource in dealing with certain types of county problems. The second portion of this report examines some of the reasons why SCOGIS has not been used. The comments presented here are based mainly on observations made of county officials over the last five years, and on discussions with other developers of information systems. Many of these comments may apply to other local nonmetropolitan governments as they become involved with the development and utilization of geo-information systems. It must be pointed out that as decision-makers, Schoharie County officials are not unique. They represent a variety of backgrounds and political convictions and possess considerable commitment to their governmental responsibilities.

The problems encountered in persuading county officials to use SCOGIS can be summarized as follows: misconceived expectations, inability to make cartographic decisions, and difficult work conditions. Lack of funds, often a major obstacle in the development and use of many projects of this type, has not been a significant factor in this case. The county provided the developmental labor costs through the use of CETA funds; the college donated computer time because of certain instructional and research benefits to be gained from the project. Consequently, the county's actual financial contribution to the construction and use of SCOGIS has been very small.

Misconceived Expectations

With a developed computerized geo-information system, county officials expected the computer, the magic black box, to generate the required data and produce the requested output without any effort from them. As one official stated: "I expected to turn on the machine, push the appropriate button, and the correct results would appear." The realization that the black box was not as magical as anticipated, occurred immediately after the completion of the initial stage of SCOGIS. Anxious to implement the system, its developers asked the county planning officials to submit a job request. A user's guide and the necessary coding forms for using SCOGIS had been developed, and the planning agency was provided with a number of copies of these materials. Without submitting a single coding form, the planning officials requested a map be made of every variable available in the system. Needless to say, such a request was impossible and shocked the program developers. With 155 variables directly retrievable from the data bank and the potential to generate thousands of other variables through transformation procedures, the creation of all these maps was not practical. The county planners assumed that, given the tremendous speed of a computer, these maps could be produced in short order. Once the impracticality of this request was explained, the planners were asked to submit requests for two or three maps and to provide through the coding forms the needed cartographic parameter data to create the maps. They were quite surprised to discover that the computer needed these data to make a map, and to learn that in theory an infinite number of maps could be produced from one variable by simply manipulating the parameter values. From their perspective, the black box was not providing them with quick and easily accessible information to alleviate their decision-making problems. Just the opposite was the case—it was requiring them to make more decisions.

SCOGIS developers learned two major lessons from this experience. First, the black-box syndrome must be overcome if information systems are going to be introduced into the rural decision-making process. Many large governmental agencies and private corporations went through this training and adjustment stage back in the 1960s when they computerized many of their operations. In many rural sections of the United States, direct exposure to computer technology is just beginning. Some of the approaches learned in the 1960s with respect to technology transfer may apply here, but it must be remembered that a rural county government is not a large governmental agency or private corporation. The second lesson learned by the SCOGIS developers was to keep the information system simple and expand on it only as its users become accustomed to its operation and request more from it. For example, many of the data in SCOGIS are in interval scale format, good for sophisticated quantitative analytical procedures. Beginning users, however, may do better to work with nominal or ordinal type data. If a user, for instance, requests a map on hardwood forests, the data bank containing nominal data can be searched to determine whether forests exist in each grid cell. The amount of forest in each cell is not in question, and thus many decisions are avoided. It is the old approach of handling everything as either black or white and ignoring any gray levels.

Cartographic Decision Making

Maps were selected as the best way to study and to handle data obtained from the geo-data bank. This decision was reached after consultation with members of the county planning office. Other methods considered were: 1) to list the data, an approach quickly dismissed because of the impracticality of analyzing large quantities of data in tabular form; and 2) to use quantitative techniques, also dismissed because few decision makers comprehend such statistical measures as standard deviation, coefficient of correlation, factor score, etc. The map was selected because large amounts of data can be displayed easily and because in general, people seem to understand maps better.

One of the major problems associated with using SCOGIS, however, is the use of the map as an analytical tool. County officials are accustomed to using established maps such as USGS topographic quadrangles and Soil Conservation soil maps, and the planners know how to draft maps. But when faced with the issue of making decisions about the content of a map, they often find themselves in the difficult situation of deciding which comes first, the chicken or the egg. In other words, if they want a map on a particular topic because of the potential information it may contain, they must make the map; but in order to make a meaningful map, they need first to obtain considerable information about the topic being mapped. Thus county officials prefer to allow experts to make the maps. The problem with this approach is that the "experts" need to know something about the topic being mapped as it relates to the geography of the county. Such experts are not readily available, and in many cases do not exist. For example, one of the few maps developed by the county using SCOGIS resulted from decisions made by the New York State Department of Environmental Conservation (DEC). DEC pointed out that winter deer yards usually occur on the south-facing slopes within a certain percent gradient range and with a certain level of forest coverage. Since each of these variables exists in the geo-data bank, a map was made showing areas containing each of these characteristics. The county was happy with this map, but to get county officials to use SCOGIS, it was necessary for other people to make decisions about map content.

County officials would be happy to allow the developers of the geo-information system to undertake the responsibility of making the necessary decisions. They would only request the maps. The developers would determine how many map classes to use, what type of class breakdowns to employ, what symbols to use, and what data to employ. In making these decisions, a condition is established for influencing county policy-making decisions. Maps can be made easily — especially with the aid of the computer — that significantly distort the magnitude of a particular problem or issue, and thereby direct the thinking of county officials along certain paths. Subsequently, county officials can blame the map maker for poor decisions that result from the patterns portrayed on a map.

This issue is a very difficult one to handle. The basic question is: "Who should make decisions concerning the content of the map, the decision maker or the map maker?" At the federal and state level, decision makers have turned this responsibility over to map makers by establishing cartographic units in various governmental agencies. In order to assist the map maker, these agencies will occasionally employ specialists on a topic for which maps are being developed; but frequently the map maker faces the problem of making decisions on his or her own without knowing much about the topic.

Large metropolitan governments have also relinquished to the map makers the job of formulating decisions about map content, either by hiring outside consultant firms, or by assigning one or two members of the planning department or the engineering department to develop the needed maps. Many non-metropolitan governments have neither the human nor the financial resources to handle the problem in this fashion. Even though higher and more affluent levels of government allow map makers to make decisions about map content, the basic question of responsibility is not resolved. Rural governments should not consider this approach the appropriate or the only model to follow, especially with the development of computerized geo-information systems and the recent rapid growth in computer graphics. In fact, rural governments, not faced with large amounts of investment in and commitment to established cartographic departments, might find it easier, with the aid of this new technology, to get decision makers involved in decisions about map content than do federal, state, or metropolitan governments. To accomplish this, basic problems of preparing and getting county officials used to making decisions must be overcome. The elimination of map-makers or government cartographic units is not being suggested, but only the need to involve the appropriate governmental officials in the process of making decisions on map content.

Difficult Work Conditions

To use a geo-information system like SCOGIS, county officials must have enough time to study the various problem areas facing the county. The research is needed to develop meaningful output from SCOGIS, output that portrays conditions in the county with reasonable accuracy. SCOGIS is a powerful research tool that can assist in analyzing a topic, but other tools and methods must be used to obtain a balanced understanding of the topic. But the typical 12- to 13-hour working day of a paid county official such as the planner consists of extinguishing brush fire problems, attempting to answer a variety of legal questions, making chamber of commerce presentations before different county groups, and seeking ways to obtain state and federal funds for various county projects. Elected officials in Schoharie County are not paid; thus they must maintain full-time jobs in addition to the responsibilities of their office. Both paid and elected county officials have little time to research in depth a topic related to a county problem; consequently, they have little time to be involved with a geo-information system. Unlike state and federal agencies, which might have the resources to undertake an in-depth examination of a problem, the planning agency and other county departments are understaffed and poorly funded. The only solution to this problem seems to be more money. Maybe a federal or state program similar to the county agricultural agent program should be established so that a county could have a resource person who would be familiar with the geography of the county, be a liaison between county decision makers and university and government research centers, and be able to assist the county in examining a problem. Geographers are well trained for these types of tasks; a county geographical agent could contribute much in assisting a county with its problems and could be trained to use a geo-information system such as SCOGIS.

Collectively, these three issues—misconceived expectations, cartographic decision making, and difficult working conditions—make it very hard to implement the use of SCOGIS at the county government level. No immediate solution exists to resolve this problem. Perhaps SCOGIS, like many innovations, will take a while to become accepted. Although technically not unique in terms of geo-information systems, SCOGIS is pioneering a new user area, the rural county government. Problems encountered and approaches tried in implementing SCOGIS should be noted so that the path for future developers of geo-information systems at the rural county level may be easier to travel.

VII. Natural Hazards: Floods and Drought

The Management of Floodplains in Nonmetropolitan Areas

Earl J. Baker and Rutherford H. Platt

INTRODUCTION

Between 140 and 180 million acres—6-8 percent of the total land area of the United States—are estimated to be subject to occasional floods. Despite federal expenditures of over $11 billion on flood protection works, flood losses in the United States are still exorbitant and on the rise. Average annual losses are estimated to be as high as $3.8 billion, with deaths exceeding 100 in 1 year out of 5 (U.S. Water Resources Council 1977; 1978). Professional geographers have long been concerned with flood problems, especially with the reasons why the sorts of land uses that are susceptible to flood damage are found in floodplains. Land-use issues continue to occupy much of the attention of individuals concerned with floodplain management. Questions and debates abound in the controversies that surround the formulation of flood policy; a number of recent reviews summarize them well (White 1975; Platt 1976; National Science Foundation 1980; Burby and French 1980). Flooding in nonmetropolitan areas per se, however, has attracted less attention than urban flood losses, which dominate headlines and public policy making. This paper will review certain aspects of flooding and the ways in which the public responds to it, which are particularly relevant to nonmetropolitan America.

TYPES OF FLOODS IN NONMETROPOLITAN AREAS

Although the most publicized flood disasters usually occur in metropolitan areas, nonmetropolitan America suffers extensive and varied losses from floods. The costs of rural and small-city flooding are not readily calculable from national data, which are classified by region and state but not generally by county or SMSA. National data are not particularly reliable; many flood losses, especially in rural areas, may not be reported (or if they are reported, they may be overestimated in order to attract maximum federal assistance). The U.S. Water Resources Council has estimated that flood losses to agriculture averaged 48 percent of total flood losses in 1975, or $1.6 billion. Estimates of regional losses are indicated in Fig. 1. Nonmetropolitan areas participate extensively in the National Flood Insurance Program, accounting for 20 percent of loss claims to date— nearly $200 million (Table 1).

Floods typically encountered in rural areas and small riverine or coastal communities are of particular types. These in turn suggest the diversity of flooding problems nationally and the need for a diversity of public and private response. The following paragraphs will consider 1) shallow riverine flooding; 2) flash flooding in narrow valleys; and 3) coastal flooding.

Shallow Riverine Flooding. A classic example of shallow riverine flooding of great frequency is found in the drainage basin of the Red River of the North. This stream flows northward into Canada, forming the border between Minnesota and North Dakota and draining a watershed of 39,199 square miles in the United States. Flooding in the Red River Valley of the North is broad, shallow, and frequent. Floods normally occur in the early spring as snow melts in headwaters at the southerly end of the basin, creating overbank flows further north. Agricultural ditching and roadways elevated on embankments (to avoid being overtopped by floodwaters) increase natural discharge and distort flowage patterns. Ring levees built to protect individual farms further exacerbate the overall flood problem (National Science Foundation 1980, p. 191). In April 1979, the Red River reached its highest peak since 1897 at Grand Forks, North Dakota. It spread up to several miles wide along a 100-mile stretch of the valley, with depths of generally a foot or two except where constricted by levees. The Corps of Engineers estimated damage at $10.1 million in North Dakota and $7.4 million in Minnesota (*The New York Times* 1979, p. D16). Lives were not generally endangered, but inconvenience and disruption of economic activity prevailed for weeks. Improvised sandbag dikes failed to protect East Grand Forks from inundation.

Flash Floods. Much greater threat to life as well as to property is posed by flash floods in constricted valleys and canyons of Appalachia, the Rocky Mountains

Table 1. Nonmetropolitan Activity of the National Flood
Insurance Program (April 8, 1981)

	SMSA	Non-SMSA	Percentage Non-SMSA
Regular program	3139	3055	49
Emergency program	2598	8236	76
No. of policies	1.4 million	603,000	30
Amount of coverage	$73 billion	$22 billion	23
Number of claims	145,110	53,024	27
Amount of claims	$781 million	$197 million	20

Source: Federal Insurance Administration Data

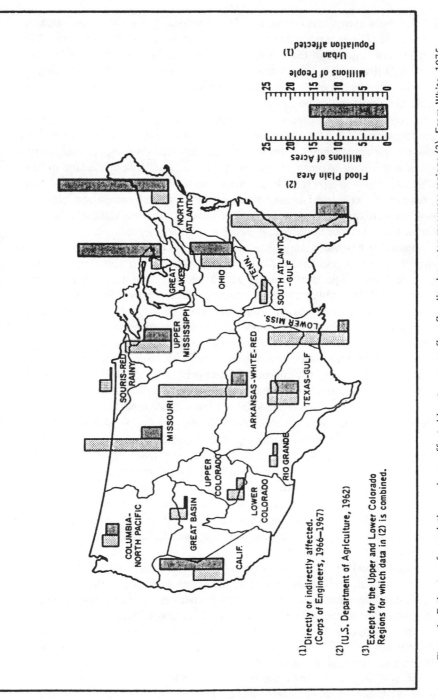

Figure 1. Estimates of population and area affected by stream overflow flooding by water resources regions (3). From White, 1975.

and elsewhere in much of nonmetropolitan America. Rapid City, South Dakota, a city of 43,000, sustained 238 deaths during its epic flash flood in June, 1972. Campers and tourists in Big Thompson Canyon, Colorado accounted for many of the 139 lives lost in a flash flood there in the summer of 1976. Throughout the West, the danger of flash floods has prompted the erection of warning signs urging the public to "climb to safety."

In Appalachia it is predominantly the residents, rather than campers and "outdoors people," who are endangered by flash floods. These people live in small mining communities, farm villages, and isolated dwellings tucked away in valleys and ravines. According to Gidez (1978, p. 3): "Most of the land in Appalachia has slopes in excess of 15 percent. This topographic limitation has caused Appalachia to have less farmland than any other area of comparable size in the lower 48 states and has resulted in greater concentration of Appalachia's population on floodplains or in other low-lying hazard-prone areas."

Appalachia has had some spectacular flood disasters, the best known perhaps being Hurricane Agnes in 1972, the recurrent disasters at Johnstown, Pennsylvania, and the tragic dam collapse at Buffalo Creek in Logan County, West Virginia. But less publicized flood disasters occur regularly in Appalachia. According to the Federal Insurance Administration, 48 percent of the communities in the country in which one or more presidential declarations of flood disasters have been made are in the twelve Appalachian states. Since January 1, 1972, 74 percent of the communities within those states with three or more flood disaster declarations are in Appalachia proper, comprising 45 percent of the nation's total of multiple declarations. Total damage in Appalachia from flooding between 1970 and April 1, 1977 exceeded $300 million with 26 reported deaths (Jimenez 1980). These totals were each exceeded during the floods of April 2-5, 1977, which caused $400 million in damage and 22 deaths in a 47-county region of Kentucky, Tennessee, Virginia, and West Virginia (Runner and Chin 1980).

The "Hill Country" of central Texas is another nonmetropolitan region with significant flood problems. In August, 1978 a 2-day rainfall amounting to 30 inches sent the Pedernales and Guadalupe Rivers over their banks, with the latter flowing at twice the previously recorded level of discharge. Small towns, dude ranches, and the LBJ Ranch were among the areas damaged, and at least 15 lives were lost.

Coastal Flooding. The nation's coastal areas have attracted extensive residential, commercial, and industrial development over the past two decades, much of it in nonmetropolitan locations. Vacation homes on isolated barrier islands and spits, offshore oil staging facilities along the Gulf Coast, lavish ocean-view homes on unstable slopes in Southern California—all occupy high-risk locations. Coastal wetlands are being filled to accommodate marinas and waterfront subdivisions, with consequent loss of natural habitats, scenic amenities, and natural buffers against erosion and storm surge. Hurricane Frederick in 1979 caused an estimated $1.8 billion in damage to public and private facilities in the Alabama coastal zone. If this storm had veered slightly to the west so as to hit New

Orleans, the damage toll in both urban and rural areas would have been much greater.

Coastal floods vary greatly in severity, time of year, and physical impact depending upon the location and type of shoreline involved. The Northeast and Middle Atlantic coasts are afflicted chiefly by storm surge and erosion due to winter storms and occasional tropical hurricanes. South Florida and the Gulf coastal region are susceptible to both hurricane-induced storm surge and inland flooding from severe rainfall. In the Houston-Galveston area, natural flooding is worsened by land subsidence due to extraction of oil and ground water, thus increasing the average probability that damaging floods will occur over time. The Pacific coast is chiefly afflicted by mudslide and landslide due to failure of slopes during heavy rains. Tsunamis are a source of coastal hazard in Hawaii and Alaska.

AWARENESS OF FLOOD RISK

The foregoing typology of nonmetropolitan flood hazards leads naturally to the question of how widely such hazards are perceived in the regions to which they apply. Perception of the hazard is the necessary prelude to informed response. This in turn raises a number of subsidiary questions, for example: 1) the most effective means of communicating risk information (maps, brochures, etc.); 2) unfamiliarity with risks (cumulative probabilities rather than annual probabilities, for instance); 3) whether the discounting of low-probability/high-consequence events can and should be overcome; and 4) whether historical examples (painting high-water marks from previous floods on telephone poles, for example) might be more effective than probabilistic approaches; and so forth.

Campaigns to increase the public's awareness of such hazards have not been very effective (Christensen and Ruch 1978; Waterstone 1978). Nor does such awareness necessarily lead to an appropriate response. People who know more about hurricanes, for example, are no more likely to evacuate low-lying areas when they are threatened (Baker 1979), although certain general surrogate measures to increase awareness of hurricanes have been related to other types of responses, most notably building practices (Cross 1979). Through the National Flood Insurance Program, people who live in floodplains or who have purchased land there are given information about the hazard, which they probably would not receive otherwise. The usefulness of this information, however, remains unknown.

An indirect measure of awareness of flood hazard is willingness to purchase flood insurance. Since 1968, flood insurance has become increasingly available through the federal government. Premiums are heavily subsidized by the government for structures already located in the floodplain, and insurance is required as a condition for a loan for new construction or acquisition of flood-prone property in communities where it is available. Nevertheless, much property in floodplains is still not insured—a most optimistic estimate would put the figure at one in three. A total of 2 million policies covering $100 billion worth of flood-prone property (as of early 1981) reflects dramatic progress over the past decade. But most policies sold, and most coverage provided, are for metropolitan areas. The four SMSAs of Miami, Tampa, New Orleans, and Houston/Galveston alone account for 38 percent of all policies sold. And aside from the occurrence of a flood, little has been shown to induce voluntary purchase of insurance. The growth cited above has primarily been the result of requiring insurance for the financing of new construction in floodplains and as a consequence of actual recent flood experience.

Psychologists and economists have made interesting findings about the way people assess risk, which suggest that many people are unlikely to purchase insurance voluntarily. Two components of that assessment are: 1) how likely people believe a flood is to occur, and 2) how bad the damages would be if the flood occurs. It is not uncommon for people to underestimate both, so it has been presumed that giving people more accurate information about the hazard should enhance their likelihood of insuring against it. It should; but recent evidence shows that because of the way most people combine perceived likelihood and expected consequences, having accurate beliefs about each will not necessarily lead to the sort of overall evaluation of risk one might expect.

Kunreuther et al. (1978) found that economists' "subjective utility model" did not predict floodplain residents' decisions whether to buy flood insurance, even when their perception of the likelihood and consequence of the hazard were known. Subsequent laboratory experiments showed that people tend to place more weight on the likelihood of something happening than on its consequences, and that they are more likely to buy insurance against a risk that has a high likelihood of occurring but small consequences than against a risk which has a low probability but major consequences. Thus people are unlikely to buy insurance unless they believe that flooding is quite likely (Slovic et al. 1976).

THE ROLE OF THE NATIONAL FLOOD INSURANCE PROGRAM

Aside from providing low-cost flood insurance, the National Flood Insurance Program (NFIP) is the nation's primary vehicle for promoting proper management of coastal and riverine flood hazard areas. A major activity of NFIP has been the identification and mapping of areas of "special flood hazards" in some 20,000 local communities, counties, and rural areas. This was completed by 1975 for all communities determined to have existing or potential flood problems. This allowed a present total of 17,000 communities (including a number of unincorporated places) to enter the program on an "emergency basis" by indicating their recognition of an existing flood hazard and undertaking certain minimal efforts to avoid further flood losses.

More important, however, to the eventual reduction of flood losses nationally is the preparation of more detailed floodplain maps and "flood insurance-rate studies." Once these are available for a community, the local government must adopt more severe restrictions on floodplain development, including limits on the type, location, elevation, and design of new construction in floodplains. If such measures are adopted so as to satisfy NFIP criteria for floodplain management (found in 24 *Code of Federal Regulations*, Sec. 1900 et seq.), the community enters the "regular phase" of NFIP. Property-owners may then qualify for much higher levels of coverage than during the emergency phase. But higher coverage, and all coverage on new structures, are sold at "actuarial rates" theoretically based on the actual risk of loss at a particular location and elevation with reference to the estimated "100 year flood level" (that is, having a one percent chance of being exceeded in any given year). If a community fails to adopt regulations sufficient to meet the NFIP "regular phase" cirteria for floodplain management, it is dropped from the program, and its property-owners can no longer obtain flood insurance. (Furthermore, the Flood Disaster Protection Act of 1973 denies federal disaster assistance and certain other benefits in non-NFIP communities).

Clearly the impact of NFIP upon floodplain management in specific communities depends upon the completion of the detailed maps and studies that bring about the "regular phase" requirements. As of early 1981, about 10 thousand detailed community flood studies had been initiated under NFIP, of which 5,800 were completed. About 6,200 of the 17 thousand communities in NFIP had entered the "regular phase." These included many nonmetropolitan communities, which accountef for 49 percent of regular program communities nationally (Table 1).

Since 1979, most floodplain management efforts at NFIP have been focussed upon larger, urban places having significant property at risk. If this policy continues, nonmetropolitan areas will receive little technical or mapping assistance. Given the extent of nonmetropolitan flood losses, this would be an unfortunate eventuality (although possibly justified in terms of national cost-effectiveness of NFIP efforts). But where smaller communities have a serious flood history, as in Appalachia, they will be scheduled for detailed attention (Jimenez 1980).

Smaller communities with flood problems have been generally slow to adopt "nonstructural" approaches to coping with floods, approaches like zoning and acquisition of the floodplain. Hutton and Mileti (1979) found, for example, that size of local government, degree of urbanization (metropolitan status), local government affluence, and staff size and expertise were all positively related to the promptness with which places agreed to participate in the National Flood Insurance Program, which made flood insurance available in communities agreeing to enact controls on development in the 100-year floodplain. Burby and French (1980) also found that floodplain management programs were stronger in places having greater financial resources, but few communities are spending much money on such efforts: only a fourth of the communities they surveyed were spending over $5000 annually, and only 15 percent were expending one person-day per week on staff time.

In any event, smaller counties and county governments need not await a federal "stick" to undertake the management of their floodplains. Even without detailed studies or maps, communities may use the best available information to get started.

FLOOD WARNINGS

It is generally known that property damage from floods is increasing in the United States. It is less well known that the death toll has trended upward since 1955, averaging 180 per year over the past few years. Most of the deaths occur in flash floods—those that rise rapidly and often affect only a relatively small watershed and channel. Many are associated with thunderstorms. Part of the problem is monitoring precipitation in such localized areas, some of which can be remote from urban areas where measuring instruments are usually located. The National Weather Service estimates that about 3,000 communities and recreation areas have serious flash flood problems and another 3,000 have moderate problems. Only 675 have site-specific flash-flood warning capability, however, and fewer than 100 new systems are being added annually (U.S. Office of Technology Assessment 1978).

The meteorological, hydrologic, logistical, and behavioral aspects of flood warning systems pose significant problems, but there might be a way to incorporate the warning/evacuation problem into other floodplain management approaches. This is clearly possible and desirable in coastal areas, where it could take many hours to evacuate some coastal areas in the event of a major hurricane, and the chances of inducing people to leave very early are remote. One community—Sanibel, Florida, an island off the southwest Gulf coast—has in fact attempted to prevent the problem by establishing a growth cap, based in part on the maximum number of people they can reasonably expect to evacuate before a major storm. Such integration of warning system objectives with other planning considerations has not been widely attempted, however, in either coastal or riverine areas.

OPPORTUNITIES FOR POST-DISASTER MITIGATION

A recent report by the U.S. Water Resources Council (Platt 1979) documented experience in a number of flood disaster sites in reducing the potential for future losses through the recovery process. Several of these involved nonmetropolitan communities: Rapid City, South Dakota; Big Thompson Canyon, Colorado; Clinchport, Tennessee; and Soldiers Grove, Wisconsin. The immediate post-disaster period affords an important opportunity to reduce future flood losses. A presidential disaster declaration releases extensive federal assistance to a community in the form of grants and loans. In addition, flood insurance proceeds, where policies are in effect, contribute to the flow of federal disaster funds.

Where rebuilding is needed, it makes sense to redesign or relocate structures so as to eliminate their vulnerability to future floods. Unfortunately, in the rush of emergency assistance, good will, publicity, and politics, longer-term considerations are often forgotten as all parties seek to help the victims return to the preflood status quo.

National policy now encourages hazard mitigation through the post-disaster recovery process. Section 406 of the Flood Disaster Relief Act of 1974 requires that states and communities receiving federal disaster aid must prepare a long-range hazard mitigation plan for the area in question. This approach was reinforced by the Carter Administration through a directive of the Office of Management and Budget (July 10, 1980) ordering all relevant federal agencies to collaborate in establishing new procedures for post-disaster hazard assessment and mitigation. Under an interagency agreement signed December 15, 1980 by twelve executive departments, the Federal Emergency Management Agency (FEMA) will coordinate the performance of post-flood investigations to determine opportunities for mitigation. FEMA's recommendations will be prepared within ten days after a flood to guide all federal efforts in the allocation of benefits to promote mitigation objectives.

The experience of the village of Soldiers Grove, Wisconsin, shows how a small rural community may rebuild itself after a flood. Soldiers Grove is a farming village of about 530 people located in the Kickapoo River Valley in the "Driftless Area" of southwestern Wisconsin. After a series of flood disasters to communities along the entire length of the Kickapoo, the Corps of Engineers planned and began construction of a flood-control dam and reservoir, 36 miles upstream from Soldiers Grove. Although some 9000 acres of farmland were acquired and the dam was two-thirds completed, construction halted in the early 1970s because of environmental objections. A Corps proposal for local levees to be funded partly at community and state expense was also rejected. Inspired by a young planner and community-development specialist, Tom Hirsch (who was hired under CETA funds), Soldiers Grove began in 1976 to develop a new approach to its flood problem, namely to relocate its entire downtown business district away from the river to a hillside. With state assistance, a suitable site was acquired by the village and prepared to receive relocated businesses.

The relocation effort assumed increased importance when a 100-year flood struck Soldiers Grove on July 4, 1978. With the support of Wisconsin's congressional delegation, a special task force was established under White House auspices to review Soldiers Grove's proposal to be a pilot project in post-disaster hazard mitigation. (The plan also involved innovative use of solar energy in the commercial structures and other imaginative features.) After considerable delay, the bulk of the community's requested budget of $5.7 million has been obtained from federal, state, local, and private sources, and the relocation of Soldiers Grove away from the Kickapoo floodplain is well underway (National Science Foundation 1980, pp. 183-190).

FLOOD HAZARD MITIGATION AND
COMPREHENSIVE PLANNING

Soldiers Grove's experience suggests the need to incorporate flood-hazard management into a community's general planning process rather than to treat it as a separate problem. The former approach can lead to more innovative joint response. If several goals are pursued simultaneously, a policy or project might be found economically feasible, whereas it might not if it achieved only a subset of the goals. Transport routes can be planned to facilitate evacuation as well as routine traffic; water and waste treatment facilities can be sited to ensure their functioning after a disaster; infrastructure that would stimulate growth in the floodplain can be redirected; and so forth.

Perhaps the greatest potential for integration of flood-hazard mitigation into the broader community planning process involves goals of environmental quality, especially provision of open space and recreation, and protection of natural areas. The growth cap in Sanibel, Florida was motivated not only by the evacuation dilemma but also by environmental concerns such as water quality and visual aesthetics. (Those motivations alone might not have been adequate to justify the cap.) Attempts to use floodprone areas in ways that are compatible with the hazard (rather than controlling the hazard) include "land use management" and "nonstructural measures," although both, particularly the latter, can include other adjustment strategies such as warning systems. A subset of nonstructural measures has the effect of preserving natural flood-prone areas, reclaiming developed floodplain land, and generally promoting open, nonintensive uses of the flood zone. These approaches can serve the community well in areas other than flood mitigation; they need to be considered more carefully when the general community planning process is going forward. Changes in federal policy should help in this area, especially in providing technical assistance to communities. Many of the more comprehensive approaches can be expensive, however, particularly if they involve the purchase of property.

CONCLUSION

Flood-hazard management is a pervasive issue in nonmetropolitan America. Small communities and county governments receive less attention from the National Flood Insurance Program than metropolitan areas. Rural jurisdictions have well-known antipathy towards land-use control or any form of interference with a property owner's whims. Yet as flood losses mount, and as some communities suffer repeated disasters, there is no choice but to exercise public planning and management responsibility over rural flood-hazard areas before the deluge arrives.

References

Baker, E. J. 1976. *Toward An Evaluation of Policy Alternatives Governing Hazard Zone Land Use.* Natural Hazards Research Working Paper No. 28. Boulder: University of Colorado Institute of Behavioral Science.

————. 1979. Predicting response to hurricane warnings. *Mass Emergencies* 4: 9-24.

Burby, R. J., and French, S.P. 1980. *Managing Flood Hazard Areas; the State of Practice.* Chapel Hill: University of North Carolina Center for Urban and Regional Studies.

Christensen, L., and Ruch, C.E. 1978. *Evaluation of Hurricane Awareness Program.* Austin: Texas Insurance Information Institute.

Cross, J. A. 1979. The association between previous residence and hurricane hazard perception and adjustments. Paper presented at the Annual Meeting of the Association of American Geographers, Philadelphia, Penn., April 22-25.

Gidez, R. M. 1978. Natural Hazards in Appalachia. *Appalachia* (June-July); 1-18.

Hutton, J. R., and Mileti, D. S. 1979. *Analysis of Adoption and Implementation of Community Land Use Regulations for Floodplains.* San Francisco: Woodward-Clyde Consultants.

Jimenez, G. 1980. A Redirection of the National Flood Insurance Program: Implications for Appalachia and the West. Mimeographed. Washington: Federal Insurance Administration.

Kunreuther, H.; Ginsberg, R.; Miller, L.; Sagi, P.; Slovic, P.; Borkon, B.; and Katz, N. 1978. *Disaster Insurance Protection: Public Policy Lessons.* Somerset, N.J.: Wiley.

National Science Foundation 1980. *A Report on Flood Hazard Mitigation.* Washington: The Foundation.

Platt, R. H. 1976. The National Flood Insurance Program: Some Midstream Perspectives. *Journal of the American Institute of Planners* (July) 42: 303-313.

————. 1979. *Options to Improve Federal Non-structural Response to Floods.* Washington: U.S. Water Resources Council.

Runner, G. S., and Chin, E. H. 1980. *Flood of April 1977 in the Appalachian Region of Kentucky, Tennessee, Virginia, and West Virginia.* Geological Survey Professional Paper 1098. Washington: U.S. Government Printing Office.

Slovic, P.; Fischoff, B.; and Lichtenstein, S. 1976. *Cognitive Processes and Societal Risk Taking.* Research Monograph 15-2. Eugene: Oregon Research Institute.

The New York Times 1979. Rain Hampers Efforts to Contain Minnesota-North Dakota Floods (April 24).

U.S. Office of Technology Assessment 1978. *Issues and Options in Flood Hazard Management.* Washington: U.S. Office of Technology Assessment.

U.S. Water Resources Council 1977. *Estimated Flood Damages, 1975-2000. Nationwide Report.* Washington: The Council.

————. 1978. *The Nation's Water Resources: 1975-2000.* Summary Volume of the Second National Water Assessment. Washington: U. S. Government Printing Office.

Waterstone, M. 1978. *Hazard Mitigation Behavior of Urban Flood Plain Residents.* Natural Hazards Research Working Paper No. 35. Boulder: University of Colorado Institute of Behavioral Science.

White, G. F. 1975. *Flood Hazard in the United States: A Research Assessment.* Technology, Environment and Man Monograph No. 6. Boulder: University of Colorado Institute of Behavioral Science.

Managing Drought Impacts on Agriculture: The Great Plains Experience

William E. Riebsame

INTRODUCTION

The Great Plains form a large agricultural region devoted chiefly to small-grains production. As defined by the Great Plains Committee (1937), the region extends from the Rocky Mountains eastward to about the 20-inch annual rainfall line and the western edge of pedalfer soils (Fig. 1). The climate of this area is semi-arid and subject to recurrent drought, the chief natural hazard facing the region's farmers. Since agricultural settlement in the 1880s, severe, Plains-wide droughts have occurred in the 1890s, 1930s, and 1950s. Scattered, locally severe droughts occurred in the 1910s, 1961, mid-1970s, and in 1980. Each drought prompted questions about appropriate land use for the region and about the necessary mixture of agricultural adjustments and government assistance for successful farming.

The recent droughts of 1974-76 and 1980 drew a great deal of attention in the popular media and provoked much government aid (Crawford 1978; Rosenberg 1980). Following the bumper crops of the 1960s, these droughts revived concerns about the stability of Plains agricultural production and the appropriateness of its technology. The important role that Great Plains wheat plays in the world food supply—it provides up to 45 percent of the world's traded wheat—lends these concerns global significance. This chapter is a review of agricultural adjustment to drought on the Great Plains. It attempts to determine which adjustments have been most successful in buffering drought impacts and in stabilizing agricultural production.

The author wishes to thank his colleagues in Clark University's Climate and Society Research Group for their contribution to this work, including: Martyn Bowden, Robert Kates, Richard Warrick, and Daniel Weiner. Part of this work was based on a project entitled "The Effect of Climate Fluctuations on Human Populations", which was funded by the National Science Foundation, Grant No. AMT 77-15019.

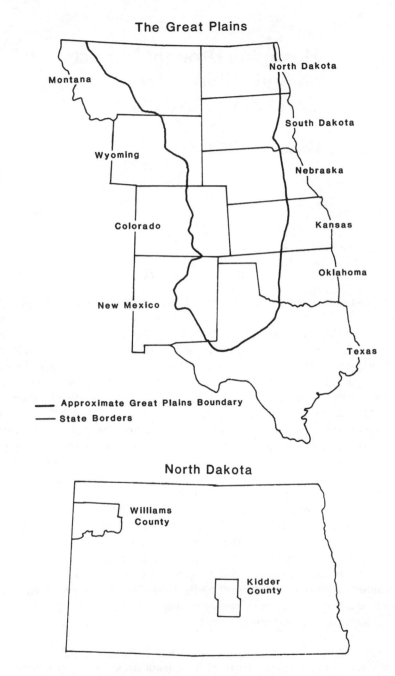

Figure 1. The Great Plains and the North Dakota study sites.

A BRIEF HISTORY

The history of agricultural settlement of the Great Plains, spanning slightly more than a century, is a dramatic record of booms, busts, and remarkable changes in land use, agricultural technologies, and social structure (Kraenzel 1955; Hargreaves 1957). A thumbnail sketch of this history begins with the first homesteaders, the "sod-busters" who moved out on to the Plains in hopes of finding agricultural abundance, and who were attracted by generous government land policies, railroad promotional campaigns, and innovative agricultural technology. Recurring periods of settlement were followed by periods of depopulation brought on by poor judgment, drought, overextension of finances, grasshoppers, and crop disease. Abandoned land was cheap, so farmers who stayed acquired larger farms, which were more efficient and less likely to fail. Contrary to the traditional view of a fluctuating frontier of agriculture that alternately advanced and retreated with runs of good and bad years (Shannon 1945), crop acreage actually remained fairly stable during the busts, and grew in a ratchetlike manner of expansion and stabilization. After the turn of the century, a rapidly expanding dry-land agricultural system was functioning on the Plains, supported by mechanization, government aid programs, and increases in farm size. The modern Great Plains, despite the effects of recurrent droughts, are the locus of wheat and sorghum production in the United States, and they contribute substantially to the world's food supply.

CHANGES IN DROUGHT IMPACTS OVER TIME

It is often assumed that the adjustments that societies make to environmental hazards result in decreased social stress when events like drought occur. In research conducted by the Climate and Society Research Group at Clark University, this assumption was examined in a series of historical case studies on the Plains. The research group's hypothesis states that the impacts of successive droughts have lessened relative to drought severity. This lessening of impacts may have been effected by technology, by changes in social organization, or by a combination of the two.

To investigate changes in drought vulnerability of the Plains over time, the research group has traced the history of drought occurrence and impacts from the late 1800s to the present. The study focussed on wheat, the region's dominant dry-land crop. The group measured drought intensity by indices computed from monthly temperature and precipitation data, using a method developed by Palmer (1965). Agricultural impacts were measured by wheat yields. Social impacts, measured by such indicators as health effects, population changes, farm transfers (sales and foreclosures), relief payments, and government programs funding, were scrutinized for changes across successive drought periods.

As described by Warrick (1980), research to date supports the lessening hypothesis, suggesting that the Great Plains agricultural system is less sensitive to drought now than it was in the past. Lessening has produced reduced social impacts. This is particularly evident in drought-related health effects, like malnutrition and starvation; once widespread, these problems have all but disappeared. The sensitivity of population changes to drought has also lessened. When drought severity is taken into consideration, population dislocations of early droughts exceed those of the well-known Dust Bowl migrations. After the 1930s, population declines during drought are indistinguishable from nondrought periods. Land abandonment and farm transfer rates, which were quite high during early droughts, have decreased with successive droughts, and population turnover rates have declined. Initial analysis of drought impacts at several county study sites also suggest decreasing adverse effects over time.

THE CAUSES OF LESSENED DROUGHT IMPACTS

Lessening of impacts is consistent with the widely-held view of the contemporary Great Plains as a technologically and socially advanced agricultural region capable of coping with the vicissitudes of nature. Several changes in Plains agriculture come immediately to mind when one seeks explanations for lessening: new tillage methods, the retirement of marginal lands, larger farm size, innovative crop technologies, and a host of government programs, from price supports to crop insurance. As pointed out at a recent conference of drought experts (Rosenberg 1980), however, we do not know which of these adjustments have contributed to lessening. Experience suggests that adjustments may become widely adopted and generally perceived as quite useful, only to be proven ineffective by subsequent research. So-called dry farming techniques promoted at the turn of the century are good examples of widely adopted, but ineffective, drought adjustments (Hargreaves 1957). Unfortunately, there have been few careful studies of the relative contribution of adjustments to the minimization of drought impacts; such a review has been recommended (Rosenberg 1980).

Modern drought adjustments have resulted from a century of research on agricultural drought problems. This effort has produced a rich body of prescriptive literature, encompassing numerous proposed drought adjustments of three main types: changes in technology, social structure, and land use.

Changes in Technology: The Techno-Fix Theme

Many researchers who observed the dust storms, withered crops, and abandoned farms of early droughts concluded that farmers were "doing something wrong" and proposed changes in one or more technical aspects of Plains agriculture. The idea that Plains agriculture can succeed with the application of proper techniques, tools, and knowledge can be labeled the "techno-fix" theme. Adjustments prescribed under this rubric include the use of drought-resistant plant breeds, fertilizers, innovative farm implements, and water and soil conservation practices like strip cropping, minimum tillage, summer fallowing, stubble mulching, and weed control.

The dry farming movement of the late 1800s (Hargreaves 1957) was an early expression of the techno-fix theme. Proponents of dry farming (e.g., Widtsoe 1911) proffered a list of tillage implements and practices aimed at conserving soil moisture during drought periods. Although many of the dry-farming methods (e.g., packing the subsurface soil to enhance capillary action) were repudiated in later research, the movement remains an important part of the adjustment history of Plains agriculture. It demonstrated the need for, and acceptance of, detailed technical advice among farmers and spurred government-supported research (Quinn 1980). The most enduring expression of the techno-fix theme has been the extensive agricultural experiment program established by the Hatch Act in 1887. Greb et al. (1979) note that most of the advances in dry-land wheat production during the last century have come from the government experiment stations.

The Social Structure Theme

Paralleling the techno-fix solution are proposed changes in the relationship between private and public sectors in Plains agriculture, and changes in the structure of Plains farms. At the societal level, adjustments proposed under this theme include government aid, disaster relief, and more enduring programs such as credit supports, price protection, and economic research. The New Deal programs of the 1930s ushered in an era of increased government involvement in drought management (Quinn 1980). The government became committed to intervening between drought and farmers, and thus it became another potential cause of lessening.

At the farm level, proponents of social adjustments have stressed the need for less tenant farming, argued that farmers should maintain large reserves for use in poor years, and called for the diversification of farm production (e.g., by adding cattle to wheat farms).

Changes in Land Use: The Misfit Theme

A final, enduring concept in Great Plains drought literature is the "misfit" theme, in which extensive crop production is portrayed as an inappropriate use of the Plains environment. John W. Powell expressed this point of view in his 1879 report on the arid lands of the West (see Stegner 1953), in which he argued that only grazing and limited, irrigated farming should be practiced on the Plains (Hargreaves 1976). Adherents to this view recommend adjustments like keeping grass cover intact, returning cultivated areas to native grasses, and re-establishing large-scale cattle-ranching. The theme's modern expression lies in the efforts of the Soil Conservation Service (SCS) and the Agricultural Stabilization and Conservation Service (ASCS) to remove marginal land from production. Proponents of the misfit theme have been evident during each Great Plains drought. The development of modern dry farming techniques and increasing world demand for grain, however, have encouraged a long-term trend toward expanding cultivation.

WHICH ADJUSTMENTS HAVE LESSENED
DROUGHT IMPACTS?

The adjustments proposed under the three themes in Great Plains drought research have widely different goals. Some are aimed at buffering the impact of drought on yields; others are attempts to mitigate the economic and social impacts of crop losses. Overall, lessened drought impacts probably resulted from the interaction of many different adjustments; but a few key adjustments can be identified under each major theme.

Techno-Fix: Mitigating the Effects of Drought on Yields

Of the three adjustment themes, the techno-fix approach appears to have dominated Plains agricultural development. In 1905, this approach was given a boost with the creation of the U.S. Department of Agriculture's Office of Dry-land Research. This office urged farmers to believe that solutions to their dry-land farming problems were forthcoming. It also put a stamp of approval on the concept of the Plains as a dry-land grain production area.

Among the adjustments adopted on the Plains in an attempt to keep yields high during droughts are the use of resistant hybrids, moisture-conserving cultivation practices, and new farm implements. According to Greb (1979), experimental research supports the notion that such methods improve the water-use efficiency of crops and thus reduce their drought vulnerability. Few researchers argue with the evidence for technologically-derived higher yields and improved quality of small grains, but debate continues as to whether the occasional impact of drought on yields has been negated. Not all researchers agree with Greb's conclusion or with his optimistic prediction that yields will continue to improve with "additional technical improvements" (Greb 1979, p. 273).

If lessened impacts have resulted chiefly from technological adjustments, the effect should be observable as a reduction of interannual variability of yields. Year-to-year variability of yields, coupled with price fluctuations, is the chief hazard to Great Plains farming, according to research on agricultural economics (e.g., Great Plains Agricultural Council 1955 and 1959). One way of searching for this signal is to analyze the residuals from a trend line fit to Great Plains wheat yields for 1890 to 1977 (Fig. 2). The ratio of actual to expected yields (percent residual) during the worst years of each drought episode shows a slight decrease with time, from about 26 percent in the 1890s to about 17 percent in the 1970s. When the differences are normalized by drought severity data available for the 1930s, 1950s, and 1970s droughts, however, no evidence for decreasing impacts is observed (Warrick 1980, p. 102).

Crop-yield/weather models developed by the Climate and Food Research Group at the University of Wisconsin-Madison (Michaels 1978) allow a more sophisticated approach to the search for lessened impacts on crop yields. Comparison of weather data and associated model wheat-yields on the Plains during 1932-75 indicate that yields were as sensitive to adverse weather in the 1970s as they were in the 1930s.

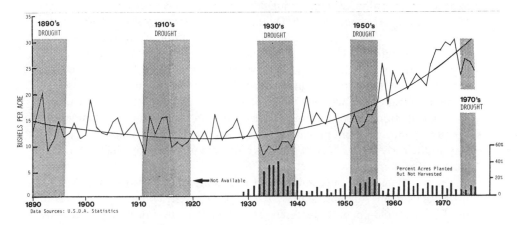

Figure 2. Wheat yields in the Great Plains 1890-1977.

Such findings raise questions about the ability of technology to protect crops from drought; similar results have shown up in other research (see National Oceanic and Atmospheric Administration 1973, and Haigh 1977). Growing concern has also been expressed about farmers' ability to control soil erosion on the Plains (Lockeretz 1978), and about their reliance on a limited number of plant varieties. The technical literature reveals substantial disagreement about the efficacy of technology in buffering drought impacts (see Perrin and Heady 1975, and Greb 1979), and there are no unequivocal findings. The results discussed here, which pertain to the Great Plains overall and may not hold at other scales of analysis, indicate that dry-land wheat yields remain sensitive to drought despite technological inputs.

Continued high yield variability may not be simply a failure of technology; it must be considered in light of several exacerbating circumstances. First, most farmers are not legally bound to carry out soil and water conservation practices, and annual acreage restriction changes cause large variations in total planting and in the quality of land planted. Second, farmers are abandoning fewer acres each year, because of better harvesting technology and higher crop prices. Thus poor-yield acres are more likely to be included in recent yield calculations. These effects might mask relative improvements in yield stability. Finally, farmers may find it difficult to achieve yields similar to those produced under experimental conditions. Nevertheless, it is clear that farmers on the Great Plains continue to experience year-to-year fluctuations in yields. This suggests that nontechnological adjustments play an important role in lessening.

The Efficacy of Social Adjustments

The range of social adjustments aimed at minimizing the impacts of poor yields is enormous—from changes in the relationship between the public and private sectors to alterations in farm structure. Estimates of total government expenditures for drought-impact mitigation on the Plains (Warrick 1975, pp. 51-52; Crawford 1978, pp. 153-156; Quinn 1980, p. 155) suggest that here may lie a major cause of the observed lessening of impacts. Contrary to the traditional view, government aid in times of drought started well before the 1930s. Seed loans to farmers were made by some Great Plains states in the late 1800s. During the drought of 1917-20, thousands of federally-funded seed and feed loans were made to Great Plains farmers, many of which were never repaid. The largest government effort to provide drought relief and simultaneously to bring American agriculture into equilibrium with the global supply/demand situation got underway in the early 1930s. Reviews of this effort are presented by McDean (1980), Quinn (1980), and Rasmussen et al. (1976).

Briefly, the goal of early government programs, spearheaded by the Agricultural Adjustment Administration's (AAA) acreage restrictions in 1933, was to reduce the build-up of large reserves of export crops (including wheat) by limiting production. This would alleviate low prices and — it was hoped — establish an economic parity between agriculture and other sectors of the economy (Agricultural Adjustment Administration 1934). Programs were also initiated to adapt agricultural practices to semi-arid, drought-prone areas. On the Plains, this included a major conservation program (Held and Clawson 1965) and a substantial land use planning effort (Hargreaves 1976). County land use planning committees were established to determine the necessary adjustments for particular areas. The most common land use changes suggested for the Great Plains were that certain acreages be reseeded to grass, that farms be enlarged, and that diversified farming become the standard, rather than the emergency, practice in the area.

Other government programs established to minimize the social impacts of drought included federal crop insurance and the Farmers' Home Administration's low-interest emergency loans. Low-interest loans, crop insurance, and disaster payments (which have been part of the acreage set-aside program since 1972) represent a powerful contemporary drought-adjustment package. Evidence suggests that these programs have contributed substantially to increased and stabilized farm income (Tweeten 1979).

Social adjustments at the farm level include changing farm operations through diversification, maintaining on-farm grain reserves, personal savings and credit reserves, altering family consumption patterns, and seeking alternative employment (Clawson et al. 1980). Throughout the Great Plains, diversification via the addition of cattle is seen as the single most effective on-farm drought adjustment. Cattle represent liquid reserves that can be converted to cash when crops are poor. As shown in the North Dakota case study discussed below, diversified farming/ranching has been practiced in some parts of the spring wheat region and has been somewhat successful in stabilizing farm income.

The Effect of Land Retirement Schemes

Conservation efforts on the Great Plains have had mixed success. Using the technical advice of the Soil Conservation Service and the financial aid provided by the Great Plains Conservation Program (GPCP), dry-land grain farmers have achieved a massive switch to conservation techniques (Vaught 1969). Unfortunately, conservation programs have not been successful in reaching the goal of permanent retirement of marginal land to grassland or to other soil building crops. The GPCP and its antecedents have been ineffective in keeping less productive and erosion-sensitive lands out of production (Pimentel et al. 1976, p. 149). Strong prices and the quest for efficiency on highly mechanized, heavily capitalized farms have encouraged the use of all available acreage. Moreover, other land use adjustment programs, such as the Agricultural Stabilization and Conservation Service's (ASCS) set-aside, base production levels on national policy, not on resource protection goals. Thus the amount of land that farmers can plant and still receive government price-protection payments fluctuates with national production and trade goals, a situation that often frustrates conservation efforts.

Wheat acreage on the Plains is a good indicator of the failure of land retirement. Only 15.5 million acres of wheat were planted on the Great Plains in 1900. In the next 3 decades, wheat acreage increased rapidly, reaching 43.3 million acres on the eve of the 1930s drought. Farm failure and land retirement programs lowered the acreage to 24.2 million in 1934, but as better weather set in during the 1940s, it rebounded to an all-time high of 54.4 million in 1949. Since then, total wheat acreage on the Plains has remained high, reaching 48.2 million acres in 1975.

According to Pimentel et al. (1976), about 71 percent of the acreage taken out of production by early government programs was put back into use during the expansion years of the late 1960s and 1970s. Clearly, marginal land-retirement schemes have had little overall impact on Great Plains agriculture. The trend of expansion to meet demand has continued to the present. In essence, then, the misfit theme and the adjustments associated with it have played relatively minor roles in reducing drought vulnerability on the Plains.

A CASE STUDY OF DROUGHT MANAGEMENT IN THE SPRING WHEAT AREA OF NORTH DAKOTA

Food production is currently the chief economic activity in North Dakota's spring wheat area, and dry-land wheat cultivation has been the dominant land use there since the late 1800s. Two study sites in the spring wheat area were chosen for detailed examination: Kidder County in central North Dakota and Williams County in the northwest corner of the state (Fig. 1).

Fieldwork was conducted during the spring and summer of 1980 to collect agricultural statistics and to interview farmers about their methods of coping with drought. It was one of the driest springs on record in many parts of the state; no measurable rain fell during the entire planting season in some central and western counties. The statewide average wheat yield for 1980 was about 18 bushels per acre, the lowest since 1961 and about 40 percent below the long-term trend. The poor crop of 1980 illustrates clearly that drought is still a major problem in the region.

North Dakota farmers tend to expect poor wheat-yields about once every 3 or 4 years, with drought being the chief cause of reduced yields. Wheat-yield records from 1900 to 1979 show that poor yields (defined here as drops of 25 percent or more below the long-term trend) occurred 28 times in Kidder County (about once every 3 years) and 16 times in Williams County (once in 5 years). The difference between the 2 counties in frequency of poor crops is especially evident in the last decade. During 1969-79, Kidder County farmers experienced three years with poor yields; in 1977, the yield was 58 percent below the long-term trend. In contrast, Williams County produced much more reliable crops, with no poor yields during the same period.

Precipitation is slightly more variable in Williams County than it is in Kidder County. Since about 1940, moisture supplies for dry-land crops have become less stable in Williams County, whereas in Kidder County they have become slightly more stable. Thus one would expect Kidder County yields to be more stable than yields in Williams County. In fact, the opposite is true, which suggests that Williams County farmers have better protected their crops from the effects of weather by applying agro-technological adjustments. Thus the search for specific drought adjustments in Williams County focused on crop-protection strategies. In Kidder County, where yields remain quite variable, the search focused on strategies aimed at buffering the impacts of poor crops on the farmer.

Techno-Fix in North Dakota: Summer Fallowing

Agriculturists in North Dakota attribute Williams County's reliable wheat-yields to summer fallowing, the practice of alternating between crop and fallow from year to year. During the fallow year, fields are kept free of weeds and are mulched with crop stubble to inhibit evaporation. Experimental trials have shown that this practice increases subsequent yields by conserving soil moisture. Summer fallowing also reduces yield variability, according to an analysis of coefficients of variation for yields of summer fallowed and continuously cropped wheat in Williams and Kidder counties (Riebsame 1981). For the last few decades, there has been a striking difference in the amount of fallowed wheat in the two counties: over 90 percent of the wheat in Williams County and only about 30 percent in Kidder County. The widespread use of this particular agro-technological adjustment in Williams County is probably the chief cause of more reliable yields compared to Kidder County.

There are several reasons why Kidder County farmers do not practice summer fallowing extensively. They feel that the opportunity costs of idled land and the need for frequent cultivation and for increased use of herbicides make it unprofitable. In addition, a review of county extension reports for the last 70 years shows that agricultural officials have not promoted summer fallowing as strongly in Kidder County as in Williams County. The reason may be the general belief that Kidder County's slightly more humid climate obviates the need for fallowing to conserve moisture.

Social Adjustments in North Dakota

The most important social adjustments that maintain farmers' well-being during crop failures take the form of government aid and on-farm diversification (the addition of cattle production to grain farms). The effectiveness of such adjustments can be measured by their impacts on farm income variability. County-level farm income data are not available on an annual basis, but at the state level, it can be shown that government payments and income from livestock sales have stabilized the interannual variability of farm income. During 1938-79, the average year-to-year change in farm income from crops alone was about 21 percent in North Dakota. When crop and livestock incomes are combined, the year-to-year change drops to 18 percent. Finally, when crop and livestock incomes are combined with government payments, the average year-to-year change drops to 16 percent. Although this analysis applies to the state overall, it is reasonable to conclude, as have most North Dakota farmers and agricultural officials, that livestock income and government payments mitigate the income-lowering effects of crop loss due to drought and other hazards (e.g., hail and excess moisture).

Most farmers in both study counties participate in government crop loss payment and crop insurance programs. Data for the two counties show that both have benefited about equally from ASCS disaster payments, which pay farmers the difference between expected and actual yields. Crop insurance data show that Kidder County farmers have continually received higher and more frequent indemnities for drought-related crop loss than have Williams County farmers. During 1959-77, Kidder County farmers received roughly $1.50 for every dollar paid in premiums, while Williams County farmers lost about half their premiums.

In terms of farm diversification, the differences between the two counties are more acute. In 1974, a cattle inventory was reported for 85 percent of the farms in Kidder County and for only about half the farms in Williams County. In the same year, Kidder County farm income was about evenly divided between cattle and crop sales, and Williams County farmers earned only about 20 percent of their income from cattle. Kidder County's highly diversified farming system has developed slowly over the last decade, with the constant urging of agricultural officials. The call for diversification first went out when North Dakota's many single-crop farms experienced massive crop failures in the early 1890s. But the lure of so-called dry farming techniques, as well as the more favorable weather and prices of the early 1900s, squelched the early diversification efforts. Interest in cattle production increased during the 1930s drought when the government became the largest beef buyer on the Plains, but it lessened again with the bumper crops of the 1940s. Diversified farming finally caught on permanently in Kidder County during the 1950s. The practice never flourished in Williams County, where yields were more reliable due to extensive summer following.

Recent experience shows the value of farm diversification. It was an important factor in maintaining the well-being of Kidder County farmers during the 1980 drought. For many, cattle income was the chief source of cash flow during the year, and record cattle sales were reported.

Land Retirement in North Dakota

As on the Great Plains as a whole, efforts to remove marginal acres from crop production have failed in the North Dakota spring wheat area. Large tracts of land retired during past droughts have been recultivated for dry-land crops. During acreage expansions in the 1960s and 1970s, wheat acreages in both Kidder and Williams counties came close to an all-time high. In 1976, Kidder County farmers devoted 143,000 acres to wheat (about 60 percent of the county's total cropland), close to the record of 156,000 acres set in 1932. Williams County farmers planted 367,000 acres of wheat (about 80 percent of their total cropland) in 1976, just under the 375,000 acres planted in 1933, the largest year on record. From agricultural settlement to the present, wheat acreages in both counties have shown a marked increase; at the same time, wheat has grown in dominance over other crops. Grass and other conservation crops have been relegated to a minor role in the region, and land retirement efforts have failed.

CONCLUSIONS

Despite recurrent drought, dry-land wheat production has become the dominant use of the American Great Plains. The impacts of drought have lessened through time, suggesting that certain adjustments have buffered drought effects success-fully. The North Dakota spring wheat area, like the Great Plains generally, relies on certain agro-technological and social adjustments to make agriculture profit-able in an uncertain environment. In some areas, adjustments that protect crops from drought damage (e.g., summer fallowing and stubble mulching) appear to have mitigated the effects of drought on agriculture by stabilizing yields. Effec-tive technological adjustments have not been adopted everywhere on the Plains, however. In areas where continuous cropping prevails, yields remain susceptible to drought damage. Some farmers have buffered drought impacts by maintaining a liquid reserve in the form of cattle, which provides income when crops fail. The Plainswide analysis of wheat-yields discussed in this paper suggests that technological stabilization of yields is the exception rather than the rule in Great Plains drought adjustment. Government aid and on-farm strategies like diversifi-cation have probably played largest role in reducing drought impacts in the long run. A third adjustment type, fundamental land use change such as the retirement of marginal acres to grassland, has often been promoted but only rarely adopted.

The next Great Plains drought will probably cause less serious social impacts than its predecessors. It will, however, reduce crop yields substantially, and income based on crop production alone is likely to remain quite variable in the future. Current efforts to discourage summer fallowing, the adjustment apparently responsible for stabilizing yields in the face of weather variability in Williams County, may cause further decreases in yield during the next drought. Also, problems not considered in this paper, like escalating energy costs and the depletion of groundwater in irrigated areas, may exacerbate future drought impacts.

Future drought adjustment in the region should be based on recognition of the relative roles of technological and social change in mitigating drought impacts. Agro-technological adjustments should be evaluated in on-farm use before they are assumed to protect crops from drought, and proven adjustments should be adopted and maintained. Social adjustments probably carry the bulk of drought impact mitigation; they should be reviewed in light of their relative importance. Recent adjustment proposals, such as the one outlined in Rosenberg (1980), pay substantial attention to social responses to drought, thus breaking a long tradition of faith in technological fixes. The importance of social adjustments suggests that more effort is needed to evaluate them; programs established during emergencies (e.g., the 1930s "Dust Bowl") should be carefully audited and, if necessary, revised to make them more flexible.

Finally, the failure of efforts to bring about basic change in land use on the Great Plains points to an economic environment that encourages greater food production for international trade, but that does not promote resource conservation. An increase in agricultural production, without a concomitant decrease in the relative variability of production, transfers the impacts of fluctuations in food supply to a larger, more vulnerable segment of the world's population. This could make the next major Great Plains drought a truly global disaster.

References

Agricultural Adjustment Administration 1934. *Agricultural Adjustment. A Report of Administration of the Agricultural Adjustment Act, May 1933 to February 1934.* Washington, DC: United States Department of Agriculture.

Clawson, M.; Ottoson, H.W.; Duncan, M.; Sharp, E.S. 1980. Report of the Task Group on Economics. In *Drought in the Great Plains: Research on Impacts and Strategies,* ed. N. J. Rosenberg, pp. 43-59. Littleton, CO: Water Resources Publications.

Crawford, A. B. 1978. State and Federal Response to the 1977 Drought. In *North American Droughts,* ed. N. J. Rosenberg, pp. 143-161. Boulder, CO: Westview Press.

Great Plains Agricultural Council, 1955. *Risk and Uncertainty in Agriculture.* Publication No. 11. Lincoln, NE.

————. 1959. *Management Strategies in Great Plains Farming.* Publication No. 19. Lincoln, NE.

Great Plains Committee, 1937. *The Future of the Great Plains.* House of Representatives Document No. 144, 75th Congress. Washington, DC: Government Printing Office.

Greb, B. W. 1979. Technology and wheat yields in the central Great Plains: commercial advances. *Journal of Soil and Water Conservation* 34: 269-273.

Greb, B. W., Smika, D. E. and Welsh, J. R. 1979. Technology and wheat yields in the central Great Plains: experiment station advances. *Journal of Soil and Water Conservation* 34: 264-268.

Haigh, P. 1977. *Separating the Effects of Weather and Management on Crop Production.* Contract report, Charles F. Kettering Foundation, Grant No. ST-77-4.

Hargreaves, M. W. 1957. *Dry Farming in the Northern Great Plains: 1900-1925.* Cambridge, MA: Harvard University Press.

———. 1976. Land-use planning in response to drought: the experience of the thirties. *Agricultural History* 50: 561-582.

Held, R. B., and Clawson, M. 1965. *Soil Conservation in Perspective.* Baltimore, MD: Johns Hopkins Press.

Kraenzel, C. F. 1955. *The Great Plains in Transition.* Norman: University of Oklahoma Press.

Lockeretz, W. 1978. The lessons of the Dust Bowl. *American Scientist* 66: 560-569.

McDean, H. C. 1980. Federal farm policy and the Dust Bowl: the half-right solution. *North Dakota History* 47: 21-31.

Michaels, P. J. 1978. *A Predictive Model for Winter Wheat Yield in the United States Great Plains.* Report No. 94. Institute of Environmental Studies. Madison: University of Wisconsin.

National Oceanic and Atmospheric Administration 1973. *The Influence of Weather and Climate on United States Grain Yields: Bumper Crops or Droughts.* Report to the Administrator. Washington, DC: United States Department of Commerce.

Palmer, W. C. 1965. *Meteorlogical Drought.* Research Paper No. 45. Washington, DC: United States Weather Bureau.

Perrin, R, K., and Heady, E. O. 1975. *Relative Contributions of Major Technological Factors and Moisture Stress to Increased Grain Yields in the Midwest, 1930-1971.* Report No. 55. Center for Agriculture and Rural Development. Ames: Iowa State University.

Pimentel, D.; Terhune, E. C.; Dyson-Hudson, R., Rochereau, S.; Samis, R.; Smith, E.; Denman, D.; Reifschneider, D. and Shepard, M. 1976. Land degradation: effects on food and energy resources. *Science* 194: 149-155.

Quinn, M. L. 1980. An Historical Survey of Drought Planning with Emphasis on the U.S. Great Plains. In *Drought in the Great Plains,* ed. N. J. Rosenberg, pp. 135-167. Littleton, CO: Water Resources Publications.

Rasmussen, W. D.; Baker, G. L. and Ward, J. S. 1976. *A Short History of Agricultural Adjustment, 1933-75.* Agricultural Information Bulletin No. 391. Economic Research Service. Washington, DC: United States Department of Agriculture.

Riebsame, W. E. 1981. *Drought Adjustment in the Spring Wheat Area of North Dakota: A Case Study of Climate Impacts on Agriculture.* Ph.D. Dissertation. Clark University, Worcester, MA.

Rosenberg, N. J., ed. 1980. *Drought in the Great Plains: Research on Impacts and Strategies.* Littleton, CO: Water Resources Publications.

Shannon, F. A. 1945. *The Farmer's Last Frontier, Agriculture 1860-1897.* New York: Farrar and Rinehart.

Stegner, W. 1953. *Beyond the Hundredth Meridian: John Wesley Powell and the Second Opening of the West.* Boston, MA: Houghton Mifflin.

Tweeten, L. G. 1979. *Foundations of Farm Policy.* Lincoln: University of Nebraska Press.

Vaught, W. L. 1969. A decade of action: Great Plains Conservation Program. *Soil Conservation* 34: 243-246.

Warrick, R. A. 1975. *Drought Hazard in the United States: A Research Assessment.* Monograph No. NSF-RA-E-75-004. Institute of Behavioral Science. Boulder: University of Colorado.

———. 1980. Drought in the Great Plains: A Case Study of Research on Climate and Society in the U.S.A. In *Climatic Constraints and Human Activities,* ed. J. Ausubel and A.K. Biswas, pp. 93-123. Oxford, United Kingdom: Pergamon Press.

Widtsoe, J. A. 1911. *Dry-Farming.* New York: MacMillan Co.

VIII. Institutions for Managing Nonmetropolitan Land

Land and Water Use Planning in the New Deal

Marion Clawson

The administration of President Franklin D. Roosevelt from 1933 to his death in 1945, commonly called the New Deal, was a period of great governmental activism compared with any preceding administration. One part of this activism was the federal government's role in land and water use planning.

The extreme economic and social conditions of the Great Depression were manifest in 1933 in unemployment of a fourth of the labor force, in extensive business bankruptcies, in shatteringly low prices for agricultural commodities, and in personal distress on a scale unknown in modern times. In that year there existed no significant unemployment compensation, no social security, no federal welfare program, and no effective program for support of commodity prices. On top of the extremely difficult economic and social conditions, there was a mood of despair, of uncertainty, and of confusion throughout the country. Roosevelt's New Deal tried various ameliorative measures during the 1933-40 period, but defense and, later, war efforts overshadowed the economic and social reforms and restorations, which had been at best only partially successful under the New Deal. This is a complex and, to me, fascinating story; I wish to focus here only on the land and water use planning aspects of that period in American history.

One of the major organizations involved in land and water use planning was the National Resources Planning Board and its predecessors (National Planning Board, National Resources Board, National Resources Committee). Although there were in succession four names, this was essentially one organization throughout. It was the only national, official, comprehensive planning agency

This essay is based upon my book *New Deal Planning: The National Resources Planning Board*, published by Johns Hopkins University Press, to which the interested reader is referred for a great deal more information than could be included here.

this country has ever had. Its operations were much broader in scope than land and water use planning, but its planning in these fields was extremely influential at the time and has greatly affected such planning over the subsequent decades.

One major approach of the New Deal was to establish (for the day) extensive public works, both for their own value and as a means of employment. There was a Works Progress Administration, under Harry Hopkins, to provide "quickie" public employment on scores of different activities. There was also a Public Works Administration, under Harold L. Ickes, to carry out major long-term public works, such as the big dams built in that period. The latter established a National Planning Board in the summer of 1933, to try to coordinate the various projects, to avoid overlaps or conflicts, and generally to seek the maximum value from the public works program. In a general organizational pattern that was maintained throughout its history, the agency had a board, consisting of Cabinet officials, and citizen members, with Harold Ickes as chairman. It was advisory to the Public Works Administration.

The National Planning Board lasted a single year, after which it was transformed into the National Resources Board, now advisory to the president but otherwise largely unchanged. This in turn lasted but a year, after which the National Industrial Recovery Act, its legal base, was declared unconstitutional. The board was succeeded by the National Resources Committee—a new name and a new legal base, but otherwise no significant change. After four years this was succeeded by the National Resources Planning Board, from which the Cabinet directing Board was dropped and replaced by a wholly citizen Board, the functions somewhat broadened, and the staffing greatly expanded.

At its very first meeting, the National Planning Board defined its functions as planning and programming of public works, coordination of federal planning, stimulation of planning at regional and state levels, and research. With modest additions, these remained the functions of the organization throughout its history. In my study of the Board and its successors, hereafter referred to as the National Resources Planning Board (NRPB), I have grouped its activities into two broad categories: (1) planning and coordination, and (2) idea stimulation. I have also argued that these were mutually inconsistent functions and that no small part of NRPB's subsequent difficulties arose from its trying to carry out inconsistent and incompatible objectives. Agency coordination is most effective when it is quiet and unobtrusive, directed primarily to the president; idea stimulation requires widespread dissemination of reports and much publicity, and it inevitably stirs controversy.

Throughout its history, NRPB had a governing board—sometimes consisting wholly of citizen members who served part-time, sometimes also of Cabinet officers who had manifold other duties. There was always a staff, which was headed throughout its whole history by Charles W. Eliot 2nd, but which expanded in numbers and functions as time went on. From early on, the board had its own regional organizations; as well as state planning organizations that were legally independent of NRPB but stimulated by it and aided by it in obtaining funds and manpower. Finally, during virtually all of its history, the board had committees and consultants. NRPB's use of committees of diverse membership was notable for its day, although the National Academy of Science and other federal organizations make extensive use of similar committees today. NRPB committees typically had leading figures from concerned federal agencies plus outstanding individuals from outside of government. These committees of NRPB, its regional organizations, and its relations with state planning agencies were among the most successful aspects of NRPB's operations.

After the first year, the NRPB group of agencies was advisory to the president. It enjoyed cordial relations with him throughout its history. It was but one of many agencies, groups, or persons who sought to influence Roosevelt. There is good evidence that he found NRPB a valuable source of ideas, though it was not his arm in day-to-day coordination of government. When the war came, Roosevelt turned to other planning and operating agencies; his contacts with NRPB diminished greatly, although he continued to support it. The board, or—more accurately—Professor Charles E. Merriam of the University of Chicago, who was a member of the board throughout its history and who was vice chairman during its final four years, insisted that an organization advisory to the president should have only the most limited and distant contacts with Congress. During the first six years, the board operated entirely on emergency funds allocated to it by the president; during its last four years, it had to seek appropriations and this exposed it to congressional scrutiny and challenge. Its relations with Congress were never good; cool and distant at first, Congress grew increasingly critical and hostile, and in 1943 when the fatal attack on NRPB was made the agency had few informed friends in Congress.

The executive order in June 1934, which established the National Resources Board as advisory to the president, directed it to come up with a report on land and water use within six months. The resulting *Report on National Planning and Public Works in Relation to Natural Resources and Including Land Use and Water Resources with Findings and Recommendations* is, in my judgment, one of the great classics of American natural resource analysis and planning. The report is long—455 pages of the oversize pages used by NRPB, full of details, thoroughly competent in a professional sense, and notable for the breadth of its coverage. It is also notable for the fact that a score or more federal agencies and over 200 named individuals participated in its preparation. Given the data bases of the day, and the state of professional arts and the analytic capacity of the day, no present group could do any better. That it was done in six months is, by modern standards, little short of a miracle.

As I contemplate the extraordinary quality of this report, I am moved to try to account for how the National Resources Board could do so well. It had, at that time, fewer than 40 of its own employees. This forced the board to rely on other persons and other agencies—and therein lies, I believe, one of its major strengths. Many of these other federal agencies had accumulated experiences and data for which they lacked other good outlets and uses. The times clearly called for imaginative approaches. Outside government, there were many professional people who were also eager to help and also lacking good professional outlets for their ideas. The combination of these, and perhaps other, factors led to the quality, comprehensiveness, and timeliness of the report.

The section of the 1934 report that dealt with land was particularly outstanding. It included a comprehensive analysis of the "conditions and tendencies influencing major land requirements," including demographic, economic, technological, and international factors; an analysis of land requirements in relation to land resources; and an extensive analysis of maladjustments in land use. The report drew heavily on earlier and ongoing studies in the Departments of Agriculture and of the Interior. The report of the water committee was also good, in relation to the times, but at that date it had available to it much less background work on which to draw than did the land committee. The report on minerals (including energy minerals) was much less comprehensive and thorough than the land report, again reflecting a poorer data and analytic base elsewhere in government.

The subsequent work of the water committee was outstanding. The committee was concerned with data collection and analysis. It introduced or made dominant two major concepts in water analysis: (1) that of river systems or river basins, wherein any development in one part of a basin affected water quantity and quality in all other parts of the basin, so that development projects could no longer be looked at in isolation from other projects; and (2) the concept of multiple-use water development, whereby flood protection, navigation improvement, power generation, irrigation, waste disposal, and other water functions were considered each in relation to the others, and the whole typically was far more productive in an economic sense than any single-purpose water development. The water committee had many able men, of whom Abel Wolman, Harlan H. Barrows, and Thorndike Saville, all from outside the federal government, were outstanding. For a considerable part of the committee's existence, Wolman was a driving force as chairman. Many other notable reports were prepared by it and published by NRPB. Among these may be included its 1936 report, *Drainage Basin Problems and Programs;* its 1938 report, *Low Dams: A Manual of Design for Small Water Storage Projects;* and its 1940 report, *Deficiencies in Hydrologic Research.* In all I identified 42 NRPB printed or mimeographed reports, totaling almost 7,000 pages, as being concerned primarily with water. The approaches to water use planning developed by NRPB's water committee have become accepted practice in all water planning in the United States today. All water planning since 1943 follows closely the concepts developed by NRPB.

The subsequent work of the land committee was good, but not as outstanding as that of the water committee. There are several reasons for this. The land committee never had a chairman with such driving force as Wolman gave to the water committee. M. L. Wilson was able, genial, a good organizer, but most of the time preoccupied with other duties; for many months there was no effective chairman. Wilson's successor, W. I. Meyers was similar—able, interested, but lacking in driving force. The feud between Ickes and Wallace during much of the 1930s over the Forest Service and the Soil Conservation Service surely inhibited the operations of the land committee. And finally, the USDA moved into rural land-use planning in a major way, making NRPB operations less necessary in this field. Many of the USDA men and women who had been so effective in preparing the 1934 report got drawn off into other activities and were generally less available to NRPB. But the land committee subsequently prepared, and NRPB published, many excellent reports. Two reports, one in 1940 and the other in 1941, dealt with public acquisition of land; another in 1941, *Land Classification in the United States;* two in 1942, *Public Works and Rural Land Use* and *Tax Delinquency and Rural Land-Use Development;* in total, 14 printed and mimeographed reports totaling over 2,000 pages dealing primarily with land. Land planning in the United States since 1943 has been strongly influenced by NRPB experience, although rather less so than water planning has been.

Space does not permit a discussion of NRPB's activities in fields other than land and water use planning. Suffice it to say that NRPB conducted or stimulated—and published—many studies on population, consumer incomes and expenditures, transportation, industrial location, housing and urban problems, security and welfare, and many other subjects. Many of them stirred much interest and discussion at the time; some of them also evoked much criticism, some of it highly emotional, from persons in Congress who in any case would have been critical or hostile to NRPB.

For the most part, NRPB stayed out of planning for agricultural adjustment, or the matching of agricultural output with effective demand, leaving this major activity to the Department of Agriculture. The New Deal included a major expansion of federal activities in agriculture, with a consequent expansion of agencies and staffing in the Department. Henry A. Wallace as Secretary, M. L. Wilson as Under Secretary, and Howard R. Tolley, as head of the Agricultural Adjustment Administration and later as chief of the Bureau of Agricultural Economics Division, sought common ground and coordinating themes among the various bureaus and programs of the Department. After the department's reorganization in 1938, land use planning became the vehicle for departmental and program integration. The states were encouraged to undertake rural land-use planning in counties, with different degrees of intensity of land-use planning proposed from Washington. A great deal of use was made of local, largely citizen, land-use planning committees. Many people who make so much of public participation in government programs these days seem totally unaware of the very extensive experience along this line in the late 1930s and early 1940s.

The work of the local and state land use planning committees was, naturally enough, variable in scope, content, emphasis, and quality; but, in my judgment, a great deal of excellent work was done. Unfortunately, most of the results of this work were not organized well or presented effectively in publications at that time, nor—apparently—have they been preserved in available records at either national or local levels. This is a pity, for that land use planning effort assembled data, made maps, and reached judgments about land that would give us a highly valuable data plane today from which to measure changes in land use that have occurred in the ensuing forty years.

In 1943 the NRPB was terminated by Congress, which withheld from it any appropriation for the 1944 fiscal year and forbade it to accept transferred emergency funds from the president. There is no single explanation for the action of Congress; a number of factors combined to enable NRPB's enemies to kill it. The agency had always lacked informed friends, as I have noted. Merriam's insistence on remaining aloof from Congress was surely a major factor here. The chairman of the board when it was a citizen board, and an influential member at all times, was Frederic A. Delano, uncle of President Roosevelt. An able man, with extensive experience in business and in city planning, he was so determined not to trade upon his relationship with the president that he was a less aggressive chairman than many another man would have been. A strong and highly emotional anti-Roosevelt sentiment was shared by many congressmen. The 1942 elections had seen a marked shift in political power to the conservatives, to the "right."

At the same time, the board cannot escape all responsibility for its own demise. The content of its social and economic reports had stirred much criticism in Congress. The timing of the release of some of these reports was unfortunate. Its work was frequently attacked as unnecessary in the war effort that then dominated American public life. Its activities in water planning had drawn the opposition of the Rivers and Harbors Congress. On top of all this, there was marked divergence between Merriam on the board, and Eliot, the staff director. In my recent research, it appears that near the end of NRPB's life, each man was scheming as to how he could circumvent or replace the other. Even before that, there had been for a long time a notable lack of agreement over emphasis of the board's work and over methods and tactics. Some of NRPB's problems would have been faced by any national planning agency at that time, but some were peculiar to this board, with its personalities, convictions, and specific approaches. In any case, the board that did exist was responsible for some outstanding land and water use planning (see earlier references). Its activities in this field have left their mark on land- and water-use planning in the United States today.

Rural Lands Aspects of the San Diego Regional Growth Management Plan

Philip R. Pryde and David C. Nielsen

INTRODUCTION

Any inclusive definition of "Nonmetropolitan America" needs to embrace areas that lie close to, and are heavily influenced by, our nation's numerous large urban complexes. Here land-use problems are most difficult. These "near-metropolitan" lands may not always be the most environmentally sensitive, but such resources and values that do exist are very vulnerable because of the accelerated tempo and economic pressures of suburban and exurban development. This chapter addresses that aspect of the rural lands problem.

GEOGRAPHICAL SETTING OF SAN DIEGO COUNTY

San Diego County is a planning paradox. The city of San Diego at its southwest corner gained 22 percent in population between 1970 and 1980, moving from fourteenth to eighth place among U.S. cities with approximately 850,000 people. The population of San Diego County increased 37 percent to about 1.8 million, of whom the vast majority live in the western third of the county bordering the Pacific Ocean (Figure 1). Of the county's land area of 4,314 square miles (larger than Delaware and Rhode Island combined), about 3,000 square miles of desert and mountains in the eastern two-thirds are inhabited by only about 22,000 people. This vast hinterland, however, is now experiencing pressures and impacts from the continuing outward growth of the urban part of the county.

Topographically, the coastal strip, along which most of the population is found, consists of a series of marine terraces dissected by the lower reaches of several streams that drain from the mountain ranges to the east. Inland from the coastal terraces is what is termed the foothills-and-valleys region. This is a combination of rolling hills, a few sharp peaks, some higher valleys, and a system of

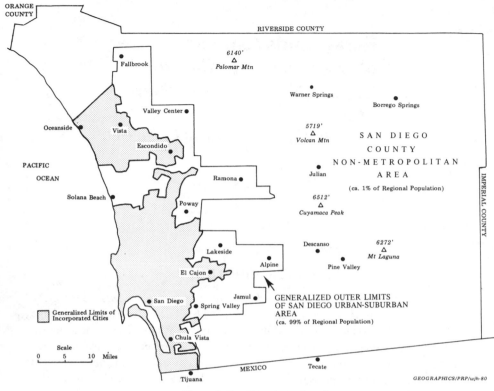

Figure 1. San Diego's rural environs.

narrower river corridors and floodplains. Through the center of the county, the 6000-foot-high Palomar, Laguna, and other mountain ranges are oriented in a northwest-southeast direction and embrace a rather heterogeneous mixture of private, federal, state, and Indian ownerships. To the east of these ranges lies the extremely arid Borrego desert, which contains several smaller mountain ranges and includes a mixture of state, private, and B.L.M. ownerships. Most is the half-million acre Anza-Borrego Desert State Park, the largest and certainly one of the most scenic state parks in the nation.

Climatically, San Diego County is semi-arid steppe along the coast, mediterranean on the west slopes of the mountain ranges, and arid desert to the east of the mountain crests. The county's diverse natural regions and its proximity to Mexico make it unusually rich in plants and birds. Several species of plants are found in the United States only within San Diego County.

About three-quarters of the region is clearly rural at present. The residents of this area think of themselves as rural, and the vast majority wish to remain that way. Most of the land is in parcel sizes of two acres or larger, and, as noted, much of it is publicly owned (Forest Service, Bureau of Land Management, California State Parks, and military land). In addition, the rural portion of the county contains seventeen Indian reservations, more than any other single county in the United States. Most individual landowners in the eastern part of the county with potentially subdividable land do not wish it to be divided into lots of less than two acres, although there are numerous corporate landowners with denser development plans.

PROBLEMS OF SAN DIEGO COUNTY

Rural San Diego County is a highly diverse and fragile area. Its agricultural lands make a half-billion dollar contribution to the local economy. Many of the publicly owned areas are major recreational resources for San Diego residents as well as for people from the rest of the state and nation. The generally pleasant climate attracts many retired persons, mobile types of industries and workers, and thousands of winter visitors.

This attraction is itself a source of significant problems. The rural area's natural beauty, unique fauna and flora, and pleasant climate, coupled with its easy access to metropolitan San Diego and Los Angeles, result in sustained and often competing developmental demands that pose a major threat to these important resources. Some of the problems are:

1. Water Availability

One of rural San Diego's greatest problems is the availability of water. Until 1947, the entire county was dependent on local water resources. The population of the county was only 300,000, but the postwar population boom had begun and the local water supply was being stretched to the limit. In 1947 the first aqueduct from the Colorado River reached San Diego. Today 98 percent of the population is served by water imported from the Colorado River and from the Feather River in Northern California. Local sources account for only ten percent of total regional consumption. The eastern two-thirds of the county is not accessible to imported water and thus is dependent primarily on groundwater. Further, because of limitations on future imported supplies, there is virtually no possibility of additional water being available to this area.

Rainfall in both the mountain and desert areas is seasonally and annually variable. In the crystalline rock mountainous areas, quantities of water in storage are quite limited. In the desert, although there is considerable water in underground aquifers, annual recharge is even less than in the crystalline rock areas. Further, crystalline rock areas are highly variable in their water-producing capacities. The long-term yield from wells is usually considerably less than initial discharge during drilling. Studies have shown that there is sufficient groundwater only for low-density residential and agricultural uses.

Problems from over-development in certain of the county's rural areas have already occurred. Near the community of Ramona, there has been interference between wells placed too close together. In the Julian area, water surface profiles show some significant declines because of groundwater extractions from nearby wells.

2. Creeping Suburbs

Some of the nonurban portions of the county do receive imported water, and this has resulted in significant development pressures in these areas. The unincorporated areas grew by 11,300 persons in 1979 alone, and are projected to grow at an average rate of 3.6 percent annually through 1995, as compared with 2.3 percent for the county as a whole.

The result has been urban encroachment into rural areas, increased demands for expensive urban services, and development patterns that, in these times of scarce energy, often make little sense.

3. Spot Development

In the more remote areas of the county, rural villages and towns have begun to experience considerable growth pressures. In the Borrego Valley, for example, during the past three years developments have been proposed that, if completed, would increase the permanent population from 1,500 to 10,000 persons by 1995. The character of this small community would be changed to that of a major resort.

4. Sanitation Problems

The county's regulations on the installation of septic systems have proved to be inadequate in the face of intensifying rural development pressures. Until now, minimum parcel sizes were based on effluent percolation tests. Such tests, however, did not take into account the impact of effluent accumulation on the water table, in particular downslope accumulation. In areas that have already high water tables and that have experienced two successive wet years, some septic systems have been unable to disperse effluents, resulting in potentially serious health problems. To alleviate such problems, already developed areas will have to install on-site package treatment systems or hook up to a regional collection system for treatment off-site. The former is very expensive and the latter may induce additional growth by providing a means to accommodate even higher densities. Clearly, what is needed is to reduce the development capability of unsewered areas to assure that septic systems do not interfere with local water supplies.

SAN DIEGO COUNTY REGIONAL GROWTH MANAGEMENT PLAN

In San Diego County there has been an interest in growth management for some time, the result of many years of rapid and sustained growth. (See Table 1.) The county's Regional Growth Management Plan was designed in part to deal with problems outlined above. In order to understand the county's program, however, a brief description is needed of certain aspects of planning in California as mandated by the state legislature.

Table 1. Population Growth in San Diego County, 1940-80,
Entire County and Unincorporated Areas

Year	County Population*	County Annual Growth Rate (%)
1940	289,348	———
1950	556,808	6.8
1960	1,033,011	6.4
1970	1,357,854	2.8
1975	1,559,505	2.8
1980 (Est.)	1,829,600	3.3

Year	Unincorporated Area Population†	Unincorporated Area Annual Growth Rate (%)
1940	48,986	———
1950	136,624	10.8
1960	227,386	5.2
1970	292,625	2.6
1975	361,756	4.3
1980 (Est.)	422,600	3.2

*Based on U.S. Census and 1975 Special Census.
†Unincorporated areas as delimited in year indicated. Actual growth rates are greater due to shrinking area.

Land Use Planning in California

The California Planning and Zoning Law requires counties and cities to "adopt a comprehensive, long-term general plan for the physical development of the county or city, and of any land outside its boundaries which in the planning agency's judgment bears relation to its planning" (*California Government Code*, Sec. 65300 et seq.). The general plan must address the following issues: 1) land use, 2) circulation, 3) housing, 4) public safety, 5) conservation, 6) open space, 7) seismic safety, 8) noise, and 9) scenic highways. Additional elements may be included in a general plan at the discretion of the local jurisdiction. The mandatory elements can be amended no more than three times during any calendar year.

The statute further requires that local zoning ordinances must be consistent with these general plans. A zoning ordinance is deemed consistent with a general plan only if:

(a) the city or county has officially adopted such a plan, and
(b) the various land uses authorized by the ordinance are compatible with the objectives, policies, general land uses, and programs specified in such a plan.

The Subdivision Map Act (*Cal. Govt. Code*, Sec. 66473.5) further requires county and local governments to regulate land subdivisions in accordance with their general plans. Subdivisions must be disapproved if:

(a) the proposed map is not consistent with applicable general and specific plans;
(b) the design or improvement of the proposed subdivision is not consistent with applicable general and specific plans;
(c) the site is not physically suitable for the type of development;
(d) the site is not physically suitable for the proposed density of development;
(e) the design of the subdivision or the proposed improvements are likely to cause substantial environmental damage or substantially and avoidably injure fish or wildlife or their habitat;
(f) the design of the subdivision or the type of improvements is likely to cause serious public health problems.

The California Environmental Quality Act requires that all local agencies prepare (or cause to be prepared by contract) an environmental impact report on any project they intend to carry out or approve which may have a significant effect on the environment (*California Public Resources Code*, Sec. 21000, et seq.). The act applies to zoning and subdivision actions as well as to major public works projects. Following the model of the National Environmental Policy Act, state environmental impact reports must address:

(a) the significant environmental effects of the proposed project;
(b) any significant environmental effects that cannot be avoided if the project is implemented;
(c) mitigation measures proposed to minimize the significant environmental effects including (but not limited to) measures to reduce wasteful, inefficient, and unnecessary consumption of energy;
(d) alternatives to the project;
(e) the relationship between local short-term uses of man's environment and the enhancement of long-term productivity;
(f) any significant irreversible environmental changes which would be involved in the proposed project should it be implemented.
(g) growth-inducing impacts of the proposed project.

The act further requires that public agencies not approve or carry out a project for which an environmental impact report has identified significant environmental impact unless one or more of the following findings can be made:

(a) changes or alterations have been required in, or incorporated into, such project which mitigate or avoid the significant environmental effects thereof as identified in the completed environmental impact report;
(b) such changes or alterations are within the responsibility and jurisdiction of another public agency and such changes have been adopted by such other agency, or can and should be adopted by such other agency;

(c) specific economic, social, or other considerations make infeasible the mitigation measures or project alternatives identified in the environmental impact report.

Background and Objectives of the San Diego Plan

The San Diego County Regional Growth Management Plan (RGMP) was prepared in the context of these state requirements. They provide local governments with the opportunity and the obligation to adopt and implement effective programs to manage growth. General plans in California cannot be ignored. They are an integral part of the process whereby land is zoned and subdivided.

At the time the RGMP was begun, the county already had important tools available to help preserve rural lands. These included provision for Resource Conservation Areas and the use of slope/density criteria in the County General Plan. Resource Conservation Areas are those parts of the county which, due to their uniqueness, value, or sensitivity, should be protected from extensive development. Specific types of Resource Conservation Areas include: (a) groundwater problem areas, (b) coastal wetlands, (c) significant native wildlife habitat, (d) construction quality sand areas, (e) littoral sand resource areas, (f) astronomical dark sky areas, and (g) archaelogical and historical sites. Over a hundred resource conservation areas have already been designated in the County General Plan and are subject to special zoning and subdivision controls.

The County Land Use Element for many years has limited the permitted density of development in rural areas through the use of slope/density criteria. These criteria relate permitted lot size to slope, i.e., the greater the slope, the larger the minimum lot size. This approach has been widely accepted and utilized throughout the county.

These tools, however, plus the county's earlier General Plan, proved inadequate to cope with problems ensuing from continued rapid growth. In 1977 the County Board of Supervisors directed the County Planning Department to prepare a Regional Growth Management Plan. Three staff persons were sent to 14 jurisdictions around the United States to learn from their growth management experience. Thereafter, a process for developing the RGMP was established, including (a) development of goals and objectives, (b) identification of potential areas for urban development, (c) preparation of a preliminary growth management plan, (d) impact analyses (economic, social, fiscal, environmental), and (e) preparation of the final plan. The process included numerous public meetings and hearings.

Objectives of the plan formally adopted by the Board of Supervisors in June, 1977, were as follows:

(a) Urban growth should be directed to areas within and adjacent to existing urban areas. The rural setting and life-style of the remaining areas of the county should be retained.

(b) Growth should be phased with essential facilities.

(c) Growth should be managed to provide affordable housing and balanced communities throughout the unincorporated area.

(d) Urban portions of the unincorporated area should be encouraged to either annex to an adjacent city or incorporate.

The San Diego County Regional Growth Management Plan as finally prepared in mid-1978 and implemented in 1979 consists of a map and set of policies. The map identifies those areas of the county best able to accommodate urban development as well as those areas which should not be developed. The policies establish appropriate intensities of use in urban and rural areas and specify conditions under which growth anywhere in the county will be permitted. The balance of this chapter addresses those provisions of the plan dealing with the first goal listed above, preservation of the rural setting and lifestyle.

Rural Preservation Policies

The Regional Growth Management Plan involves four tasks or elements that seek to guide development away from unsuitable rural lands. These are: 1) identification of "urban development areas"; 2) urban limit lines; 3) rural groundwater policy; and 4) a septic effluent accumulation study.

Urban Development Areas. The identification of areas suitable (or unsuitable) for future development involved a complex series of analyses. First, a total of 14 growth management objectives were selected. Second, a nonnumerical rating system was employed to indicate the degree of compatibility of specific sites with each objective. Third, criteria were developed to indicate the ability of specific areas to accommodate new growth harmoniously with the objectives. (See Appendix 1 for objectives and criteria.)

The areal unit of analysis used was the Traffic Analysis Zone (TAZ), a geographic unit developed by the California Department of Transportation to facilitate detailed regional studies. Its size is based on population and is generally half the size of a census tract.

Only those areas receiving imported water were included in the analysis, since they were the only areas where urban levels of growth were allowed. The study was carried out as follows:

(1) 261 areas (TAZs) were evaluated in terms of 95 separate criteria. A total of 8,000 separate analyses were required to complete the study.

(2) After these areas were evaluated, a composite score or overall rating was assigned to each.

(3) The overall ratings were then tested and evaluated to assure consistency and accuracy.

(4) TAZs were combined to coincide with community and subregional boundaries.

(5) These larger units were given an overall rating and the ratings once again tested for accuracy and consistency.

The ratings used were as follows:

+   Growth in this area is highly compatible with the objective and should be encouraged.

0   Growth in this area has a "neutral" impact upon the objective.

—   Growth in this area is not compatible with the objective and should be discouraged.

X   This area contains a fundamental restraint to development. (The area is outside the boundaries of a water district supplying imported water; the area is a floodplain or lagoon, etc.)

Use of this methodology provided a technically and politically viable approach for the identification of the boundary between urban and rural lands. It took objectives, defined through the political process, and provided a systematic way to achieve them. It provided a basis for containing urban development within specified areas and for applying strategies to protect rural lands from urban encroachment. The results of this effort, with certain exceptions (see below), have survived intense public scrutiny, public debate, and one legal challenge.

Urban Limit Lines. Once areas suitable for future urban levels of development were identified, an effort was made to further ensure that such development would be contained within these areas through the use of urban limit lines. These lines were drawn on the county general plan land use map in two areas: around the large contiguous suburban zone surrounding the city of San Diego and nearby satellite cities, and around outlying country towns not contiguous with the coastal urbanized areas.

These lines define the areas within which all developmental densities of one dwelling unit per acre or denser must be contained. Outside the urban limit lines, the policies of the estate and rural development categories of the general plan, permitting lots only of two acres or larger in size, must apply. Through this technique, the small outlying towns can, one hopes, be prevented from sprawling all over the rural back country.

Rural Groundwater Policy. As discussed earlier, approximately two-thirds of the county land area is totally dependent on groundwater. Rainfall in these areas is variable. Aquifer recharge and storage are limited. Some communities have already experienced problems, and it is likely that others will in the not too distant future.

When the county's general plan was originally developed, it did not take water availability into account in establishing permitted intensities of use, although since then the environmental review process has provided a degree of protection. The extent of groundwater resources in rural San Diego County still has not been adequately quantified.

To begin solving the problem, the Regional Growth Management Plan included a rural groundwater policy, which has since been approved and is now being implemented. The purpose of the policy is to assure that the demands created by new development not exceed the long-term availability of local groundwater resources. To accomplish this, the policy proposes the following:

(1) interim residential density controls in areas not served by imported water;
(2) a program of comprehensive geological studies to determine long-term groundwater availability;
(3) establishment of a county hydrogeologist position in the County Department of Planning and Land Use.

The policy establishes interim density controls for new subdivisions of land not receiving imported water. The parcel sizes range from 5 to 20 acres and are based on calculations of recharge. The calculations are based on available data, the adequacy of which can be questioned in some cases. Assumptions concerning infiltration and soil moisture capacity may have understated the extent of the problem in certain areas. Nevertheless, on an interim basis, the policy provides more protection than is currently available in the county general plan and zoning ordinance.

Exemptions from the density controls can be granted in three ways:

(1) Projects receiving water from a mutual water company or other water service agency will be exempt if the agency is operated in conformance with a groundwater management plan certified by the county and the proposed project is consistent with the plan.
(2) Projects in the Borrego Valley are exempt, pending completion of special studies of the area (see below).
(3) Projects elsewhere can be exempted if satisfactory proof of groundwater availability is submitted to the county hydrogeologist.

The policy directs that the county hydrogeologist prepare and implement a program to evaluate fully and monitor the long-term availability of groundwater resources in those areas not served by imported water. The program will define specific areas based on hydrogeologic factors. Studies, to be assigned on a priority basis to those areas experiencing greatest development pressures, will investigate groundwater recharge, use, and quality. If the results of these studies dictate, the interim density controls described above will be modified.

The county hydrogeologist will implement the policy. Duties of the position will include preparation of guidelines for hydrologic studies and groundwater management plans, review of all studies and plans submitted pursuant to the policy, and technical oversight of studies to determine long-term groundwater availability.

Septic Effluent Accumulation Study. The county has begun to deal with the sanitation problems discussed above. On an interim basis, detailed hydrogeologic studies are being required for development proposals requiring septic tanks in areas with known high groundwater problems. The results of these studies will be used to determine the number of lots that can be safely created.

During the coming fiscal year, long-term solutions to this problem will be evaluated by staff in conjunction with a task force of experts.

Public Acceptance and Implementation

The San Diego Regional Growth Management Plan has been gradually accepted as a planning tool by the public, though not universally among the development community. The probable reason why it has not produced any concerted opposition is that the term "management" in the RGMP relates primarily to *where* new development will take place, rather than to any abridgement of the total amount. The RGMP places no predetermined limitation on expected county population growth, but rather accepts and makes use of the year 1995 population projections produced by the region's council of governments (the San Diego Association of Governments). This figure is 2.4 million, which equates to an annual population growth rate of about 2.3 percent. Thus developers generally perceive no overall threat to their industry from the RGMP, simply a new set of ground rules on where they should invest in raw land. On the other hand, there are many present residents who would favor a much slower regional rate of growth, and who would fault the RGMP for not inhibiting growth. If net immigration were to rise enough so that the projected 2.3 percent annual growth rate were to be significantly exceeded, however, then the RGMP (if not amended) might act as a form of brake on total potential for regional development.

There have been some problems in implementing the RGMP. In general, these have occurred in specific communities (or on certain individual large property holdings) where prior expectations exceeded the new promise of the RGMP. Preserving productive agricultural land has proven to be an especially difficult task. In addition, the effects of California's famed Proposition 13 need to be examined. Each of these considerations will be reviewed briefly below.

One aspect of land development in rural San Diego County that has created problems for implementing the RGMP has been what might be termed the "splittable lot promotion" concept. Many large parcel owners have filed subdivision maps over the years to divide their property into lots of a size a little more than twice the minimum zoning on the property. For example, if the area is zoned for two acre lots, they might subdivide their parcel into a number of five-acre lots. This provides an attractive sales approach, persuading the prospective buyer that the lot will be an income producer because the buyer can later split it into two lots and sell one at what will undoubtedly be an appreciated price. Thus in many close-in rural areas, if the RGMP staff was recommending two-acre lots, many of the residents would prefer one-acre zoning; or if staff suggested four acres, the larger land holders wanted two. This proved to be a significant problem in the areas around such communities as Alpine and Fallbrook. In Alpine, for example, several square miles recommended for two-acre lots were zoned for one acre due to landowner pressure. To do this, the urban limit line of this small community had to be expanded to about fifteen square miles.

Larger sensitive areas have posed special problems. The vicinity of Borrego Springs, for instance, not only lies in a typically fragile desert biome, but is also an enclave within the highly scenic Anza Borrego Desert State Park. The key issue here concerns the amount of groundwater available over the long run, an issue over which there is much disagreement and a lack of data. The county has designated this region a Special Study Area, pending further information. But preliminary approval of two or three very large developments occurred some years ago; how long these developers (who claim that plenty of water is available) can be asked to delay their plans is unclear. One was approved in early 1980. It is certain that current zoning for the privately owned portion of the Borrego Valley, which now supports about 1,500 year round residents, would allow an ultimate population of about 20,000. Whether this represents a viable long-term carrying capacity for this small corner of the Sonoran Desert is open to considerable debate and was the reason for the Special Study Area designation in the RGMP.

Preserving the region's better agricultural lands has been especially trying. A long-studied agricultural element for the county's general plan was turned down in the autumn of 1979. A major stumbling block to the passage of an agricultural element was the high degree of existing subdivision of agricultural land. Very little crop land in the county is in large holdings (e.g., more than 160 acres). A significant percentage (perhaps as much as half) of all agricultural income in the county comes from parcels of five acres or less, consisting primarily of "gentlemen farmer" orchards maintained for secondary income or as a hobby. An associated problem is that the owner of larger parcels is apt to be a corporation that leases the land out for farming on a temporary basis, rather than an individual "serious" farmer. Thus there is no "farming lobby" in the county.

Simply defining "prime agricultural soil" within the context of San Diego County agriculture was a basic problem. Two of the main agricultural products, eggs and greenhouse flowers, can be produced on nonagricultural soils, and two other primary products, avocados and cattle, are most often raised on Class III to Class VI soils. The greenhouse operators, in fact, could claim that they *had* to have an underlying residential zone, or banks would not lend them the money they need to stay in the greenhouse business!

When farmland is proposed for development, many arguments are offered that it is no longer viable as agricultural land. Some complaints, such as avocado root rot, foreign competition for the local flower businesses, occasional frosts or floods, and increasing costs of imported water (up to $300 per acre-foot) are unquestionably legitimate. A few of the other economic arguments that are occasionally presented could probably be challenged. Decision makers are rarely privy to the necessary economic data that would be necessary to make such a challenge, however. Thus the subdivider's case, whether it be sound or not, can seldom be countered.

The main opposition to the agricultural element, which would have placed all areas having favorable agricultural soils into a permanent agricultural zone, came less from the large landholders than from the smaller ones, who wanted to reserve the right to re-divide their land at some future date. Politically, they were able to carry the day before the County Board of Supervisors.

California's well-known Proposition 13 limited property taxes to one percent of fair market value. This served to restrict government spending by sharply reducing the ability of local governments to raise revenue from bonds. The taxation provisions of Proposition 13 have had the effect of greatly reducing the tax pressures on rural lands, and in fact, generally cut rural land taxes to a greater degree than does the Williamson Act, which limits property taxes on agricultural land by assessing the land only for its agricultural, rather than developmental, potential. Used together, the two measures essentially eliminate the argument that farmers are being taxed off their land in California. But neither measure is able to counter the temptation to sell the land for profit to a developer, and to take one's farming operations to a more remote location.

The reduction in local governmental income (resulting from the reduced property tax rates) has had two serious repercussions. The first was predictable. Since local jurisdictions needed to cut budgets and spend less money, it was natural that they would cease volunteering to pay for local developmental infrastructures (roads, parks, schools, sewers, etc.) out of municipal budgets, but instead impose these costs upon developers. This has been done, often with great constituent (taxpayer) approval. But this, of course, has helped to raise the already high cost of local housing.

The second ramification was less expected, but hardly surprising. Since local special districts (particularly school and sewer) have less revenue, and since Proposition 13's other provisions make it hard to pass new bond issues, these districts have found it financially very hard to expand their services to new areas. As a result, some developers have encountered great difficulty in securing the services necessary to take care of their subdivisions. Proposition 13 thus surprisingly may turn out to be one of the more effective growth control measures ever passed in California.

Proposition 9, to effect a similar cut in California's state income tax, was on the ballot in June, 1980. Its intended effects would have been similar to Proposition 13's. Interestingly, this time around, the builders opposed Proposition 9, and the voters turned it down.

The San Diego experience in preserving rural values and the essence of the regional rural landscape suggests certain areas where additional research is needed. Certainly one of the primary areas is in the carrying capacity of those subregions that are dependent on groundwater. In fact, such studies are needed for the county as a whole.

Another need is a better understanding of the political viability of various agricultural protection policies in San Diego County. County planners clearly did not expect the intensity of opposition to the proposed agricultural element that was encountered. A politically acceptable mechanism to preserve prime agricultural land in the county has not yet been discovered.

The experience with the agricultural element and with land-use problems generally points to the need for a better understanding of the local political process. In particular, there is a need to understand more clearly the various constituencies who influence land use policy, their motivations, and the manner in which they operate. Such knowledge is necessary in order to predict the outcomes of major policy deliberations as well as to prepare policy proposals that are technically valid and politically workable.

References

Conservation Element, San Diego County General Plan, 1976. County of San Diego.

County Groundwater Policy, 1979. In *Board of Supervisors Policy Manual,* County of San Diego.

Land Use Element, San Diego County General Plan, 1979. County of San Diego.

Regional Growth Management Plan, County of San Diego, 1978.

Lough, C. F. 1976. *Groundwater Resources, Ramona Planning Area.* County of San Diego Integrated Planning Office.

Mayo, A. L. 1977. Groundwater in San Diego County. In *Geologic Hazards in San Diego County,* ed. P. L. Abbott and J. K. Victoria, pp. 60-69. John Porter Dexter Memorial Publications, San Diego Society of Natural History, San Diego.

Appendix
Urban Development Area Selection Criteria

Policy Area	Objectives	Growth Will Be Encouraged in TAZs:
Land Use	Locate urban development within and adjacent to existing urban areas	Where 40% to 80% of planned holding capacity has been reached.
	Preserve and expand agricultural uses	Where there is no potential for agricultural uses.
Capital Facilities	Fully utilize existing capacities	Where sufficient capacity exists for projected population.
	Extend facilities to contiguous areas	Which are within or adjacent to the service areas of service providing agencies.
		Where transit service exists currently, or current land use designations are compatible with future public transit provision.
Environmental	Protect lagoons, flood plains, sand, rock deposits, mountains and deserts	Where there are no environmentally sensitive areas.
	Locate growth in temperate areas to reduce energy needs	Where average heating degree days are below 2,600.
	Limit development to areas where imported water is available	Which lie within the boundaries of County Water Authority.

Policy Area	Objectives	Growth Will Be Encouraged in TAZ's:
Environmental (cont.)	Minimize transportation needs and trip frequency	Where at least 40 acres of commercial and industrial land are available.
Housing	Increase low and moderate income housing availability	Where planned residential densities average or exceed 7.3 dwelling units per acre. (Priority will be given to areas over 14.5 average dwelling units per acre).
Social	Meet needs of special populations according to —socio-economic status	Which lie within one of the census tracts ranking low socio-economically based on income, unemployment, welfare needs, occupational level and disease incidence.
	—employment availability	Which lie proximal to one of the region's ten top employment generating subregional areas.
	—economic stability	Which lie within census tracts relatively sensitive to changes in land use and economic conditions based on measures of mobility, homeownership, fixed incomes and growth rates.
Economic	Optimize tax base with land use mix to encourage incorporation	Where the ratio of commercial/industrial assessed valuation to total AV is above average.
	Urbanize where county expenditures and revenues balance	Where per capita AV is above average for the county.
	Encourage urbanized areas to annex	Which lie within the sphere of influence of an incorporated area and land use designations are compatible with the incorporating city's designations.

Can Environmental Mediation Make Things Happen?

David A. Aggerholm

Mediation, the voluntary coming together of parties in a dispute to try to reach some resolution with the help of a facilitator or mediator, has long been an accepted form of labor dispute settlement. During the 1960s, mediation was tried with some success and still is used as a means to resolve community level disputes, especially in low-income areas.

In the early 1970s, with the rapid growth of the environmental movement and particularly the passage of federal and state impact legislation, mediation came to be viewed as a possible alternative to the costly and time-consuming litigative route being used to resolve the burgeoning numbers of environmental and labor union disputes.

Today, by all accounts, environmental mediation is alive and well and growing slowly but steadily. So it must work—or does it? Without question, mediation has had its share of success stories—some of them impressive. Even more important, perhaps, I believe that widespread training for resource professionals in conflict resolution and mediation skills that they could use in their day-to-day work could prevent many conflicts from ever happening. Unfortunately, very little such training exists.

Mediation, like everything else, has its limits. I learned first-hand about some of those during the past two years while I was working to implement perhaps the best known and reputedly successful environmental mediation effort of all—the Snohomish Basin Mediated Agreement. The Snohomish mediation was the first major environmental mediation and has served as a significant catalyst to the growth of environmental mediation. Five years after the agreement was concluded, I am convinced that it will never be implemented. In the following paragraphs I outline some of my experience of the mediation process, some lessons learned and what they mean for environmental mediation.

SETTING AND BACKGROUND

The Snohomish River Basin lies just east and south of the Seattle metropolitan area, less than an hour's drive from 1.5 million people. Flanked by the forested and spectacular Cascade range on the west, the valley has remained relatively undeveloped and sparsely populated. The principal industries are timber and agriculture, and there are numerous forms of recreation. How has the Basin remained so unspoiled and bucolic in the face of strong developmental pressures? Flooding is the answer—frequent and serious flooding that causes damages of approximately $4.5 million per year.

Beginning in 1960, the Corps of Engineers labored to find a solution to the flooding problem. In 1968 and again in 1969 the Corps recommended major structural packages, which valley residents liked but which environmentalists— whose star was rising fast—wouldn't buy. Battle was joined on a stormy January night in 1970 in the small mountain town of North Bend when 800 angry citizens, representing both sides, confronted the Chief of Engineers, who had flown from Washington to attend the Corps public meeting on the proposed project.

In November 1970, Dan Evans, the state's strongly environmentalist Governor, stepped in. Governors play a key role in Corps projects in that they must endorse a proposed Corps action for it to move forward for further executive branch and congressional consideration and approval. Saying he needed more information to decide whether or not to endorse the Corps proposal, Evans called for a joint federal-state study of alternatives. Almost three years later, the study presented eleven alternatives. Shortly thereafter, the Governor rejected the Corps's 1969 structural package.

So after 13 years of frustrating study and debate, valley residents seemed no closer to a solution to the chronic flooding problem. Most of them, it should be noted, agreed with the environmentalists that the Basin's environmental values should be preserved, but they also wanted relief from flooding. It was beginning to appear that the wisdom of Solomon would be required to resolve this all-too-frequent dilemma of the environmental age.

ENTER ENVIRONMENTAL MEDIATION

In 1973 environmental mediation was but a gleam in very few eyes. But it happened that one pair of those eyes belonged to Gerald Cormack, a successful community dispute mediator from Washington University in St. Louis. Cormack had just convinced the Ford Foundation to sponsor a test of environmental mediation. It also happened that the Ford project officer, Jane McCarthy, was familiar with the Snohomish Basin impasse through her acquaintance with Sydney Steinborn, the Corps's Seattle District Engineering Chief. Steinborn, a strong advocate of public involvement and intensely committed to finding a workable solution for the Snohomish, convinced McCarthy and Cormack, who were unsuccessfully casting about for a pilot conflict, that they should select the Snohomish. Finally they agreed; they went to the governor and convinced him to formally sponsor a mediation of the longstanding dispute. In early 1974, a group of a dozen farmers, environmentalists, and valley townspeople got together with McCarthy and Cormack, serving as mediators, to try to resolve the dilemma of providing flood protection without sacrificing the valley.

In December, after months of long, hard bargaining and compromise, they finally spawned the Snohomish Basin Mediated Agreement. The agreement, which was basically a plan or blueprint for the future growth of the Basin, called for a very limited structural program combined with land-use controls, flood-plain acquisition, and institutional measures. The governor immediately endorsed it. Within a year an interim Basin Coordinating Committee was established, which fleshed out more details. A Corps preliminary feasibility study found the Agreement economically feasible, Everyone was euphoric. The dilemma was resolved. Mediation worked. All that remained was to implement it.

SUBSEQUENT EXPERIENCE

What has happened since those happy days in 1975? First, it is important to understand that all the structural elements of the agreement—a dam and some limited levees—and much of the nonstructural portion—particularly floodplain acquisition—were expected to be implemented by the Corps at a cost of several hundred million dollars. And, as noted, preliminary Corps studies looked favorable. But soon after the agreement was reached, Steinborn, its strong advocate in the Corps, retired. His successors were much less enamored with the agreement, which one high official terms a "flaky" solution to flooding. Neither were they pleased at the loss of their earlier structural package, which they viewed as the "right" solution. Progress on the all-important detailed feasibility studies virtually came to a halt, a victim of "higher priorities."

Second, a key requirement in the justification of the proposed dam was to find a local buyer for the considerable Municipal and Industrial (M & I) water supply that the dam would provide. (In fact, more than 50 percent of the projected benefits of the proposed dam were water supply benefits—the flood control benefits alone being insufficient to justify the dam.) The only possible buyer, the city of Seattle, had already decided on another supposedly cheaper source and wasn't budging on its position.

Third, the agreement was signed by state, county, and local government bodies that shared responsibility for its implementation. As events unfolded, it became clear that these parties were not all marching to the same drummer. A variety of strategies and agendas began to emerge. By early summer 1978, 18 years after the Corps got into the act and three years after the "Agreement to end all Agreements," little progress had been made toward implementation.

This is where I came into the picture—borrowed from the federal government by King County to help break the logjam. For the next year my full-time occupation was to try to make things move. Before the year ended, Senators Magnuson and Jackson (no political lightweights) and much of Washington's congressional delegation were deeply involved. In the executive branch, the Council on Environmental Quality, the Office of Management and Budget, the Water Resources Council, the Office of the Secretary of the Army, the Executive Office of the President, and untold numbers of Corps officials marched across our stage. At the local level the governor and elected officials from all the involved jurisdictions played active roles.

What do we have to show for all this frenetic, intense, and costly activity?

(1) Much more money for the Corps study and a congressional deadline to complete the feasibility study by fall 1981.

(2) A strong federal policy from Washington, D.C. *against* federal investment in floodplain acquisition in the Snohomish Basin (or almost anywhere). We did manage to raise an ominous spectre to the federal government of untold numbers of local governments lining up at the federal trough for funds to acquire all of their floodplain lands.

(3) Continuing strong resistance by the city of Seattle to buying the water.

(4) An escalation of state-local gaming, compounded by the efforts of some of the citizen members of the original mediation group.

So today, 20 years after they began, the Corps studies are now moving smartly along toward an expected conclusion that *no* federal investment in any element of the agreement is warranted. A few local officials and a few citizens from the mediating group gather periodically and dutifully at meetings of the Basin Coordinating Council—the only recommendation of the agreement actually implemented—to review progress, plot new strategies, and ponder what went wrong. And in the valley most residents still cling to the hope that somehow the Corps's original plan will be revived.

What have I learned from all this? Some lessons now seem obvious and fundamental. For example, it is clear that those with the responsibility, power, authority, and means to implement a mediated agreement (or any land-use decision) must either be among the parties to the agreement or be committed *and able* to implement it.

In this case, none of the implementors was at the table. And while many of the key players were supportive, some of the most crucial ones weren't—notably the Corps and the city of Seattle (which, by the way, had always felt excluded even from the periphery of the mediation). Further, the "strong" nominal support of many others was found to have conditions or prices attached. It has also become clear, as indicated earlier, that many local officials and valley residents have gone along with the agreement only because it was the only show in town. Most preferred the Corps's original proposal (and still do).

Closely related to these is the fact that the more players there are, the more difficult it is to keep them moving in a united way. We had a pretty effective state-local coalition going at first, but when things began to turn sour, factions tended to form that diluted their effectiveness—especially in transactions with the federal government. Today, in my opinion, there is no effective intergovernmental coordination.

Another obvious lesson is that the more hoops that have to be jumped through—rules, regulations, approvals—the less likely a mediated agreement or any land use plan is to survive. The problem is compounded exponentially for each level of government that must be involved, and it is especially critical if a mediated solution must be subjected to rigid benefit-cost or other analysis after the fact. In our case, it did; and I think most of us involved have had to admit grudgingly that the structural components of the agreement do not comprise a cost-effective or even a good solution to the flooding problem. And there is little doubt that a major federal investment in these components is *not* warranted. In fact, the "flaky" label given by the Corps official wasn't too far off, when applied to the structural elements.

Passage of time exacerbated an already difficult situation. The more complex a process is in terms of those involved and the policy and procedural hoops required, the more time will be necessary to implement it. And the more time it takes, the more likely it is that someone or something important to implementation will change. (It is interesting to note, for example, that the average time between the beginning of a Corps feasibility study and the beginning of construction is 20 years.)

Perhaps the mediators tried to do too much by attempting to resolve the flooding problem with what in effect was an innovative and creative floodplain management and land-use "plan" for the entire Basin. There was just too much to accomplish; almost none of it could be implemented locally, and much of it was not feasible in terms of current federal policy and procedures.

I think they also made a mistake by inserting an all-or-nothing condition in the agreement, which states very clearly that "the specific pre-conditions included in these joint recommendations are acceptable only as a total package." This was evidently viewed as a lever on the Corps to achieve full implementation rather than just the structural components, but I believe it turned out to be more of an albatross, for several reasons. It has become clear, for example, that floodplain acquisition and many of the other nonstructural elements are not going to be federally funded and therefore are not going to be realized. Thus, by its own definition, the agreement becomes void when the Corps issues its findings on these elements.

But there still is flooding, and there still is a well-funded Corps study that might be able to recommend an acceptable and federally fundable solution to that problem. And the Basin Coordinating Council (BCC) has been established as the state-local implementing institution. But the citizen leaders of the BCC— the only active members—steadfastly refuse to use the council as a medium to reopen talks aimed at revising the agreement. These leaders continue to stress that as far as this agreement is concerned, it's all or nothing, and they cling to the hope that something will happen to turn things around.

In retrospect, I think those of us involved knew or sensed most of the potential problems and pitfalls, but we felt we could pull it off with our impressive political clout and fancy footwork. And we almost did. It is unfortunate that the current situation is so inflexible that no flood-damage relief is in the offing.

I want to add one further lesson that emerged from this—the vital importance of one or two key people in the right places. In fact, I think the whole thing might have ended quite differently and with much less melodrama and pain if one key person in the drama—Sydney Steinborn of the Corps—hadn't left the stage when he did.

As I stated earlier, Steinborn was sympathetic and committed to the implementation of the agreement. If he had stayed, the Corps Seattle district might have pursued the feasibility study and sought ways to make it work as had been done when Steinborn was in charge. If current nonstructural policy and procedures didn't work, he might have sought a revision of the agreement to implement the nonstructural elements independently.

It is also important to recognize that most of the Corps's resistance all the way up the line was not over questions of substantive merit—that came later when we wouldn't stop pushing—but over the Corps's unbending adherence to the *organizational* principle that the local district engineer knows best about his district and must be supported at virtually all costs. Steinborn might have pushed at the edges of existing policy and procedure to find a way. Instead, the Corps Seattle district pulled those restrictive policies and procedures around itself as a protective cloak.

CONCLUSIONS

The Snohomish Basin conflict should not have been mediated. Nor should any conflicts like it be mediated—conflicts in which implementation responsibilities and requirements are so complex, diffuse, costly, and time-consuming that the chances of implementation are nil. (It is interesting to note that Jane McCarthy, the Ford project officer and one of the mediators in the dispute, was always apprehensive about using the Snohomish as a case study, for some of these very reasons.)

Mediation can make things happen—can solve problems—but conflicts must be chosen carefully. My own view is that local environmental and land use disputes in which implementation authority is simple and clear cut and in which solutions can be implemented quickly and neatly are the most suitable. But I see a disturbing trend toward applying mediation to bigger and more complex issues even in the national policy realm. I don't think this will work.

Meanwhile the Snohomish saga goes on. What of the future? I am concerned that all of that beautiful floodplain is still vulnerable to development, even though the federal government maintains steadfastly that local land use regulation will save it. Maybe a large and prosperous county like King County can do it (it recently passed a $50 million agricultural land acquisition program, which may help). But most local government-elected officials don't seem able to stand development pressures in spite of regulations on the books—though there is always room for the exception(s).

Clearly the federal government must re-evaluate its floodplain management policies and procedures. In particular, there is a vast gap between the rather liberal provisions of the president's *policies* on floodplain management and the much more restrictive implementing *procedures*, particularly the evaluation criteria required under the Water Resources Council's *Principles and Standards.*

With regard to flood control, I suspect that when the 50- or 100-year storm hits, the Corps will dust off its old plan, local support will coalesce behind it, and if we still have Jackson or his equivalent in Congress, the basin will have one or more shiny new dams. That doesn't say anything about environmental mediation—it just says something about how things work—even today.

IX. Land Use Impacts of Energy Development

Energy Change
and Evolving Nonmetropolitan
Land Use Patterns

Lawrence M. Sommers and Donald J. Zeigler

The cheap-energy era that facilitated mechanization, technological development, and urban growth and sprawl came to an abrupt end with the Arab oil embargo in 1973. Since that time, it has become increasingly obvious that the people of the United States must make major adjustments in their use of resources and significant adaptations in their life-styles in order to cope with resource limitations, rising prices, and new forms of resources.

The petroleum- and automobile-dependent settlement patterns of the present need to be replaced by energy-efficient structures and patterns for living and working (Koenig and Sommers 1980). Rising energy costs and shifts to non-liquid fossil fuels and renewable resources will eventually curtail urban sprawl and redirect urban growth toward greater densities in nucleated cities and villages. The nonmetropolitan land-use areas located between the nucleated centers are now threatened by encroaching and penetrating urban functions. One hopes this is one of the major areas in which future urban sprawl can be controlled. As the cost, availability, and technical form of our energy sources shift with time, so also will the physical and social organizational characteristics of the way people utilize the land resources. The objective of this paper is to analyze briefly the implications of the changing energy picture for the land-use and human settlement patterns of these nonmetropolitan areas.

THE IMPENDING CHANGE IN SETTLEMENT PATTERNS

Figure 1 indicates in broad outline the major characteristics of the contemporary and future metropolis. In a general analysis of the two situations, the decreasing influence of the automobile in the future is pronounced. The present highly

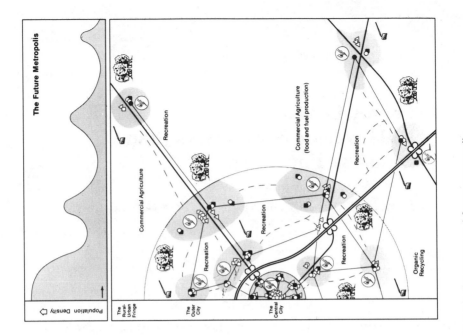

The Contemporary Metropolis

Population Density

The Rural-Urban Fringe

The Outer City

The Central City

Recreation

Vacant Land (formerly agricultural)

Vacant Land

Recreation

Residential Areas

Co-Generation/ District Heating

Garden Farming

Fast-Growing Woodlots

Activity Nodes
- ○ Retail Centers
- □ Professional Centers
- ■ Education and Civic Centers
- △ Industrial Centers
- ● Mass Transit Centers

Transportation Arterials
- Interstate Highways
- Major Secondary Highways
- Major Mass Transit Lines
- Bicycle Trails

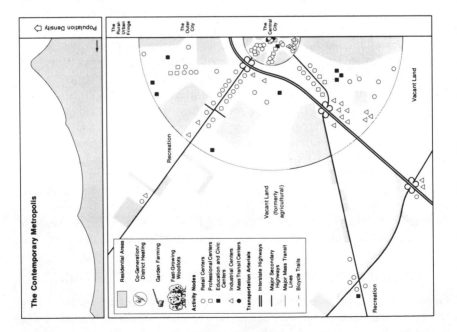

The Future Metropolis

Population Density

The Rural-Urban Fringe

The Outer City

The Central City

Commercial Agriculture

Recreation

Recreation

Recreation

Recreation

Recreation

Commercial Agriculture (food and fuel production)

Organic Recycling

Figure 1. The spatial organization/energy relationships of land use in the current and future metropolis.

specialized and linear patterns of activity nodes dispersed along major thorough-fares and made possible by flexible automobile transportation will probably be replaced by a clustering of activities in community centers. Future activity nodes will be highly diversified, compactly organized, and accessible by walking, bicycling, and public transportation as well as the automobile. Outside the central city, urban functions will be concentrated at points of maximum accessi-bility by mass-transit lines and nonautomobile transportation. In order for this concentration to be accomplished, changes must take place in nonmetropolitan land areas.

ACTIVITY CENTERS

A considerable amount of urban-type activity is spread throughout otherwise largely rural land in present-day nonmetropolitan areas, as shown in Figure 2. Isolated gasoline service stations, garages, schools, grain elevators, bars, churches, and occasional factories are scattered along rural or county roads. At intersec-tions there may be a rural village or town with a business district or the remnants of a once-active commercial center. Each establishment is dependent upon the automobile for transporting the majority of its customers; thus parking lots are an important feature associated with each activity or service.

As energy becomes more expensive and changes in form, rural activity nodes will become more diversified, more compact, and centered at transportation crossing points such as road intersections. The business sections of rural villages will be revitalized with a greater variety of retail stores and service activities. Small industries based on local resources such as food processing may develop.

RESIDENTIAL AREAS

Future zoning regulations will probably prevent the construction of scattered nonfarm houses, isolated subdivisions, and homes on large lots (up to ten acres in size). The result will be higher densities in and around rural trade centers. The availability of renewable forms of energy—wind, solar radiation, and biomass—may facilitate the spread of scattered settlements in certain areas. This predic-tion is based on the assumption that a renewable form of energy or a combina-tion of sources eventually would largely eliminate the need for fossil fuels.

AGRICULTURAL LAND AND OPEN SPACE

In areas near large cities today, the amount of vacant or idle land has been in-creasing. This phenomenon is due partly to land speculation resulting in high prices for locating potential urban type functions and partly to the high tax rate on agricultural land.

Prime agricultural land near cities should be protected in the future for food production. More land near cities will be reserved for local recreational facilities

	ACTIVITY NODES		RESIDENTIAL AREAS		OPEN SPACE	
	CONTEMPORARY METROPOLIS	FUTURE METROPOLIS	CONTEMPORARY METROPOLIS	FUTURE METROPOLIS	CONTEMPORARY METROPOLIS	FUTURE METROPOLIS
GENERAL COMPARISON	Activity nodes highly specialized and widely separate, e.g., industrial parks, commercial strips, office complexes, school and college campuses ----- Dispersed along major thoroughfares in linear patterns.	Activity nodes highly diversified and compactly organized to facilitate accessibility by a pedestrian or pedaling population. ----- Larger centers have functionally specialized districts within the context of overall diversity. ----- Clustered around points at maximum accessibility where they take on the function of community centers. ----- Organized into a hierarchy of service centers.	Residential areas oriented to highways and divorced from employment, commercial, and other types of service centers. ----- As distance from the city center increases, there is a trend toward lower density and larger lots.	Residential areas clustered around activity nodes throughout the metropolitan area. Greater density achieved by planned unit development of single family residences and a greater emphasis on townhouses and apartments.	Large expanses of un- or under-used open spaces; much vacant land.	Open space between communities used as a valuable urban or rural resource; little land that is truly vacant.
THE CENTRAL CITY	CBD comparatively small as a result of being poorly adapted to the automobile. ----- Beyond the CBD, activity nodes arranged in a linear pattern allow major thoroughfares.	Revitalized CBD re-emerges as the point of maximum accessibility for the metropolis as a whole as a result of being the focus of mass transit lines. ----- Beyond the CBD, activity nodes clustered at points of maximum accessibility and served by mass transit.	Much abandonment of residential areas in the central city, particularly around the CBD.	Central city becomes a desirable place to live as older, higher density residential areas are renovated and supplemented by new medium- and high-density housing development.	Open space often not used to its full advantage, often taking the form of vacant lots, lands awaiting development, and private lots.	Open space recognized as a valuable resource and fully used for recreation, aesthetics, education, and for shaping community development.

THE OUTER CITY	Specialized and widely separated activity nodes consume much land and exert little influence on the location of residential development. ----- Often comprised of services that cater not only to nearby communities but also to metropolitan populations as a whole (formerly a function of CBD).	Diversified and compactly organized, activity nodes become the nuclei around which other development coalesces. ----- Comprised of services geared to the community rather than the metropolitan market. ----- Lower order nuclei (schools and convenience stores) emerge in larger communities.	Dormitory suburbs with no community centers. ----- Accessibility to activities and services tied to the use of motorized vehicles.	Coalescence of residential areas around community centers resulting in more self-contained communities. ----- Accessibility to activities and services possible by foot and cycle as well as by cars; mass transit provides access to more distant service centers.	Open space often studded by isolated dwellings, or abandoned farms; left-overs from leap-frog development held by land speculators.	Open space areas separate communities and provide sites for recreation, community gardening, fast-growing woodlots, and inter-community transport corridors.
THE RURAL URBAN FRINGE	Activity nodes are most (1) "free-standing" services such as convenience stores, schools, and churches strung out along rural thoroughfares or oriented to inter-changes; (2) the remnants of once-active business districts in rural towns and villages.	More diversified and compactly organized activity nodes take form in areas that are already heavily populated, around points of maximum accessibility, and in the old down-towns of revital-ized rural villages.	Rural, nonfarm residences of three types: (1) smaller housing sub-divisions along major secondary highways; (2) in-dividual housing units strung out along rural highways; ----- (3) single-family homes on large lots or abandoned farms completely isolated from other residential units.	Rural, nonfarm residences are replaced by: (1) family-scale farms and (2) higher density rural trade centers serving the surrounding population and hosting some food processing or packaging industries (likely to be revitalized small towns already in existence).	Much formerly agricultural land now vacant. ----- Some recreation but generally accessible only by motorized vehicles.	Vacant land re-placed by parks, recreation sites, nature preserves, fast-growing wood-lots, bicycle and mass transit cor-ridors, and commercial agriculture pro-ducing food and fuel crops.

Figure 2. Major contrasts in various segments of the current and future metropolis.

in order to conserve energy. The family farm or intensive horticultural activities will probably re-emerge as an important part of the agricultural scene near urban centers. Fast-growing trees in small but numerous woodlots may appear to help supply the energy needs of city residents. The increase of garden farming in the areas between nucleated centers will reduce the length of the food chain. Corridors for mass transit will likely connect village and town nucleations with the suburbs and large cities.

The net result will be a clearer separation between rural and urban land-use categories in the nonmetropolitan areas. The emerging activity and land-use patterns will be more energy-efficient. The cities and nucleated centers will gradually become more compact, and the urban encroachment into nonmetropolitan land can be slowed and in many areas will cease. The keys to such change are the decisions that will be made by both the private and public sectors.

THE FRAMEWORK FOR PUBLIC AND PRIVATE CHOICE

Public and private decisions involved in reducing the energy intensity of human settlements and adapting them to the use of alternatives to liquid and gaseous fuels can be organized into a hierarchy of goals, physical facilities and processes, and private and social decisions, as illustrated in Figure 3.

The hierarchy begins with individuals and progresses through the components of human settlements (houses, buildings, farms) to the organization of those elements into settlement patterns on the landscape. If objectives related to the creation of energy efficiencies at all levels in the hierarchy are pursued over time, the result will be the evolution of conservation-oriented processes influencing the nature of the flows of people, goods, and information, and the integration of those processes into a more totally resource-efficient metropolitan system.

The recommendations for the support of community initiatives are logically structured around five major areas in the hierarchy of Figure 3.

1. Behavioral: The creation of values, attitudes, practices, and skills that stimulate personal energy efficiency. The ultimate goal is to create more energy-efficient individuals.
2. Technological: The creation of energy-efficient housing units; commercial and public establishments; recreational facilities; farms, gardens, and woodlots; and modes of transportation. The ultimate goal is to create energy-efficient components of human settlements.
3. Land Use: The creation of patterns on the landscape that minimize the distances over which people need to travel and over which goods need to be moved; this is achieved by guiding the location of socioeconomic activities so as to increase the density and functional diversity of human settlements. The ultimate goal is to create more energy-efficient land use patterns.
4. Urban Physical Infrastructure: The creation of energy-efficient processes to expedite the flow of people, goods, and services (public utilities).

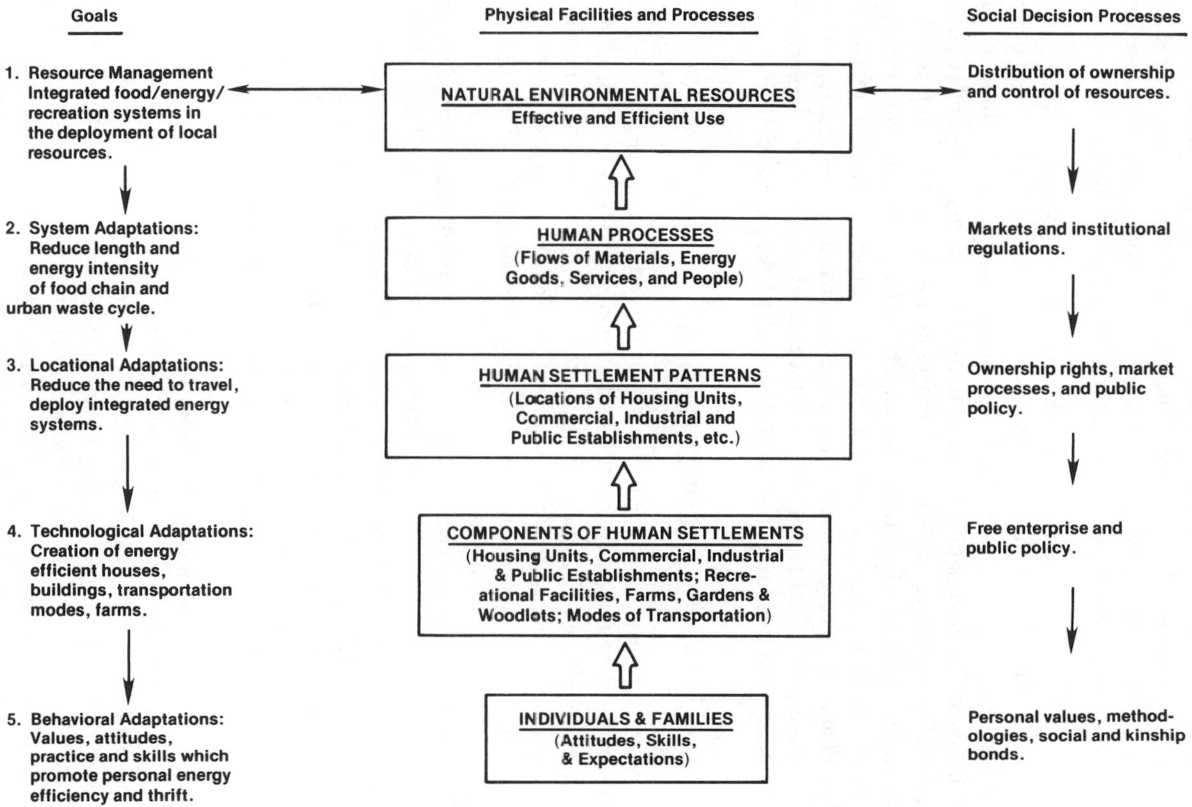
Goals
Physical Facilities and Processes
Social Decision Processes
1. Resource Management Integrated food/energy/recreation systems in the deployment of local resources.
NATURAL ENVIRONMENTAL RESOURCES
Effective and Efficient Use
Distribution of ownership and control of resources.
2. System Adaptations: Reduce length and energy intensity of food chain and urban waste cycle.
HUMAN PROCESSES
(Flows of Materials, Energy Goods, Services, and People)
Markets and institutional regulations.
3. Locational Adaptations: Reduce the need to travel, deploy integrated energy systems.
HUMAN SETTLEMENT PATTERNS
(Locations of Housing Units, Commercial, Industrial and Public Establishments, etc.)
Ownership rights, market processes, and public policy.
4. Technological Adaptations: Creation of energy efficient houses, buildings, transportation modes, farms.
COMPONENTS OF HUMAN SETTLEMENTS
(Housing Units, Commercial, Industrial & Public Establishments; Recreational Facilities, Farms, Gardens & Woodlots; Modes of Transportation)
Free enterprise and public policy.
5. Behavioral Adaptations: Values, attitudes, practice and skills which promote personal energy efficiency and thrift.
INDIVIDUALS & FAMILIES
(Attitudes, Skills, & Expectations)
Personal values, methodologies, social and kinship bonds.

Figure 3. The decision-making process involved in adapting energy efficient human settlements.

The ultimate goal is to create energy-efficient physical infrastructures.
5. Regional Resource Deployment: The creation of more energy self-reliant metropolises through the integration of energy/food/activity systems. The ultimate goal is effective and efficient use of regional resources.

Thus the land use patterns, population densities, physical infrastructure, technologies, and other elements of adaptation selected as targets for human settlement change are critically dependent upon the interrelationships of the local economic, political, and social conditions and the community and regional resources. The particular policies and programs for motivating and assisting timely energy-efficient adaptations also depend critically on local and regional conditions. Thus energy- and resource-efficient urban forms are regionally dependent and must be grounded in local and regional initiatives. State government, however, must facilitate and monitor the process and moderate interregional shifts in terms of their overall social costs and benefits to the area at large.

CONCLUSIONS

In summary, the energy-inefficient automobile-dependent settlement system of the present must be replaced by patterns of human activity and living structures that are energy-efficient. Population densities must be increased to make possible such energy-conserving technology as district heating and mass transportation. Such change can be effected only by developing a process and a desire to bring about innovations in current patterns of living.

These changes should include: 1) reduction of current energy consumption through conservation practices; 2) implementation of energy-efficient transportation systems over the long term; 3) raising the levels of thrift and durability of products used daily, such as automobiles and appliances; 4) reducing the need for travel and transport for business, social, and recreation purposes; 5) increasing the use of integrated cogeneration electric and heat energy systems; 6) shortening the distance for obtaining food and local renewable resources and for disposing of urban wastes.

The major result of such measures would be a reversal of the current trends of rapid urban sprawl into nonmetropolitan land areas. Prime agricultural land near cities would be retained for food production. Other areas could be reserved for such uses as recreation, the growing of wood for energy, and market gardens. Population densities could be increased selectively in the urban areas by infilling vacant land; smaller, more nucleated settlements would develop around the smaller settlements now scattered around the large city. The objective would be a more energy-efficient urban and rural landscape that would help alleviate the rising costs of energy and, with proper planning, provide an improved quality of life.

Reference

Koenig, H.E. and Sommers, L.M. 1980. *Energy and the Adaptation of Human Settlements: A Prototype Process in Genesee County, Michigan.* E. Lansing, Mich.: Mich. State University.

Impacts of Coal Mining and Conversion in Northern Plains States

Lloyd D. Bender, Thomas F. Stinson, George S. Temple, Larry C. Parcels, and Stanley W. Voelker

Interest in the mining and utilization of coal reserves in the Northern Great Plains increased in the 1970s. This region contains 64 percent of the nation's low-sulfur compliance coal reserves (Smith et al. 1976). Subbituminous coal is found in the Powder River Basin of northeastern Wyoming and southeastern Montana. Lignite is found in extreme eastern Montana and extends through North Dakota into Canada. Large amounts of these reserves are strippable and are in thick seams with relatively shallow overburdens. The quantities of coal expected to be mined in the Northern Plains have created concerns about the associated impacts.

This discussion reviews the effects of environmental regulations on coal mining in the region, designates those portions of the region to be affected most, and estimates local population and employment effects. Concluding remarks speculate that changes in institutions governing property rights in the broadest sense of the concept will have the greatest and most lasting effect on land use patterns, not only in the Plains states, but throughout the nation.

OVERVIEW OF ENVIRONMENTAL REGULATIONS

The environmental regulations, which began in 1970 and have been complicated by other events since then, set the stage for early coal development in the Northern Plains and influenced forecasts of future production. Renewed interest in Northern Plains' coal reserves was stimulated by the Clean Air Act of 1970. New coal-fired facilities could meet New Source Performance Standards (NSPS) for sulfur dioxide emissions by burning low-sulfur coal without expensive flue-gas desulfurization. The standard remained in effect until the amendments of 1977. New plants built under the standards of the 1970 act will be coming on stream until the early 1980s.

313

These initial sulfur dioxide standards prepared the way for a burst of development of the low-sulfur coal in the Northern Plains. The standards allowed low-sulfur coal to be substituted for flue-gas scrubbing as long as emissions contained less than 1.2 pounds of sulfur dioxide per million Btus of coal burned.

Two provisions of the Clean Air Amendments of 1977 successively altered forecasts of western low-sulfur coal usage. At first it was thought that demand for western coal would decline because sulfur control equipment was mandated by these amendments. Later it was recognized that low-sulfur coal demand would be enhanced by clean air standards.

The feature of the 1977 amendments that dominated forecasts immediately after the amendments were passed was the mandating of Best Available Control Technology (BACT). Some form of sulfur control was required. The economic incentive to use low-sulfur western coal was reduced (Gordon 1978). A 1977 Argonne National Laboratory study concluded that "any BACT scenario has the effect of trading off Northern Plains and Midwestern production, especially after 1985. . . ." (Krohm, Dux, and VanKuiken 1977).

The second major feature of the 1977 amendments, one that has received recent attention, concerns PSD—Prevention of Significant Deterioration—which enhances demand for low-sulfur coal. Limits were imposed on pollution increases in areas with air quality already higher than required by basic standards (Gordon 1978). Further, more stringent rules applied to areas not in compliance with air-quality standards. Two effects of the PSD regulations are becoming apparent. First, PSD regulations influence the location of new industry in the nation, and hence regional coal demand and land-use patterns. Second, they severely restrict the siting alternatives for new power plants unless low-sulfur coal is used. Fisher and Cukor (1980), in an analysis by Teknekron, Inc., conclude:

> It is only in some cases that the New Source Performance Standards will represent the governing degree of control. The majority of the newly constructed power plants will be more severely constrained by Prevention of Significant Deterioration regulations than by the revised New Source Performance Standards—and the PSD regulations will significantly limit the sulfur content of coal that can be burned even if the most efficient scrubbing systems are used.

They also point out that "none of the modeling efforts undertaken by federal agencies . . . considers the additional limitations imposed by PSD. . . ."

Finally, revised New Source Performance Standards permit 70 percent partial scrubbing (wet or dry) if emissions are below 0.6 pounds of sulfur dioxide per million Btu, and an increasing amount of scrubbing up to 90 percent with emissions up to 1.2 lbs. per million Btu (Coal Outlook 1980a). Reduction through coal preparation is credited. These NSPS allow a partial substitution of low-sulfur coal for scrubbing.

COAL MINING IN THE NORTHERN PLAINS IN THE 1970s

Early environmental regulations soon altered the sources of coal and supply patterns. Western coal was a nominal source for midwest utilities in 1970. By 1976, western coal was supplying more than 10 percent of utility consumption, or 96 million metric tons per year (mmtpy), in 11 midwestern and 4 southeastern states (Krohm, Dux, and VanKuiken 1977). A 1977 report found that only 39 percent of new U.S. utility capacity planned through 1985 was to be fitted with flue-gas desulfurization equipment (Krohm, Dux, and VanKuiken 1977).

The effect on coal production in the Northern Plains was just as dramatic. Production in Montana, Wyoming, and North Dakota increased from less than 10 mmtpy in 1965 to 100 mmtpy in 1978 (Fig. 1). The fact that the early standards applied to plants planned through 1977 means that demand for their low-sulfur coal needs will extend into the early 1980s. Continued promulgation of current PSD standards implies even greater demands for low-sulfur coal than was originally anticipated.

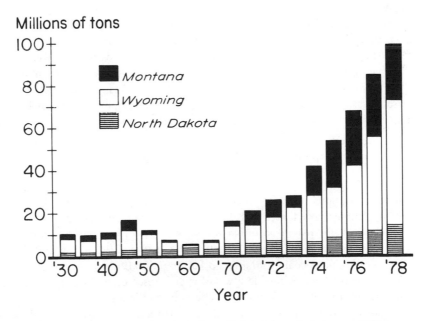

Figure 1. Coal production, Northern Great Plains states, selected years, 1930 to 1978. 1930 to 1975, Annual editions of "Minerals Yearbook," Volume II, Area Reports, Domestic U.S. Bureau of Mines, Washington, D.C.: 1976 to 1978, Department of Energy, *Energy Data Reports*, Washington, D.C., Energy Information Administration.

FORECASTS FOR THE FUTURE

The Northern Plains states are scheduled for large increases in coal production in the next decade. Prediction of future coal development in the Northern Plains is, however, clouded by several uncertainties. These include petroleum prices, rates of conversion from petroleum to coal, the future of nuclear power, and synfuels development. In addition are changes in environmental regulations, the state of the economy, leasing of federal coal reserves, and rates of technical progress in the coal industry.

A major determinant of coal use is the growth rate of electrical consumption. Utilities are the major users of coal. Utility use in 1977 was 475 million tons, over 70 percent of the national total of 673 million tons. Declines in the growth rate of electrical consumption have accompanied higher prices. Thus demand for electricity in markets served by Northern Plains coal will be a major determinant of production.

The Department of Energy (DOE) projects western coal production capacity to be 710 million tons by 1990 (DOE 1979). By comparison, that is greater than total production in the nation in 1977. Capacity projections are based upon mines planned by private companies. But annual production of large western strip mines can be increased very rapidly by simply accelerating the rate of mining at existing sites.

A recent study for the Department of Energy, using the ICF, Inc. interregional coal model, projected national coal production of about 1.4 billion tons in 1990 (Fig. 2). Northern Plains production was projected to be between 458 and 587 mmtpy, depending upon rail rates, or 32 to 40 percent of national production in 1990 (Coal Outlook 1980b). Northern Plains coal production will increase, regardless of what happens with synfuel development, nuclear power plants, environmental regulations, petroleum prices, and transportation rates.

LOCATION OF COAL DEVELOPMENT IN THE NORTHERN PLAINS

The general locations of future Northern Plains coal production can easily be identified, although exact sites will depend upon leasing and transport linkages. The Northern Plains region accounts for 46 percent of the nation's mineable reserves, but 76 percent of the strippable low sulfur coal (Hamilton and White 1975). Subbituminous coal (containing 8,100 to 9,600 Btu per pound) accounts for 71 percent of these strippable low-sulfur coal reserves, and lignite (6,100 to 7,250 Btu) the remaining 29 percent. The subbituminous coal is exported to other regions of the United States. Although strippable coal is contained in at least 44 counties of the region, only 13 of these contain subbituminous reserves; more precisely, 93 percent is located in only 4 contiguous counties in northern Wyoming and southeastern Montana—Campbell, Wyoming; and Big Horn, Powder River, and Rosebud, Montana (Fig. 3). The future development of coal in the Powder River Basin awaits additional rail linkages and federal leasing.

Figure 2. Forecasted U.S. coal production by region, 1990. From Department of Energy ICF, Inc. *Interregional Coal Model Coal Outlook*, Jan. 14, 1980.

The location of initial coal development in the Plains was confined to existing leases. A moratorium on federal coal leasing was imposed selectively in 1970, and nationwide in 1971 (Cannon 1978). In Wyoming, 96 federal leases covered 214,821 acres, and 1,568 state leases covered 1,235,229 acres in 1977. Montana only had 17 federal leases in 1977, covering 36,293 acres, and 51,947 leased state acres. Only 25 percent of North Dakota coal acreage is federal. These lease constraints, combined with dual surface and mineral ownership and with transportation linkages, set the stage for siting new coal mines in the Northern Plains in the 1970s.

New and prospective mines are enumerated in the Department of Energy's Western Coal Development Monitoring System (1979). Of the 96 mmtpy total capacity for Montana in 1990, 86 mmtpy (90 percent) is scheduled for Rosebud and Big Horn Counties. Included in the Montana subbituminous area are the Crow and Northern Cheyenne Indian Reservations. In Wyoming, 300 mmtpy capacity is envisioned by 1990, of which 200 mmtpy is in Campbell County. Converse and Sheridan Counties are scheduled for 13 and 10 mmtpy respectively. The 1990 capacity in Mercer and McLean Counties, North Dakota is projected to be 35 mmtpy out of a 45 mmtpy total (not including a gasification plant in Dunn County). Thus the very large increases in coal mining scheduled for the Northern Plains will be concentrated heavily in only 7 counties (including the spillover effects into Sheridan County, Wyoming).

The location of coal conversion plants in the Northern Plains would add to these demands for coal and would add to the impacts of mining and on-site electricity generation. Coal conversion technologies such as gasification and liquefaction are proposed in order to utilize the vast coal reserves of the nation. Probable locations are near large mineable reserves such as those in Montana, Wyoming, and North Dakota. Although it is impossible to anticipate whether advanced coal conversion plants will be built or precisely where they will be located, it is prudent to evaluate the impacts of such eventualities.

LOCAL POPULATION EFFECTS

The employment and population effects of large increases in Northern Plains' coal mining can easily be exaggerated because our perspective and historical bases of comparison are Midwestern and Appalachian experiences. Reviews of environmental impact statements for western development show consistent

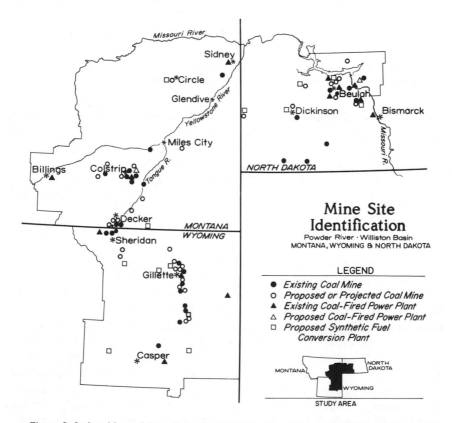

Figure 3. Strippable coal deposits in the Northern Great Plains coal field. From Missouri River Basin Commission, *Fact Book for Western Coal/Energy Development*, Resource and Land Investigations Program, Reston, Virginia. January 1979.

overestimates of employment and population (Coddington 1980). There are several reasons for this. First, Northern Plains mining is concentrated rather than spread throughout the region. Second, mine productivity is many times greater in large western strip mines than in mines elsewhere. The average number of miners per million tons of production in 1979 was 32 in Montana and 45 in Wyoming (Coal Outlook 1980c). The average for strip mines nationally is about 143 miners per million tons, a factor 3 to 4 times higher than in Wyoming and Montana. The average underground labor requirement is 400 miners per million tons capacity, a factor 9 to 13 times higher. Third, employment multipliers are very low in the simple rural economies of the Northern Plains. Induced local consumption is typically the only important local effect of industrial expansion, since manufacturing and processing are negligible parts of these economies. Fourth, local and regional labor can supply part of the employment increases because western strip mining uses uncomplicated technologies. Finally, rural economies in the Plains are experiencing many of the structural changes such as increases in service employment and labor-force participation rates that are evident in rural economies throughout the nation, and these changes are often confused with mining impacts.

Coal development will have relatively large impacts on local economic growth, even though the aggregate changes are less than those often anticipated by observers. The relative impacts on population are illustrated by (a) population changes in cities and towns in coal counties during the 1970s, and (b) by anticipated changes to 1990 in the major coal counties.

Population Changes Since 1970

The effects of coal development are concentrated in towns and cities near the coal projects rather than being spread out within the major coal reserve counties and the region. These are small towns in sparsely settled parts of the region. The population of the major cities and towns in the seven Northern Plains coal counties listed in Table 1 demonstrate this fact.

The populations of the small towns nearest to coal mines and new power plants have had large relative changes. Although these changes reflect national trends influencing rural areas throughout the nation and changes in other mineral exploitation and farming as well as coal development, there can be no mistaking the dominant effects of new coal mines and electricity-generating plants near rapidly growing places.

Towns affected by the Decker, Montana mines (which produced nearly 10 mmtpy in 1978) are Decker, Montana and Sheridan, Wyoming. In Rosebud County, the company town of Colstrip is near mines (producing 13 mmtpy in 1978) and Colstrip thermogenerator plants I and II, which started operation in late 1975. Forsyth is the nearest city.

Coal production in Mercer and McLean Counties reached about 6 mmtpy in 1978. Nearly 2,700 megawatt (MWe) capacity was in operation or being built in 1978 in these two counties.

Table 1. Population of Major Cities and Towns in Coal Counties
of the Northern Great Plains

County	City	Population		Population change	
		1970	1980	Number	Percentage
Montana					
Big Horn	Hardin	2,733	3,300	567	21
	Lodge Grass	806	771	−35	−4
Rosebud	Forsyth	1,873	2,553	680	36
North Dakota					
McLean	Underwood	781	1,329	548	70
	Washburn	804	1,767	963	120
Mercer	Beulah	1,344	2,878	1,534	114
	Hazen	1,240	2,365	1,125	91
	Stanton	517	623	106	21
	Zap	271	511	240	89
Wyoming*					
Campbell	Gillette	7,194	12,134	4,940	69
Converse	Douglas	2,677	6,030	3,353	125
	Glenrock	1,515	2,736	1,221	81
Sheridan	Dayton	396	701	305	77
	Ranchester	208	655	447	215
	Sheridan	10,856	15,146	4,290	40

Source: U.S. Census of Population, Bureau of Census, PHC 80, Vols. 28, 36, and 52, 1981.
*Other mineral exploitation important in these counties.

Campbell County coal production was 29 mmtpy in 1978, and the 330-MWe Wyodak number 1 was coming on stream. Glenrock is near the 788-MWe Dave Johnston plant, and about 3 mmtpy of coal was produced in Converse County in 1978 in addition to other minerals.

Population Changes Due to Anticipated Energy Development Beyond 1978

Changes in population are generally assumed to reflect the timing and magnitude of impacts. But many factors influence local population changes in response to employment changes. Foremost among these are the local multiplier effects, labor-force participation rates, the demographic composition of the population, and the extent of commuting.

Local county employment multipliers are small in the rural parts of the Northern Plains, because of the simple economies that serve agriculture and provide basic consumer services. Similar patterns are expected to hold true in coal counties. Labor-force participation rates and the demographic composition of the labor force change as employment increases rapidly in a rural area. During construction periods, for instance, much of the new labor is composed of single workers with extremely high participation rates. The participation rate of residents also increases during periods of high local labor demands. The combined effect is that population rises at a slower rate than employment. Finally, workers may commute long distances to jobs if local housing is unavailable or expensive. In this case, population impacts are distributed over a wide geographic area along major commuting routes.

Baseline projections for Rosebud, Campbell, and Mercer Counties compared with projections that anticipate coal development show the population effects of additional coal development. Although unrealistic, the baseline assumes no additional coal mine or conversion development after 1978. Anticipated capacity additions are conservative estimates of new mining and conversion facilities through 1990. These are built up from mine plans, a knowledge of the area, and assumed labor productivities. No synfuels conversion is included, and tonnages are less than those published by the Department of Energy.

The COALTOWN impact simulation model was used to estimate population and other impact parameters (Bender et. al. 1980; Temple 1978). This model, which is relatively simple, forecasts economic indicators from a set of stochastic equations. The coefficients of the equations were originally estimated using 1970-74 data for 181 nonmetropolitan Northern Plains counties.

Population in each county would continue to grow slowly to 1990 even under baseline assumptions without new energy developments or expansions after 1978 (Figs. 4-6). This growth would be due to the effect of development before 1978, to secular national trends, and to agricultural and other industrial production. Differences in population changes among counties can also be attributed to the initial demographic composition of the population and to the location of the county with respect to regional trade centers. Secular changes in the national economy that are reflected in the Northern Plains are increases in income, innovations in the retail trade sectors, and in the later 1980s a stabilizing labor-force participation rate.

In general, these conditions would tend to encourage slow but steady secular increases in employment and population over the next decade even without additional coal mining and conversion. Campbell County's population could increase to 21,600 by 1990, largely through immigration of about 4,500 people between 1979 and 1990 (Table 2). The increases in Rosebud and Mercer Counties would be modest and could mean about 13,000 and 8,000 people respectively in each county by 1990.

The coal mining and conversion expected by 1990 could bring population increases of up to 188, 150, and 142 percent of 1978 levels in Campbell, Rosebud, and Mercer Counties respectively (Figs. 4-6). At that time, Campbell County may produce 135 mmtpy of coal and generate 660-MWe of electricity. Rosebud County coal production is expected to be about 24 mmtpy and power generating capacity 2060-MWe. Mercer County will have at least 1662-2060-MWe capacity and about 13 mmtpy coal production. Much of this growth will have taken place by the early 1980s in Rosebud and Mercer Counties, but coal production in Campbell County is expected to continue to grow throughout the period. It is to be noted that mine expansion plans in Montana are constrained due to federal leasing actions.

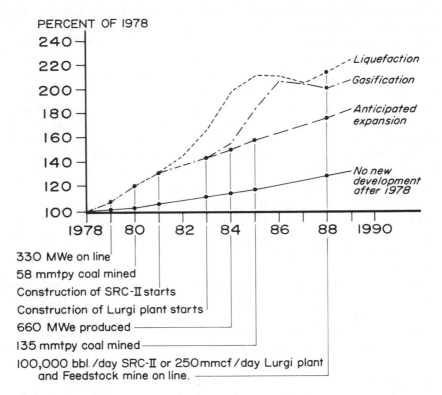

Figure 4. Indexes of simulated population estimates 1978-90, Campbell County, and assumed energy developments. From EDD/ESCS/USDA Energy Impact Team.

Hypothetical Synfuel Developments

Two types of coal conversion facilities are evaluated for Northern Plains sites—coal gasification and coal liquefaction. These two types of technologies define the upper and lower boundaries of impacts within which other advanced coal conversion options would fall. The facilities to be evaluated are (a) one 250 million cubic feet per day (MMcfd) Lurgi gasification plant, and (b) one 100,000 barrels per day (bbl/day) SRC-II liquefaction plant (Environmental Protection Agency 1979). Each facility is added separately to baseline cases in three counties in the Northern Plains.

Gasification. The construction and operation of a coal gasification plant requires a large work force. Construction uses over 10,000 worker-years with a peak of 4,800 in the fourth year. The operating work force is estimated to be about 600 workers (EPA 1979). To be on line in 1988, construction would begin in 1983 and continue over a 5-year period, not counting preplanning, site selection, and permitting time. A feedstock mine of approximately 10 million tons is assumed to come on line in 1988.

The largest absolute population impact due to a gasification plant is in Mercer County (5,930) followed by Campbell (3,940) and Rosebud (3,670) Counties (Table 2). This is the additional population assuming other coal mines and generating plants continue to expand as anticipated. Total population would exceed 1978 levels, however, by 224, 214, and 187 percent in Mercer, Campbell, and Rosebud Counties respectively, because of gasification and all other anticipated coal development (Figs. 4-6).

Population changes are largest in the first 4 years of construction (Figs. 4-6). The population peaks would be larger than shown if construction workers were to bring their families to live with them at the site. It is important during the construction period to provide temporary living quarters for immigrating single workers. Not only is the new population localized near the site, but also population change, labor turnover, social problems, and the need for state and local

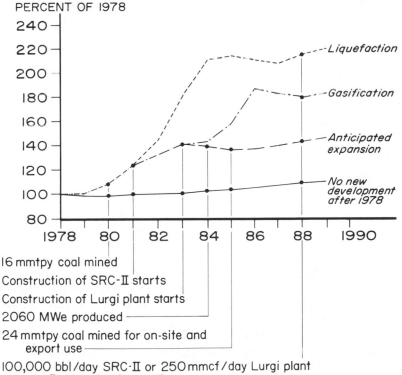

Figure 5. Indexes of simulated population estimates 1978-90, Rosebud County, and assumed energy developments. From EDD/ESCS/USDA Energy Impact Team.

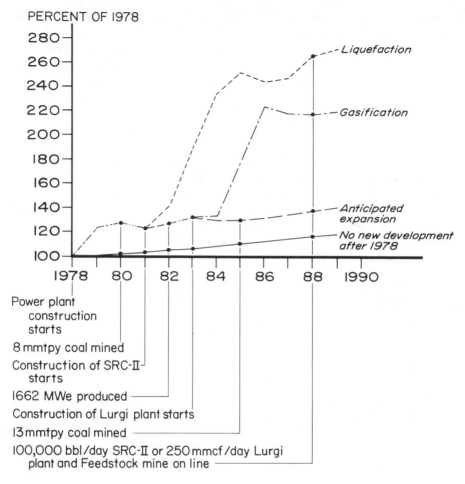

Figure 6. Indexes of simulated population estimates 1978-90, Mercer County, and assumed energy developments. From EDD/ESCS/USDA Energy Impact Team.

government services are minimized. Thus the peak in population can be reduced, and a longer transition period can be provided to arrive at the new stable population during the operation stage.

Liquefaction. A 100,000 barrels per day (bbl/day) SRC-II liquefaction plant is a very large facility; the associated population impact provides an outer boundary within which other energy conversion options may fall. Construction would require as many as 22,000 worker-years spread over 7 years. The peak construction work force is estimated to be 5,600, 6,500, and 4,600 in years 4, 5, and 6, respectively. Operation of the plant could require 1,600 workers (EPA 1979). A 12- to 14-mmtpy coal mine would supply the plant's feedstock. The assumption is made that group quarters are available for construction workers, and that most of them will not be accompanied by families.

The effect of construction of the plant is spread over a large number of years (Figs. 4-6). The peak population is maintained over perhaps 4 years; population tends to increase after operations begin, because of the stability of the operation work force and the presence of members' families. In this case also, the assumed presence of group living quarters and the presence of workers without the accompaniment of families smoothes the population changes from the construction to the operating phase.

Population could increase to 272, 229, and 225 percent of 1978 levels in Mercer, Campbell, and Rosebud Counties respectively (Figs. 4-6). That is a result of the liquefaction plant and all coal development expected in 1990. Absolute population changes due to the liquefaction plant alone above the anticipated coal development to 1990 are estimated to be 9,655, 7,370, and 6,140 in Mercer, Rosebud, and Campbell Counties respectively, in 1990.

Table 2. Estimated 1990 Employment, Population, and Migration Indicators for 4 Assumed Energy Development Levels; 3 Northern Plains Counties

Item	Direct[a] Coal-Related Jobs	Total Jobs[b]	Total Population[c]	Accumulated Net Migration[d]
		Campbell County		
Baseline				
No expansion after 1978	1,025	12,025	21,625	4,475
Anticipated expansion after 1978	5,150	18,260	28,800	12,010
Gasification on line 1988	6,090	19,860	32,740	15,790
Liquefaction on line 1988	7,201	21,660	34,940	17,875
		Rosebud County		
Baseline				
No expansion after 1978	680	5,945	13,090	720
Anticipated expansion after 1978	1,280	7,130	14,630	4,010
Gasification on line 1988	2,205	8,750	18,300	7,570
Liquefaction on line 1988	3,305	10,600	22,000	11,100
		Mercer County		
Baseline				
No expansion after 1978	443	4,130	7,940	890
Anticipated expansion after 1978	987	5,240	10,470	2,460
Gasification on line 1988	2,077	7,070	16,400	8,250
Liquefaction on line 1988	3,245	9,000	20,125	11,800

Source: COALTOWN Impact Assessment Model (Bender et al. 1980, and Temple 1978).

[a]Includes construction and operating work forces of coal mines, electricity generating plants, and gasification and liquefaction plants.

[b]Jobs include multiple, part-time, or full-time positions. Employment is lower by the number of people with multiple jobs.

[c]Changes in employment and population are influenced by changes in nonenergy industries sectors.

[d]Net migration 1979-90.

The population increase, in each case, is supplied through net migration of people into the county. This is the key indicator of the need and demand for permanent housing and for local government services. Labor-force participation rates and wages remain high in all counties after construction of the liquefaction plant.

FISCAL IMPACTS ON STATE AND LOCAL GOVERNMENT

The distribution of revenues frequently does not match the needs generated by energy facilities. The combined tax revenues of all government units do appear to be sufficient to cover the cost of additional services for the new population, although it remains problematic how great all social costs might be over the life of coal exploitation. Few long-term fiscal shortfalls should occur in state governments, counties, and school districts that contain energy facilities. Cities and school districts receiving additional population will fare poorly if they do not have access to this new tax base. Their large potential deficits can be made up only through increased taxes on residents or through impact aid from state and federal governments. In North Dakota, for example, intergovernmental transfers are the major source of revenues of local governments. In any case, short-term fiscal strains will arise because the timing of impacts will precede new revenues or impact aids from energy developments.

Precise projection of future revenues and expenditures is difficult. Tax law and rate changes, and lags that occur in revenues as energy facilities are constructed, are also impossible to portray accurately. Similarly, only general expenditure averages of governments are available. As a result, wide confidence bands should be placed around expenditure and revenue projections.

Revenue projections for the year 1990 are presented in Tables 3-6 for states, counties, school districts, and municipalities, assuming four development cases. The four cases are (1) no energy development expansion after 1978; (2) energy developments as now anticipated after 1978; (3) a gasification plant coming on line in 1988; and (4) a liquefaction plant coming on line in 1988. The last two cases are each added separately to case (2), which assumes anticipated energy development. Revenues reflect all activities for an operating year expressed in 1978 dollars.

State government revenues are projected to be considerably larger than average per capita state expenditures at present levels (Table 3). State revenues are net of intergovernmental transfers and are expressed in dollars per person in each county. Expenditures are 1977 levels adjusted to 1978 prices, but do not reflect additional state programs that will be adopted as a result of sustained energy development.

County revenues are projected to be higher than expenditure levels in Wyoming and North Dakota but lower in Montana; but these comparisons can be very misleading (Table 4). County government infrastructure likely will adapt to new demands, which could prove to be large. An example is the county road

Table 3. State per Capita Revenues Projected for Alternative 1990 Development
Cases in 3 Counties, and Average per Capita State Expenditures[a]

Item	Rosebud County Montana	Mercer County North Dakota	Campbell County Wyoming
	1978 dollars per capita		
Development case for 1990			
Baseline growth	2,606	1,509	1,400
Anticipated growth after 1978	3,833	2,234	4,574
Anticipated growth after 1978 plus operation of a 250 mil. cu. ft./da.			
Lurgi gasification plant by 1988	4,951	2,706	4,351
Anticipated growth after 1978 plus operation of a 100,000 bbl./da.			
SRC-II liquefaction plant by 1988	4,475	2,903	4,174
Expenditures			
Total	654	863	697
Capital and debt	177	288	222
Operation and maintenance	477	575	475

Source: Revenues are estimated by COALTOWN and ENGYTX simulation models (Bender et. al. 1980, and Temple 1978). Expenditures are taken from *Census of Governments, 1977*, U.S. Bureau of Census, Washington, D.C.
[a]Revenue projections are based on laws and tax rates existing in 1978 and are net of earmarked intergovernmental transfers.

Table 4. County per Capita Revenues Projected for Alternative 1990 Development
Cases in 3 Counties, and Average per Capita County Expenditures[a]

Item	Rosebud County Montana	Mercer County North Dakota	Campbell County Wyoming
	1978 dollars per capita		
Development case for 1990			
Baseline growth	104	199	424
Anticipated growth after 1978	177	295	889
Anticipated growth after 1978 plus operation of a 250 mil. cu. ft./da.			
Lurgi gasification plant by 1988	256	280	890
Anticipated growth after 1978 plus operation of a 100,000 bbl./da.			
SRC-II liquefaction plant by 1988	232	280	884
Expenditures			
Total	313	165	384
Capital and debt	37	32	43
Operation and maintenance	276	133	341

Source: Revenues are estimated by COALTOWN and ENGYTX simulation models (Bender et. al. 1980, and Temple 1978). Expenditures are taken from *Census of Governments, 1977*, U.S. Bureau of Census, Washington, D.C.
[a]Revenue projections are based on laws and tax rates existing in 1978 and are net of earmarked intergovernmental transfers.

Table 5. School per Pupil Revenues Projected for Alternative 1990 Development Cases in 3 Counties, and Average per Pupil School Expenditures[a]

Item	Rosebud County Montana	Mercer County North Dakota	Campbell County Wyoming
	1978 dollars per capita		
Development case for 1990			
Baseline growth	1,903	1,052	4,195
Anticipated growth after 1978	2,233	1,552	8,394
Anticipated growth after 1978 plus operation of a 250 mil. cu. ft./da. Lurgi gasification plant by 1988	2,635	1,554	7,898
Anticipated growth after 1978 plus operation of a 100,000 bbl./da. SRC-II liquefaction plant by 1988	2,611	1,362	8,450
Expenditures			
Total	1,786	1,671	2,239
Capital and debt	101	100	398
Operation and maintenance	1,685	1,571	1,841

Source: Revenues are estimated by COALTOWN and ENGYTX simulation models (Bender et. al. 1980, and Temple 1978). Expenditures are taken from Census of Governments, 1977, U.S. Bureau of Census, Washington, D.C.

[a]Revenue projections are based on laws and tax rates existing in 1978 and are net of earmarked intergovernmental transfers.

Table 6. City per Capita Revenues Projected for Alternative 1990 Development Cases in 3 Counties, and Average per Capita Municipal Expenditures[a]

Item	Rosebud County Montana	Mercer County North Dakota	Campbell County Wyoming
	1978 dollars per capita		
Development case for 1990			
Baseline growth	40	206	88
Anticipated growth after 1978	42	249	104
Anticipated growth after 1978 plus operation of a 250 mil. cu. ft./da. Lurgi gasification plant by 1988	44	260	103
Anticipated growth after 1978 plus operation of a 100,000 bbl./da. SRC-II liquefaction plant by 1988	46	275	104
Expenditures			
Total	228	202	286
Capital and debt	71	60	69
Operation and maintenance	157	142	217

Source: Revenues are estimated by COALTOWN and ENGYTX simulation models (Bender et. al. 1980, and Temple 1978). Expenditures are taken from Census of Governments, 1977, U.S. Bureau of Census, Washington, D.C.

[a]Revenue projections are based on laws and tax rates existing in 1978 and are net of earmarked intergovernmental transfers.

network that will have to be built and maintained in largely roadless areas. Furthermore, incremental capital costs for new facilities will be much greater than those of the past due to inflation. The gross proceeds of coal mines are taxable property in both Wyoming and Montana, and small changes in mill levies can generate large changes in revenue. Wyoming counties especially can generate large revenues from energy facilities because of their dependence on local taxes as sources of revenue. County governments in North Dakota, on the other hand, tend to be dependent upon state aids rather than local property taxes, and present aids may prove inadequate.

School districts in Montana and Wyoming appear to receive enough revenues to meet expenditure levels assuming 1978 tax levies (Table 5). Projected revenues in North Dakota for schools fall somewhat short of expected levels. School foundation programs in each state will tend to support operations.

City governments in Montana and Wyoming will clearly suffer financial hardships unless additional state or federal aid is made available (Table 6). City expenditures average $228 and $286 in Montana and Wyoming respectively. Projected per capita revenues are not above $46 in Montana and $104 in Wyoming in any development case. The problem is attributed to the fact that energy facilities are located outside city limits and thus are not subject to city property taxes. North Dakota meets this problem by providing a direct aid to cities from its state tax on coal and coal conversion.

The results of these fiscal analyses agree generally with those of other studies (Murdock and Leistritz 1979) that suggest long-term fiscal shortfalls should prove no insurmountable problem for those state and local governments that contain energy developments. The exceptions to this general conclusion are extremely important and numerous, however. First, cities and school districts without access to energy tax bases will be affected. Sheridan County, Wyoming, for instance, will be the home of many southern Montana miners. Second, short-term deficits during early development phases will pose problems. Third, limits on local taxes and bonded indebtedness could severely constrain the local governments' management of their finances. Fourth, the level, mix, and cost of local governments will undoubtedly change, especially during rapid growth. Fifth, many social costs other than government infrastructure are incurred as a result of rapid and sustained energy development. Sixth, Indian tribes face special problems. Finally, the institutions defining the rights to and uses of resources will be changed by energy development. The remaining discussion is addressed to this last point.

RESOURCE AND LAND-USE ISSUES OF NORTHERN PLAINS COAL DEVELOPMENT

Northern Plains and western coal development have accelerated a subtle yet pervasive pressure to change the institutions that define access to, use of, and returns from resources. A sudden presence of large profits motivates rent-seekers to alter the system of rights to those resources and their use. Northern Plains coal development provides that stimulus. Some of these changes will set precedents for future legislative and judicial decisions affecting the national system of resources.

It seems reasonable, then, to highlight five institutions presently undergoing change as a result of expanded western coal production. Illustrated are types of property rights that are fundamental determinants of resource use and that, once changed, will influence resource use in the nation for years to come.

Taxation

Taxation is one state power that alters land-use policy and land-use patterns. State powers to tax severed minerals have been upheld by the U.S. Supreme Court numerous times (Hellerstein 1978). Nevertheless, renewed judicial and legislative challenges are being made to change those state powers. In the Montana Supreme Court, a group of coal and utility companies from six midwestern and southern states challenged the constitutionality of Montana's coal severance tax. This is a landmark case that Montana won in the U.S. Supreme Court. In addition, recent measures introduced in the U.S. Congress seek to impose ceilings on states' coal severance tax rates. Although they would affect only Montana and Wyoming at present, other states and other minerals could be the subject of future actions. Whatever the outcome, the extent and location of resource use in the nation will be affected.

Water Rights

Concern over water demands of large-scale energy projects in the arid west is accelerating changes in water-rights institutions. Montana, Wyoming, Colorado, and Idaho are suppliers of large amounts of water to downstream users (Gray 1979). In some jurisdictions, water rights are being sold to energy companies. Other states are changing water rights. A four-year effort is underway in Montana requiring the filing of water rights claims. The goal of the program is to make Montanans' rights to water secure in any future disputes, and these could be used in negotiations with large-scale energy projects and downstream users.

Environmental Regulations

A greater dependence on coal, together with the environmental regulations governing coal conversion, have extremely important consequences for land-use patterns. Among the many problems associated with increases in sulfur dioxide and nitrous oxide emissions is that of acid rain (Teknekron 1979). Already, lakes in some northern regions are barren because of acidity, and the eastern portion of the United States is also subject to acid rain. The increased use of coal in new locations will produce additional acid rain problems affecting land use, and the environmental regulations designed to control such emissions will inevitably influence industrial location.

Facility Siting

States, localities, and citizen groups now have many ways to control the timing and location of new coal mines and conversion facilities. Two federal initiatives—the federal coal leasing program and proposed federal legislation streamlining the siting of coal conversion facilities—will alter the control of siting. Each of these affects siting directly, but together they are only a part of the larger issue of federal ownership and control of resources in the West.

Federal land and resource use in the West set the stage for industrial development and population distribution. Federal and state governments own or control about 57 percent of the land surface in the mountain states of the West (personal communications, H. Thomas Frey, Geographer, Economic Research Service, USDA, February 25, 1980), and are the major owners of coal reserves there. About 30 percent of Montana's and 48 percent of Wyoming's surface are in federal land ownership (U.S. Department of the Interior 1977). About 76 percent of the total acreage in Montana's known recoverable coal resource area (KRCRA) is under federal mineral ownership, and about 85 percent of the Wyoming KRCRA acreage is under federal mineral ownership (Butler 1978).

Federal land-use policies, siting legislation, and mineral leasing will directly affect patterns of development and resource use in the West and will indirectly alter resource use elsewhere.

Indian Rights

Heightened interest in western coal has forced Indian tribes into a sustained effort to define, formalize, and institutionalize their rights. Perhaps as much as 25 percent of the nation's energy resources are owned by Indians. About 10 percent of Northern Plains coal is owned by the Crow and Northern Cheyenne.

Associated with energy development on reservations are issues such as water rights, control of non-Indians on reservations, control of mineral leasing, and taxation. Important Indian rights to resources and their use are being defended by Indian tribes, although the process is long and arduous. The cases dealing with energy resources will establish precedents for judicial action in numerous other areas of Indian rights.

SUMMARY

Future coal mining in the western United States could furnish 30 to 40 percent of the nation's supply by 1990. The Northern Plains will provide much of that. Despite the seemingly great magnitude of this coal development, direct local impacts will be concentrated largely in seven mining counties in the Great Plains. Relative population changes in these counties will be large, although smaller than that which would be anticipated in other coal mining areas, and relatively small from a national perspective.

Increases in the tax base of state and local governments due to coal mining and conversion are generally adequate to cover the local impacts that are near

term. Problems arise in the distribution of revenues among governmental jurisdictions and in the timing of revenue flows relative to the timing of impacts.
Special cases are communities that are affected but do not share in the tax base
of a mine or coal conversion facility. The timing of revenues is especially critical
in the initial stages of project planning, when uncertainty is high; the construction phase, when large numbers of temporary workers may be present; and the
shut-down phase, when the economic base of the community may disappear.

Resource and land-use issues being generated by coal development, especially
in the Northern Plains, are of great importance to the nation. Institutions governing access to, use of, and returns from resources will change as the various
interest groups vie for position to capitalize on the vast coal resources of the
Great Plains.

Property rights are the threads of the fabric that form the economic system.
They define access to resources and returns from those resources. Rights, whether
formal or informal, influence resource use. A revolution in rights is being pre-
cipitated by heightened coal development because of the sudden rise in economic rents evident there. Once established, the institutions upholding those rights
are slow to change without renewed incentives. The precedents established by a
change in property rights form the basis for re-evaluation of numerous other
rights institutions throughout the nation. Although the machinery of change
moves slowly, its momentum is powerful. Changes in institutions governing
access to and use of resources could be the major and the longest-lasting impact
from Northern Plains and western coal development, eventually overshadowing
the local population and employment impacts that receive attention today.

References

Bender, L. D. 1980. The effect of trends in economic structures on population change in
    rural areas. In *New Directions in Urban-Rural Migration: The Population Turnaround in
    Nonmetropolitan America*, ed. D. L. Brown and J. M. Wardwell, ch. 6, pp. 137-162.
    New York: Academic Press.

Bender, L. D.; Temple, G. S.; and Parcels, L. C. 1980. An Introduction to the COALTOWN
    Impact Assessment Model. Washington, D.C.: USDA Economics, Statistics, and Coop-
    eratives Service, and EPA Office of Environmental Engineering and Technology, EPA-
    600/7-80-146 (August).

Butler, J. 1978. Federal coal leasing and 1985 and 1990 regional coal production forecasts.
    Washington, D.C.: Department of Energy, Leasing Policy Development Office, un-
    published.

Cannon, J. S. 1978. *Mine Control: Western Coal Leasing and Development.* New York:
    Council on Economic Priorities.

Coal Outlook. 1980a. *EPA Sticks with Partial Scrubbing Rule* (February 11): 2.

————. 1980b. *ICF Sees Coal Pipelines as Hedge Against Escalating Rail Rates.* (January
    14): 4-5.

————. 1980c. *Operators Boosted Productivity in 1979's Third Quarter* (February 25): 4-5.

Coddington, D. 1980. Research needs in local impact assessment. *Proceedings of Great
    Plains Council Coordinating Committee 8 Conference on Energy Impacts, March 17-18,
    1980, Denver, Colorado.*

Environmental Protection Agency. 1979. Energy from the West. Energy Resource Development Systems Report Vol. II: *Coal*. Washington, D.C.: Environmental Protection Agency, Office of Energy Minerals and Industry, EPA-600/7-79-06b.

Fisher, K., and Cukor, P. 1980. Coal supply for Texas utilities. Prepared by Teknekron, Inc., Berkeley, CA for presentation at the Second Conference on Air Quality Management in the Electric Power Industry, Austin, Texas, January 22-25, (mimeographed).

Gordon, R. L. 1978. Hobbling coal. *Regulation* (July/August): 36-45.

Gray, S. L.; Sparling, E. W.; and Whittlesey, N. K. 1979. Water for Energy Development in the Northern Great Plains and Rocky Mountain Regions. Washington, D.C.: USDA Economics, Statistics, and Cooperatives Service, Staff Report NRED 80-103.

Hamilton, P. A., and White, Jr., D. H. 1975. The Reserve Base of U.S. Coals by Sulfur Content: Part 2. Washington, D.C.: DOI U.S. Bureau of Mines, Information Circular 8693.

Hellerstein, W. 1978. Constitutional constraints on State taxation of energy resources. *National Tax Journal* 31(3) (September): 245-256.

Krohm, G. C.; Dux, C. D.; and VanKuiken, J. C. 1977. Effects on Regional Coal Markets of the 'Best Available Control Technology' Policy for Sulfur Emissions. Argonne, Illinois: Argonne National Laboratory, ANL/AA-16.

McMartin, W.; Whetzel, V.; and Myers, P. R. 1980. People, agricultural resources and coal development. Washington, D.C.: USDA Economics, Statistics, and Cooperative Service, Natural Resources Division (unpublished).

Murdock, S. H., and Leistritz, F. L. 1979. *Energy Development in the Western United States — Impact on Rural Areas*. New York: Praeger.

Myers, P. R.; Hines, F. K.; and Conopask, J. 1978. A Socioeconomic Profile of the Northern Great Plains Coal Region. Washington, D.C.: USDA Economics, Statistics, and Cooperatives Service, Agricultural Economics Report 400.

Rieber, M. 1975. Low sulfur coal: A revision of reserve and supply estimates. *Journal of Environmental Economics and Management* 2: 40-59.

Smith, A. E.; Walsko, T. D.; and Cirillo, R. 1976. Coal Supply and Air Quality Limitations on Fossil-Fueled Energy Centers. Argonne, Illinois: Argonne National Laboratory. August.

Stinson, T. F., and Voelker, S. W. 1978. Coal Development in the Northern Great Plains: The Impact on Revenues of State and Local Governments. Washington, D.C.: USDA Economics, Statistics, and Cooperatives Service, Agricultural Economics Report 394.

Teknekron Research Inc. 1979. An integrated monitoring network for acid deposition. Prepared for EPA, R-023-EPA-79, Interim Report, November (mimeographed).

Temple, G. S. 1978. A dynamic systems community impact model applied to coal development in the Northern Great Plains. Bozeman: Montana State University, Ph.D. dissertation.

U.S. Department of Commerce. 1981. Census of Population and Housing. Washington, D.C.: Bureau of Census PHC 80, Vols. 28, 36, and 52.

U.S. Department of Energy. 1979. Western Coal Development Monitoring System. Washington, D.C.: Dept. of Energy, Division of Coal Production Technology, Office of Coal Supply Development, DOE/RA-0045.

U.S. Department of the Interior. 1977. Public Land Statistics. Washington, D.C.: Bureau of Land Management.

Yandle, B. 1978. The emerging market in air pollution rights. *Regulation* (July/August): 21-29.

Environmental Impacts of Synthetic Liquid Fuels Development in the Ohio River Basin

Gary L. Fowler, J. C. Randolph, and Steven I. Gordon

The development of a large-scale synthetic and alcohol fuels industry in the United States has been proposed as one way to reduce the nation's dependency on foreign petroleum imports. S932, the Energy Security Act, Title I, Synthetic Fuels, sets a production goal of 500,000 barrels per day (bpd) crude oil equivalent, primarily from coal and oil shale, by 1987 and increasing to two million bpd by 1992. Title II, the Biomass Energy Act of 1980, calls for an alcohol production level of 60,000 bpd by 1982, and a production level equivalent to at least 10 percent of estimated gasoline consumption by 1990. Significant public investment and institutional support through the Synthetic Fuels Corporation are integral parts of the act.

A high level of uncertainty characterizes the planning for synthetic fuels development. Debate over feasible production goals and the level of support from the federal government has intensified with the change from the Carter to the Reagan administration. The debate over environmental impacts has also continued. Although numerous studies have examined the technological and economic feasibility of candidate technologies, the lack of operating experience

This paper is based in part on reserach conducted for the Ohio River Basin Energy Study (ORBES). The ORBES project has been funded by the U.S. Environmental Protection Agency as part of the Integrated Assessment Program. The contents of this paper do not necessarily reflect the views and policies of the Environmental Protection Agency, nor does mention of trade names or commercial products constitute endorsement or recommendation for use.

The maps were produced by Raymond M. Brod of the Cartography Laboratory, Department of Geography, University of Illinois at Chicago. Steven D. Jansen, Energy Resources Center, University of Illinois at Chicago, coordinated the mapping work for ORBES. Michael A. Ewert and William W. Jones, Environmental Sciences Applications Center (ESAC), School of Public and Environmental Affairs, Indiana University compiled the data on coal and biomass resources.

in the United States with commercial-scale plants poses significant questions about the impacts of the technologies upon the environment and host communities. Environmental research programs are designed to reduce the level of uncertainty by the mid-1980s. In the meantime, sufficient information is available to design assessments of synthetic fuel technologies that will focus upon environmental policy issues relevant to those regions of the country in which the industry may be located.

The purpose of this essay is to define the environmental policy issues that may be associated with synthetic fuel development in the Ohio River Basin. This is a region whose abundant coal resources have supported urban-industrial development and whose rich agricultural lands have contributed significantly to the nation's food production. Over the next two decades, projected patterns of regional energy development from conventional fuels indicate that significant additional stress may be placed upon selected land, water, and air resources. The location of a synthetic fuel industry in the Ohio River Basin is likely to change the nature, magnitude, and the geographical distribution of environmental impacts in a way that will challenge land use and energy policy in the nonmetropolitan areas of the eastern United States.

SYNTHETIC FUEL DEVELOPMENT IN THE OHIO RIVER BASIN

The Ohio River Basin region has rich reserves of coal and biomass resources that can be used as feedstocks for synthetic and alcohol fuels. These include the coal reserves of the Eastern Interior Basin and the Appalachian Basin, as well as conventional grain crops and lignocellulosic materials from the region's agricultural lands and ecological systems. The Ohio River Basin includes the two areas in the eastern United States that have been identified as resource regions for coal-derived fuel development (U.S. Department of Energy—USDOE—1980; Rickert et al. 1979).

Coal Resources

In 1976, the Ohio River Basin region produced 468.7 million tons of coal (Willard et al. 1980). Kentucky was the largest producer, followed by West Virginia and Pennsylvania. Most of the coal from West Virginia, Pennsylvania, and Illinois came from deep mines. Surface mine production was the principal source of coal in the other states, especially Indiana. More than two-thirds of the coal mined in the region is used to generate electricity.

Each state has coal resources that are potentially available for synthetic fuel development. Illinois has the largest reserve base, followed by West Virginia, Kentucky, Pennsylvania, Ohio and Indiana. Deep-mineable reserves exceed strippable reserves in each state. In the Eastern Interior Basin, deep mineable reserves are located in the interior, primarily in Illinois, whereas the surface-mineable reserves are located on the periphery of the basin (Figs. 1 and 2). The

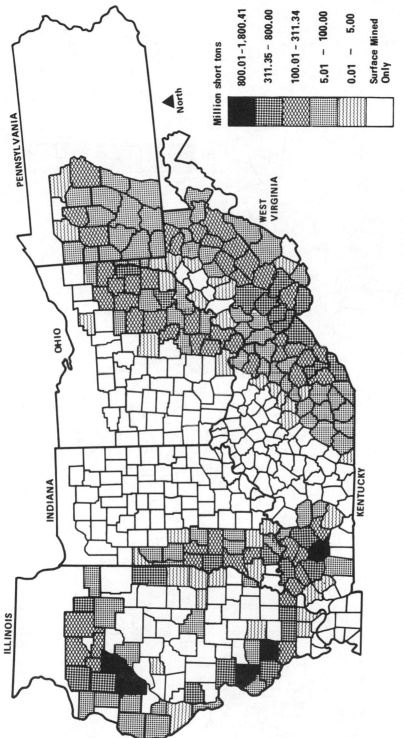

Million short tons

800.01–1,800.41

311.35 – 800.00

100.01 – 311.34

5.01 – 100.00

0.01 – 5.00

Surface Mined
Only

Figure 1. Deep mineable reserves in 1974. From Willard et al., 1980. Parts of states on this and subsequent maps that do not have county boundaries are outside the Ohio River Basin study region.

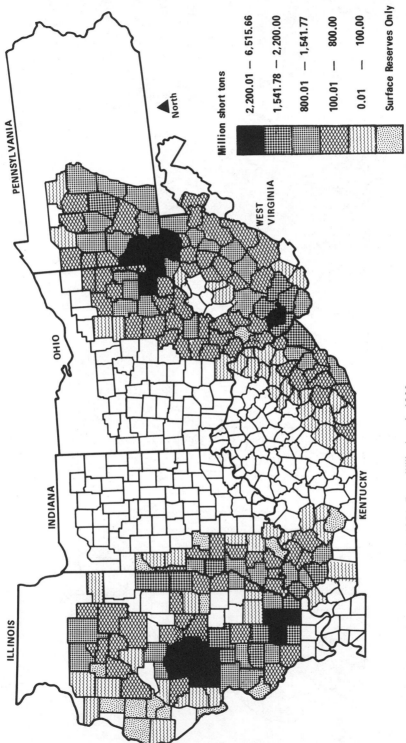

Million short tons

2,200.01 — 6,515.66

1,541.78 — 2,200.00

800.01 — 1,541.77

100.01 — 800.00

0.01 — 100.00

Surface Reserves Only

Figure 2. Surface mineable reserves in 1974. From Willard et al., 1980.

surface-mineable reserves in the Appalachian Basin are concentrated in eastern Ohio and in the central Appalachian highlands of West Virginia and Eastern Kentucky. Elsewhere, the geographical distribution of the deep-mineable and surface-mineable reserves are closely associated. Most of the region's coal resources have a high sulfur content.

Thirteen coal hydrogenation projects are located or planned for sites in the Ohio River Basin (U.S. Congress, Senate 1979; Ohio River Basin Commission 1978). Kentucky has six of these, and all except one of the coal liquefaction projects (Jones 1980). All of the proposed plants are located on the mainstream of the Ohio River and its major tributaries near the coal fields of the Eastern Interior and the Appalachian Basins. Whereas a typical small mine can produce the amount of coal needed by pilot plants, demonstration plants require the production of a moderate to large-size mine. None of the synthetic fuel from coal plants in the basin operates at commercial scale. However, the total production of two or three of the largest mines currently operating in the basin would be necessary to provide coal feedstocks to commercial scale plants.

Biomass Resources

The feedstocks for bioenergy come from several sources. They include wood from commercial forest land; grass and legume herbage from hay and pasture land; ethanol and lignocellulosic materials from intensive agriculture; and biogas from animal and agricultural wastes. The Office of Technology Assessment (Congress, OTA 1980) has estimated the energy potential from all sources at national scale for 1985 and the year 2000. In the long term, wood from commercial forests and other sources of lignocellulosic material has the greatest energy potential. Virtually none of these sources is currently used to produce energy. In the short term, ethanol from cereal grains and sugar crops can be used as alcohol fuels.

The Ohio River Basin is rich in biomass resources (Randolph and Jones 1980). Approximately 85 percent of the total area is in agriculture or in nonfederal forests. Agriculture, which is the dominant type of land use in the region, is concentrated in Illinois, northern and central Indiana, and northwestern Ohio. The distribution of Class I and II soils defines the potentially most productive agricultural lands (Fig. 3). Prime farmlands, defined as Class I and II soils, account for 39 percent of the total area in the region and 72 percent of the agricultural lands. Corn is the most important crop, with much smaller acreages in soybeans and winter wheat. These and other conventional cereal grains, which are concentrated on prime agricultural lands, are important sources of food and feed. They are also the most important sources of crop residues for biomass energy (Tyner and Bottum 1979; Welch 1979).

Nonfederally owned forests occupy an additional 31 percent of the region (Fig. 4). These forests, most of which are small privately-owned tracts, represent the biomass resource base of wood from commercial forests. The forest land is concentrated in the eastern part of the basin, especially in the Appalachian areas

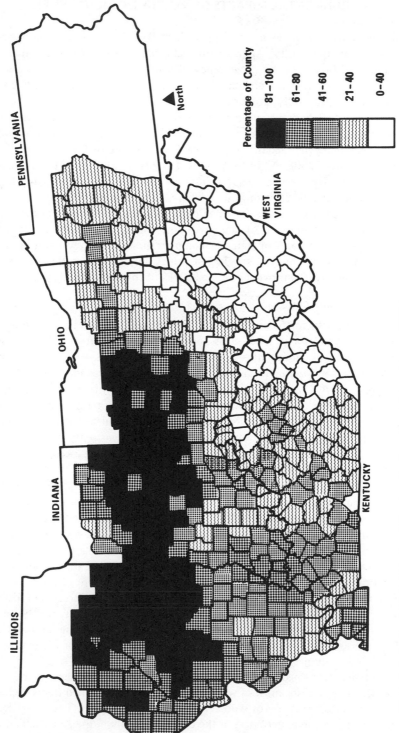

Figure 3. Agricultural lands: Class I and Class II soils. From Randolph and Jones, 1980.

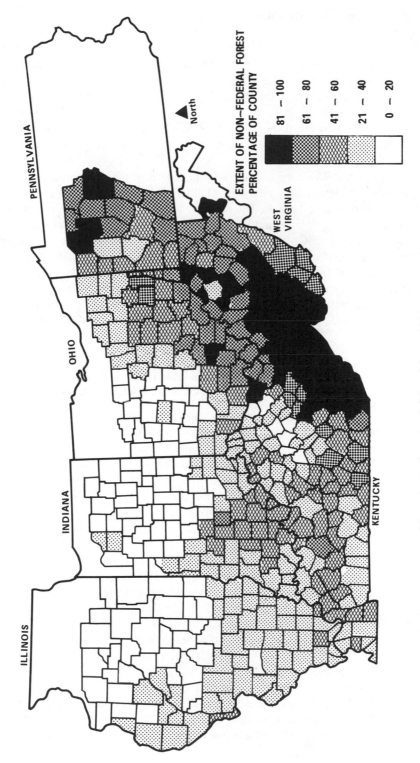

Figure 4. Ownership and management of forest lands. From Randolph and Jones, 1980.

EXTENT OF NON-FEDERAL FOREST
PERCENTAGE OF COUNTY

81 – 100
61 – 80
41 – 60
21 – 40
0 – 20

North

PENNSYLVANIA

WEST VIRGINIA

OHIO

INDIANA

ILLINOIS

KENTUCKY

of eastern Kentucky, southeastern Ohio, West Virginia, and western Pennylvania. Currently, forest products are primarily hardwoods that are used for manu-factured wood products. The Shawnee National Forest in Illinois, the Hoosier National Forest in Indiana, the Wayne National Forest in Ohio, and the Daniel Boone National Forest in Kentucky and West Virginia are the region's largest areas of publicly-owned forest lands. They are 12 percent of the total land area and could be added to the biomass resource base if this were in accord with federal forest-management policy.

Although the inventory of energy produced from biomass resources in the basin is incomplete, commercial-scale facilities are available for the production of ethanol from cereal grains. The primary Midwestern supplier of ethanol for gasohol fuels is located in central Illinois. Proposals for several large-scale facilities in Ohio with a capacity of 113-123 million gallons per year have been announced (Ohio Department of Energy, personal communication), and the feasibility of alcohol fuels in Indiana has been examined (Computer Sciences Corporation 1980). Additional distillation capacity is available in grain alcohol distilleries that either recently have ceased production or are under-utilized (*Energy Users Report*, No. 335, January 10, 1980, pp. 4-5). Many of the distilleries are in Kentucky.

REGIONAL ENVIRONMENTAL IMPACTS FROM SYNTHETIC LIQUID FUELS DEVELOPMENT

Significant environmental impacts are associated with the use of coal and biomass resources of the Ohio River Basin for producing synthetic liquid fuels. A rigorous quantitative assessment of the impacts requires details on technology and site-specific effects that are not yet available because of limited operating experience, especially with the coal-derived processes. The Ohio River Basin Energy Study (1981) considered only the potential environmental impacts of conventional fuels; and USDOE (1980) did not assess the impacts that might be associated with coal mining, waste disposal, or with liquid fuels from biomass. Sufficient material is available, however, to define qualitatively the potential environmental impacts and policy issues that are associated with synthetic fuels development, and the land use conflicts that may develop because of the geo-graphical distribution of coal and biomass resources in the Ohio River Basin.

Air Pollution

Coal conversion processes result in significant emissions of sulfur dioxide and particulates. Morris et al. (1979) have estimated that air pollutant residuals from the SRC-II direct liquefaction process are less than from the direct combustion of coal in central station electricity generating facilities. Furthermore, a signifi-cant portion of the emission sources is shifted from the end use and conversion sites to hydrogenation sites and coal mining areas. Because synthetic liquid fuels can be transported economically over long distances, mine-mouth siting is attractive. Combustion tests of SRC materials have led USDOE (1980) to conclude that current technology is sufficient to control air pollutant emissions from hydrogenation facilities under existing air quality regulations. Particulates from surface mining, which primarily result from removing the overburden, are not expected to be a major environmental problem.

Acid precipitation is a relatively recent and controversial environmental issue (Council on Environmental Quality 1980). Acid precipitation is formed when oxides of sulfur and nitrogen, released when fossil fuels are burned, combine with moisture in the atmosphere and fall to earth. The sulfur and nitrogen oxides come largely from industries and utilities that use coal-fired power plants. Acid precipitation can result in decreased productivity from crops and the Ohio River Basin region has been identified as a major source region for acid precipitation in the eastern part of the United States (Ohio River Basin Energy Study 1981). Coal hydrogenation technologies have lower fuel cycle emissions of sulfur dioxide than coal combustion technologies but higher emissions than the natural gas or oil that their synthetic fuels might replace (Morris et al. 1979).

The air-quality impacts from biomass production are less clearly defined. Distilleries may use coal-fired power, and thus contribute to sulfur dioxide concentrations. But particulates from agricultural activities may become the principal air-quality issue in bioenergy. In the short term, intensive mechanical disturbance of the fine loam soils of prime agricultural lands could be a problem equivalent to a nonpoint source of air pollution. The contribution of biomass energy production to suspended particulates could increase significantly if the intensive cultivation of energy crops is expanded to marginal, less productive, and more erosive land.

Particulates are important air residuals in the Ohio River Basin (Ohio River Basin Energy Study 1981). More areas fail to attain National Ambient Air Quality Standards because of particulate concentrations than sulfur dioxide. Particulates contribute to visibility impairment, and they may affect ecosystem productivity by reducing the amount of sunlight available for photosynthesis.

Water Quality

A wide variety of constituents are associated with coal liquefaction. Most of the stable elements occur in coal, and many of these have been detected in various forms at appreciable concentrations in liquefaction process waters, wastewaters, or solid waste leachates. In addition, hundreds of organic compounds have already been identified in coal liquefaction process waters, products and wastes. Many of these organic and inorganic contaminants are known to be highly toxic (USDOE 1980). Given the potential environmental problems, Bailey et al. (1979) recommend that coal conversion plants in the Ohio River Basin should be zero-discharge facilities.

The aqueous leaching and dissolution of solid waste materials has the greatest potential for the release of hazardous inorganic constituents. Also, contaminants can enter the ground water through acid mine drainage as well as leaching of waste materials from surface coal mining activities. Acid mine drainage is a regional problem in the Northern Appalachian Basin, and in portions of southern Illinois and Indiana (Rickert et al. 1979). Siltation and sedimentation in surface waters because of soil erosion is a local problem in surface mining areas. Underground mining may disrupt aquifers that serve as regional water supplies.

Degradation of water quality by pesticides and chemicals is an issue in biomass energy. Expanding intensive agricultural production, especially corn and conventional cereal grains, to provide feedstocks for bioenergy may result in the use of more pesticides and fertilizers to maintain crop yields on marginal agricultural lands. These lands and crops characteristically result in more erosion, which may lead to problems of siltation and sedimentation.

Water Use

Large supplies of water are needed for coal hydrogenation technologies. The SRC-II process requires more make-up water than any other coal process and has more total water use than a central station electricity generation unit with flue-gas desulfurization (Morris et al. 1979). Extraordinary water use for the intensive agricultural production of biomass sources is not expected, as irrigating energy crops is generally not considered to be economically viable, or necessary, in the eastern United States (Tyner and Bottum 1979). Some water is consumed in the fermentation of biomass materials, especially in large-scale facilities. However, the need to have large supplies of water available for coal hydrogenation is the primary issue in water use.

Solid Waste Disposal

Solid waste handling and disposal pose significant environmental problems, especially for synthetic fuels from coal. The wastes from coal hydrogenation technologies are more hazardous and require more special handling than flue-gas desulfurization scrubber sludges and fly ash from electric generating facilities using coal (Morris et al. 1979). Aqueous leaching and dissolution of solid waste materials are the major issues. Coal-derived processes may shift the location of the production of solid wastes away from conversion sites and end use to the point of hydrogenation and coal mining activities, where more land is available for waste disposal. The problem of leaching remains, however.

Problems in the disposal of solid waste from the distillation of cereal grain depend upon the scale of the operation. Waste from small-scale facilities can be disposed of in the environment without major difficulty, or converted to livestock feed. Disposing of wastes from large facilities may be more difficult, as the volumes involved require larger land areas for handling and disposal.

The effect of the 1976 Resource Conservation and Recovery Act (RCRA; Public Law 94-580) on synthetic liquid fuels development is uncertain. The legislation deals with the management of solid and hazardous wastes and encourages energy and resource recovery. The hazardous waste management provisions are of considerable concern if wastes produced by various technologies, especially coal, are identified as hazardous. This has led USDOE (1980) and others (Cal-zonetti 1979; Carnes 1979) to consider that RCRA may become a major constraint on siting synthetic fuels from coal plants.

Land Use and Terrestrial Ecosystems

Both coal hydrogenation and biomass processes potentially have significant impacts on land resources and terrestrial ecosystems. Because of high demands for coal, large areas of productive agricultural and forest land may be temporarily or permanently converted because of mining. A mine operator must disturb more land in the Appalachian Basin per ton of coal than in the Eastern Interior Basin (Willard et al. 1980). Although the future expansion of surface mine production in the Eastern Interior Basin would affect significantly less acreage than in Appalachia, much of the reserve base underlies prime agricultural lands and other lands that are suitable for producing biomass resources.

Soil erosion from surface-mined lands may contribute to the degradation of water quality, and underground mining may result in surface subsidence. To the extent that coal mining affects surface and subsurface hydrology and stream characteristics, coal hydrogenation will increase flood hazards. Particulates in the air may result in a decline in agricultural and natural ecosystem productivity because of reduced photosynthesis.

Producing liquid fuels from biomass may result in different impacts (Fletcher 1980; National Agricultural Lands Study 1981). In the short term, the sources of ethanol will remain concentrated on prime agricultural lands where yields from conventional grain crops are high. Future increased production may come from improved production techniques and species, and from the conversion of cropland and pasture intensive cultivation. Set-aside land is also a potential source of "new" land (Tyner and Bottum 1980). Any future expansion of hayland, cropland and non-cropland pasture, and lignocellulosic crops probably will be restricted to marginal lands where the proportion of land used for agriculture is less. These crops are not likely to displace conventional grain production from prime agricultural lands. Increased soil erosion and the depletion of soil nutrients may occur when crop residues are removed, however, and when intensively cultivated cereal grains, especially corn, are grown on marginal, less productive, and more erosive land (cf. U.S. Congress, Office of Technology Assessment—OTA—1980; and Tyner and Bottum 1980). Removing residues from crop lands also results in a decline in land quality, although techniques are available to accommodate the change. If fertilizers (to replace nitrogen) and pesticides are added to the land, they may contribute to the degradation of water quality.

In the long term, lightly managed ecosystems, such as forests, may be transformed into intensively managed monocultures. This is especially likely if the source of biomass feedstocks changes to lignocellulosic materials and large-scale silviculture plantations are developed from commercial forests. Although the extent of the forest land is not expected to change significantly, the overall productivity may increase because of improved forest management. The possibility of soil erosion, stream sedimentation, and flooding may also increase (U.S. Congress, OTA 1980).

COMPARATIVE ANALYSIS

Comparative analysis of the potential environmental impacts suggest four conclusions:

- *Biomass has the potential to be a source of liquid fuels that has relatively few significant environmental problems and some important environmental benefits.*

  The potential environmental impacts of biomass production are less severe than those associated with coal hydrogenation technologies. However, a vigorous expansion of bioenergy production could cause serious environmental damage unless the resource ecosystems are properly managed.

- *Ethanol produced from conventional cereal grains and other sources has more severe environmental impacts than those associated with processes that use lignocellulosic materials.*

  Wood, wastes, and grasses have potentially few adverse environmental impacts, whereas impacts from using crop and logging residues will depend upon resource management.

- *Coal hydrogenation technologies that produce liquid fuel have more severe environmental impacts than those from the direct combustion of oil and gas, but somewhat less severe impacts in selected areas than from coal-fired electricity generating conversion plants.*

  The relative environmental advantages of synthetic fuels from coal, however, depends upon the technology and stage in the fuel cycle. The problems of solid waste disposal are especially serious because of the impacts on land use and water quality.

- *A significant portion of the pollutant emission sources, and hence the environmental impacts, will be located in the coal and biomass resource areas.*

  For coal-derived fuels, this may represent a shift away from places of end use and conversion to the hydrogenation and mining sites as relatively clean fuels derived from coal are used as boiler fuels in electricity generating units.

Several benefits might result from reducing air pollutant emissions from the direct use of coal in the Ohio River Basin and distributing part of the source locations to less densely populated nonmetropolitan areas in the region. For example (Morris et al. 1979), fewer people would be exposed to pollutants, thus reducing the risk to public health; and larger areas would be available for solid waste disposal. Also, siting electrical generating units in or near non-attainment areas would be easier if the units burned clean fuels. The Ohio River Basin currently has significant air-quality problems that are related to the direct combustion of coal, especially with regard to the long-range transport of sulfur dioxide and acid precipitation (Ohio River Basin Energy Study 1981). The effects upon air quality of producing synthetic fuels from coal in the region are open to question. However, the pilot and demonstration plants for synthetic fuel from coal in the region are located at sites along the Ohio River and its major tributaries that are accessible to coal resources. If commercial plants follow this pattern, they would still add to the concentration of pollutants in the Ohio River corridor even while reducing emissions elsewhere.

Coal-mining areas, on the other hand, would bear extraordinary impacts across a range of environmental systems that already suffer problems under current patterns of use. These include acid-mine drainage, soil erosion, degradation of water quality, and, in surface-mined areas, large-scale changes in land use and ecological productivity. Water quality and land-use impacts closely parallel coal use. The environmental impacts of hydrogenation plants will be localized, except for pollutants that are transported from the site. But the impacts associated with coal mining cover a much more extensive area. Their extent depends on the size of the facility and technology. Coal liquefaction and similar low-efficiency processes demand the most coal and have the greatest impact in the coal resource regions.

Issues in the use of biomass resources depend on the sources of fuel feedstocks. In the short term, biomass for fuel could compete with food and feed crops for the limited base of arable land. Some additional supplies of ethanol can be produced by substituting one crop for another (e.g., corn for soybeans) without increasing the acreage in conventional grain crops. New cropland can be brought into intensive cultivation for producing energy crops, although most of the land is marginal and erosive. OTA (U.S. Congress, OTA 1980) concludes that although the potential for competition between bioenergy and agriculture involves only a small fraction of the total biomass resource base, that fraction is capable of causing major conflict.

The competition between land use for bioenergy and agriculture in the region could become even more serious if, in the future, surface-mineable reserves that underlie agricultural lands are brought into coal production. The potential for conflict between farming prime agricultural lands and extracting surface-mineable reserves that underlie them is highest in counties that have large surface-mineable reserves and in which Class I and Class II soils are a large proportion of the land area (Willard et al. 1980; and Fig. 5). These counties are concentrated in the periphery of the Eastern Interior Basin, where recent and projected expansion of surface mining in Illinois and Indiana are in areas that also have extensive acreages of prime farmlands. State energy development programs may conflict with agricultural land-preservation policies (e.g., Benda 1980). In the face of such conflicts, the principal issue is the disturbance of prime farmland from mining

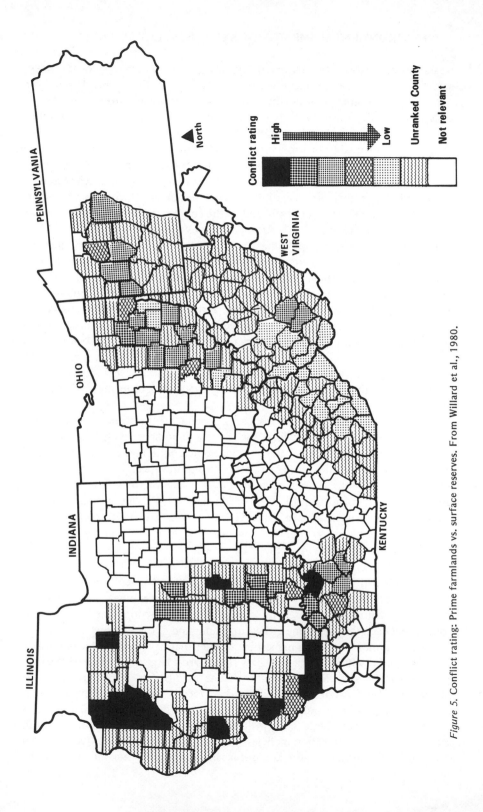

Figure 5. Conflict rating: Prime farmlands vs. surface reserves. From Willard et al., 1980.

and the rate and level of land reclamation. The recovery time of prime agricultural land in Illinois that has been surface-mined can be relatively short, given the necessary management and financial resources.

In the long term, a shift in the source of biomass energy to lignocellulosic crops, forage, pasture, wood and wastes could greatly increase the total biomass energy supply without any significant effect on food production or prices (U.S. Congress, OTA 1980). The potential for competition with surface-mined coal, however, would also increase. This would include relatively large areas of agricultural land on the periphery of the prime farmlands in the Eastern Interior basin as well as much of the nonfederal forest land in the Appalachian Basin. If the expansion of coal mining in the Eastern Interior Basin comes primarily from underground mines, the conflicts between using land for coal and agriculture would decrease. In the Appalachian Basin, the potential for land use conflicts between coal and biomass as sources of liquid fuels are great regardless of the type of mining. Large-scale expansion of coal mining could result in decreased productivity of the biomass resource base. The land would be more erosive and difficult to manage, and intensively managed forest ecosystems might be more subject to land-use and water impacts from underground as well as surface mines.

The size and location of the coal and biomass conversion facilities raise further environmental issues. USDOE (1980) has suggested two options for synthetic coal development, each of which would produce different environmental impacts and would require different regulatory and institutional structures. Large coal conversion facilities ($\geqslant$100,000 barrels per day, or bpd) located at a few sites would "concentrate" or "contain" environmental impacts at the site. Higher rates of resource consumption and residual production occurring over several jurisdictions might require centralized decision-making and regional permitting. A large number of small (28-35,000 bpd) to medium-size (40-60,000 bpd) facilities located at several sites would disperse environmental impacts, however. Coal conversion facilities are expected to be located at mine-mouth sites in either case because of their large demands for coal and the relatively low cost of shipping synthetic oil and gas products to markets. But environmental impacts will be concentrated in the coal resource regions whether the facilities are geographically dispersed or not.

Biomass resources are likely to be used in the areas where they are produced (U.S. Congress, OTA 1980). Large-scale ethanol production can use idle or underutilized capacity in commercial grain distilleries, whereas large-scale methanol plants may need to be constructed. The dispersed geography of biomass resource production favors small energy conversion facilities. Small facilities offer opportunities for decentralized production that can take advantage of the assimilative capacity of the local environment. There are questions of environmental trade-offs, however (U.S. Congress, OTA 1980). Impacts that are primarily local in nature, such as damage from fugitive dust and toxic waste disposal, are less severe at a given site but occur with greater frequency.

POLICY ISSUES

The potential environmental impacts from the production of liquid fuels from coal and biomass pose significant challenges to environmental and energy development policy in the Ohio River Basin. The policy issues, posed here as questions with comments, include the following:

- *In view of existing and projected regional air quality from conventional emission sources, are current air-quality policies and regulations sufficient to prevent further environmental damage and permit synthetic liquid fuel development?*

  Policies relevant to sulfur dioxide emissions and related issues of long-range transport and acid precipitation are of concern to coal processes whereas particulates may be the major issue for biomass.

- *Considering the sources of contaminants from coal processes and biomass, are current water-quality policies and regulations sufficient to prevent the further degradation of the region's water supplies?*

  This issue is particularly important with respect to the constituents associated with coal liquefaction processes and the pesticides, herbicides, and fertilizers that potentially may be used in large-scale biomass production.

- *Coal liquefaction processes typically require large amounts of water. Will supplies of water be adequate?*

  Agricultural production for biomass could compete with both food production and liquefaction processes for available water.

- *In view of the potential environmental impacts associated with waste handling and disposal, especially coal processes, are current and proposed regulations and policies sufficient to prevent environmental damage?*

  The definition of toxic substances, and the application of RCRA, are major uncertainties in the development of a synthetic fuels industry in the region. The issue is important because wastes are sources of materials that can pollute water supplies.

- *Production of large volumes of liquid fuels from biomass processes will require greatly increased land areas. What policies are necessary to balance the more important competing land uses?*

  This issue includes the need to manage carefully the consequences of emerging interdependence between agriculture and energy, surface mining for coal, and forest production for fuel, timber, and wildlife habitat, recreation and natural areas. The issue is of current importance because of the USEPA agricultural lands-protection policy (1979) and similar policies in states such as Illinois.

- *Production of large volumes of liquid fuels from coal processes will require large quantities of coal. Will current policies and regulations affecting coal mining and reclamation provide adequate protection for land and water quality?*

The new federal surface-mine reclamation regulations (SMRCA) are of primary concern, as are factors that may affect the mix of surface and underground mining.

- *Should policies be designed to bring new cropland under intensive cultivation for the production of energy crops?*

Because of potential competition with food, fiber, and feed, the efficacy of various uses of "new" lands (e.g., set-aside land and marginal lands) for displacing imported fuels should be examined. This issue is important in the short term for the production of ethanol.

A second set of policy issues concern energy supplies:

- *Should policies be implemented that favor and encourage the long-term development of liquid fuels production from renewable resources such as biomass, even though there may be numerous short-term problems and constraints?*

Although our reserves of coal are very large, coal, like petroleum, is a non-renewable natural resource. Under proper management, biomass is a renewable natural resource of infinite capacity, although prime agricultural lands for biomass production are definitely limited. Residuals-based taxes, fines, and penalties are one means of favoring biomass over coal.

- *Should policies be designed to encourage the early shift of biomass production from conventional cereal grains and ethanol to methanol production from lignocellulosic materials, especially forests?*

Assessments of sources of biomass energy indicate that methanol production from lignocellulosic materials has positive advantages in terms of environmental impacts, absence of competition with food, fuel, and fiber crops, and potential for displacing petroleum fuels.

- *From an environmental perspective, should relatively small-scale, dispersed conversion facilities be encouraged and subsidized rather than developing large, centralized facilities?*

At issue is the dispersal of environmental impacts, as well as the type and scale of decision making that is necessary in order to plan, develop, and regulate a synthetic fuels industry.

Finally,

- *The common characteristics of coal and biomass production and their environmental impacts exist throughout the Ohio River Basin. Should the states cooperate in planning, developing, and regulating synthetic liquid fuels production along with other energy developments?*

USDOE (1980) has identified this as an important, perhaps critical issue. The Ohio River Basin Energy Study (1980) has also suggested increased interstate cooperation in energy and environmental issues associated with conventional fuels. The Ohio River Basin Commission (1979) is one of several existing regional organizations with these concerns.

CONCLUSION

The large-scale production of synthetic liquid fuels from coal and oil shale, and alcohol fuels from biomass, has been proposed as a way to decrease the nation's dependence on foreign oil. Whereas extensive deposits of coal and oil shale are located in the western United States, the eastern part of the country has rich resources of coal and biomass. The development of these resources for a synthetic fuels industry in regions such as the Ohio River Basin, where energy production from conventional fuels already has placed considerable stress on the environment, raises significant issues of environmental and energy development policy.

A comparison of the potential environmental impacts from producing liquid fuels from coal and biomass suggests that biomass has potentially fewer significant environmental problems and some important environmental benefits. Ethanol produced from conventional cereal grains presents the most serious environmental problems. Methanol produced from lignocellulosic materials, especially wood, is less problematic. Coal hydrogenation technologies have less severe impacts in certain areas than occur from the direct combustion of coal. Both coal and biomass conversion processes will concentrate environmental impacts in the resource regions.

The potential environmental issues pose specific questions for environmental and energy development policy. One set concerns environmental issues; a second set addresses regional energy production. Currently, the increased use of high-sulfur coal from the Eastern Interior and Appalachian Basins has received the most attention from federal and state officials and industry groups. On the basis of our comparative analysis, we suggest that the use of biomass resources in the region for producing liquid fuels should receive more consideration.

References

Bailey, R. E.; Hendendorf, P.; Skidmore, D. R.; Fong, F. Ku; Sykes, R. M.; and Stiefel, R. C. 1979. *Wastewater Production and Treatment for Synthetic Fuel Processes in the Ohio River Basin*. Prepared for the Ohio River Basin Commission. Columbus, Ohio: Water Resources Center, The Ohio State University (August).

Benda, G. 1980. Reconciling Conflicting Objectives of State Agencies. In *Proceedings of The Governor's Conference on the Preservation of Agricultural Lands*, pp. 58-64. Doc. No. 80/26; Springfield, Illinois: Illinois Institute of Natural Resources (November).

Calzonetti, F. J. 1979. *Impact of the Resource Conservation and Recovery Act on the Siting of Coal Conversion Energy Facilities in the United States*. ORNL/OEPA-12. Oak Ridge, Tennessee: Oak Ridge National Laboratory (February).

Carnes, S. 1979. *The Siting and Institutional Impacts of RCRA.* CONF-790499-1 Oak Ridge, Tennessee: Oak Ridge National Laboratory.

Computer Sciences Corporation 1980. *Fuel Alcohol Opportunities for Indiana.* Washington, D.C.: National Alcohol Fuels Commission (August).

Council on Environmental Quality 1980. *Environmental Quality 1980.* Eleventh Annual Report. Washington, D.C.: Council on Environmental Quality.

Fletcher, W. W. 1980. *Farmland and Energy: Conflicts in the Making.* NALS Interim Report No. 3. Washington, D.C.: National Agricultural Lands Study (March).

Jones, J. E. Jr. 1980. Synthetic Fuel Development in Kentucky. In *Conservation and Alternative Energy for Illinois and the Midwest, Proceedings of the 8th Annual Illinois Energy Conference,* pp. 195-214. Chicago: Energy Resources Center, University of Illinois at Chicago Circle.

Morris, S.C.; Maskowitz, P.D.; Sevian, W.A.; Silberstein, S.; and Hamilton, L.D. 1979. "Coal Conversion Technologies: Some Health and Environmental Effects." *Science* 206 (November 9): 654-662.

National Agricultural Lands Study (NALS) and Fred Hart Associates. 1981. *Balancing Energy Needs with Agricultural Land Availability.* NALS Technical Paper XVI; Washington, D.C.: NASL.

Ohio River Basin Commission. 1978. *The Ohio River Basin: The Regional Water and Land Resources Plan, Draft Environmental, Economic and Social Impact Statements.* Cincinnati, Ohio: Ohio River Basin Commission (July).

Ohio River Basin Energy Study. Final Report. 1981. Washington, D.C.: U.S. Environmental Protection Agency, Office of Research and Development.

Peart, R. M.; Doering, O. C. III; Tyner, W. E.; Lechtenberg, V. L.; and Barber, S. A. 1979. Problems and Potential of Alcohol from Agriculture. In *Petroleum and National Gas in Illinois, Proceedings of the Seventh Annual Illinois Energy Conference,* pp. 237-246. Chicago: Energy Resources Center, University of Illinois at Chicago Circle (October).

Randolph, J. C. and Jones, W. W. 1980. *Ohio River Basin Energy Study: Land Use and Terrestrial Ecology.* Washington, D.C.: U.S. Environmental Protection Agency, Office of Research and Development.

Rickert, D.A.; Ulman, W. J.; and Hampton, E. R., eds. 1979. *Synthetic Fuels Development: Earth-Science Considerations.* Washington, D.C.: U.S. Department of the Interior/Geological Survey, U.S. Government Printing Office.

Schanz, J. J. Jr.; Sawyer, J. W. Jr.; and Perry, H. 1979. *The Optimal Future Regional Distribution of National Synthetic Fuel Capacity.* Washington, D.C.: Resources for the Future (June).

Tyner, W. 1980. *The Potential of Using Biomass for Energy in the United States.* Publication Series No. 80-3; West Lafayette, Indiana: Institute for Interdisciplinary Engineering Studies, Purdue University (May).

————; and Bottum, J. Carrol 1979. *Agricultural Energy Production: Economic and Policy Issues.* Station Bulletin No. 240; West Lafayette, Indiana: Department of Agricultural Economics, Agricultural Experiment Station, Purdue University (September).

U.S. Congress 1979a. *Gasohol: A Technical Memorandum.* Washington, D.C.: U.S. Government Printing Office.

————. 1979b. Senate. Committee on the Budget, Subcommittee on Synthetic Fuels. *Synthetic Fuels.* Committee Print, 96th Congress, 1st sess., September 27, 1979. Washington, D.C.: U.S. Government Printing Office.

————. 1980. Office of Technology Assessment. *Energy From Biological Processes.* Washington, D.C.: Office of Technology Assessment.

U.S. Department of Energy 1980. Assistant Secretary for Environment, Office of Technology Impacts. *Synthetic Fuels and the Environment: An Environmental and Regulatory Impacts Analysis.* Washington, D.C.: U.S. Department of Energy.

U.S. Environmental Protection Agency 1978. "EPA Policy to Protect Environmentally Significant Agricultural Lands." Washington, D.C.: U.S. EPA (September 8).

Welch, L.F. 1979. An Inventory of the Energy Potential from Biomass in Illinois. In *Petroleum and Natural Gas in Illinois. Proceedings* of the Seventh Annual Illinois Energy Conference, pp. 224-36. Chicago: Energy Resources Center, University of Illinois at Chicago Circle (October).

Willard, D. E.; Ewert, M. A.; Hogan, M. E.; and Martin, J. D. 1980. *A Land Use Analysis of Existing and Potential Coal Surface Mining Areas in the Ohio River Basin Energy Study Region.* Washington, D.C.: U.S. Environmental Protection Agency, Office of Research and Development.

Hazardous Waste Management: Land Use Implications for Nonmetropolitan America

Roy C. Herndon

In recognition of growing public concern over hazardous wastes, ABC aired on prime-time TV an hour-long documentary called "The Killing Ground" (ABC News 1979), which was seen by millions of Americans. This documentary put into sharp focus the problems America faces in the handling and disposal of hazardous wastes. Incidents in New York, Louisiana, Kentucky, New Jersey, and other locations vividly portrayed the consequences of improper or careless hazardous waste disposal procedures.

Why should the recent wave of concern over hazardous waste disposal be of unique interest to nonmetropolitan America? The question may be put another way. After the rules and regulations governing hazardous waste disposal are passed and implemented, where are the most likely hazardous waste disposal sites? The likely sites will be nonmetropolitan, i.e., areas removed from cities or other population centers. Hazardous waste sites in such locations pose a minimal immediate threat to existing population centers. But hazardous waste remains a potential problem for both metropolitan and nonmetropolitan America regardless of its final location.

BASIC CONSIDERATIONS

The production of hazardous waste is not a new phenomenon. What is relatively new is man's awareness that the improper handling of such wastes can cause major environmental and human health problems. Ironically, the possibility of land pollution has increased as science and technology have facilitated more successful and efficient air- and water-pollution controls.

A hazardous waste is "any waste which requires special management provisions in waste handling (process, storage, collection, hauling and disposal) because of its acute and/or chronic effects on the public health and welfare, the individuals who handle it, or on the environment" (State of Washington 1973, p. 3). For this paper, a more technical definition is not needed. Rules and regulations governing the disposal of hazardous waste, however, require establishment of more specific criteria for concentrations, tolerances, cutoff levels and threshholds. Also, the possible cumulative effect of certain chemicals in the body must be considered.

QUANTITY AND QUALITY

Two aspects to the problem that must be considered in devising an appropriate management scheme are first, the quantity of the waste generated and second, its nature or quality. These are interrelated in the management problem. Extremely small quantities of some hazardous wastes are potentially dangerous, while substantial quantities of less toxic materials may often be handled safely through conventional disposal practices.

Our highly industrialized society generates billions of tons of solid waste each year. Most of it is managed by land disposal techniques (U.S. Environmental Protection Agency 1978, hereinafter cited as U.S. EPA). In the United States the five major sources of waste are mining, agriculture, industry, municipalities, and sewage. (Radioactive wastes are considered separately below.) Although the volume of mining wastes is far greater than that generated by other sources, this waste is largely made up of overburden, which does not usually pose so great a threat to the environment or to human health as does the waste from the manufacturing or industrial sector. Similarly, agricultural wastes are largely crop and feed lot wastes, which are potentially less hazardous than industrial wastes and can be handled more easily.

Of the billions of tons of solid waste produced each year, about 350 million wet tons are produced by the industrial sector of the economy (U.S. EPA 1978). Of this industrial waste, about 50 million tons of potentially hazardous wastes are produced by the manufacturing sector and as a result of pollution control technology (U.S. EPA 1978). These industrial wastes come from a variety of specific manufactured products. For example, the accompanying tabulation illustrates some of the more common products and their associated hazardous wastes:

Product	Hazardous Waste Generated
Plastics	Organic chlorine compounds
Pesticides	Organic chlorine compounds, organic phosphate compounds
Medicines	Organic solvents and residues, heavy metals (mercury and zinc, for example)
Paints	Heavy metals, pigments, solvents, organic residues
Oil, gasoline, and other petroleum products	Oil, phenols, and other organic compounds, heavy metals, ammonia salts, acids, caustics
Metals	Heavy metals, fluorides, cyanides, acid and alkaline cleaners, solvents, pigments, abrasives, plating salts, oils, phenols
Leather	Heavy metals, organic solvents
Textiles	Heavy metals, dyes, organic chlorine compounds, solvents

These potentially hazardous industrial wastes are of primary concern here. In the past, this waste has generally been deposited in or on the land, at times with severe negative human impacts. Recent examples point clearly to the need for proper land-disposal techniques if potentially hazardous wastes are to be managed safely over both the short and long term (U.S. EPA 1980; U.S. Congress 1979).

The Resource Conservation and Recovery Act of 1976 (P.L. 94-580) requires every state to have a program to manage its hazardous waste properly. Eventually, it may be economically and technically feasible to eliminate or reduce greatly the quantity of hazardous waste generated. By treating the waste at the point of generation, it may be possible to render it sufficiently harmless so that conventional disposal may be used. It is unlikely, however, that there will be a reasonable alternative to land disposal for much of the hazardous waste generated in the next few years. As each state tries to comply with the rules and regulations resulting from P.L. 94-580, disposal sites will have to be found. These disposal sites will not likely be in or even close to metropolitan areas. Rather, these sites will be in rural areas where both population density and the cost of land are low. Also, economies of scale make it plausible for large tracts of land to be set aside in one location enabling a particular site to be used for a number of years before closing.

Transportation of wastes is also a concern. Accidents and spillage from shipments of hazardous waste will not be confined to nonmetropolitan America; all communities must be prepared to cope with such occurrences. As regulations are implemented, more of this waste will be transported away from the generator to disposal sites at considerable distances.

Monitoring of disposal sites over the long run is another significant concern to land-use managers in nonmetropolitan areas. Some hazardous wastes persist for indefinite periods of time (such as certain pesticides and some special-purpose industrial chemicals). Even after the site is no longer active, the area must be monitored and its future use restricted.

A recent EPA report states that 30,000 or more sites in the United States may contain hazardous wastes of one sort or another (Fred C. Hart Associates, Inc. 1979). Not until the 1980s, however, will a nationwide survey of all open dumps provide a better estimate of the geographic dimensions of this problem.

Alternatives to surface land disposal which might prove adequate and safe are subsurface land disposal (well injection), disposal in water, recycling, incineration and pyrolysis, above or below ground short-term storage, above ground long-term storage, waste elimination and/or decontamination at the source, and waste decontamination after collection but prior to disposal. Each alternative has both advantages and disadvantages. The most appropriate option can be selected only after a specific set of conditions has been analyzed. These conditions include factors such as the type and quantity of waste to be managed, as well as economic considerations.

Issues other than health and safety must be considered in the selection of hazardous waste sites. Individuals or groups from metropolitan as well as nonmetropolitan areas may object to the aesthetic impairment of land adjacent or close to such a site. In addition, individuals may object to the real economic loss attendant upon lower land values for property near these sites.

The land-use planner must recognize the need for guidance from those outside the field of planning if he is to select and evaluate hazardous waste management alternatives properly. Expert help may be needed to assess the biological, ecological, hydrological, and socioeconomic aspects of hazardous waste management schemes.

Because land disposal will probably be the keystone of hazardous waste programs in the near future, the determination of land needs for surface disposal over the next 20 years becomes important. If we use the estimated figure of 50 million tons of hazardous waste produced each year in the United States, and if we assume an average specific gravity of the wet waste of about 3 and an average load depth of 1 meter, then approximately 10 square kilometers per year will be needed. Assuming that secondary pollution effects (due to flooding and leaching) might increase the land made unavailable for other uses by a factor of 100, this would mean that 1000 square kilometers per year would be needed for the surface land disposal of hazardous waste. If we assume further that the lifetime of the hazardous waste is 20 years, then over the next 20 years about 20,000 square kilometers would be used for hazardous waste sites, which would then be unavailable for other uses. This amounts to 0.2 percent of the total land area of the United States.

A few caveats are needed at this point. First, there are many hazardous wastes whose lifetimes far exceed 20 years, so that the land made unavailable for other uses may extend well beyond the 20-year period assumed. On the other hand, by choosing and preparing a site properly, the secondary effects might be ameliorated to a point that less surface land would be required than we originally estimated. Further, over the next 20 years the amount of hazardous waste to be disposed of on land might either increase or decrease significantly, thus changing the total land needed for hazardous waste disposal. Nevertheless, we are talking about less (possibly much less) than 1 percent of the total land area of the United States.

RADIOACTIVE WASTES

There is one class of potentially hazardous waste that deserves special consideration. This is the radioactive waste that emanates from the nuclear industry, both military and civilian. Radioactive wastes are generated at various points in the nuclear fuel cycle from the mining and milling of uranium ore through reprocessing (if performed) and final disposal of the waste. Reprocessing involves sending spent reactor fuel to a plant where the usable fissionable material is extracted from it and reenters the fuel cycle as a feedstock in the fabrication of more nuclear fuel.

In 1978 the president established an Interagency Review Group on Nuclear

Waste Management (IRG) to examine the long-term management and disposal of all types of nuclear waste. Its report (IRG 1979, p. 15) defined the following major classes of nuclear wastes:

- High-Level Wastes (HLW)—These wastes include either intact fuel assemblies that are discarded after use or the portion of wastes generated in the reprocessing of spent fuel. These wastes are being considered for disposal in geologic repositories or by other options designed to provide long-term isolation of the wastes from the biosphere.

- Transuranic (TRU) Wastes—These wastes result mainly from spent fuel reprocessing, the fabrication of plutonium to make nuclear weapons, and possibly plutonium fuel fabrication for recycle to reactors. TRU waste is defined as material containing more than ten nanocuries of transuranic activity per gram of material. These wastes would be disposed of in a similar manner to that used for HLW.

- Low-Level Wastes (LLW)—These wastes contain less than ten nanocuries of transuranic contaminants per gram of material, require little or no shielding, and have low but potentially hazardous quantities of radionuclides. LLW are generated in almost all activities involving radioactive materials and are presently being disposed of by shallow land burial.

- Uranium mine and mill tailings are the residues from uranium mining and milling operations and contain low concentrations of naturally occurring radioactive materials. The tailings are generated in very large volumes and are stored on-site.

- Gaseous effluents are released into the biosphere and become diluted and dispersed (they were not considered in this report).

The primary objective of the nuclear waste management program is to ensure that "Existing and future nuclear waste from military and civilian activities should be isolated from the biosphere and pose no significant threat to public health and safety" (IRG 1979, p. 15). To accomplish this end, the technology chosen must meet all the relevant radiological protection criteria as well as any other regulatory requirements.

The IRG examined six technologies as candidates for use in final disposal of high-level and transuranic wastes:

- Placement in mined repositories
- Placement in deep ocean sediments
- Placement in very deep drill holes
- Placement in a mined cavity with rock melting
- Partitioning of reprocessing wastes, transmutation of heavy radionuclides, and geologic disposal of fission products
- Ejection into space

Of these six options, the IRG thought land disposal in the form of mined repositories (i.e., geologic formations) would be available soonest. The IRG believed interim surface storage of spent fuel at reactors or at away-from-reactors storage facilities would be an important component of its overall waste management program until repositories are available. According to the IRG, however, surface storage should not be viewed as an alternative to ultimate disposal.

Because of the need to isolate high-level and transuranic wastes from the biosphere for relatively long periods of time, and because disposal in mined repositories is the nearest term option, the IRG identified the following important technical findings believed to be representative of informed opinion:

- A systems approach should be used to select the geologic environment, respository site and waste form.
- Overall scientific and technological knowledge is adequate to proceed with region selection and site characterization.
- Detailed studies of specific, potential respository sites in different geologic environments should begin at once.
- The actinide activity in transuranic and high-level wastes suggests that both waste types present problems of comparable magnitude for the long term.
- The degree of long-term isolation provided by a repository and the effects of changes in repository design, geology, climate, and human activities on the public health and safety can only be assessed through analytical modeling.
- The effects of future human activity must be evaluated more carefully.

The IRG position was that the federal government should maintain a technically conservative approach in pursuing the development of mined repositories for high-level and transuranic wastes disposal (IRG 1979).

The IRG further recommended that by 1981 the Department of Energy and the Nuclear Regulatory Commission should review existing and alternative low-level waste disposal techniques and determine whether any should be adopted in the near future.

The nature and scope of nuclear waste management problems demand a planning and decision-making process that is open to wide participation by state and local governments, including federally recognized Indian groups. To insure this participation, the IRG recommended that the federal agencies responsible for the design, development, and implementation of the nuclear waste management program involve all interested and affected parties directly and extensively.

The IRG also reviewed the cost and financing of nuclear waste management. It estimated that total government costs through the end of the century for research and development, interim storage, and ultimate disposal (including commercial and defense wastes) would be between $15 billion and $25 billion (IRG 1979).

As a result of this IRG report, a detailed assessment of nuclear waste disposal options was made in an environmental impact study on the management of commercially generated radioactive waste (U.S. Department of Energy 1979).

Defense and military wastes were excluded from this study, although they were considered in the IRG report to the president. In response to criticism that earlier studies were biased toward conventional geological disposal methods, care was taken to evaluate all disposal options.

This generic environmental impact statement characterizes the wastes to be managed from an assumed generation scenario of 10,000 GWe-year (billion watts electric year) of power over a 65-year period ending in the year 2040 with the last reactor to be built in the year 2000. Should other quantities of nuclear power be used, the impacts would be proportional.

This study indicates that the "state of technology" stands out as the major factor in the decision-making process. As a result, the geologic land-disposal option again appears more favorable than the other options considered. The cost of waste disposal is about 0.6 mills per kilowatt hour compared to the energy production cost of 25-35 mills per kilowatt hour and is not decisive in the choice of disposal alternatives (U.S. Department of Energy 1979).

Because most of high-level commercial nuclear waste will emanate from power reactors, it is useful to have an estimate of the order of magnitude of high-level waste from that sector. A typical light-water reactor (the kind used commercially in the United States at this time) produces about 30 megawatts (MW) of thermal power per metric ton of fuel, or about 10 MW of electrical power per metric ton of fuel for a 33 percent efficient system. A reasonably sized reactor would contain about 100 metric tons of nuclear fuel, which would mean about 1000 MW of electrical energy could be generated. Each year a third of this fuel needs to be replaced, which means that 30 metric tons per year of spent fuel becomes available as high-level waste from each 1000 megawatts-electric (MWe) nuclear power plant. Currently, the United States has about 70 commercial nuclear reactors generating about 50,000 MW of electrical power and about 1650 metric tons of spent fuel each year.

Because of its concern over nuclear proliferation and possible diversion of fissile material, the Carter Administration did not favor reprocessing fissile material from commercially generated spent fuel. This means that spent fuel assemblies constitute high-level wastes from the commercial reactor sector of the nuclear industry.

If there is no commercial reprocessing, there will soon be a serious shortage of places to store the spent reactor assemblies prior to providing a final resting place for the waste. For each metric ton of spent fuel from a typical 1000 MWe light-water reactor, there are about 8 kilograms of plutonium produced. This amounts to 240 kilograms of plutonium per year per 1000 MWe reactor. If, for example, there were 1000 such reactors operating in the United States, there would be between 200 and 300 metric tons of plutonium generated. Because it takes considerably less than 100 kilograms of plutonium to fashion a reasonably effective nuclear device, the concern about the management of such quantities of plutonium seems justified. (I might mention that the amount needed to fashion a single explosive device represents less than 0.01 percent of the plutonium generated in the above scenario. Thus an extremely accurate accounting procedure would be needed in order to know if a few kilograms of plutonium had been diverted illegally.) It should be kept in mind that the spent fuel is actually a potential resource; however, for political and social reasons it is considered a waste product requiring special, long-term management techniques.

A few examples concerning what can (and did) happen if proper management procedures are not followed are presented below. In West Valley, New York a commercial reprocessing plant (now shut down) stored about 600,000 gallons of high-level liquid waste in a carbon steel tank (Lester and Rose 1977). Because the company is no longer in business, the question becomes what to do with the waste when the tank corrodes, and who will pay for corrective action. The point is that in the management of certain types of waste, the private sector may not have built-in mechanisms to deal effectively and equitably with issues such as perpetual monitoring, corporation "death," and public health and safety. Of course, merely shifting the burden to the public or governmental sector does not insure success. At a government plant in Hanford, Washington (first built to produce plutonium for nuclear weapons), most of the high-level waste is stored in underground tanks. A total of 152 of these tanks were constructed for the storage of 150 million liters of high-level liquid waste (each tank holds about 1 million liters, or 300,000 gallons). Since 1956, about 2 million liters of these wastes have leaked from various pipes and from 18 of these carbon steel tanks onto the land (U.S. Energy Research and Development Administration — ERDA — 1975). A large leak in 1973 went undiscovered for almost 2 months. Approximately 115,000 gallons of high-level liquid waste leaked into the ground (U.S. ERDA 1975). The irony of this accident was that the readings of the tank levels were systematically and properly recorded, but no one compared previous readings with current ones (U.S. ERDA 1975). This is a clear example of careless management techniques.

Although this discussion has been primarily about high-level nuclear waste, the intermediate and low-level wastes are also of concern. For example, at the Hanford facility, nonhigh-level liquid waste was disposed of in earthern cribs. Liquid waste was discharged directly into a subsurface crib until radioactivity as monitored beneath the crib reached a specific level. When this happened, the crib was abandoned and a new one was constructed. As a result of poor management, the following took place: "Due to the quantity of plutonium contained in the soil (about 100 kilograms in 1800 cubic feet of soil) of the Z9 crib, it is possible to conceive of conditions (flooding or heavy rains concentrating the plutonium) which could result in a nuclear chain reaction (excursion). Removal of the contaminated soil will eliminate any possibility of such an event . . .." (U.S. Atomic Energy Commission 1975). Proper management would have anticipated such a potential hazard, and an unnecessary risk could have been avoided.

Low-level wastes are generated in almost all activities involving radioactive materials (such as medical laboratories, universities, and hospitals) and are presently disposed of by shallow-land burial. Uranium mining and milling operations produce tailings that contain low concentrations of naturally occurring radioactive materials. The tailings are generated in very large volumes and are stored on-site. In Grand Junction, Colorado these tailings were used as construction fill dirt for over 15 years. Public buildings including schools, shopping centers, and homes were built on these low-level radioactive wastes. In Florida the phosphate mining industry produces vast quantities of slightly radioactive mining waste, and residential subdivisions have been built using this reclaimed land. Not all experts agree as to the potential danger presented by such low-level wastes, but it is better to err on the side of caution when dealing with such wastes. The proper management of these wastes presents a challenge to the land use manager because the only practical management at this time is land disposal.

An interesting aspect of nuclear waste disposal, and of high-level wastes in particular, is that the total land area needed to dispose of the waste is relatively small: "the mass and volume of the waste generated by nuclear power activities are very small—all such waste that will be produced by the operation of all nuclear electric power plants between now and the end of the century will have a volume of less than 500,000 cubic feet—the volume of a one-story warehouse 200 feet on a side" (Pittman 1975). This statement applies only to high-level wastes. Low-level reactor wastes, although 10 to 20 times the volume of the high-level wastes, are much easier to handle because heat and penetrating radiations are considerably lower. In addition, volume reduction techniques could reduce these lower-level reactor wastes to about the same volume as that of the high-level wastes.

It should be understood that only commercial reactor waste was considered in this example and the volume was calculated on the basis of reprocessed fuel with residual waste solidification. It is important to keep in mind that the policy of the United States, out of concern for nuclear proliferation and possible diversion of fissile material, is to prohibit commercial reprocessing of reactor fuel. This means that in the United States, at the present time, the spent reactor fuel is itself the high-level waste and will require more space for disposal than if it were reprocessed. Even a volume increase of 10 or 100 does not represent an inordinate land area, however. (There are, of course, radioactive wastes from defense installations, which increase the total volume of wastes; but these wastes can still be reprocessed.)

It should be emphasized that although the total land area needed for disposal of all radioactive wastes may be relatively small, the potential for large-scale environmental contamination may be quite large. The time required for containment of these high-level wastes until they decay to safe levels ranges from a few hundred to many thousands of years. Leakage of these wastes into the biosphere could render vast land areas (and water supplies) unsafe for many years.

By way of conclusion, it is fair to say that the "marriage" of hazardous waste to land-disposal techniques has not been without problems. The offspring from such a marriage have often been unwanted and uncared for by their parents. These undesirable effects will certainly be seen and felt in the rural and nonmetropolitan areas where the hazardous waste sites are located. However, the impacts can easily reach into the metropolitan areas by way of environmental damage such as ground and surface water contamination.

The following recommendations summarize the best procedures to be followed in the management of these hazardous wastes:

- Minimize the amounts generated by modifying the industrial process involved.
- Transfer the waste to another industry that can use it.
- Reprocess the waste to recover energy or materials.
- Separate hazardous from nonhazardous waste at the source and concentrate it, with reduced handling, transportation, and disposal costs.
- Incinerate the waste, or subject it to treatment that makes it nonhazardous.
- Dispose of the waste in a secure landfill (one that is located, designed, operated, and monitored—even after it is closed—in a manner that protects life and the environment).

During the next decade the challenge of handling hazardous wastes properly must be met and resolved. Land-use planners and managers in nonmetropolitan areas face an enormous challenge and responsibility in this regard. Geographers can help solve this problem by using their analytical skills to understand better the areal distributions of hazardous wastes and their spatial relationships. Certainly, nonmetropolitan America could benefit greatly from help in hazardous waste management.

References

ABC News Closeup. 1979. The Killing Ground, Thursday, March 29 (10-11 PM, EST).

Fred C. Hart Associates, Inc. 1979. *Preliminary Assessment of Clean-up Costs for National Hazardous Waste Problem.* Report prepared for the U.S. EPA.

Interagency Review Group on Nuclear Waste Management. 1979. *Report to the President.* Washington, D.C.: U.S. Government Printing Office.

Lester, R. K., and Rose, D. J. 1977. Nuclear Wastes at West Valley, New York. *Technology Review* 79, no. 6 (May): 20-29.

Pittman, F. K. 1975. Management of Radioactive Wastes. *Water, Air and Soil Pollution* 4: 215-219.

State of Washington, Department of Ecology. 1973. *A Report on Industrial and Hazardous Wastes.* Olympia, Washington.

U.S. Atomic Energy Commission. 1972. *Wash-1520, Contaminated Soil Removal Facility.* Richland, Washington.

U.S. Congress. 1979. *Hearing before the Subcommittee on Oversight and Investigations of the Committee on Interstate and Foreign Commerce,* Washington, D.C.: U.S. Government Printing Office.

U.S. Department of Energy. 1979. *Management of Commercially-Generated Radioactive Waste.*

U.S. Environmental Protection Agency 1979. *Solid Waste Facts.* SW-694.

————. 1980. *Everybody's Problem Problem: Hazardous Waste.* SW-826.

U.S. ERDA 1975. *Waste Management Operations, Hanford, Washington.* Final Environmental Impact Statement (2 volumes).

Nuclear Power Station Hazards and Responses in Nonmetropolitan America

James Kenneth Mitchell

The protection of humans from excessive nuclear radiation has recently become a major public issue in the United States. The accident at Three Mile Island on March 28, 1979 called into question safety considerations in the design, construction, and operation of commercial reactors and the adequacy of plans for coping with nuclear emergencies (U.S. Nuclear Regulatory Commission 1979a, pp. 35-60). (Hereinafter this agency will be cited as NRC.) Formulation of a National Plan for Nuclear Waste Management was announced in early 1980. (White House 1980.) There is a continuing debate about the long-term effects of exposure to low-level radiation in the workplace and elsewhere. (U.S. Council on Environmental Quality 1979, pp. 206-210.) Soil contamination as a result of nuclear testing at Enewetak (Eniwetok) Atoll still makes headlines 20 years after the last explosion (U.S. General Accounting Office 1979a). Operations were recently suspended at several New England reactors because of fears about the reliability of computer programs for evaluating seismic risks (NRC 1979b). In 1979, the governors of Nevada, Washington, and South Carolina temporarily closed or restricted dumping at the nation's three low-level waste disposal sites because of concern about packaging and shipping defects (U.S. General Accounting Office 1980a).

Clearly, there are potential health and safety hazards associated with most aspects of nuclear energy—quite apart from its military uses (Kates 1978, pp. 95-97). Whether these hazards are greater than others to which populations are exposed is difficult to assess. Some writers on nuclear radiation contend that nuclear accidents are viewed more gravely than other disasters because their effects are poorly understood (NRC Environmental Protection Agency 1978, App. pp. 1-2). As measured by numbers of emergencies declared by state governors, radiation accidents comprise 7 percent of all extreme events (National Governors Association 1978, p. 10). Most of the nation is exposed to hazards from one or another phase of the nuclear cycle. Wyoming and Utah contain most of the uranium mines and mills. Many commercial reactors are located in the eastern half of the nation, and along the Pacific coast (Fig. 1). Nuclear fuel processing and fabrication plants are found mainly in Washington, California, Tennessee, Virginia, Pennsylvania, and New England (NRC 1980f. pp. 1-19 to 1-20). Waste burial facilities are sited in Washington and Illinois.

Among these various sources of nuclear hazard, this chapter will address particularly issues affecting commercial nuclear reactor stations themselves and their impact upon surrounding nonmetropolitan areas. Of 187 reactors in existence or planned, 128 are outside SMSAs. All have the potential for releasing large quantities of radionucleii into the ambient environment and have thus engendered high levels of public concern (Hohenemser, Kasperson, and Kates 1977). Finally, there is a strong possibility that existing and proposed safety regulations may significantly influence land uses and life-styles in areas surrounding such facilities, particularly in still sparsely developed nonmetropolitan areas.

Analysis of the need for nuclear energy logically precedes discussion of power station hazards. The extent to which commercial nuclear power should continue to be produced, however, is both a divisive public issue and a complex subject, one that requires more detailed exploration than is possible here. This paper is not concerned with the economic, ecological, technological, or political viability of nuclear power, or about the numbers of reactors that might be necessary to serve the U.S. market. Rather, it addresses questions affecting the siting and regulation of power stations and the management of radiological safety programs in their hinterlands.

THE STATUS OF NUCLEAR POWER IN NONMETROPOLITAN AMERICA

As of November 1, 1980, there were 70 licensed, operating reactors at 48 sites in the United States (*Nuclear Safety* 1981, pp. 105-109). Three others have operating licenses but are shut down indefinitely (Three Mile Island 2, Indian Point 1, Humboldt Bay). Construction or operating license applications for 114 other reactors are under review. Most operable reactors are located in New England and the Middle Atlantic states (25), the upper Midwest (19), and the Southeast (17) (Fig. 1).

Forty-four operating reactors are sited outside SMSAs (Table 1). They are scattered across 21 states but are most conspicuous in Wisconsin (4 reactors, 3 sites), Michigan (4 reactors, 3 sites), Virginia (4 reactors, 2 sites), and South Carolina (4 reactors, 2 sites). By contrast, most of the 29 reactors in SMSAs are located in only 3 states: New York (6 reactors, 4 sites); Pennsylvania (5 reactors, 3 sites); and Illinois (4 reactors, 2 sites). Despite early proposals to build them inside municipal boundaries of New York, none are located in major cities. On the other hand, there are few commercial reactors in remote areas far removed from substantial populations. Siting characteristics vary, but power stations are

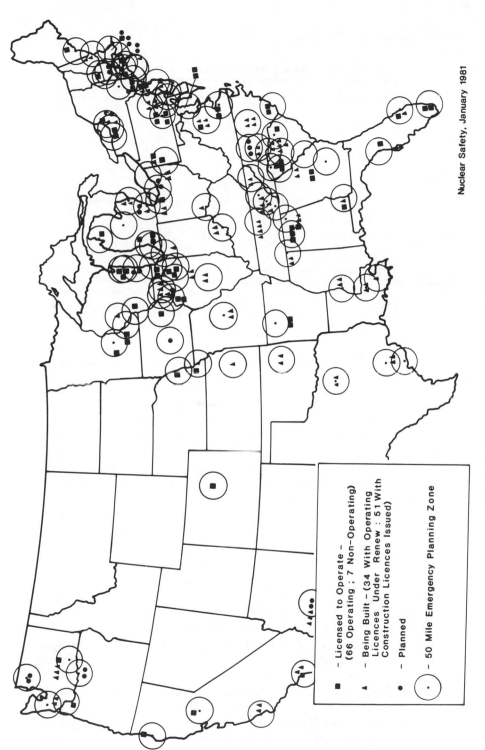

Figure 1. Nuclear power reactors in the United States.

Legend:

■ – Licensed to Operate – (66 Operating ; 7 Non-Operating)

▲ – Being Built – (34 With Operating Licences Under Renew : 51 With Construction Licences Issued)

● – Planned

⊙ – 50 Mile Emergency Planning Zone

Table 1. Urban and Nonurban Nuclear Reactors

Operating Reactors*	N (Sites)	N (Reactors)
Located in SMSAs†	17	29
Located outside SMSAs	32	44
	49	73
License Applications under review		
Located in SMSAs	17	30
Located outside SMSAs	39	84
	56	114

*Includes Indian Pt. 1, TMI 2, Humboldt Bay.
†SMSAs as defined in 1979.

Table 2. Trends in Nuclear Reactors (1960-80)

Period	Number of Reactors Licensed	Number of Reactors Located Outside SMSAs	Percentage Reactors Located Outside SMSAs
1960-66	5	4	80
1967-73	32	20	62.5
1974-80	36	20	56

typically found on—or just beyond—the fringes of metropolitan areas. Given the continuing growth and dispersion of metropolitan populations, it is likely that a majority of existing nuclear reactors may soon be found within metropolitan boundaries. Nonetheless, if all planned reactors are constructed, some nonmetropolitan regions will experience marked increases in exposure to potential hazard. Thirty-six new reactors are scheduled for rural areas of Tennessee (10), Illinois (8), Washington (7), South Carolina (6), and Texas (5). By 1994, of the 48 contiguous states, only West Virginia, Kentucky, Montana, North Dakota, South Dakota, Wyoming, Nevada, Utah, and New Mexico will lack commercial nuclear reactors.

Although most are located outside major metropolitan areas, nuclear power stations raise issues for both urban and rural residents. Most supply power to urban and rural populations. Many threaten to be caught up in spreading exurban development, or to face increasing competition for the use of recreation and amenity resources that can often be found in association with power plant sites. Accidents involving the dumping of radioactive waste water into rivers and lakes, or the release of radioactive gases, have the potential to affect the health and welfare of large numbers of people. Moreover, industries in rural and metropolitan fringe areas frequently generate, attract, or otherwise encourage, nearby population growth and economic development. This is especially true of large-scale energy development facilities. New mining enterprises or oil and gas processing plants have sometimes given rise to boomtowns characterized by narrowly based economies and drastic social change. If nuclear power stations are involved, the implications are doubly serious. Small communities face physical, social, and economic disruption, and incoming new residents, attracted by employment opportunities, defeat the intent to locate reactors in areas of low population.

Reactors And Small-Community Development

Although there is little doubt that nuclear research and development stimulated the growth of Oak Ridge, Tennessee and a few other towns, it is much less certain that commercial nuclear power plants per se cause substantial socioeconomic and demographic changes. Utility companies argue that nuclear power plants bring jobs and tax revenue into host communities. Certainly, nuclear power stations have benefitted some small rural communities in this way. In 1974, for example, 87 percent of the tax revenues of Lower Alloways Creek Township, New Jersey were contributed by two reactors (New Jersey, Department of Community Affairs 1974). At least before the Three Mile Island accident, nuclear power stations were perceived by most local governments as stable, clean, safe, job-producing, revenue-generating entities. As such they were welcome additions to small communities.

Many areas near nuclear power stations are growing rapidly. For example, the site of Indiana's Bailley power station is flanked by the Burns Harbor Bethlehem Steel Works, which employs 3,500 people, and the heavily used beaches of the Indiana Dunes National Lakeshore (U.S. Congress 1979b, p. 21). This southern fringe of Lake Michigan is rapidly being converted into an industrial and residential exurban appendage of metropolitan Chicago. Likewise, major population increases have occurred in the hinterland of the Oyster Creek (New Jersey) power station. In 1965, when a construction permit was granted by the Atomic Energy Commission, there were 3,162 houses located within 4 miles of this site. By 1976, the same area contained 9,507 houses (Morell and Kinder 1977). Large residential, commercial, and recreational developments are planned for the Pismo Beach and Avila areas within 8 miles of California's Diablo Canyon reactor site (NRC 1980c, pp. 3-82). Similar trends have been observed at other sites.

NRC recognizes that certain plant locations have major growth potential. Twenty-one have been identified as "high growth population density sites" (NRC 1979e, pp. 1-5 and 1-6) (Table 3). Between 1970 and 2000 it is expected that their combined population within 10 miles will rise from 2,599,000 to 4,196,000—a 61.5 percent increase. Most of these places already exceed population density guidelines for reactor siting. By the year 2000 they will probably contain an average of 636 persons per square mile, with areas near Indian Point and Zion surpassing 1,400 per square mile. In short, there is no hard evidence that nuclear power stations generate population growth or attract industry; but it is abundantly clear that they are often sited sufficiently near growing areas that they may eventually be surrounded by housing or other intensive land uses unless ameliorative action is taken. Without such action, the potential for disaster may grow to unmanageable proportions.

Table 3. High Population Density Sites

Power Station Site	Operating Status	State	Population within 10 miles	
			1970	2000
Indian Point	Operating	New York	329,000	444,000
Zion	Operating	Illinois	282,000	441,000
Limerick	1982	Pennsylvania	281,000	420,000
Enrico Fermi	1981	Michigan	185,000	326,000
Beaver Valley	Operating	Pennsylvania	154,000	184,000
Three Mile Island*	Operating	Pennsylvania	121,000	183,000
Millstone	Operating	Connecticut	119,000	170,000
Bailley	1983	Indiana	103,000	166,000
Turkey Point	Operating	Florida	99,000	269,000
Seabrook	1983	New Hampshire	99,000	185,000
Shoreham	1984	New York	95,000	182,000
Oyster Creek	Operating	New Jersey	83,000	164,000
Perry	1982	Ohio	94,000	146,000
Midland	1980	Michigan	90,000	141,000
Duane Arnold	Operating	Iowa	79,000	120,000
Haddam Neck	Operating	Connecticut	57,000	117,000
St. Lucie	Operating	Florida	47,000	114,000
Salem	Operating	New Jersey	78,000	111,000
Trojan	Operating	Oregon	71,000	108,000
San Onofre	Operating	California	67,000	105,000
Catawba	1981	South Carolina	66,000	100,000

Source: NRC 1979d, pp. 1-6.
*Unit 2 not operating because of the accident.

Assessing Disaster Potential

Planning for technological and natural hazards is beset by uncertainties about probability of occurrence and scale of impacts and consequences. Ideally, comprehensive hazard management attempts to protect against events of a specified magnitude or level of risk with backup provisions for events exceeding that magnitude. Comprehensive floodplain management, for instance, might include levees capable of containing a "100-year flood," with warning and evacuation systems, and flood insurance to deal with larger floods. Nuclear accident planning so far has not employed this kind of integrated response system (Lewis 1980, pp. 53-65).

NRC recognizes nine classes of possible reactor accidents, ranging from trivial releases of radioactivity that can be treated in a routine fashion (Class 1), to combinations of component failures that result in "meltdown" of a reactor core and/or breaching of its containment (Class 9) (NRC 1980c, p. 96). On the basis of a 1975 reactor safety study—the Rasmussen Report (U.S. Atomic Energy Commission 1974)—it was widely believed that the *probability* of a catastrophic

(Class 9) accident was vanishingly small. Hence the NRC failed to include planning for the consequences of such accidents in the reactor regulation process. Events at Three Mile Island do not quite satisfy the criteria for inclusion in Class 9, but they clearly underscore the possibility of very serious power station accidents. Whether the Three Mile Island experience will cause accident probability estimates to be revised upwards is not yet known (*Federal Register* 1980a, pp. 40101-40104). There is no doubt, however, that the accident has focused attention on the need to plan for the potential *consequences* of nuclear accidents — however remote their chances of occurrence (NRC 1980c, p. 96).

The health effects of a core meltdown have been variously estimated. According to a joint NRC/EPA Task Force report (1978, pp. 1-45), a core meltdown followed by large-scale release of airborne radioactive particles could spread potentially damaging effects very widely. If a damaging radiation threshold value of 5 rem for whole body exposure is assumed, people living up to 115 miles from a stricken reactor could be affected. Thyroid-threatening doses could be carried much farther. Whole body exposure of 200 rem or greater, which may produce significant "early health effects" (including death and serious injury) shortly after an accident, would occur within 10 miles of a reactor. Other studies project higher death tolls. The "Rasmussen Report" anticipates 3,300 prompt fatalities and 45,000 latent fatalities as possible consequences of an "extremely serious accident" (U.S. Atomic Energy Commission 1974). The Council on Environmental Quality (1980) has concluded that between 200 and 23,000 additional cancer deaths could occur in an area *beyond* 50 miles from a given power plant.

A variety of other problems would also arise. Land, water, vegetation, and animals could be extensively contaminated. Society would be forced to shoulder heavy costs for emergency care, evacuation, decontamination, and compensation of victims. Inhabitants and businesses might permanently leave the region of the disaster. The affected population would bear a burden of fears of living foreshortened, sickly lives, and the spectre of genetic defects in future generations.

These are "worst case" possibilities. Past accidents have not produced such stark consequences. Annual whole-body dose rates in the United States, from all sources, are approximately 210 mR (National Academy of Sciences 1972). Maximum radiation levels measured around Three Mile Island on March 28, 1979 did not exceed 365 mR per hour. (NRC 1979c, p. 386). There, the total release of radioactive iodine (I^{131}) was approximately 12 curies—some 0.2 percent of the amount released in the Windscale (U.K.) accident of 1957 (U.S. Congress 1979b, p. 8). No fatalities or injuries were reported among the surrounding population at Windscale.

RESPONSES TO REACTOR HAZARDS

Possible avenues of response to the hazards posed by nuclear reactors include:

- improved reactor safety technology;
- limitations on the siting of reactors;
- land use and population controls in areas at risk; and
- emergency response plans

These will be considered in some detail.

Reactor Technology

Most engineering systems are improved by repeated testing to the point of failure, and by incorporating revisions based on operating experience. With nuclear reactors, these practices do not apply. The systems must be designed to operate to the highest possible degree of reliability, without the opportunity to learn from actual failures (Lewis 1980, pp. 56-57). These include automatic shutdown and cooling systems and heavily reinforced containment facilities.

The Three Mile Island accident tested these systems to their limits. Reactor shutdown occurred as intended, and neither the reactor vessel nor the containment building was breached. But, through a combination of valve failures, faulty instrumentation, and human error, fuel assemblies were left uncooled for several hours. Zirconium cladding began to oxidize, leading to the formation of hydrogen gas. An explosion was feared which might damage the containment building and release large amounts of radioactivity into surrounding areas.

Proponents of nuclear power argue that for 25 years, the United States has experienced no deaths as a result of commercial reactor accidents. This has been attributed to the success of technological "defense-in-depth." But Three Mile Island has demonstrated that potentially serious accidents can occur. The fact that this type of accident was not anticipated in previous safety studies, underscores the likelihood that other modes of failure remain to be discovered. Planning for the safety of lives and property in the vicinity of nuclear power stations is thus an important public policy issue.

Reactor Siting

Reactor siting policies and procedures have varied significantly over the past 35 years (Weinberg 1979, pp. 179-208). Thus reactors occupy a wide range of locations with differing hazard potential for adjacent populations. Although the first U.S. nuclear fission experiments were conducted in the City of Chicago, most reactors built by the Atomic Energy Commission between 1946 and 1954 were located relatively far from heavily populated areas, e.g., Hanford, Washington; Idaho Falls, Idaho; Los Alamos, New Mexico; Oak Ridge, Tennessee; Savannah River, South Carolina.

Private development of nuclear power reactors was encouraged by the Atomic Energy Act of 1954. Achievement of maximum reliable power supply at least financial cost became a guiding principle, and new siting criteria emerged. These tended to emphasize locations close to load centers and ample supplies of cooling water. As a result, nuclear power stations were increasingly located in river valleys or on shorelines, close to or within metropolitan areas.

The hazard potential of reactor sites is a function of present and future population distributions. Other factors being equal, reactors in sparsely settled areas pose less hazard than those close to large concentrations of population. Among 68 operating reactors surveyed, 29 are located in counties with average population densities less than 50 per square mile (Table 4). Fewer people are at risk in such areas, but those who do live there have no less cause for concern.

Table 4. Population Densities in Counties Near Nuclear Power Stations

Population per Square Mile*	Number of Operable Nuclear Reactors	Percentage
Less than 10	4	5.9
10-49.9	25	36.8
50-249.9	21	30.9
250 or more	18	26.4
	68	100.0

Source: U.S. Census of Population, 1970.

*U.S. population density (1970)—57.5 per square mile; about 75 per square mile in 48 states.

Alternative Siting Policies and Practices

It has long been NRC practice to evaluate power station sites with reference to their environmental constraints, the design and operations characteristics of proposed reactors, population density, and land use. Consideration is given to alternative sites if certain population-density criteria are exceeded (Table 5). Since these criteria were published in 1974, no applications for construction permits that exceeded the criteria have been received (U.S. Congress 1979b, pp. 140-143). Even if a site was discovered to have unfavorable characteristics, it could still be judged acceptable if enough engineering safety features were designed into the reactor system to compensate for site deficiencies. In 1979, a NRC task force recommended changes in current policy. These were designed to separate siting from reactor design considerations in the licensing process, and to take into account accidents that could exceed safety provisions incorporated into reactor design (NRC 1979d; *Nuclear Safety* 1980b). A year later, NRC adopted these proposed changes (*Federal Register* 1980b, pp. 50350-50355).

Table 5. Maximum Allowable Population Near Nuclear Reactors

Distance from Plant (miles)	Maximum Allowable Population
5	30,000
20	500,000
40	2,000,000

Source: NRC Population Distribution Around Nuclear Power Plant Sites, September 1974.

Even locating a nuclear power station at a remote site does not guarantee public safety in the event of an accidental release of airborne nuclear contaminants. The orientation and width of the dispersion plume of radionucleii can vary greatly depending on prevailing wind conditions during the period following their emission. There is no agreement about how far such plants should be removed from major population centers, or about NRC emergency planning procedures generally. At least five major alternatives seem possible:

1. Selective closing and decommissioning of reactors sited in areas of greatest hazard potential;
2. cessation of further reactor construction;
3. confinement of new reactors to remote sites not presently scheduled for development;
4. selective concentration of new reactors in nuclear complexes at existing or proposed sites;
5. continuation of existing market-oriented site development programs.

Several of these alternatives may be combined, e.g., selective closings and concentrations of new reactors in remote clusters. Each scenario has its respective advantages and drawbacks to local populations, private utilities, and the nation. Whichever alternative is selected, it is likely that governments will play increasing roles in the choice process (NRC 1980d). In the past, governmental intervention has meant subjecting private site selection to regulatory veto on the basis of technical feasibility (NRC 1980e). Experience shows that this has not produced acceptable results: "it will be necessary to develop new institutional arrangements and siting methodologies [to manage future siting of such hazardous facilities]" (National Academy of Sciences 1980, pp. 150-158; 165-167).

EMERGENCY PLANNING AROUND NUCLEAR POWER STATIONS

The responsibility for emergency planning is shared between operating utilities and surrounding governments, but the development of emergency plans is the responsibility of the power plant licensee. Critics allege that emergency plans have a low priority among NRC tasks, although even before Three Mile Island, NRC was attempting to improve emergency planning procedures. Pertinent features of existing and proposed procedures are considered below.

Utility Emergency Plans

Utilities must develop plans to be approved by NRC for managing onsite emergencies and for the protection of people who live within a limited distance of each reactor. They are not responsible for implementing offsite responses. They are merely required to notify appropriate public authorities about the existence and nature of an emergency. A typical utility emergency plan addresses:

- types of radiological emergencies;
- plant personnel responsibilities;
- plant control centers;
- contact with public authorities;
- off-site monitoring;
- medical treatment;
- surrounding population and road networks;
- emergency training programs; and
- expected dosage rates.

Emergency plans generally apply only to specified areas surrounding power stations. Plant operators must maintain an "exclusion area" around their premises, rarely more than a quarter-mile in radius. This area is usually owned by the utility and closed to the public. Beyond " the exclusion area" lies the Low Population Zone (LPZ), which is the basis for current emergency planning regulations. The LPZ is defined as an area whose "total number and density of residents are such that there is a reasonable probability that appropriate protective measures would be taken in their behalf in the event of a serious accident" (U.S. Congress 1979a, p. 41). Another measure is the "Population Center distance," defined as the distance between a reactor and the nearest boundary of a densely populated area containing more than 25,000 people.

Critics contend that these are vague and normative concepts that lead to irrational results (U.S. General Accounting Office 1979b). Thus the LPZ radius for Indian Point is 0.6 miles, for Three Mile Island it is 2 miles, and at Oconee, South Carolina—a relatively remote facility—it is approximately 6 miles (U.S. Congress 1979a, pp. 42-43). NRC approves emergency plans for smaller areas around reactors in densely populated regions and larger areas in sparsely populated districts. It is assumed that additional technological safeguards applied to reactor systems will compensate for reductions in the spatial extent of emergency planning. But, as determined by the U.S. President's Commission on the Accident at Three Mile Island (1979, p. 16):

> The LPZ approach has serious shortcomings. First . . . LPZs for many nuclear power plants are relatively small areas. Second, if an accident as serious as the one used to calculate the LPZ were actually to occur, it is evident that many people living outside the LPZ would receive smaller, but still massive doses of radiation. Third, the TMI accident shows that the LPZ has little relevance to the protection of the public—the NRC itself was considering evacuation distances as far as 20 miles even though the accident was far less serious than those postulated during siting. We have therefore concluded that the entire concept is flawed, [and] . . . we recommend that [it] be abandoned in siting and emergency planning.

Other analysts have reached similar conclusions. For example, the joint NRC/EPA task force (1978) recommended that a protective zone of 10 miles in radius be established around each plant.

Apart from the questionable validity of the LPZ, and the fact that utilities are not legally responsible for offsite protection, most utilities do not conform to NRC's 1975 guidelines for emergency planning. In 1979, only four facilities met this test. A recent report summarizes the problem. "The fact that this guide is not a binding regulation and has not been applied retroactively is suggestive of past failure on the part of both industry and the NRC to take seriously the entire question of emergency planning" (NRC 1980b, p. 6).

State and Local Emergency Plans

Municipalities, counties, and state governments are responsible for protecting and evacuating people who live in impact areas beyond plant boundaries. NRC does not require state and local emergency plans to be prepared before licensing a reactor. The commission does, however, provide technical assistance to governments that wish to improve their radiological planning capabilities. It also "concurs" in state plans which meet its existing review standards. Before the TMI accident, only 9 of 25 states with licensed reactors had emergency plans with NRC concurrence (U.S. Congress 1979a, p. 31). By early 1980, this number had risen to 16. According to a congressional report, "State and local officials sometimes do not even know of the existence of the utility plan and the responsibilities it assigns to them" (U.S. Congress 1979a, p. 34). As a result, there has often been little coordination between utilities' plans and those of adjacent state governments.

Local radiological plans are not reviewed by the NRC, which assumes that states will integrate municipal and county plans into a mutually compatible strategy. Available evidence suggests that such integrated planning is lacking in most states. In 1979, for example, only one of four counties within four miles of Indian Point had an emergency plan (U.S. Congress 1979a, p. 35).

Proposed Revisions

NRC has issued new interim criteria and guidelines for emergency planning (*Federal Register* 1979, pp. 75167-75174). They are intended for use by states, local governments, plant operators, and relevant federal agencies.

The new rules, if adopted, pose far-reaching implications for land use in the vicinity of plants in nonmetropolitan areas. The relatively small LPZs would be replaced by two much larger Emergency Planning Zones (EPZs) (Fig. 2). The inner "Exposure EPZ" encompasses land within about ten miles of a nuclear power station. Here, the main planning goal is to reduce human exposure to radiation by a combination of evacuation, sheltering, and use of thyroid blocking agents to mitigate the effects of inhaled airborne contaminants. The outer "Ingestion EPZ" includes areas within 50 miles of power stations. Here emergency planning is chiefly concerned with preventing contamination or consumption of food supplies such as water, dairy products, and other foodstuffs.

It is further proposed that: (1) protective measures to be taken within each EPZ shall be specified; (2) the NRC must concur in state and local government

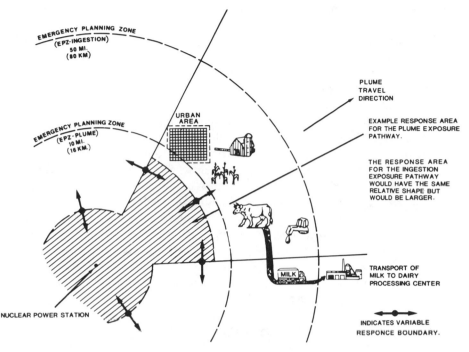

Figure 2. Concept of emergency planning zones.

emergency plans if licensing of a reactor is to be approved or continued; (3) plans shall be reviewed annually by persons not directly responsible for their preparation or operation; and (4) persons within the Plume Exposure EPZ will receive information about accident probabilities, potential effects, methods of warning notification, and protective action annually. It is not yet clear how responsibility for all these measures would be allocated, nor whether a plant would be suspended for failure to satisfy the new regulations.

The proposed rules still leave many emergency planning issues undecided. Evacuation, sheltering, thyroid medication, restrictions on foodstuffs, and controls on entry to contaminated areas are key elements of an emergency plan, but their relative contributions have not been established for different environmental, socioeconomic, temporal, and spatial contexts, nor for different degrees of exposure to hazard.

Each adjustment poses special problems. In the case of evacuation, for example, how should planning for low-density rural areas differ from high-density urban areas? Smaller populations are not necessarily easy to evacuate: the Maine Yankee plant at Wiscasset is located at the convergence of several long peninsulas, which lack good escape routes. Similar problems arise where power stations lie near barrier islands. Should everyone be evacuated or only selected groups, e.g., pregnant women, children, and elderly? How should planners cope with the effects of mass evacuation upon recipient areas? How can reception of warnings be assured, especially where people are likely to be out of reach by telephone, radio, or television? At least half the homes within ten miles of the Maricopa County (Arizona) nuclear plant do not have telephones. During the summer, most Wiscasset area residents are likely to be out of doors in daylight hours. To what degree might there be widespread public involvement in emergency evacuation drills?

Fifty-mile emergency planning zones would encompass some states in their entirety (e.g., Connecticut, Rhode Island, Massachusetts), and large parts of many others (Fig. 1). Might there be restrictions on farming, especially dairying, or other uses (e.g. watershed lands, well fields)? Should new developments be prevented, controlled, or reviewed in either of the two proposed emergency zones? Will federal authority over such zones be enlarged?

There is no consensus on the allocation of roles among those likely to be involved in preparing, reviewing, approving, funding, or implementing plans—including the public for whom these plans are now being developed. Given the primacy of the federal government in nuclear affairs, does this mean an expansion of federal regulatory authority throughout either or both of the emergency planning zones? Yet variations in local conditions call into question the usefullness of a detailed federal level planning effort and argue for locally informed site-specific approval procedures (NRC 1980, pp. 3-188; 3-287). Since many reactors are sited near rivers or other water bodies which also mark local, state, or national boundaries, this raises the issue of which governmental units should be involved in local emergency planning. How can their coordination be ensured? Will utilities, the federal government, states, or municipalities pay for emergency planning?

Most important, it is not clear what will be the role of emergency planning (1) in relation to other nuclear hazard adjustments, and (2) within the reactor licensing process. Emergency planning does not address post-disaster recovery and redevelopment, nor does it confront the problem of compensation to persons or communities harmed or threatened by nuclear accidents. The National Academy of Public Administration has recommended that "the eligibility of state and local governments with nuclear power plants in or adjacent to their jurisdictions for funds under the Disaster Relief Act of 1974 should be conditional on participation in [a utility-supported program of grants for emergency preparedness training and operations]" (NRC 1980b, p. 44). Nuclear disaster relief programs or broad-based nuclear insurance programs have received little discussion as policy alternatives, however.

Land Use and Population Controls

The scope and effectiveness of emergency plans are closely related to population and land-use characteristics of the area in which a facility is located. It has been noted earlier that evacuation poses different problems in urban and rural settings. As demographic and land use conditions change through time, plans must be updated.

There have been few attempts to control population density or land use with the objective of reducing exposure to hazards from nuclear accidents. The California Energy Resources Conservation and Development Commission is required to insure that population densities do not exceed safe limits. It is authorized to purchase developments rights or apply restrictive zoning to achieve these ends (Nero et al. 1977, p. 10). More recently, California's Nuclear Power Plant Emergency Review Panel has recommended that anything which inhibits the execution of local emergency plans be included within the purview of the state's Environmental Quality Act (NRC 1980b, pp. 3-123). This would require the preparation of "Environmental Impact Reports" for new developments near nuclear facilities. New Jersey in 1976 placed a moratorium on all developments near its two nuclear power stations (Morrell and Kinder 1977). Since both sites lie within the state's coastal zone, subsequent development proposals have been reviewed by the Department of Environmental Protection. A small hotel has been approved for construction, but a 448-unit housing development has been turned down.)

Nuclear power stations are often sited in floodplains or on waterfronts susceptible to inundation and storm damage. Hence their adjacent areas may be eligible for special regulation under the provisions of floodplain or coastal zone management statutes. Elsewhere, amenity conservation and agricultural land preservation statutes might serve similar ends. Thus far, the NRC has not devoted much effort to examining the potential role of land use or density controls for extended areas near power stations. It is a subject that deserves more attention.

SUMMARY AND CONCLUSIONS

The disaster potential of nuclear power stations is not uniformly distributed throughout the United States. It varies according to the age, design, and number of reactors at a given site. Moreover, although siting characteristics themselves vary widely, most operating reactors are located within pockets of low population density, on or near the fringes of metropolitan areas. Completion of planned reactors will increase the hazardousness of some states, but the future distribution of power stations will tend to conform to the existing pattern. Even if no further operating licenses are issued, total disaster potential will continue to increase as present facilities are engulfed by expanding metropolitan areas.

Four sets of alternative measures may be adopted to reduce nuclear power station hazards. They include: 1) improved reactor safety technology; 2) siting restrictions; 3) emergency response planning; and 4) land use and population-density controls. Since Three Mile Island, NRC, states and local governments are placing more emphasis on power station siting controls and on emergency planning. Given the uncertainty which surrounds licensing of additional reactors, the implications of new siting policies are still unclear (unless they are applied retroactively). It is possible that future reactors may be built on truly remote sites, however, and that multiple reactor energy centers may replace scattered individual sites. In any event, the 50-mile emergency planning zones, if implemented, would expand the sphere of influence of nuclear plants in nonmetropolitan areas.

The hazards of nuclear power stations cannot be considered in isolation. They are nested within larger issues of even greater complexity. How can the national mix of energy sources be modified to reduce the total hazard burden? Will society be willing to trade off hazards against lower energy costs or security and longevity of supplies? In expanding the range of response to nuclear hazards, the total impact of power stations on the lives of people who live in surrounding areas may be increased. So long as safety was equated with "failsafe" engineering, nearby residents did not have to formally concern themselves with questions of emergency readiness or appropriate land uses. Now they may be embroiled in problems that require sophisticated analysis, sensitive implementation of responses, and—perhaps—increased local costs. Nonmetropolitan county and local governments are underfinanced and unprepared to face the technical concerns of nuclear hazard planning, let alone the divisive debates that may accompany development of effective hazard management systems.

Whatever the final disposition of new nuclear safety programs, they are likely to add to the expense and complexities of using this energy source. Hence it is also necessary to re-examine the total costs of nuclear power as a contributor to the national energy budget. This should be a comparative assessment which includes all sources of unconventional and conventional energy. Notwithstanding the argument that nuclear power is widely regarded as a substantially different, and dangerous, energy form—and therefore deserving of special evaluation and management—such a comparative assessment is necessary before the United States can pursue an effective and safe national energy policy.

References

Federal Register 1979. Vol. 44, No. 245, December 19.
————. 1980a. Vol. 45, No. 116, June 13.
————. 1980b. Vol. 45, No. 147, July 29.
Hohenemser, C.; Kasperson, R.; and Kates, R.W. 1977. The Distrust of Nuclear Power. Science 196 (April 1).
Kates, R.W. 1978. Risk Assessment of Environmental Hazard. Scope Report No. 8. New York: John Wiley and Sons.
Lewis, H. W. 1980. The Safety of Fission Reactors. Scientific American 242 (3).
Morell, D., and Kinder, G.D. 1977. Housing Growth in the Vicinity of Nuclear Power Plants: A Case Study. Report to the Energy Policy Analysis Group, Brookhaven National Laboratory. Princeton: Center for Environmental Studies.
National Academy of Sciences. 1972. The Effects on Populations of Exposure to Low Levels of Ionizing Radiation. Report of the Advisory Committee on the Biological Effects of Ionizing Radiation. Washington, D.C.
————. 1980. Long-Range Environmental Outlook. Proceedings of a Workshop, November 14-16, 1979. Washington.
National Governors Association. 1978. Emergency Preparedness Project, Final Report. Washington.
Nero, A.V.; Schroeder, C.H.; and Yen, W.W.S. 1977. Control of Population Densities Surrounding Nuclear Power Plants. Vol. 5 of the Final Report on Health and Safety Impacts

of Nuclear, Geothermal and Fossil-Fuel Electric Generation in California. LBL- 5921. Berkeley: Lawrence Berkeley Laboratory.

New Jersey. Department of Community Affairs. 1974. *Thirty-Seventh Annual Report of the Division of Local Government Services, 1974.* Trenton: Division of Local Government Services.

Nuclear Safety. 1980. Technical Note: Report of the NRC Siting Policy Task Force. 21(3).

————. 1981. Operating U.S. Power Reactors. 22(1).

U.S. Atomic Energy Commission 1974. *Reactor Safety Study.* WASH-1400. Washington.

U.S. Congress 1979a. *Emergency Planning Around U.S. Nuclear Powerplants: Nuclear Regulatory Commission Oversight.* House Report No. 96-413, August 8, 1979. (96th Congress, 1st Session) Washington: U.S.G.P.O.

————. 1979b. Senate Committee on Governmental Affairs. *Radiation Protection:* Hearing before the Subcommittee on Energy Nuclear Proliferation and Federal Services, May 9, 1979, Part 3. (96th Congress, 1st Session) Washington: Government Printing Office.

U.S. Council on Environmental Quality. 1979. *Environmental Quality – 1979.* Washington: Government Printing Office.

————. 1980. Some Long-Term Consequences of Hypothetical Major Releases of Radioactivity to the Atmosphere from Three Mile Island. By Jan Beyea. Washington: U.S.G.P.O.

U.S. General Accounting Office. 1979a. *Enewetak Atoll – Cleaning Up Nuclear Contamination.* PSAD-79-54, May 8. Washington.

————. 1979b. *Emergency Preparedness Around the Rancho Seco Nuclear Powerplant: A Case Study.* EMD-79-103, October 2. Washington.

————. 1980a. *The Problem of Disposing of Nuclear Low-Level Waste: Where do we go from Here?* EMD-80-68, March 31. Washington.

————. 1980b. *Existing Nuclear Sites Can be Used for New Powerplants and Nuclear Waste Storage.* EMD-80-67, April 1. Washington.

U.S. Nuclear Regulatory Commission/Environmental Protection Agency. 1978. *Planning Basis for the Development of State and Local Government Radiological Emergency Response Plans in Support of Light Water Nuclear Power Plants.* NUREG 0396 and EPA 520/1-78-016. Office of State Programs, Office of Nuclear Reactor Regulation: Office of Radiation Protection. Washington.

U.S. Nuclear Regulatory Commission. 1979a. *Annual Report.* Washington: Government Printing Office.

————. 1979b. Office of Public Affairs: Press Release, No. 79-52. (March 13). Washington.

————. 1979c. *Three Mile Island: A Report to the Commissioners and to the Public.* Special Inquiry Group. Vol. II, Part 3. NUREG/CR-1250. Washington.

————. 1979d. *Report of the Siting Policy Task Force.* SECY-79-493. (August 16). Washington.

————. 1979e. *Beyond Defense-in-Depth: Cost and Funding of State and Local Government Radiological Emergency Response Plans and Preparedness in Support of Commercial Nuclear Power Stations.* NUREG-0553. Office of State Programs. Washington.

————. 1980a. *NRC Staff Preliminary Analysis of Public Comments on Advance Notice of Proposed Rulemaking on Emergency Planning.* NUREG-0628. Office of Standards Development. Washington.

————. 1980b. *Major Alternatives for Government Policies, Organizational Structures and Actions in Civilian Nuclear Reactor Emergency Management in the United States.* NUREG/CR-1225. Washington. (January)

————. 1980c. *Criteria for Preparation and Evaluation of Radiological Emergency Response Plans and Preparedness in Support of Nuclear Power Plants.* NUREG-0654 and FEMA-REP-1. Washington.

————. 1980d. *Federal-State Cooperation in Nuclear Power Plant Licensing.* NUREG-0398. Washington.

————. 1980e. *A Review of NRC Regulatory Processes and Functions.* NUREG-0642. Washington.

————. 1980f. *Status of Nuclear Power Reactors Under NRC Purview—May 23, 1980.* NUREG-0380, Vol. 4, No. 5. Washington.

U.S. President's Commission on the Accident at Three Mile Island. 1979. *The Need for Change: Legacy of TMI.* Washington.

Weinberg, A.M. 1979. Can we Fix Nuclear Energy? Reprinted in U.S. Senate Committee on Governmental Affairs. *Radiation Protection:* Hearing before the Subcommittee on Energy, Nuclear Proliferation and Federal Services, Part 3. 96th Congress, 1st Session, Washington. (May 9)

White House. 1980. *The President's Program on Radioactive Waste Management.* February 12.

Recapitulation

George Macinko

In his chapter on the Natural Resources Planning Board, Marion Clawson puts
the activities of the board into two broad categories: 1) idea stimulation, and 2)
planning and coordination. Clawson believes these to be mutually contradictory
functions and judges attempts by any one agency to do both as a sure-fire
prescription for failure. By analogy, one might argue that for any one volume to
attempt to do both is similarly foolhardy. The Conference on Nonmetropolitan
Land Use, from which this book developed, avoided this trap by focusing on
idea stimulation—and left the task of putting the ideas to work as its unfinished
agenda. Although the conference did not pretend to be an action blueprint, it
performed admirably in its role of idea stimulator, generating valuable perspectives and providing the basic information indispensable to intelligently directed
action.

The AAG proposal to the National Science Foundation cited as goals of the
conference the identification of emerging nonmetropolitan land-use trends and
issues, and the presentation of recent research findings in geography and other
disciplines relating to these issues. Other objectives, though important, were
derivative from the above and included the stimulation of multidisciplinary research; facilitation of communication between academics and public agencies;
and the promotion of cross fertilization among disciplines.

How well did the conference meet this imposing list of objectives? Very well
indeed, as a reading of the volume attests. But the published proceedings do not
tell the whole story. The plenary session format, in which single papers were
presented serially, figured prominently in the success of the conference. It eliminated the distractions inherent in multi-session efforts and allowed the full
weight of the total assemblage to be focused on each paper in turn. Trends,
issues, perspectives, and premises seen in stark relief led to uninhibited and
wide-ranging discussions in which formal disciplinary associations were completely

ignored. The insights developed as the result of this spontaneous interplay amply fulfilled the hopes of the conference organizers.

The conference was far too rich in its presentation of basic information, its delimiting of trends and issues, and its setting forth of perspectives and insights to be summarized fully here. Nor shall I presume to do so. Instead, I shall focus on one paper—an especially rich one—as a means to present some accomplishments of the conference and to suggest what yet remains to be done. I shall then give a much more limited review and explication of selected other papers.

The paper by Healy and Short identifies the trend in which current land use tends increasingly to conceal both owner identity and intent, and then goes on to examine the issues attendant therein. It observes that the cornfield on the fringe of the metropolitan area may present a properly bucolic appearance though owned, not by a farmer, but, instead, by a realtor biding his time for the proper moment to unearth his subdivision plans. In an era when rural land often becomes the vehicle for investors more interested in capital gains than commodity production, it is important to be able to detect such camouflage; Healy and Short suggest one means of doing so. They see the land market as the precursor to land-use change. Expectations of change are frequently revealed in the land market far in advance of any actual change in land use. For example, expectations that rural land will be put to urban use are often reflected in land prices long before actual construction begins on the land.

But, despite the importance of understanding the land market, there are great gaps in our knowledge of how it works and where market trends are taking us. Much more research must be done on how rural land prices are set, how individual land ownerships change through time, and, especially, on how the many new demands now being placed on rural lands will affect the productive efficiency of rural land resources. When the urban-born move to the country in search of rural amenities and then object to the noise of the predawn tractor, or the smell of the upwind hog farm, what consequences for farm production ensue? Little is known about the long-term effects of such sociological phenomena.

Brown and Beale, reacting to the declining birth rates of the last decade, project a decline in the rate of household formation between 1985 and 1995, and, on that basis, see a possible lessening of pressure for rural land conversion. Healy and Short, on the other hand, see a marked increase in the number of elderly over roughly the same time span. Given that the ranks of the elderly will nearly double by the turn of the century; and given their increasing penchant for rural retirement sites (even now retirees are second only to farmers as owners of rural acreage); will rural retirees exert enough pressure for rural land conversion to offset the decline in pressure projected by Brown and Beale? We do not know, in part because such opposing sets of data are usually expressed in isolation. The conference format, however, literally forced participants to take notice of each other. It outlines sharply the need for further research to resolve such differences, which bear heavily on the adequacy of rural lands to meet their manifold future demands.

In particular, the thorny question of whether or not deliberate steps to preserve farmland are mandated can be addressed better as the result of conference deliberations. This question, on which there is a full gamut of opinion and nothing approaching consensus, is customarily expressed in terms of the ability of technological advances in agriculture to offset the loss of farmland due to conversion—most often conversion to urban uses.

Healy and Short add to the factors bearing on this issue by noting that land parcellation generally impairs productivity, and continued parcellation poses a serious threat to efficient commodity production. While one hears much of the decline in farm populations and the attendant increase in farm size, the concommitant fact of parcellation is the hidden part of the same equation. Here again, more research is needed before an assessment of balance can be accomplished. Clearly, more study of the parcellation phenomenon is in order, particularly where large-lot zoning is in place. Such zoning, locking up land in parcels too small for efficient production, has been a significant factor in the high rates of parcellation characterizing the past two decades. And "locking up" is probably not an overstatement, for Healy and Short find parcel splitting to be a well-nigh irreversible process. Small parcel size and scattered ownerships resulting from parcellation present serious barriers to future regrouping of forest and agricultural lands into efficiently sized units.

Finally, Healy and Short emphasize that the use of the land market as precursor to land-use change is based on a deliberate attempt to look further ahead than is customary. But what is the most appropriate time frame for land-use planning? As noted previously, Brown and Beale project a lessening demand for rural land conversion during 1985-95, largely because the baby-boom generation will have already formed its households, and smaller numbers will then be in the household formation stage. But, shortly after the turn of the century, the children of the baby-boom generation, already on the way and causing a reversal of the recent decline in births, will themselves enter the household stage, and the pressure on rural land conversion may well increase. Reduction or expansion of pressures for rural land conversion attributable to projected rates of household formation is clearly a matter of time scales. How far down the pike should one look? Surely the question of appropriate time frames is itself worthy of more serious examination and debate than it has received thus far.

Brown and Beale, who admit to no great overall concern for farmland preservation, observe that the top 100 agricultural countries (those that produce 22 percent of crops by value), are experiencing disproportionately high rates of population growth and land conversion. Therefore, regardless of the overall fate of agricultural lands, it is difficult to escape concern for these particular lands, some of which produce domestically irreplaceable fruit and winter vegetable crops. But all schemes of farmland preservation, whether at national or regional scales, are flawed, and point to the need for new institutional arrangements.

Zinn points out a "Catch-22" situation whereby those farm exports most depended on to reduce a national balance of payments deficit, occasioned by a heavy dependence on imported petroleum products, are those that need the most energy to produce. This situation is made to order for a net energy analysis which, given the lesser energy required for production on prime farmlands, should include the energy inputs needed by farmland category as well as crop type.

Zinn also observes that theoretical economists see no need for legislative protection of farmlands—in great part because of the presumed substitutability of other lands for farmlands. But he also observes that, when looking to future land requirements, foresters, agriculturalists, and urbanologists all tend to look to the same land to satisfy their specific needs. This situation calls for an integrated, multidisciplinary assessment of the entire rural scene rather than the isolated, single-aspect studies that are now the rule.

Riebsame's study of drought adjustments in the Great Plains, an area producing up to 45 percent of the world's wheat trade, discloses that land conservation measures are the neglected portion of the adjustment triumvirate that also includes technological fixes and social adjustment efforts. Although the failure of conservation programs is multifaceted, much of it can be attributed to a national policy that emphasizes production levels over resource protection. For example, the amount of land that can be planted to wheat and still receive price protection payments is determined by national production and trade goals rather than conservation needs. Such policy differs in no substantial way from the much-criticized policy of the Soviet Union, which, in field and factory, accords higher priorities to production goals than to maintenance requirements. Herein we confront a classic dilemma. The general long-term societal interest demands a stop to the wholesale loss of topsoil caused by overly intensive farming practices. Yet the short-term private (farmer) and bureaucratic (in this case, Agricultural Stabilization and Commodity Service) interests see the present desirability of the opposite course of action. Close monitoring of the ecological integrity of an agricultural system stressed by balance of payments considerations would seem to be a prudent investment.

Berry suggests strongly that agriculture may be in the throes of a major discontinuity, as there are growing indications that the remarkable yield increases of the recent past may be entering a plateau phase. This should be monitored closely because, if true, it calls for a thorough reconstruction of agricultural policy and its derivatives.

The monitoring tasks needed may be helped along by the newly emergent remote sensing techniques described by Cowen and Baumann. Baumann, however, adds a disquieting note when he relates the almost complete failure of local officials to make use of the data provided by such monitoring techniques. Information alone is not enough. King Hubbert, the renowned petroleum geologist, is fond of saying, "most facts are useless." That is, many are trivial, some are significant but improperly delivered, and others are treated as trivial by poorly trained or weakly motivated recipients. More work needs to be done on how best to transmit information to maximize its practical utility. Throughout a long and distinguished career, the botanist Paul Sears, though not denying the need for more research and new information, argued compellingly that it was even more important to devise ways to use information already available sensitively and sensibly. That need still exists.

Pryde and Nielsen treat the subject of growth management. Comparable to the preservation of agricultural lands, this too is a thorny issue subject to widely differing opinions. Basic to the San Diego approach is the accommodation of growth—not its limitation. Again, one bumps into the appropriateness of the time scale to be used. Given the power of the exponential, accommodation to any positive rate of consumptive land use must eventually end in a situation precluding further growth. This may come later in the vastness of San Diego County than in the midst of megalopolis, but the issue remains: when is the appropriate time to face squarely the proposition that growth accommodation is ultimately a temporizing measure, no matter how cleverly conceived? And therefore, in any finite space, growth limitation is an issue that cannot be avoided.

Finally, both Bender et al. and Fowler et al., in their studies of the impacts of coal mining and conversion upon the communities of the Northern Great Plains and the potential environmental impacts of coal and biomass development in the Ohio River Basin, suggest that truly comprehensive and integrated studies are needed to determine the overall effect of the many combined pressures on nonmetropolitan lands. As with Zinn, the specter is raised that the very same land is looked to as a reserve to support the future expansion of often mutually incompatible uses such as coal, biomass, cropland, forestry, recreation, watershed, wildlife, grazing, and housing. We do not yet know how to synthesize such comprehensive efforts successfully, but the failure to meet this challenge exacts an increasingly heavy toll.

CONCLUSION

The Nonmetropolitan Land Use Conference proved to be an effective interdisciplinary and interagency forum for the interaction of a diverse group of participants deeply interested in identifying concerns and questions of land use and, in the context of substantive research results, exploring future research themes. A number of research themes were suggested directly by participants; an even greater number are likely to emerge as the result of the stimulation provided by the free-wheeling exchange that characterized the conference. Although each of us viewed the rich tapestry of the conference proceedings through his or her own set of spectacles, we were all enriched by the process and made better able to cope with present and emerging problems of rural land use.

Contributors

David A. Aggerholm. Currently, Mr. Aggerholm is a Senior Water Quality Management Adviser at EPA in Washington, D.C., on loan to King County, Washington, to assist in the development and implementation of water and land use related programs. Since 1965, he has held a variety of federal positions concerned with water resources. Between 1974 and 1976, Mr. Aggerholm managed a transportation planning grant at the University of Massachusetts. He has served as a consultant to the National Commission on Water Quality and the U.S. Council on Environmental Quality. Mr. Aggerholm holds a B.S. in forestry from Michigan State and two master's degrees from Pennsylvania State University.

Earl J. Baker. Dr. Baker is associate professor of geography and director of the Environmental Hazards Center at Florida State University in Tallahassee. He received his Ph.D. in geography in 1974 from the University of Colorado at Boulder. His research has addressed the management of natural hazards including hurricanes, floods, and drought. He is editor of a forthcoming collection of papers concerning societal response to hurricanes. Dr. Baker has conducted projects for the U.S. Nuclear Regulatory Commission, the Federal Emergency Management Agency, the National Oceanic and Atmospheric Administration, and several state agencies.

Paul R. Baumann. Professor Baumann is associate professor of geography at SUNY-Oneonta. He received his academic training at Indiana University and the University of Cincinnati. His research and instructional interests include geo-information systems, computer cartography, remote-sensing pattern recognition and computer-based instruction. He has written a number of papers and monographs on these topics. Mr. Baumann is also the director of the Laboratory for Computer Graphics at Oneonta and is a consultant to NASA with respect to computer-quantitative pattern recognition techniques.

Calvin L. Beale. Dr. Beale heads the Population Studies Group of the Economics, Statistics, and Cooperative Service in the U.S. Department of Agriculture. He is a demographer and geographer by training. Before joining USDA, he was with the Bureau of the Census. Dr. Beale's research has focused on American rural demography especially the regrowth of rural population in recent years, ethnic minority studies and regional studies. He is the author of many reports and studies on nonmetropolitan demographic shifts.

Lloyd D. Bender. Since 1975, Dr. Bender has served as project leader of a nation-wide team for the EDD Energy Impact Project. The project goals are to esti-mate population, employment, income, taxation and other changes due to energy development. Current analyses are on mine, power plant, and synfuel impacts. Under his supervision, this work is carried out at various universities. Dr. Bender holds a Ph.D. in agricultural economics from the University of Missouri at Columbia, and is presently an economist with EDD/ERS/USDA at Montana State University. He currently is Leader of the Rural Policy Impact Group team of researchers within the EDD.

Norman A. Berg. Mr. Berg was born in Iowa but grew up on a farm in Pine County, Minnesota. He received his B.S. from the University of Minnesota and his M.S. in public administration from Harvard University. Mr. Berg served in several key field positions in Idaho and South Dakota with the Soil Conservation Service. During World War II, he took three years' leave for service in the Marine Corps. He was appointed Assistant to the Administrator, SCS, in Washington, D.C. in 1960. From July 1965 to December 1968, he served as Deputy Administrator for Field Services. In January 1969, Mr. Berg assumed the position of Associate Administrator and was appointed to his present position as chief on September 12, 1979. He is a charter member and fellow of the Soil Conservation Society of America and has received the USDA's Distinguished Service Award.

David Berry. Dr. Berry is a senior analyst at ABT Associates in Cambridge, Mas-sachusetts. Previously, he was visiting assistant professor of urban and regional planning at the University of Illinois and a research associate at the Regional Science Research Institute in Philadelphia. His principal research interests are in rural geography, including agriculture, rural labor markets, and the evo-lution of small towns. Dr. Berry attended Syracuse University and received a Ph.D. in regional science from the University of Pennsylvania in 1973. Currently, he is involved in the National Rural Community Facilities Assess-ment Study for the Farmers Home Administration.

John R. Borchert. Professor Borchert's interests have been in natural resource systems, land development, and planning. His research over the past two decades has focused on the evolution of the U.S. urban system, regional urban growth trends, and land uses. He has served on the faculty of the Uni-versity of Minnesota since 1949. He was urban research director of the Upper Midwest Economic Study from 1961-64; director of the university's center for Urban and Regional Affairs, 1968-76; and leader of the research and development division of the Minnesota Land Management Information System, 1964-75. He has served frequently as a consultant to the Minnesota legislature and State Planning Agency, and occasionally to other state and federal agencies and legislative bodies. He is a past president of the Association of American Geographers; former chairman of the Earth Sciences Division, National Research Council; and a member of the National Academy of Sciences.

Ronald Briggs. Dr. Briggs's interests include transportation planning and analysis, population studies, location analysis, and urban geography. His research and writings have been on such topics as transportation resources for the rural poor, transportation and human needs, and transportation problems in low population density areas. He teaches geography and political economics at the University of Texas at Dallas and is a research affiliate at the Southwest Center for Economic and Community Development. Dr. Briggs was educated in the United States and England.

David L. Brown. Dr. Brown earned his B.A. from Miami University, Oxford, Ohio, and his M.S. and Ph.D. in sociology from the University of Wisconsin at Madison. He had conducted demographic research for the U.S. Department of Agriculture since 1972. He represented the USDA in the National Agricultural Lands Study. His research interests include population distribution, migration, commuting, population composition, and service delivery in sparsely populated areas. He has published over two dozen articles and chapters in books.

Marion Clawson. Dr. Marion Clawson served with the Bureau of Agricultural Economics of the U.S. Department of Agriculture in various capacities from 1929 until 1946. He moved to the Bureau of Land Management, U.S. Department of the Interior, in 1947, assuming the position of Director of BLM, from 1948 until 1953. In 1955, he joined Resources for the Future, Inc., in Washington, D.C., where he has held many positions: Director of Land Use and Management Studies; Director of Land and Water Studies; Acting President (March 1974-June 1975); Vice President (July-December 1975); and thereafter, consultant (January 1976-present). His scholarly output has averaged nearly a book a year in the fields of land and water resource management, public lands, agricultural policy, economics of recreation, and the land-development process. Dr. Clawson holds B.S. and M.S. degrees from the University of Nevada and a Ph.D. in economics from Harvard.

David J. Cowen. Dr. David J. Cowen is professor of geography and director of the Social and Behavioral Sciences Laboratory at the University of South Carolina. He has been at the University since 1970 after receiving his B.A. and M.A. in Geography from SUNY at Buffalo and his Ph.D. from Ohio State University. He has extensive teaching and research experience in areas of computer mapping, geographical information systems, and location theory. He is presently working closely with the University's Graphics Section of Computer Services in the development and implementation of geographical information systems to support the needs of various state agencies. Among these activities has been applications of the Census GBF/DIME files, the South Carolina Land-Use Information System, and the Land Use/Land Cover files of the USGS.

Gary L. Fowler. Professor Fowler received his Ph.D. in geography from Syracuse University in 1969. Before joining the Department of Geography at the University of Illinois at Chicago in 1972, he taught at the University of Kentucky and Indiana University. Dr. Fowler's research interests include interdisciplinary technology assessment of regional energy development. He was co-principal investigator of the three-year, EPA-sponsored Ohio River Basin Study of power-plant siting. His current research concerns metropolitan energy management and planning.

Glenn V. Fuguitt. Dr. Fuguitt received his Ph.D. in sociology from the University of Wisconsin at Madison in 1956. Since that time he has been on the faculty of the Department of Rural Sociology there. His major research activities have concerned part-time farming, the demographic structure and change of villages and nonmetropolitan cities, and population redistribution, particularly as it affects nonmetropolitan areas in the United States. Dr. Fuguitt is a native of Florida.

Robert G. Healy. Dr. Healy is a senior associate at The Conservation Foundation, Washington, D.C., where he directs the foundation's rural land market project. Over the years, he has done research on a wide variety of topics related to land use, including land-use regulation, housing, landscape protection, agricultural and forest policy, and industrial siting. He is author or co-author of *Land Use and the States, The Lands Nobody Wanted,* and *Protecting the Golden Shore.* Currently, he is completing a book on the rural land market in the U.S. Before joining the Conservation Foundation in 1975, Dr. Healy was associated with the Urban Institute, Resources for the Future, and Harvard University. He holds a Ph.D. in economics from UCLA.

Roy C. Herndon. Dr. Herndon is director of research for the Resource Analysis Center of the Institute of Science and Public Affairs at Florida State University and university coordinator for the Florida Sea Grant Program. He is also director of the institute's Hazardous Waste Program and serves as executive director of the governor's Hazardous Waste Policy Advisory Council. His research interests include environmental, nuclear, and solid-state physics. He has served as project director of Florida's statewide hazardous waste study and as project coordinator and co-principal investigator for the assessment of the economic impact of Florida's proposed hazardous waste control program. He also directed the development of the Leon County Solid Waste Management Plan. Invited in 1977-78 and in 1979 and 1981 to the Université de Lausanne as a visiting scientist, Dr. Herndon lectured on the problem of high-level radioactive waste disposal in the United States. He holds a Ph.D. in physics from Florida State University.

Harley E. Johansen. Dr. Johansen's interests in rural settlement and agricultural activities grew out of childhood experiences in a rural community of Scandinavian immigrants in northwestern Wisconsin. After receiving a B.A. degree in geography from Wisconsin State University at River Falls and M.S. and Ph.D. degrees from the University of Wisconsin, he joined the Department of Geography and the Regional Research Institute at West Virginia University in Morgantown. The characteristics and processes of change in social, demographic, and economic activities in rural areas are the focus of Dr. Johansen's research. Current research activities involve the process of change in population and business activities in small towns, and the effects of community characteristics and development efforts on this process. He is now head of the Department of Geography at the University of Idaho.

Peirce F. Lewis. Peirce Lewis is professor of geography at the Pennsylvania State University in University Park, where he teaches and writes about the ordinary landscapes of North America—what they look like, how they originated, and what they seem to mean.

George Macinko. Dr. Macinko, Professor of Geography and Director of Environmental Studies at Central Washington University, traces his interest in conservation and resource use to a boyhood spent in the strip-mine country of the Eastern Pennsylvania Anthracite Coal Fields. After early work in mining and geological engineering, he earned a degree in philosophy from the University of Idaho. As a Woodrow Wilson Fellow in philosophy at the University of Michigan, he encountered the field of geography, in which he received a Ph.D. in 1961. A post-doctoral year in Natural Resources followed in 1965. He served as co-director of an AAG project that culminated in *A Sourcebook on the Environment*, published by the University of Chicago Press in 1978.

James Kenneth Mitchell. Dr. Mitchell was born in Northern Ireland and received his undergraduate education at the Queens University of Belfast. He came to the United States in 1965 and earned master's degrees in geography and planning from the University of Cincinnati and a Ph.D. in geography from the University of Chicago in 1973. For the past decade he has been a faculty member at Rutgers University, where he is now director of the geography graduate program and acting chairman of the department of human ecology and social science. His major research is concerned with human adjustment to extreme environmental and social stresses. Current projects involve social violence in plural societies, human responses to natural and technological hazards, and several coastal zone management studies. He is chairman of the Scientific Committee on the Outer Continental Shelf of the U.S. Department of the Interior.

David C. Nielsen. In preparation for his position as growth management director for San Diego County, California, Mr. Nielsen studied growth management programs in 13 jurisdictions throughout the United States. Previously, he was director of the county's Environmental Impact Report program and conducted an evaluation of certain county air-pollution control rules. He has made formal presentations at national conferences of the National Association of Home Builders and American Institute of Planners as well as locally in California. Mr. Nielsen holds a bachelor's degree from Wheaton College in Illinois and an M.P.A. from the University of Washington at Seattle.

Larry C. Parcels. Dr. Parcels is a regional economist working on the Energy Impact Project as an adjunct assistant professor at Montana State University, Bozeman. His current responsibilities include impact assessment modeling applied to rapid economic changes in rural localities. Dr. Parcels received a Ph.D. from Cornell University in 1979.

Rutherford H. Platt. Dr. Platt is associate professor of geography and planning law at the University of Massachusetts at Amherst. His professional interests encompass many aspects of land and water resource management in the United States. He has served as consultant to several federal agencies on floodplain management and was formerly staff attorney with a private environmental organization in Chicago. Dr. Platt holds a B.A. in political science from Yale and a law degree and Ph.D. in geography from the University of Chicago. He is the principal investigator for the grants to the AAG under which this conference was organized, and he has served as overall conference coordinator.

Philip R. Pryde. Dr. Pryde is a specialist on land use planning and environmental analysis in the Department of Geography at San Diego State University. He received his B.A. in economics from Amherst College, and his M.A. and Ph.D. in geography from the University of Washington. In addition to numerous articles, he is the author of *Conservation in the Soviet Union* and the editor and partial author of *San Diego: An Introduction to the Region.* He has served on several regional land use commissions and committees, including the San Diego County Planning Commission, and has recently completed a term as its chairman. He helped prepare the San Diego County ordinance mandating solar hot-water heating in rural parts of the county.

J. C. Randolph. J. C. Randolph completed undergraduate and graduate degrees at the University of Texas at Austin and completed his Ph.D. in ecology from Carleton University (Ottawa) in 1972. Dr. Randolph was a staff ecologist in the Environmental Sciences Division at Oak Ridge National Laboratory from 1972 to 1974. He joined the School of Public and Environmental Affairs at Indiana University in 1974 and in 1977 was named Director of Environmental analysis. He was concerned with terrestrial ecology and land use issues as one of the core team members of the three-year, U.S. EPA-sponsored Ohio River Basin Energy Study.

William E. Riebsame. Bill Riebsame received his Ph.D. in geography from Clark University in 1981. He specializes in the study of climatology and resources management. He recently completed a post-doctoral fellowship with the International Council of Scientific Unions' Scientific Committee on Problems of the Environment (ICSU/SCOPE) as coordinator of SCOPE's methodological review of climate impact assessment. He is currently teaching at the University of Wyoming. Dr. Riebsame's recent research has focused on the impacts of drought on Great Plains agriculture and the use of records of extreme weather events for identifying periods of climate stress.

Howard G. Roepke. Dr. Roepke has taught in the Department of Geography at the University of Illinois-Champaign since 1952. Development and industrial location are his major research interests; he has published a number of books and articles on these subjects. A certified industrial developer, he is a fellow member of the American Economic Development Council, and past president of the Great Lakes Area Development Council and Illinois Development Council; currently he is a research fellow of the Urban Land Institute and editor of the AEDC *Journal.* Dr. Roepke received his B.A. and M.A. from the University of Wisconsin-Madison and his Ph.D. from Northwestern University.

James L. Short. Dr. Short is professor of real estate and land studies at San Diego State University, where he teaches courses in land economics, land-use policy, and real estate. He has been a consultant to government agencies, private real estate investors, and environmental organizations. He has written on housing, new towns, exurban land use changes, and rural land market issues. Recent articles have appeared in *The Appraisal Journal* and the *Journal of the American Planning Association.* Dr. Short is currently participating in the Rural Land Market Project conducted by The Conservation Foundation, under the direction of Robert G. Healy. The results of this study are the basis for a forthcoming book on rural lands. Dr. Short received his Ph.D. degree in urban land economics from UCLA.

Barry Smit. Dr. Smit attained an M.A. in geography at the University of Auckland and later a Ph.D. from McMaster University. He has been at the University of Guelph since 1976 and has published articles on farm enlargement, farm labor, rural land markets, land use policy and planning, attitudes toward exurban development, and service provision in rural areas. He is a director of the Land Evaluation Project at Guelph, an interdisciplinary study which evaluates alternative uses of lands under possible future scenarios in cooperation with Agriculture Canada and the Ontario Ministry of Agriculture and Food.

Lawrence M. Sommers. Dr. Sommers received his B.S. and Ph.M. from the University of Wisconsin and his Ph.D. from Northwestern University. Upon completing his degree, Dr. Sommers joined the faculty of Michigan State University, where he was chairman for 24 years and is now professor of geography. Among his publications are 9 books and monographs and approximately 30 articles in American and European journals on a variety of geographical topics. His interests lie in the development geography of Western Europe, especially Norway; North Sea oil and natural gas developments; resource, land use and energy problems in Michigan; and the history and methodology of geography. Dr. Sommers has served the AAG as a councilor and on many committees. He has served on the executive board and nominating committee of the National Council on Geographic Education and the committee on geography of the Office of Naval Research.

Larry K. Stephenson. After completing undergraduate and M.S. degrees at Arizona State University, Dr. Stephenson rounded out his geographic education at the University of Cinncinati, where he received a Ph.D. After several years on the faculty of the University of Hawaii at Hilo, he returned to Arizona. He has held visiting faculty appointments at Arizona State University and the University of Arizona. Currently, he is a planner for the Arizona Department of Health Services; adjunct faculty in the Department of Geography at Arizona State University; a member of the teaching faculty of the University of Phoenix; and an instructor for Golden Gate University. He has taught in the fields of planning, public administration, business, and health services administration as well as geography. His current research interests include regional planning, environmental policy, and land-use regulation, while his past publications encompass a range of social, economic, methodological, and educational topics.

Thomas F. Stinson. Dr. Stinson is an economist with the Economic Development Division, ESS, USDA, stationed at the University of Minnesota, St. Paul, specializing in local government finance in rural areas. Recent research has addressed mineral taxation, and tax revenues and expenditures associated with mining. He developed the tax and revenue models of local governments that were used in this report. Dr. Stinson received the Ph.D. in economics at the University of Minnesota in 1972.

Kirk H. Stone. Professor Stone is a population geographer. His lifetime professional specialty is the rural settling process and rural settlement form, particularly on and in world frontiers. He has published widely on this subject. In recent years, his efforts have been focused on refining the large and diverse nonmetropolitan category of population into smaller units using remote sensing techniques. Professor Stone trained at the University of Michigan and Syracuse University. He has taught at the Universities of Georgia, Wisconsin, and Toledo.

George S. Temple. Dr. Temple is a former research associate at the University of Minnesota. He authored the impact assessment model used in the preparation of this report while completing the Ph.D. in economics at Montana State University. Before that, Dr. Temple received the M.S. in economics at the University of Wisconsin and taught economics while a resident of Canada. He is currently studying law at the University of Minnesota.

Stanley W. Voelker. Mr. Voelker is retired economist, Economics and Statistics Service, USDA, formerly stationed at North Dakota State University, Fargo. He received the M.S. from Montana State University, Bozeman, and spent a career studying the rural development of the Northern Plains. He has devoted the past five years to resource and taxation issues related to rapid rural economic change.

Donald J. Ziegler. Dr. Ziegler obtained his Ph.D. from Michigan State University in 1980. He is an assistant professor, Department of Geography, Old Dominion University, Norfolk, Virginia. He is a joint author of a monograph on Three

Mile Island. His research and teaching specializations include energy and population.

Jeffrey A. Zinn. An analyst with the Congressional Research Service, Dr. Zinn's areas of policy research center on coastal zone and land use management issues, particularly agricultural lands. He has been a consultant to the USDA reviewing conversion of land and water conservation programs for a Senate oversight committee. For two years, he worked with the Conservation Foundation on a variety of natural resource projects. He received his B.A. from the University of Vermont (1967), his M.A. from the University of Rhode Island (1970), and his Ph.D. from Oregon State University (1972).

Index

Index

Numbers in italics refer to the pages on which complete references are listed. Numbers in parentheses refer to pages written by the person indicated.